T0389716

Novel Perspectives on Communication Practices in Antiquity

Papyrologica Lugduno-Batava

Edidit

Institutum Papyrologicum Universitatis Lugduno-Batavae

Moderantibus

W. Clarysse, K. Donker van Heel, F. A. J. Hoogendijk, S. P. Vleeming

VOLUMEN XLI

The titles published in this series are listed at *brill.com/plb*

Novel Perspectives on Communication Practices in Antiquity

Towards a Historical Social-Semiotic Approach

Edited by

Klaas Bentein
Yasmine Amory

BRILL

LEIDEN | BOSTON

Cover illustrations: Papyrus drawing from M. J. Raven, *Papyrus van bies tot boekrol* (1982), p. 24; A second-century tax receipt, BGU III 718 (103 CE). © Staatliche Museen zu Berlin—Ägyptisches Museum und Papyrussammlung, Photo: Sandra Steiß, P 7882.

Library of Congress Cataloging-in-Publication Data

Names: Bentein, Klaas, editor. | Amory, Yasmine, editor. | Novel
    Perspectives on Communication Practices in Antiquity: Towards a
    Historical Socio-Semiotic Approach (Conference) (2019 : Ghent, Belgium)
Title: Novel perspectives on communication practices in antiquity : towards
    a historical social-semiotic approach / edited by Klaas Bentein, Yasmine
    Amory.
Description: Leiden ; Boston : Brill, [2023] | Series: Papyrologica
    lugduno-batava, 0169-9652 ; volumen XLI | "This volume contains selected
    and thoroughly revised versions of papers presented at the international
    conference "Novel Perspectives on Communication Practices in Antiquity:
    Towards a Historical Socio-Semiotic Approach." Held at the cultural
    center Het Pand in Ghent from October 3 to 5, 2019" | Includes
    bibliographical references and index.
Identifiers: LCCN 2022043636 (print) | LCCN 2022043637 (ebook) |
    ISBN 9789004526518 (hardback ; acid-free paper) | ISBN 9789004526525
    (ebook)
Subjects: LCSH: Manuscripts, Classical (Papyri)—Congresses. | Communication
    —History—To 1500—Congresses. | Semiotics—Social aspects—Congresses. |
    LCGFT: Conference papers and proceedings.
Classification: LCC PA3343 .N68 2023 (print) | LCC PA3343 (ebook) |
    DDC 302.2093—dc23/eng/20221006
LC record available at https://lccn.loc.gov/2022043636
LC ebook record available at https://lccn.loc.gov/2022043637

Typeface for the Latin, Greek, and Cyrillic scripts: "Brill". See and download: brill.com/brill-typeface.

ISSN 0169-9652
ISBN 978-90-04-52651-8 (hardback)
ISBN 978-90-04-52652-5 (e-book)

Contents

Acknowledgments VII
Notes on Contributors VIII
Editorial Notation IX

Introduction: Developing a Historical Social-Semiotic Approach to
Communication Practices in Antiquity 1
  Klaas Bentein and Yasmine Amory

PART 1
*A Novel Approach to the Visual and Material Characteristics of
Ancient Documents*

1 Beyond the Text or the Contribution of "Paléographie signifiante" in Documentary
   Papyrology: The Example of Formats in Late Antiquity 17
     Jean-Luc Fournet

2 BIG & Small: The Size of Documents as a Semiotic Resource for
   Graeco-Roman Egypt 29
     Marco Stroppa

3 Notes on Ostraca and Scribal Practice 39
     Sofía Torallas Tovar

4 Visual Signs of Deference in Late Antique Greek Letters on Papyrus 54
     Yasmine Amory

5 The Spread and Persistence of Roman Features in Some Greek Papyrus Letters of
   the High Chancery 65
     Eleonora Angela Conti

6 Applied Category Analysis for Interpreting a List in the Late Antique Documentary
   Tradition: Some Preliminary Considerations 72
     Antonella Ghignoli

PART 2
A Multi-Modal Approach to Ancient Sources

7 The Textualization of Women's Letters from Roman Egypt: Analyzing Historical
   Framing Practices from a Multi-Modal Point of View 89
     Klaas Bentein

8 Towards a Socio-Semiotic Analysis of Greek Medical Prescriptions
   on Papyrus 113
     Nicola Reggiani

9   Imagining Faith: Images, Scripts, and Texts of Early Christian Inscriptions from the
     Roman Near East   131
       James Wolfe

10   The "Exposed Writings": Semiotic Contributions to the Analysis of Linguistic
     Variability in Archaic Greek Inscriptions   146
       Sarah Béthume

PART 3
A Quantitative Approach to Linguistic Variation in Papyri

11   Ὀκτώ or ὀκτώι: Reconsidering Orthographic Hypercorrection in Antiquity   171
       Geert De Mol

12   Word-Split Frequency in Greek Documentary Papyri (with an Appendix on
     Syllabification)   184
       Mark Depauw

     Index of Passages Cited   191
     Index of Subjects   196

Acknowledgments

This volume contains selected and thoroughly revised versions of papers presented at the international conference "Novel Perspectives on Communication Practices in Antiquity: Towards a Historical Socio-Semiotic Approach." Held at the cultural center Het Pand in Ghent from October 3 to 5, 2019, the conference occurred in the context of the ERC project "Everyday Writing in Graeco-Roman and Late Antique Egypt: A Socio-Semiotic Study of Communicative Variation" and benefitted from the financial support of the *Historical Sociolinguistics Research and Training Program Research Network* (FWO) as well as Brill. Various junior colleagues provided practical help during that conference, for which we would like to express our gratitude. We would also like to thank all the people who have been involved in bringing this book project to its completion, including Giulia Moriconi, associate editor for Classical Studies at Brill, for her patience and support; Melinda Johnston, our copy-editor, for the invaluable help she provided in formatting and proofreading the individual chapters; the anonymous reviewer at Brill, for their useful comments and suggestions; and last but not least, our contributors, for the enthusiasm and attentiveness they displayed at the conference, and the eagerness with which they contributed to this volume.

Klaas Bentein & Yasmine Amory
Ghent, June 2022

Notes on Contributors

Yasmine Amory
PhD (2018), École Pratique des Hautes Études, is a post-doctoral research fellow at Ghent University. She has published many articles on communication practices in antiquity and compiles editions of unpublished papyri from different collections around the world.

Klaas Bentein
PhD (2012), is an associate research professor at Ghent University and PI of the ERC project EVWRIT (www.evwrit.ugent.be). He has published widely in the fields of Ancient Greek linguistics and papyrology, including *Verbal Periphrasis in Ancient Greek: Have- and Be- Constructions* (OUP 2016).

Sarah Béthume
PhD (2022), is a lecturer at UCLouvain (Belgium). She studies the correlation between socio-orthographic and dialectal variability and the pragmatic dimension of the archaic inscriptions from Argolid.

Eleonora Conti
PhD (2010), worked for many years at the Istituto Papirologico "G. Vitelli," University of Florence, with which she still collaborates. She deals with literary papyrology (attic oratory) and documentary papyrology, most of all with the study of Ancient Greek letters and paleography.

Mark Depauw
is a full professor of Ancient History at KU Leuven. Originally a specialist in Demotic Egyptian, he now spends most of his time directing the research platform Trismegistos (www.trismegistos.org), on the basis of which he builds his quantitative research.

Geert De Mol
is a PhD candidate at Ghent University and collaborator of the ERC project EVWRIT. His research focuses on the social meaning of spelling variation—more specifically, on orthographic hypercorrection in Ancient Greek papyri.

Jean-Luc Fournet
is a professor at the Collège de France, which created its first chair of papyrology, "Written Culture in Late Antiquity and Byzantine Papyrology," for him in 2015. He is also a professor at the École Pratique des Hautes Études. He is a French papyrologist and has a special interest in the culture of late antiquity—particularly poetry, multilingualism, and modalities of written culture.

Antonella Ghignoli
is a full professor in palaeography at Sapienza University of Rome and PI of the ERC project NOTAE. Since 1991 she has published extensively in the fields of Latin palaeography and diplomatics, covering a wide range of topics from the early Middle Ages to the Renaissance. Her current research is focused on literacy and written culture in late antiquity and the early Middle Ages.

Nicola Reggiani
is a research fellow (Ricercatore) in papyrology at the University of Parma. His main current research interests are unpublished papyri from Tebtunis (he is editing P.Tebt. vol. VII); digital papyrology, including authoring *Digital Papyrology I* (De Gruyter 2017) and editing *Digital Papyrology II* (De Gruyter 2018); and Greek medical papyri, which he studies from a material viewpoint.

Marco Stroppa
PhD (2015), is employed at the Papyrological Institute "G. Vitelli" of the University of Florence. He has published widely in the field of papyrology, including *I bandi liturgici nell'Egitto romano* (FUP 2017), especially first editions of literary and documentary Greek texts.

Sofía Torallas Tovar
PhD (1995), is a professor of classics at the University of Chicago, curator of the papyrus collection at the Abbey of Montserrat, and co-PI of the project "Transmission of Magical Knowledge: Magical Handbooks on Papyrus." She has published widely on different aspects of papyrology, including linguistics, early Christianity, and the materiality of books and documents.

James Wolfe
PhD (2020), is the Alex and Marie Manoogian postdoctoral research fellow in Armenian history at the Center for Armenian Studies and Department of History at the University of Michigan. His research focuses on the experiences of Armenian and Syriac-speaking communities in the late antique and medieval Middle East. In multiple forthcoming publications, he explores issues of genre and literary composition in Armenian and Syriac historiography.

Editorial Notation

The transcription of Greek texts employs the following editorial conventions (the so-called "Leiden system"):

… dots under letters (α̣β̣γ̣) indicate uncertain letters, plain dots (. . .) indicate the approximate number of illegible or lost letters
(   ) indicates the solution to an abbreviation or symbol
[   ] indicates a lacuna in the original
⟨   ⟩ indicates an omission by the ancient scribe
{   } indicates a cancellation by the editor of the text
〚   〛 indicates a deletion by the ancient scribe
`   ´ indicates an interlinear addition

In addition to that,
| denotes the start of a new line on the papyrus where we have not printed the text in the same configuration as on the papyrus

The transcription of inscriptions employs a similar system of symbols.

α̲β̲   indicates letters seen by an earlier editor but no longer visible on the stone
[- - -]   indicates lost lines of an uncertain number
| denotes the start of a new line on the stone where we have not printed the text in the same configuration as on the stone. Note that the vertical stroke also occurs as reproduction of a sign in the inscription (sign or symbol with undetermined function, trace, separating vertical stroke, etc).

Introduction: Developing a Historical Social-Semiotic Approach to Communication Practices in Antiquity

Klaas Bentein and Yasmine Amory

1 Setting the Stage*

Recent studies in epigraphy and papyrology have on various occasions referred to two methodological "turns" (sometimes called "revolutions" or "paradigm shifts"),[1] both of which are considered to be materially oriented.[2] The first turn, also known as "the material turn," concerns a new interest in the production of written artifacts, both the raw materials of writing (the material substrate) and the act of writing itself. For this, the availability of digital images has been critical, especially in papyrology. Because of this availability, scholars are now able to study much greater quantities of documents, in much greater detail, and to illustrate their findings. For example, Roger S. Bagnall and Raffaella Cribiore have been able to exhaustively analyze the corpus of women's letters, taking into consideration not just handwriting, but also layout, document format, and writing material,[3] while more systematic accounts of these elements in ancient letters have been given by Antonia Sarri and Jean-Luc Fournet, among others.[4]

The second turn, which is known as "the spatial turn," concerns an interest in the archeological context, and the spatial context of writing. As Bagnall suggests,[5] this turn is more complicated than the first, because it concerns a two-way direction: papyrologists, for example, may ask what they can learn about their documents from an investigation of the archeological context, but vice versa, they can also ask what there is to learn about an archeological context from the documents that are found in it. An early example of this type of approach is the work of Peter van Minnen, who considered the relationship between papyri and the context in which they were found, focusing on Roman Karanis.[6] While some skepticism can be voiced about the relationship between movable objects such as papyri and their place of discovery,[7] this is less of a problem for inscriptions. A good example is the recent study by Polly Lohmann,[8] who not only situates Pompeian graffiti in different types of houses, but also enquires about how those texts were produced, who was behind them, and how they were integrated within domestic spaces. Rather than viewing graffiti as passive objects, Lohmann considers the texts as "actors" which can convey intention or evoke reactions.

As Bagnall notes, work on the material and spatial aspects of ancient documents has enabled scholars to reconstruct the "ecosystem" of writing, or in other words, the social dimensions of writing in antiquity; that is, "who wrote; how they were educated in different types of writing competence; what materials they used when, where, and for what purposes; how they displayed their education, importance, and concern for their correspondents by the way they laid out, wrote, and marked up what they wrote."[9] Such concerns have been central to scholars working on the language of documentary sources, too, a field of research which is often not taken into consideration (consciously or unconsciously) by scholars working on the materiality of ancient documents.[10] Indeed, Bagnall's comment almost echoes the title of a paper that was foundational to modern-day sociolinguistics, Joshua Fishman's famous "Who Speaks What Language to Whom and When"

---

* This chapter was written in the context of the ERC Starting Grant project EVWRIT ('Everyday writing in Graeco-Roman and Late Antique Egypt. A socio-semiotic study of communicative variation', PI Klaas Bentein), a project which has received funding from the European Research Council under the Horizon 2020 research and innovation programme (Grant Agreement No. 756487). Ninety percent of the chapter was written by the first author, Klaas Bentein.

1   For an overview, see Bagnall 2016.

2   Roger Bagnall (2016, 80) refers to "materializing revolutions," noting that documentary disciplines have undergone other fundamental changes, too, especially in the areas of digitization and internationalization. Various edited volumes have appeared in recent years on the "materiality" of ancient documents. See, among others, Boschung and Bremmer 2015; Petrovic, Petrovic, and Thomas 2018; Hoogendijk and van Gompel 2019; Caputo and Lougovaya 2020.

3   Bagnall and Cribiore 2006, 2nd, online edition published in 2008 (https://www.fulcrum.org/concern/monographs/79407z10h).

4   Sarri 2018; Fournet 2007, 2009.

5   Bagnall 2016, 82.

6   van Minnen 1994.

7   See Bagnall 2016, 83. For discussion of this problem with regard to the archive of Claudius Tiberianus, see Stephan and Verhoogt 2005.

8   Lohmann 2017.

9   Bagnall 2016, 81–82.

10 Lohmann (2017, 58), for example, explicitly states that she will not concern herself with philological/linguistic matters. A notable exception is Bagnall and Cribiore 2006, which makes many relevant linguistic observations.

(1965).[11] While in 2010 it was possible for Trevor Evans and Dirk Obbink to say of documentary papyri that "we are still dealing today with linguistic resources of extraordinary richness which have hardly begun to be explored,"[12] in recent years considerable progress has been made in areas such as language contact and multilingualism, the role of scribes, and linguistic register; perhaps sufficiently so to speak of a third, "linguistic" turn in the study of documentary texts.[13]

This volume, and the conference out of which it results, is based on the conviction that the studies mentioned above (whether embedded in a "material," "spatial," or "linguistic" turn) all have something in common: a central concern for the *dialogical* relationship between social agents and contexts of communication. With this, we mean that the context of writing may impose a certain framework on social agents, while at the same time social agents may go beyond these frameworks through creative acts of writing. Questions about the centrality of texts in society and their role in the shaping of "discourse" have received in-depth treatment by scholars such as Michel Foucault, Jürgen Habermas, Martin Nystrand, Norman Fairclough, and others. It is only fairly recently, however, that scholars have started looking at this question from a micro-perspective; that is, how the shape of written artifacts relates to their social context. This research branch is known as "social semiotics."[14] What makes this approach unique is that it takes a *systematic* approach to the question, by mapping the different ways in which writers can make meaning, but also by outlining the types of meaning that these writers can make.

Noticeably, social semiotics explicitly profiles itself as a study of modern-day communication, as indicated in the title of one of its main textbooks: *Multimodality: A Social Semiotic Approach to* Contemporary *communication*[15] (our emphasis). The main purpose of this volume is to analyze whether similar questions can be asked for antiquity, and whether similar, or at least related methods can be applied. In pursuing such a *historical* social-semiotic approach for the first time, we have intentionally taken a broad approach. While seeking to develop a more holistic and systematic approach to communication practices in antiquity, we did not ask that all contributors investigate

the combination of linguistic, visual, and material characteristics, but rather gave them the freedom to focus on specific elements. Nor did we expect that they should apply a predetermined theoretical framework: rather, we suggested that they explore approaches that they considered tailored to the questions they were dealing with. As such, we conceive of historical social semiotics as an umbrella term, a "house with many rooms," as we further discuss below (§ 2.4).

In terms of subject matter, too, the volume covers a broad area, with not only Greek but also Latin and Syriac texts. Papyri are discussed in various contributions, but potsherds and inscriptions are also taken into account, as are paraliterary texts. Most contributions focus on the Roman and late antique period, but some go back to the Ptolemaic or even Archaic/Classical period. Egypt is the main place of interest, but some contributions look at other regions, such as the Latin West, Greece, or Syria. As such, it is our hope that the volume will give interested readers a taste of what historical social-semiotic questions can look like, and that it will function as a platform for follow-up studies on the same theme.

2   Social Semiotics: Some Key Concepts

2.1   *Engaging with Semiotics: A Masochistic Exercise?*

Semiotics—the study of signs in the broadest sense—has had a bad press.[16] Engaging with this field is even considered by many a "masochistic exercise," because of semioticians' love of complex terms and opaque distinctions. In a sense, it should not come as a surprise that semiotics has a complicated way of describing things, since its objects of study are genuinely complicated: after all, semiotics as the study of signs covers a very broad area, including words, images, sounds, gestures, and objects—"anything which 'stands for' something else," as one scholar put it.[17]

In actual practice, semiotics has largely focused on language—the most extensive but also the most familiar semiotic system—to such an extent that the history of semiotics and linguistics are closely intertwined. While the insights gained by semiotics' founding fathers, Ferdinand de Saussure and Charles Sanders Peirce, such as the distinction between "language" and "parole" as levels of analysis, or between "symbols," "icons," and "indices" as types of signs, can be considered foundational, their work does promote an image of language as a decontextualized and

---

11   These questions can in turn be traced back to antiquity. See Leiwo 2021, 19 on Isidorus (ca. 560–636 CE).

12   Evans and Obbink 2010, 2.

13   In this area, too, various edited volumes have appeared in recent years: see, e.g., Leiwo, Halla-aho, and Vierros 2012; Cromwell and Grossman 2018; Bentein and Janse 2021.

14   For further discussion, see § 2.

15   Kress 2010.

16   See Bateman, Wildfeuer, and Hiippala 2017, 51.

17   Chandler 2007, 2.

dematerialized system. It was another linguist, Michael Halliday, who first proposed we view language as a *social semiotic system*,"[18] using this term to argue against the separation between language and society, instead viewing language as a device used to express meaning in context.

Despite being a linguist, Halliday recognized that "there are many other modes of meaning, in any culture, which are outside the realm of language," and that these other "modes" are "all bearers of meaning in culture," which can be defined as a "set of semiotic systems, as a set of systems of meaning, all of which interrelate."[19] Because of its orientation towards context, and its recognition of text as a semantic (rather than a formal) unit, Halliday's framework, known as "Systemic Functional Linguistics," opened the door to approaches which did in fact take into account other semiotic systems. Particularly well known in this regard is the work of Gunther Kress and Theo van Leeuwen,[20] an approach which has come to be known as "Social Semiotics."

2.2 *Meaning in Context: Social Semiotics*

One of Halliday's key insights was that communication is not only multimodal (that is, involving multiple "modes" of meaning), but also polyfunctional. Halliday hypothesized that there are three kinds of "meaning" (so-called "metafunctions"),[21] which he refers to as "ideational," "textual," and "interpersonal."[22] Scholars working in the Systemic Functional tradition have analyzed the workings of these three functions in other types of communication, visual communication in particular.

One of the most important and influential studies undertaken in this regard is Kress and van Leeuwen's *Reading Images: The Grammar of Visual Design* (1996),[23] a book that intended to set out a "grammar" of the meaning-making possibilities available in visual-based communicative artifacts. The authors do so by splitting up meaning in terms of Halliday's three metafunctions, and by discussing the systems of choice available for each. Thus, for example, Kress and van Leeuwen distinguish between the systems of "information value," "salience," and "framing" for the textual metafunction. With regard to information value, they argue that content placed on the left-hand side of images tends to be "given," whereas new information tends to be placed on the right-hand side, similarly to what we know to be the case in language.

In their study of visual design and other types of communication, Kress and van Leeuwen introduced some fundamental concepts, three of which we would like to mention here. A first central concept is that of (semiotic) mode, which can be defined as "a socially shaped and culturally given semiotic resource for making meaning."[24] Examples of such modes include image, writing, layout, music, and speech, among others. A term that is closely related to mode, as can also be seen in Kress's definition, is that of semiotic resource, which, unlike "mode," can be used with various degrees of abstractness, referring to anything that carries meaning, as indicated in the following definition: "the actions and artifacts we use to communicate, whether they are produced physiologically ... or by means of technologies—with pen, ink and paper; with computer hardware and software; with fabrics, scissors and sewing machines, etc."[25] Furthermore, van Leeuwen notes that the notion of a semiotic resource can be related to that of "sign" in traditional semiotic theory, but is preferable because it avoids the impression that what the sign stands for is pre-given. The third notion worth highlighting here is that of design: social semioticians adopt a rhetorical approach to communication, whereby they conceptualize the sender of a message as "rhetor." Document design can then be seen as "the translation of rhetorical intent into semiotic implementation."[26]

2.3 *Mapping Meaning to Form: Multimodality*

While heavily focusing on situating communication in its social context, and mapping systems of choice in specific semiotic modes, Kress and van Leeuwen also paid attention to the relations between different semiotic modes, a branch of research that is now known as "multimodality." While subsequent scholarship in the area of multimodality has built on and advanced Kress and van Leeuwen's pioneering insights,[27] their approach was criticized by others,[28] because of the fluidity of fundamental concepts such as mode, the difficulty to empirically verify some of the claims that were made, and the extension of a

---

18 See the title of Halliday's book, *Language as Social Semiotic* (1978).

19 Halliday 1978, 4.

20 See, e.g., Kress and van Leeuwen 1996; van Leeuwen 2005; Kress 2010.

21 Alternatively, more semiotically oriented labels are "presentational," "organizational," and "orientational." See Lemke 2002, 304–5.

22 See Bentein (this volume) for further discussion.

23 Second edition published in 2006.

24 Kress 2010, 79.

25 van Leeuwen 2005, 3.

26 Kress 2010, 49.

27 See, e.g., Jewitt and Kress 2003; Lim 2004; Matthiessen 2007.

28 See, e.g., Bateman 2008, 38–57.

conceptual framework that was designed for language to other areas of communication.[29]

Scholars such as Tuomo Hiippala and John Bateman have therefore elaborated a new approach that is less oriented towards social context and more towards the development of a descriptive model that can be used for the corpus-based study of multimodal artifacts. Known as the GeM (Genre and Multimodality) model, it distinguishes between various annotation layers, such as a layout layer, a rhetorical layer, or a navigation layer. At the same time, these scholars have attempted to refine and reconceptualize basic concepts such as "mode." Bateman, for example, conceptualizes semiotic modes as consisting of three strata.[30] The first stratum is the *material substrate*, which can be utilized by a certain group of users as a tool for making meaning. A material substrate carries *semiotic resources* of differing complexity (language, images, gestures, etc.), which form the second stratum. The third and last component is the stratum of *discourse semantics*, which guides the contextual interpretation of the semiotic resources, directing the reader towards the correct interpretation in a given context.[31]

2.4 *Historical Social Semiotics: A House with Many Rooms*

In proposing to extend social semiotics as a discipline to *historical* social semiotics, we are following a trend in linguistics research to extend the analysis of modern-day spoken and written language to the past. The best-known case of such an extension is arguably the development of historical sociolinguistics out of (variationist) sociolinguistics.[32] Sociolinguists initially showed little concern for texts from the past; William Labov, the founding father of sociolinguistics, famously characterizing historical linguistics as "the art of making the best use of bad data."[33] This restricted view was criticized by scholars such as Suzanne Romaine, who found that "a sociolinguistic theory which cannot handle written language is very restricted in scope and application, and cannot claim to be a theory of 'language'."[34] This then led to the extension of sociolinguistics to texts from the past under

the heading of "historical sociolinguistics" (initially called "socio-historical linguistics"), a discipline which has come to maturity over the last thirty years.

While the application of "the tenets of contemporary sociolinguistic research to the interpretation of material from the past"[35] has been a central goal of historical sociolinguistics, methodologically the discipline is certainly not confined to the sort of variationist research that has played a central role in contemporary sociolinguistics. Historical sociolinguistics is a house with many rooms, so much so that a broad definition of the discipline as "the reconstruction of the history of a given language in its socio-cultural context"[36] is more adequate and inclusive. More broadly speaking, it also does not mean that historical sociolinguistics should restrict itself to the application of mainstream sociolinguistic methods and questions. Given the radically different nature of the source material, it is only logical that historical sociolinguistics should develop its own methods and questions. In fact, it has recently been argued that the data historical sociolinguists are working with are not necessarily bad as long as they are treated on their own terms; that is, when scholars design inquiries for which the data that we possess are suited.[37]

We consider the same to be true for historical social semiotics: approaching historical data with models that have been designed for contemporary communication will undoubtedly lead to new questions and methods. At the same time, approaching texts from a historical social-semiotic perspective can be done through various frameworks, which may be more tailored to the specific questions that are asked. One approach that we would like to highlight in this context is Fournet's "paléographie signifiante."[38] In observing that "l'analyse materielle d'un document peut être porteuse de sens,"[39] not only when it comes to text type, but also with regard to the socio-cultural context of writing, and the provenance of the document, Fournet has argued that paleography should go beyond the purely descriptive analysis of documents, and should pay much more attention to the interrelationship between material features and context. Ultimately, this is very much in line with what we are proposing here.

29   E.g., the extension of "information value" to visual language, as we saw above.

30   See Bateman 2011.

31   Bateman 2011, 21; Hiippala 2014, 115.

32   Another field where such an extension can be witnessed is Politeness Theory, which has now come to be expanded to Historical Politeness Theory. See, e.g., Kádár and Culpeper 2010 and, with a focus on ancient languages, Kádár and Ridelagh 2019.

33   Labov 1994, 11.

34   Romaine 1982, 122.

35   Conde Silvestre and Hernández Campoy 2012, 1.

36   Conde Silvestre and Hernández Campoy 2012.

37   Stenroos 2018.

38   As Fournet (this volume) notes, paleography should be understood in a broad sense, including the study of scripts, writing supports, formats, and layouts.

39   Fournet 2007, 353.

3 Outline of the Volume

Thematically, the volume is divided into three main parts. The first consists of contributions focusing on the visual and material characteristics of ancient documents, as well as their relationship with the context of writing. To open, Fournet (Ch. 1) discusses the importance and relevance of documentary paleography (in the broadest sense, including the study of scripts, writing supports, formats, and layouts), which, he argues, should go beyond a purely descriptive approach. Under the heading "paléographie signifiante," Fournet intends to capture aspects of social meaning such as the nature and purpose of the document, the context of its writing, the personality of the writer, and the conventions regulating its drafting. To illustrate this approach, he discusses the particular case of documentary formats/layouts in late antiquity: during this period, writers no longer exclusively wrote along the fibers, but also adopted the mode of transfibral writing. Fournet outlines the general trend from a diachronic point of view, while being simultaneously attentive to synchronic diversification in terms of regional provenance and text type.

With the same focus on the interrelationship between genre and visual/material characteristics, Marco Stroppa (Ch. 2) looks at one of the most recognizable external characteristics of documentary sources, their size, and asks whether this could be considered a semiotic resource; that is, whether very large and very small papyri were written for special purposes. He argues that in considering a document "large" or "small," one should not only consider its dimensions, but also the relationship between the format and the size of the letters. Documents that are large in this relative sense are often associated with power, such as festive or prefectural letters, and in such cases, writers could opt for a large size to impress the reader and give more strength to their words thanks to the document's format. In the second part of his contribution, Stroppa looks at documents that have a small size: fragments are the best-known type of small document, but there are also small documents that are completely preserved, such as notes, receipts, and orders. Stroppa focuses on one, informal type of small document—party invitations—suggesting they were so small because they were made for a private purpose and an individual use: they could easily be carried or hidden, and perhaps even served as a sort of entrance ticket.

Sofía Torallas Tovar (Ch. 3) aims to better understand how the choice for a specific writing material—the ostracon—influenced visual choices. Potsherds have previously been considered a low-cost solution or an opportunity medium, with little analysis being performed on their materiality. Nevertheless, about one third of the documents that come from Egypt have been written on pottery or stone ostraca, many of them showing signs of having been written by professional scribes. Torallas Tovar discusses the use of ostracon for several text types (tax receipts, lists and accounts, letters), and compares their format and layout with that of documents written on papyrus. She discusses to what extent material aspects of writing itself (posture, holding the document) and the substrate (throwing lines, etc.) may have had an impact.

Building on Fournet's approach, Yasmine Amory (Ch. 4) analyzes how writers could convey deference in late antique letters through a number of visual means—such as graphic style, letter size, the use of blank spaces, and the disposition of the text—in order to predispose the addressee to the request—developing as it were a "visual politeness theory." At the same time, senders could adapt these visual means with the aim of humbling themselves and enhancing their inferior position. Thus, Amory suggests that "a play of oppositions" was at work in late antique letters, to which both senders and addressees were sensitive, possibly under the influence of a graphic education, as is suggested by some exercises on wooden tablets and papyri.

Eleonora Conti (Ch. 5) focuses on the features that characterize fourth-century Greek official letters from the high chancery. She notes that these letters are often multilingual, in the sense that they combine a Greek body with a Latin date. Such documents, however, also have a number of characteristic visual features: the greeting formula, for example, is attached to the text and is written in a more rapid *ductus*, and the date is written partly at the bottom and partly in the left margin. Conti argues that such features not only guaranteed the authenticity of the document but also underlined its official nature; as such they played an instrumental role in signaling social identity and formality. Conti also provides an overview of the relevant papyrological documentation, from earlier and later periods, and offers a comparison with Latin specimens of official letters.

Latin documentary sources are also central to Antonella Ghignoli's contribution (Ch. 6), which focuses on the representation of a sequence of things in the form of a list. Ghignoli reflects on the external features of lists in the rich documentation of documentary papyri from Roman and late antique Egypt, which can be used in the identification of lists (and the like) in fragmentary papyri. Relevant features include the arrangement of the text on a papyrus sheet, its alignment, the use of punctuation marks, the presence of graphic (Christian) symbols, a particular type of handwriting, and titles, among others.

Ghignoli uses these features as a basis for a comparative analysis of similar practices in documentary sources from the Roman West, the transmission of which is much poorer. Her analysis focuses on one specific, sixth-century Latin unpublished documentary papyrus.

The second part of the volume consists of contributions that explicitly relate visual and material features to the linguistic characteristics of texts. Klaas Bentein (Ch. 7) argues that in order to better understand the process of "textualization"—the coming into being of a non-literary text—a multi-modal approach is advisable. He argues for the central importance of the concept "framing" to understand communication practices in antiquity, suggesting we distinguish between "linguistic" and "typographic" framing, and relating framing features to three different levels ("micro," "meso," and "macro"). Focusing on women's letters from Roman Egypt, Bentein argues that based on linguistic and typographic framing practices, documents can be placed on a continuum that ranges from minimal to maximal discourse planning. Bentein concludes his contribution by situating textualization practices in their wider social context, exploring the relationship that seems to exist between framing and the letters' communicative functions. From this point of view, a certain type of textualization can be understood as a communicative strategy, rather than the result of (a lack of) education.

The same sort of multi-modal approach is advanced in Nicola Reggiani's chapter (Ch. 8). Reggiani focuses on paraliterary texts, more particularly papyri with a medical content, which he considers particularly suitable for a social-semiotic analysis. Reggiani looks into prescriptions as one of the better attested subcorpora: because each prescription conveys a single and unique message, there is ample use of what are called "paratextual" devices, such as *ekthesis*, *paragraphos*, *koronis*, and blank space, to divide prescriptions from each other. Reggiani also pays attention to the complementarity of these paratextual devices with formulaic markers such as ἄλλο and πρός. Such short expressions are sometimes represented in the form of a monogram, which could be viewed as the symbolic identifier of the starting point of a new recipe. Furthermore, these paratextual devices had a role to play at the text-structural level, which consisted of three distinct phases: "header," "pharmacological composition," and "practical instructions for preparation and administration." Reggiani notes that differences in layout features may have a connection with the context and the different audiences the prescriptions were meant for.

James Wolfe (Ch. 9) also considers inscriptions as "multimedial," communicative objects, but focuses on a different time and place: Roman Syria. He discusses how

the choice of a script could be meaningful on its own, independent of lexical information. He argues that script could function as a visual form of communication, and that the choice of Greek vs. Syriac in this region could function as a communicative image that supplemented the lexical information, by engaging in and reaffirming certain generic, institutional, and societal expectations. Wolfe argues that the use of Syriac signaled belonging to a local, civic community. At the same time, certain visual features (such as the directionality of the script, carving techniques, and letter forms) suggest an awareness of and accounting for the visual typologies of Greek monumental epigraphy. Wolfe discusses these multiple layers in terms of simultaneous communication in multiple "registers." As a second case study, Wolfe discusses the use of the acronyms ΧΜΓ and ΙΧΘΥΣ in Greek inscriptions: he argues that these could communicate multiple, discrete independent messages simultaneously. Like the use of a particular script, it could signal belonging to a certain community. At the same time, Wolfe argues against a priori connections between, for example, scripts and aspects of identity: rather, it is necessary to examine each inscription and its choice of script as a communicative act.

Sarah Béthume (Ch. 10) discusses the multitude of (ortho)graphic variants one is faced with in archaic and classical inscriptions, and the difficulty inherent in determining their nature; in particular, whether they have a phonetic/phonological reality in spoken language. Béthume argues that current interpretations often lack sensitivity to the particular nature of the source material. In reconsidering the so-called "hypercorrect aspiration," Béthume argues that one should not see epigraphic texts as transcriptions of oral utterances, but as written utterances inscribed with their own communicative goals. Béthume bases her approach on Jean-Marie Klinkenberg and Stéphane Polis's "scripturology," which views writing as a semiotic system in its own right. She concludes that the phenomenon under analysis is better viewed as a "hyperarchaism" or "hyperdialecticism," which formed part of a local graphic standard.

The third part sees the volume close with two contributions that put language central: in these chapters, linguistic variation is studied in relation to the context of writing by means of a quantitative approach. Geert De Mol (Ch. 11) focuses on orthographic hypercorrection in non-literary papyri. More particularly, he investigates the rendering of the number eight as either ὀκτώ or ὀκτώι; contrary to what one would perhaps expect, the latter form is attested with some frequency in the papyrological corpus. De Mol closely investigates the social contexts in which these forms can be found (in terms of genre, personal preferences, the relationship between sender and addressee), in order to provide a clearer answer to the question whether we are in fact dealing with a case of "quantitative" or "qualitative" hypercorrection, as distinguished in modern-day sociolinguistic treatments. He concludes that the notion of quantitative hypercorrection best characterizes the phenomenon under investigation, even if it does not entirely accord with modern-day characterizations in terms of its social distribution.

A quantitative approach towards linguistic variation is also pursued by Mark Depauw (Ch. 12), who investigates the phenomenon of word splitting, a textual practice that has received little to no attention so far. Depauw starts from the observation that whereas in Egyptian and Demotic texts words are seldomly split, in Greek texts word splits do not seem to be so infrequent. Using the data made available through recently developed Trismegistos tools such as Trismegistos Words and Trismegistos Text Irregularities, he investigates which influence linguistic and extralinguistic factors such as word length, formality (private vs. official), and time period (Ptolemaic vs. Roman) have on word splitting practices in Greek papyri, letters in particular. Depauw concludes by relating word splitting to related practices, such as abbreviations and syllabification, noting the need for further research.

4 Ten Challenges for Future Research

Now that we have outlined the book's content, we would like to conclude the introduction by briefly sketching ten key challenges for future research in the field of historical social semiotics. Evidently, there are many more challenges to be mentioned; what we present here, then, are the concerns that emerged from our conference discussions and from the chapters published in this volume.

1. Paying attention to the medium. In both epigraphy and papyrology, attention has been paid to the different writing materials that were available, and the connection of those writing materials to certain communicative purposes, usually discussed in terms of text types or families of text types (e.g., the use of the codex for literary purposes, potsherds for shorter texts such as receipts, lead for curse tablets, etc.). There has been relatively little reflection beyond this, however. An important distinction that could move the discussion forward is that between "material" and "medium": in some cases, a material, if it is steadily used to fulfil some communicative purpose, can establish itself into a full-blown medium: the newspaper is an example of a medium that "evolved to support

the fast-paced production and consumption of news by adopting a particular type of low-cost paper—newsprint."[40] In the case of antiquity, one could, for example, consider papyrus-based documents with a vertical format and perfibral writing direction as a specific type of medium.

A second point to consider in this regard is the relationship between material/medium and mode: whereas earlier scholarship conceived of these two concepts as independent from each other, modes "los[ing] their tie to a specific form of material realization"[41] and being conceived of in abstract ways, more recently it has been suggested that the two should be intimately related to each other. In Bateman's abovementioned GeM model,[42] it is explicitly acknowledged that different types of material substrates, such as the printed page, have different affordances: fonts may need to have a certain minimum size, for example. Other types of constraints associated with materiality are also taken into account, including production and consumption constraints. As Torallas Tovar shows in her chapter on Greek ostraca, referring to such affordances and constraints adds considerable detail to our understanding of writing practices in antiquity.

2. Rethinking the visual dimension. Scholars working in the areas of social semiotics and multimodality like to stress the fundamentally different nature of present-day communication: Bateman for example, explicitly situates the "ascendency of the multimodal document" in modern times, noting that what he calls "multimodal density" was fundamentally different in earlier periods.[43] Other scholars have been more careful with such claims: Anthony Baldry and Paul Thibault, for example, note that "there is, of course, no such thing as a monomodal page: there never has been and never will be."[44] At the same time, they recognize that some documents (present-day ones) are more obviously multimodal than others, because they combine traditional semiotic resources such as language and layout, with more modern ones such as color and photographs.

Such considerations urge us to attend to the role of elements that are considered visual in modern-day communication—such as images, diagrams, symbols—in documents from antiquity. While some research has been done on drawings accompanying (primarily Roman)

---

40   Hiippala 2017, 278.
41   Kress and van Leeuwen 2001, 22.
42   Bateman 2008, 15–19.
43   Bateman 2008, 2.
44   Baldry and Thibault 2006, 58.

inscriptions,[45] less work has been done on non-literary papyri, where sketches and drawings are perhaps infrequent but not completely absent.[46] Ildar Garipzanov has recently argued that the rise of what he calls "graphicacy" (referring to the use and understanding of graphic devices such as graphic symbols, geometric patterns, graphic images, diagrams, maps, etc. in various types of writing) should be situated long before the modern age.[47] The ongoing ERC project NOTAE (NOT A wriTtEn word but graphic symbols: An evidence-based reconstruction of another written world in pragmatic literacy from late antiquity to early medieval Europe; PI Antonella Ghignoli, Sapienza University of Rome), which aims to investigate the presence of graphic symbols in documentary texts from late antiquity to the early Middle Ages, will certainly shed light on this understudied research field.[48]

More fundamentally perhaps, we should reconsider how visual communication was achieved in antiquity: already in the earliest periods of writing, non-sensical inscriptions, consisting of letters that do not form meaningful words can be found as a decorative element.[49] Similarly, in archaic sculpture, writing is not used to frame the image, as in modern times, but rather is included in the field of the sculpted image, thus forming part of the material and figurative form of the object on which it was inscribed.[50] Curse tablets were sometimes given the shape of the object that was cursed, such as a foot or a tongue, or their materiality and writing (punctured lead; scrambled, or backwards written letters) could otherwise support the desired effect.[51] In the field of papyrology, Fournet has suggested that aspects such as the orientation of the document and the writing direction gave an immediate suggestion of the type of communication that was involved. Such evidence suggests that while the ancients did not usually include images as we know them in their documents, the visual was far from neglected.

3. Recognizing patterns. With its focus on larger corpora and document structure, it should come as no surprise that the multimodal research carried out by Bateman and others has focused on the recognition of patterns across documents, conceptualized as "multimodal genres." When it comes to language, genres have traditionally been described as linear and staged. Thus, for example, the petition as a genre can be described in terms of four stages: an opening (*prescriptio*), a background to the request (*narratio*), the actual request (*preces* or *precatio*), and the closing.[52] Relying on a principle of linearity becomes problematic, however, when multimodal considerations are made. Genre therefore needs to be approached as a multi-stratal phenomenon, a task that scholars working with the GeM model have started to undertake; in fact, next to the different layers described above (§2.3), Bateman recognizes a fifth layer, the "genre layer," "a representation of the grouping of elements from other layers into generically recognizable configurations distinctive for particular genres or document types,"[53] though it is much less developed and more hypothetical than the other layers.

Preliminary suggestions have also addressed how similarities between genres can be represented. Two main modes of representation for modeling genres can be mentioned in this regard: one, referred to as "typological" (representing genre families in terms of networks of choices), and another, "topological" (representing genres in terms of a genre space where one genre may be closer to another on the basis of a number of dimensions of comparison), both of which remain to be further explored. For a long time, relationships between genres have only been noted in passing by scholars working in antiquity and have rarely been conceptualized in the just-mentioned modern sense.[54] Recent scholarship has started to fill this gap:[55] mention can be made, among others, of the "Grammateus"[56] project led by Paul Schubert at the University of Geneva, which aims to produce a comprehensive typology of Greek documentary papyri and to assess the relationship between them through the analysis

---

45   See, e.g., Langner 2001; Lohmann 2017, 243–328.

46   See Horak 1992, and more recently Whitehouse 2007. For magical papyri, see, e.g., Martín Hernández 2012; Dijkstra 2015.

47   Garipzanov 2015.

48   See Ghignoli 2019 for an overview of the project. On the use of paratextual symbols and diacritic marks in Egyptian texts, from the pharaonic period until the Arabic period, see also Carlig et al. 2020.

49   See, e.g., Snodgrass 2000, 29–30. In the sphere of magic, we also find mystical letters forming words that are not commonly known (*ephesia grammata*) and magical signs (*charakteres*).

50   See Dietrich 2017, 315.

51   See Eidinow 2019, 364–67.

52   See, e.g., White 1972 and, more recently, Fournet 2019 with a focus on the evolution and changes of the late antique petition.

53   Bateman 2008, 108.

54   See, e.g., Guarducci 1969, 2:58, on the relationship between laws, decrees, and official letters in the domain of epigraphy.

55   See, e.g., Schubert 2018a on the typology of warrants, whose format was influenced by the petition and, later on, by the changing format of private business notes.

56   https://www.unige.ch/lettres/antic/unites/grec/enseignants/schubert/grammateus/.

of their "architecture"; that is, the material aspects, layout, and content.

4. Acknowledging differences in writing competence. Apart from studying larger patterns such as genres and registers, recent scholarship has made an effort to study the language of the individual (idiolects) in documentary papyri.[57] Such research has drawn attention to the existence of various linguistic competences: Evans, for example, divides writers in the Zenon archive into four groups, ranging from those with a clearly high education to those struggling with spelling and syntax.[58] In a similar vein, Amory has proposed we distinguish between different types of writers, based on the nature and quality of their handwriting.[59]

Questions about the interrelation between linguistic and graphic competence have rarely been asked: the general assumption seems to be that there should be a correspondence between the two competences, or, when such a correspondence is absent, that it can be related to the influence of a scribe taking down dictation. Bagnall and Cribiore have drawn attention, however, to some women's letters where the linguistic level is much higher than the graphic level, which are more difficult to explain.[60] Some of these questions are explored by Bentein in this volume in his discussion of "framing" as a multimodal principle.

Intimately related to the question of competence is the issue of schooling: while we have a fairly good knowledge of levels of schooling and the program, there is much less evidence for a graphic schooling, a topic further discussed by Amory in her contribution to this volume. Another question that deserves further reflection, but is even more difficult to answer, concerns reading competences: it stands to reason that people would not only have had different competences in producing written material, but also in engaging with it, depending on their exposure to such material.[61] Some research has been done on scribes guiding people through the use of blank spaces,[62] and on how barely literate people would still have been able

to recognize text types,[63] but further research would be welcome.

5. Accounting for diachronic change. While diachronic change has been a central topic in linguistics, we have much less understanding of the development of the make-up of multimodal artifacts, both within and across genres. The development of the Greek letter genre, particularly in late antiquity,[64] and the interconnections that seem to exist between rhetorical structure, document format, writing direction, and language—a topic that is treated by Fournet in this volume—has been an exception to this general trend. While social semiotic studies acknowledge that change is a feature inherent to all semiotic systems, there is still relatively little knowledge about the effects of such change on multimodality: as noticed by Hiippala, there is little knowledge "where processes of change originate and what drives them forward."[65]

A number of concepts have been developed that may be beneficial for discussions of antiquity, too. For example, scholars have applied the principles of change developed by Halliday and Christian Matthiessen[66] for language as a semiotic system—called "logogenesis" (the level of the actual language use, the text), "ontogenesis" (the level of the language user and their development, the degree to which they have knowledge of the semiotic system), and "phylogenesis" (the level of human language in general)— and applied them to the study of artifact structure. From the perspective of phylogenesis, change could be seen as enabling the expansion of "meaning," in an adaptation to new discursive and non-discursive (physical/biological) environments.[67] So, for example, in the modern age the introduction of the screen as a material substrate could be seen as forming a new discursive environment, which stimulated the novel combination of semiotic resources.[68]

6. Engaging in cross-cultural comparison. Research on multilingual inscriptions has brought to light interesting correspondences between documents from different cultural traditions. For example, it appears that writers sometimes consciously maintained linguistic symmetry, even if that meant departing from the linguistic norm in one

---

57   See, e.g., Evans 2010; Nachtergaele 2015; Leiwo 2017; Vierros 2020.
58   Evans 2012.
59   Amory, forthcoming.
60   Bagnall and Cribiore 2006.
61   Experienced readers, too, may have had different reading strategies depending on previous experience and reading goals.
62   See Schubert 2018b.

63   See, e.g., Kruschwitz and Campbell 2009 on the visual patterns associated with document types in Roman Pompei.
64   For a broader discussion of the development of the characteristics of Greek letters in the Graeco-Roman period, see Sarri 2018.
65   Hiippala 2016, 76.
66   Halliday and Matthiessen 1999, 17–18.
67   See Martin 1997, 9.
68   See Hiippala 2016, 78.

language, while in some cases, this even meant adopting another script to suggest closeness (a phenomenon sometimes called "allotography"). Even inscriptions written purely in one language sometimes consciously seem to adopt linguistic features from another linguistic tradition to display attachment to that tradition.[69]

It would be interesting to extend this sort of research beyond purely linguistic observations and to analyze which differences and (conscious/unconscious) similarities existed between different writing traditions. This is a topic treated here in the contributions of Wolfe (Greek and Syriac) and Conti (Greek and Latin), but it has also been of some interest in recent scholarship on modern-day writing practices. Bateman and Judy Delin, for example, have compared English and Japanese instruction manuals,[70] and Hiippala the Finnish and English versions of the same tourist brochure.[71]

7. Developing quantitative approaches. Most work to date on the materiality and by extension social semiotics of ancient documents has been done from a qualitative perspective. This is not just because scholars working in the field are most familiar with a qualitative approach: at present, there are simply no tools available that allow us to annotate large amounts of data in a user-friendly way. This is not to say that digital papyrology has not made a lot of progress in recent years: the papers published in *Digital Papyrology II: Case Studies on the Digital Edition of Ancient Greek Papyri* (2018, edited by Nicola Reggiani) give a good overview of some of the latest methods and tools developed in this field. These tools particularly concern the level of the text/document, including its diplomatic transcription, metadata, image(s), and secondary literature. Less progress has been made on levels lower than the text, although some of the functionalities developed by Trismegistos, such as Trismegistos Words and Text Irregularities,[72] form a notable exception to this trend, and some very valuable research findings have been made in this regard,[73] as also shown by Depauw in his contribution to this volume.

In order to engage in multi-modal research, we need digital tools that are able to make annotations not only at different textual levels but also on different types of objects (texts and images), preferably in a (semi)automated manner, and to link those annotations to each other in sophisticated ways, so that they can be queried. This is a challenge all researchers working in the field of multimodality face; to give one example, for his multimodal analysis of tourist brochures, Hiippala analyzed a corpus of "just" 89 documents.[74] Computer vision and machine learning are rapidly developing fields which address many of the issues relevant to multimodal analysis. Learning techniques from these fields, or even communicating and collaborating with its scholars, would open up further opportunities/possibilities for classicists. Exemplary in this regard has been the project led by Isabelle Marthot-Santaniello at the University of Basel, "Reuniting Fragments, Identifying Scribes and Characterizing Scripts: The Digital Paleography of Greek and Coptic Papyri,"[75] which is attempting to apply techniques such as document binarization to the papyrological corpus for purposes such as writer identification.[76]

8. Integrating theoretical models. When new digital tools are developed, it is important that they not only allow new possibilities on the digital side; they should also be based on the latest theoretical insights, concerning, for example, document structure. Above, we have described the progress that has been made by scholars such as Bateman in developing a "corpus-based" approach to multimodal analysis, which clearly distinguishes between different analytical layers for annotation. Bateman's framework is firmly based on findings from other disciplines, including not only social semiotics, but also design theory and rhetorical structure theory.

Scholars working in the areas of multimodality and social semiotics more broadly have drawn on a variety of theoretical frameworks to improve and enrich their analyses, including politeness theory, critical discourse analysis, cognitive linguistics, construction grammar, relevance theory, and visual rhetoric.[77] While these primarily linguistic frameworks have been applied (to various extents) to the analysis of the Ancient Greek language, their relevance for documents in their entirety remains to be explored, a point that is made in this volume by Amory for politeness theory.

69　　See Adams and Swain 2002, 7–8. Conversely, there are bilingual inscriptions with two texts that are similar but seem to follow their own cultural traditions (see Taylor 2002, 321).

70　　Bateman and Delin 2003.

71　　Hiippala 2012.

72　　These functionalities can be utilized at https://www.trismegistos.org/words/ and https://www.trismegistos.org/textirregularities/ respectively.

73　　See, e.g., Stolk and Depauw 2015; Keersmaekers 2020.

74　　Hiippala 2016.

75　　https://d-scribes.philhist.unibas.ch/en/.

76　　For recent publications, see, e.g., Mohammed, Marthot-Santaniello, and Margner 2019; Pratikakis et al. 2019.

77　　See van Leeuwen and Kress 1995; Bowker 2013; Forceville 2014; Cohn 2016.

9. Allowing for complementary perspectives. While the introduction of multiple analytical layers for documentation annotation, as in social semiotic and multimodal approaches, considerably facilitates and clarifies the analysis of (ancient) documents, it begs the question to what extent such approaches constitute an abstraction. Lemke has suggested in this context that we try to adopt a "phenomenological" perspective, questioning "whether the division of meaning making into language, gesture, drawing, action etc. is not mostly artificial."[78] In actual practice, it is probable that the different aspects of the multimodal artifacts that people produce and encounter are actually perceived of as unitary phenomena. In a similar vein, scholars have criticized the fact that in most social semiotic and multimodal theories the process of meaning making is approached (whether implicitly or explicitly) from the point of view of the speaker/producer/author. One may just as well put the hearer/recipient/reader at the center, focusing on the question of "how ... recipients integrate the different modalities like text, picture, sound, and design into a coherent meaning."[79]

While linguistic studies have demonstrated the value of including a "meta-perspective" on how language users perceived linguistic variation and varieties,[80] exploring such alternative perspectives on document design and composition is far from evident for the source material we are dealing with, though perhaps not entirely out of the question.[81] This is shown by Béthume in this volume, who challenges the adequacy of modern scholarship's use of the term "hypercorrection," arguing for the need to see inscriptions as written utterances that were perceived visually in antiquity. The same topic, but for a different corpus and time period, is also taken up by De Mol, whose chapter shows that in terms of social context, the use of a linguistic term such as hypercorrection is less straightforward than it may seem at first sight.

10. Mapping communicative situations. When it comes to contexts of writing in antiquity, scholarship has mostly concentrated its effort on recording stable characteristics such as the names of the persons involved in the communicative event, and their place and time of writing (the Trismegistos portal being the best-known source for such metadata). More recent scholarship has also attempted to map characteristics that are more dynamic, and therefore require close reading of the actual text, such as the relationship between the sender and the addressee, their occupation at the time of writing, the social distance, among others. This is now being exhaustively undertaken in the context of the ERC-funded EVWRIT project (Everyday writing in Graeco-Roman and late antique Egypt: A socio-semiotic study of communicative variation), which is led by Klaas Bentein at Ghent University.[82]

Both approaches are essentially participant- rather than communication-based, which can be partly attributed to the fact that they are focused on a fixed set of text types, such as letters, petitions, and contracts. In order to be able to make a broader comparison of communicative situations, and to gain a more comprehensive understanding of the functions of written communication in society, both synchronically and diachronically, one would have to develop a set of parameters that specifically target the nature of the different communicative situations, such as the social domain (administrative, family and friendship, transactional, religious, etc.),[83] the directionality of the social interaction (e.g., unidirectional [a sermon] vs. interdirectional [a dialogue]), and the type of interaction (e.g., embodied [direct contact] vs. disembodied [indirect contact]).[84] Taking into account such a broader set of communicative parameters would enable scholars to detect similarities and differences not only across text types, but also across fields that are traditionally not studied together—papyrology and epigraphy, literary and non-literary texts—which may be considered a crucial step towards a better understanding of the history of writing practices in antiquity.

Reference List

Adams, J. N., and Simon Swain. 2002. "Introduction." In *Bilingualism in Ancient Society*, edited by J. N. Adams, Mark Janse, and Simon Swain, 1–20. Oxford: Oxford University Press.

Amory, Yasmine. Forthcoming. "More than a Simple Intuition: Towards a Categorization of Paleographical Features in Greek Documentary Papyri." *Comparative Oriental Manuscript Studies Bulletin.*

Bagnall, Roger S. 2016. "Materializing Ancient Documents." *Daedalus* 145, no. 2: 79–87.

---

78   Lemke 2014, 166.
79   Bucher 2017, 91.
80   See, e.g., Colvin 2014; Van Rooy 2016; Bentein 2021.
81   Letter writing manuals, for example, constitute an interesting source for such a meta-perspective.

82   See www.evwrit.ugent.be. For an inventory of potential social parameters and their impact on particle usage in documentary papyri, see, e.g., Bentein 2015.
83   See, e.g., Ong 2015, 194–226.
84   See, e.g., Clark 1999.

Bagnall, Roger S., and Raffaella Cribiore. 2006. *Women's Letters from Ancient Egypt, 300 BC–AD 800*. Ann Arbor: University of Michigan Press.

Baldry, Anthony, and Paul J. Thibault. 2006. *Multimodal Transcription and Text Analysis: A Multimodal Toolkit and Coursebook with Associated On-line Course*. London: Equinox.

Bateman, John A. 2008. *Multimodality and Genre: A Foundation for the Systematic Analysis of Multimodal Documents*. Basingstoke: Palgrave Macmillan.

Bateman, John A. 2011. "The Decomposability of Semiotic Modes." In *Multimodal Studies: Multiple Approaches and Domains*, edited by Kay O'Halloran and Bradley Smith, 17–38. London: Routledge.

Bateman, John A., and Judy Delin. 2003. "Genre and Multimodality: Expanding the Context for Comparison across Languages." In *Contrastive Analysis in Language*, edited by Dominique Willems, Bart Defrancq, Timothy Colleman, and Dirk Noël, 230–66. London: Palgrave.

Bateman, John A., Janina Wildfeuer, and Tuomo Hiippala. 2017. *Multimodality: Foundations, Research and Analysis; A Problem-Oriented Introduction*. Berlin: De Gruyter Mouton.

Bentein, Klaas. 2015. "Particle-Usage in Documentary Papyri (I–IV A.D.): An Integrated Sociolinguistically-Informed Approach." *GRBS* 55, no. 3: 721–53.

Bentein, Klaas. 2021. "The Distinctiveness of Syntax for Varieties of Post-Classical and Byzantine Greek: Linguistic 'Upgrading' from the Third Century BCE to the Tenth Century CE." In Bentein and Janse 2021, 381–414.

Bentein, Klaas, and Mark Janse, eds. 2021. *Varieties of Post-Classical and Byzantine Greek*. Berlin: De Gruyter Mouton.

Boschung, Dietrich, and Jan N. Bremmer. 2015. *The Materiality of Magic*. Paderborn: Wilhelm Fink.

Bowker, Janet. 2013. "Variation across Spoken and Written Registers in Internal Corporate Communication: Multimodality and Blending in Evolving Genres." In *Variation and Change in Spoken and Written Discourse: Perspectives from Corpus Linguistics*, edited by Julia Bamford, Silvia Cavalieri, and Giuliana Diani, 47–64. Amsterdam: John Benjamins Publishing.

Bucher, Hans-Juergen. 2017. "Understanding Multimodal Meaning Making: Theories of Multimodality in the Light of Reception Studies." In *New Studies in Multimodality: Conceptual and Methodological Elaborations*, edited by Ognyan Seizov and Janina Wildfeuer, 91–123. London: Bloomsbury Academic.

Caputo, Clementina, and Julia Lougovaya, eds. 2020. *Using Ostraca in the Ancient World: New Discoveries and Methodologies*. Berlin: De Gruyter.

Carlig, Nathan, Aurore Motte, Guillaume Lescuyer, and Nathalie Sojic, eds. 2020. *Signes dans les textes. Continuités et ruptures des pratiques scribales en Égypte pharaonique, gréco-romaine et byzantine, Actes du colloque international de Liège (2–4 juin 2016)*. Liège: Presses Universitaires de Liège.

Chandler, Daniel. 2007. *Semiotics: The Basics*. 2nd ed. London: Routledge.

Clark, Herbert H. 1999. "How Do Real People Communicate with Virtual Partners?" In *Proceedings of 1999 AAAI Fall Symposium, Psychological Models of Communication in Collaborative Systems, 5–7 November, North Falmouth*. Menlo Park, CA: AAAI Press.

Cohn, Neil. 2016. "A Multimodal Parallel Architecture: A Cognitive Framework for Multimodal Interactions." *Cognition* 146: 304–23.

Colvin, Stephen. 2014. "Perception synchroniques des dialectes et de la koinè." In *Diffusion de l'attique et expansion des* koinai *dans le Péloponnèse et en Grèce centrale*, edited by Sophie Minon, 19–28. Geneva: Droz.

Conde Silvestre, Juan Camilo, and Juan Manuel Hernández Campoy. 2012. "Introduction." In *The Handbook of Historical Sociolinguistics*, 1–8. Chichester: Wiley-Blackwell.

Cromwell, Jennifer, and Eitan Grossman, eds. 2018. *Scribal Repertoires in Egypt from the New Kingdom to the Early Islamic Period*. Oxford: Oxford University Press.

Dietrich, Nikolaus. 2017. "Framing Archaic Greek Sculpture: Figure, Ornament and Script." In *The Frame in Classical Art*, edited by Verity Platt and Michael Squire, 270–316. Cambridge: Cambridge University Press.

Dijkstra, Jitse. 2015. "The Interplay between Image and Text on Greek Amulets Containing Christian Elements from Late Antique Egypt." In *The Materiality of Magic: An Artefactual Investigation into Ritual Practices and Popular Beliefs*, edited by Ceri Houlbrook and Natalie Armitage, 271–92. Philadelphia: Oxbow.

Eidinow, Esther. 2019. "Binding Spells on Tablets and Papyri." In *Guide to the Study of Ancient Magic*, edited by David Frankfurter, 351–87. Leiden: Brill.

Evans, Trevor V. 2010. "Identifying the Language of the Individual in the Zenon Archive." In Evans and Obbink 2010, 51–70.

Evans, Trevor V. 2012. "Linguistic and Stylistic Variation in the Zenon Archive." In *Variation and Change in Greek and Latin*, edited by Martti Leiwo, Hilla Halla-aho, and Marja Vierros, 25–40. Helsinki: Finnish Institute at Athens.

Evans, Trevor V., and Dirk D. Obbink. 2010. "Introduction." In *The Language of the Papyri*, edited by Trevor V. Evans and Dirk D. Obbink, 1–12. Oxford: Oxford University Press.

Fishman, Joshua A. 1965. "Who Speaks What Language to Whom and When?" *Ling* 1, no. 2: 67–88.

Forceville, Charles. 2014. "Relevance Theory as Model for Analysing Visual and Multimodal Communication." In *Visual Communication*, edited by David Machin, 51–70. Berlin: De Gruyter.

Fournet, Jean-Luc. 2007. "Disposition et réalisation graphique des lettres et des pétitions protobyzantines: pour une paléographie 'signifiante' des papyrus documentaires." In *Proceedings of the 24th International Congress of Papyrology, Helsinki, 1–7 August, 2004*, edited by Jaakko Frösén, Tiina Purola, and Erja Salmenkivi, 1:353–67. Helsinki: Societas Scientarum Fennica.

Fournet, Jean-Luc. 2009. "Esquisse d'une anatomie de la lettre antique tardive d'après les papyrus." In *Correspondances. Documents pour l'histoire de l'Antiquité tardive. Actes du colloque international, université Charles-de-Gaulle-Lille 3, 20–22 novembre 2003*, edited by Roland Delmaire, Janine Desmulliez, and Pierre-Louis Gatier, 23–66. Lyon: Maison de l'Orient et de la Méditerranée Jean Pouilloux.

Fournet, Jean-Luc. 2019. "Anatomie d'un genre en mutation: la pétition de l'Antiquité tardive." In *Proceedings of the 28th Congress of Papyrology; 2016 August 1–6*, edited by Alberto Nodar and Sofía Torallas Tovar, 571–90. Barcelona: Publicacions de l'Abadia de Montserrat.

Garipzanov, Ildar. 2015. "The Rise of Graphicacy in Late Antiquity and the Early Middle Ages." *Viator* 46, no. 2: 1–21.

Ghignoli, Antonella. 2019. "The NOTAE Project: A Research between East and West, Late Antiquity and Early Middle Ages." *Comparative Oriental Manuscript Studies Bulletin* 5: 29–42.

Guarducci, Margherita. 1969. *Epigrafia greca*. Vol. 2. Rome: Istituto poligrafico dello Stato, Libreria dello Stato.

Halliday, M. A. K. 1978. *Language as Social Semiotic: The Social Interpretation of Language and Meaning*. Baltimore: University Park Press.

Halliday, M. A. K., and Christian M. I. M. Matthiessen. 1999. *Construing Experience through Meaning: A Language-Based Approach to Cognition*. New York: Cassell.

Hiippala, Tuomo. 2012. "The Localisation of Advertising Print Media as a Multimodal Process." In *Multimodal Texts from Around the World: Cultural and Linguistic Insights*, edited by Wendy L. Bowcher, 97–122. London: Palgrave Macmillan.

Hiippala, Tuomo. 2014. "Multimodal Genre Analysis." In *Interactions, Images and Texts: A Reader in Multimodality*, edited by Sigrid Norris and Carmen Daniela Maier, 111–23. Berlin: De Gruyter.

Hiippala, Tuomo. 2016. *The Structure of Multimodal Documents: An Empirical Approach*. New York: Routledge.

Hiippala, Tuomo. 2017. "An Overview of Research within the Genre and Multimodality Framework." *Discourse, Context & Media* 20: 276–84.

Hoogendijk, Francisca A. J., and Steffie M. T. van Gompel, eds. 2019. *The Materiality of Texts from Ancient Egypt: New Approaches to the Study of Textual Material from the Early Pharaonic to the Late Antique Period*. 1st ed. Boston: Brill.

Horak, Ulrike. 1992. *Illuminierte Papyri, Pergamente und Papiere I*. Pegasus Oriens 1. Vienna: Holzhausen.

Jewitt, Carey, and Gunther R. Kress, eds. 2003. *Multimodal Literacy*. New York: Peter Lang.

Kádár, Dániel Z., and Jonathan Culpeper. 2010. "Historical (Im)Politeness: An Introduction." In *Historical (Im)Politeness*, edited by Dániel Z. Kádár and Jonathan Culpeper, 9–38. Bern: Peter Lang.

Kádár, Dániel Z., and Kim Ridealgh. 2019. "Introduction." *Journal of Historical Pragmatics* 20, no. 2: 169–85.

Keersmaekers, Alek. 2020. "A Computational Approach to the Greek Papyri: Developing a Corpus to Study Variation and Change in the Post-Classical Greek Complementation System." PhD diss., KU Leuven.

Kress, Gunther R. 2010. *Multimodality: A Social Semiotic Approach to Contemporary Communication*. London: Routledge.

Kress, Gunther R., and Theo van Leeuwen. 1996. *Reading Images: The Grammar of Visual Design*. London: Routledge.

Kress, Gunther R., and Theo van Leeuwen. 2001. *Multimodal Discourse: The Modes and Media of Contemporary Communication*. London: Arnold.

Kruschwitz, Peter, and Virginia L. Campbell. 2009. "What the Pompeians Saw: Representations of Document Types in Pompeian Drawings and Paintings (and Their Value for Linguistic Research)." *Arctos* 43: 57–84.

Labov, William. 1994. *Principles of Linguistic Change*. Oxford: Blackwell.

Langner, Martin. 2001. *Antike Graffitizeichnungen: Motive, Gestaltung und Bedeutung*. Wiesbaden: Ludwig Reichert.

Leiwo, Martti. 2021. "Tracking down Lects in Roman Egypt." In Bentein and Janse 2021, 17–38.

Leiwo, Martti. 2017. "Confusion of Moods in Greek Private Letters of Roman Egypt?" In *Variation and Change in Ancient Greek Tense, Aspect and Modality*, edited by Klaas Bentein, Mark Janse, and Jorie Soltic, 242–60. Leiden: Brill.

Leiwo, Martti, Hilla Halla-aho, and Marja Vierros. 2012. *Variation and Change in Greek and Latin*. Helsinki: Finnish Institute at Athens.

Lemke, Jay L. 2014. "Multimodality, Identity and Time." In *The Routledge Handbook of Multimodal Analysis*, 2nd ed., edited by C. Jewitt, 165–75. Abingdon: Routledge.

Lemke, Jay L. 2002. "Travels in Hypermodality." *Visual Communication* 1, no. 3: 299–325.

Lim, Fei Victor. 2004. "Developing an Integrative Multi-Semiotic Model." In *Multimodal Discourse Analysis*, edited by Kay O'Halloran, 220–46. London: Continuum.

Lohmann, Polly. 2017. *Graffiti als Interaktionsform: Geritzte Inschriften in den Wohnhäusern Pompejis*. Berlin: De Gruyter.

Martín Hernández, Raquel. 2012. "Reading Magical Drawings in the Greek Magical Papyri." In *Actes Du 26e Congrès*

International de Papyrologie, Genève, 16–21 Août 2010, edited by Paul Schubert, 491–98. Geneva: Droz.

Martin, J. R. 1997. "Analysing Genre: Functional Parameters." In *Genres and Institutions: Social Processes in the Workplace and School*, edited by Frances Christie and J. R. Martin, 3–39. London: Cassell.

Matthiessen, Christian M. I. M. 2007. "The Multimodal Page: A Systematic Functional Exploration." In *New Directions in the Analysis of Multimodal Discourse*, edited by Terry D. Royce and Wendy Bowcher, 1–62. Mahwah, NJ: Lawrence Erlbaum Associates.

Mohammed, Hussein, Isabelle Marthot-Santaniello, and Volker Margner. 2019. "GRK-Papyri: A Dataset of Greek Handwriting on Papyri for the Task of Writer Identification." In *2019 International Conference on Document Analysis and Recognition (ICDAR)*, 726–31. Sydney: IEEE.

Nachtergaele, Delphine. 2015. "The Formulaic Language of the Greek Private Papyrus Letters." PhD diss., Ghent University.

Ong, Hughson T. 2015. *The Multilingual Jesus and the Sociolinguistic World of the New Testament*. Leiden: Brill.

Petrovic, Andrej, Ivana Petrovic, and Edmund Thomas, eds. 2018. *The Materiality of Text: Placement, Perception, and Presence of Inscribed Texts in Classical Antiquity*. Leiden: Brill.

Pratikakis, Ioannis, Konstantinos Zagoris, Xenofon Karagiannis, Lazaros Tsochatzidis, Tanmoy Mondal, and Isabelle Marthot-Santaniello. 2019. "ICDAR 2019 Competition on Document Image Binarization (DIBCO 2019)." In *2019 International Conference on Document Analysis and Recognition (ICDAR)*, 1547–56. Sydney: IEEE.

Reggiani, Nicola, ed. 2018. *Digital Papyrology II: Case Studies on the Digital Edition of Ancient Greek Papyri*. Berlin: De Gruyter.

Romaine, Suzanne. 1982. *Socio-Historical Linguistics: Its Status and Methodology*. Cambridge: Cambridge University Press.

Sarri, Antonia. 2018. *Material Aspects of Letter Writing in the Graeco-Roman World 500 BC–AD 300*. Berlin: De Gruyter.

Schubert, Paul. 2018a. "Warrants: Some Further Considerations on Their Typology." *BASP* 55: 253–74.

Schubert, Paul. 2018b. "Who Needed Writing in Graeco-Roman Egypt, and for What Purpose? Document Layout as a Tool of Literacy." In *Literacy in Ancient Everyday Life*, edited by Anne Kolb, 335–50. Berlin: De Gruyter.

Snodgrass, Anthony. 2000. "The Uses of Writing on Early Greek Painted Pottery." In *Word and Image in Ancient Greece*, edited by Keith Rutter and Brian Sparkes, 22–34. Edinburgh: Edinburgh University Press.

Stenroos, Merja. 2018. "From Scribal Repertoire to Text Community: The Challenge of Variable Writing Systems." In *Scribal Repertoires in Egypt from the New Kingdom to the Early Islamic Period*, edited by Eitan Grossman and Jennifer Cromwell, 20–40. Oxford: Oxford University Press.

Stephan, Robert P., and Arthur Verhoogt. 2005. "Text and Context in the Archive of Tiberianus (Karanis, Egypt; 2nd Century AD)." *BASP* 42: 189–201.

Stolk, Joanne, and Mark Depauw. 2015. "Linguistic Variation in Greek Papyri: Towards a New Tool for Quantitative Study." *GRBS* 55, no. 1: 196–220.

Taylor, David G. K. 2002. "Bilingualism and Diglossia in Late Antique Syria and Mesopotamia." In *Bilingualism in Ancient Society: Language Contact and the Written Text*, edited by J. N. Adams, Mark Janse, and Simon Swain, 298–331. Oxford: Oxford University Press.

van Leeuwen, Theo. 2005. *Introducing Social Semiotics*. London: Routledge.

van Leeuwen, Theo, and Gunther Kress. 1995. "Critical Layout Analysis." *Internationale Schulbuchforschung* 17, no. 1: 25–43.

van Minnen, Peter. 1994. "House-to-House Enquiries: An Interdisciplinary Approach to Roman Karanis." *ZPE* 100: 227–51.

Van Rooy, Raf. 2016. "'What Is a "Dialect"?' Some New Perspectives on the History of the Term Διάλεκτος and Its Interpretations in Ancient Greece and Byzantium." *Glotta* 92, no. 1: 244–79.

Vierros, Marja. 2021. "Idiolect in Focus: Two Brothers in the Memphis Sarapeion (II BCE)." In Bentein and Janse 2021, 39–74.

White, John L. 1972. *The Form and Structure of the Official Petition: A Study in Greek Epistolography*. Missoula, MT: Society of Biblical Literature.

Whitehouse, Helen. 2007. "Drawing a Fine Line in Oxyrhynchus." In *Oxyrhynchus: A City and Its Texts*, edited by Alan Bowman, Revel A. Coles, Nikolaos Gonis, and Peter Parsons, 296–306. London: Egypt Exploration Society.

PART 1

A Novel Approach to the Visual and Material Characteristics of Ancient Documents

∴

Beyond the Text or the Contribution of "Paléographie signifiante" in Documentary Papyrology: The Example of Formats in Late Antiquity

Jean-Luc Fournet

Introduction

Paleography[1] has always maintained a privileged relationship with literary papyrology: it is in the field of literary papyri that scripts and bibliology tend to be considered as important as textual data. It is for this reason that we have no thorough and systematic studies of the papyrological scripts and layouts beyond literary papyri. In contrast, in the field of documentary papyrology, paleography has long played a minor role: it is usually taken into account only for dating. It suffers, for the rest, from the competition of the very text which constitutes the almost exclusive interest of documentary papyri for editors and readers of their editions, who are often historians naturally more interested in meaning than in form. Moreover, the much greater number of documentary papyri compared to literary papyri has meant that papyrologists, having to make choices, have neglected formal aspects to concentrate on content.

Yet I do not see why the study of scripts and formats would be less necessary in the documentary field than in the literary one, as they are two sides of the same coin: the written culture. Applied to documents, paleography has a lot to say. First, on a macro-cultural level, it illuminates a whole system of conventions that regulate the act of writing. Taught at school, in notaries' offices, or in chancelleries, these codes determine the choice of writing styles, writing materials, and their layout. They thus constitute the most tangible (since they are immediately visible) and at the same time the most profound part of the written culture. Second, on a micro-cultural level, it conveys information on how an individual puts into practice the codes of this written culture. It helps provide a clearer idea of their cultural and socio-professional profile, as I have shown elsewhere, particularly through the use of diacritic signs in documents.[2] Third, from a more pragmatic point of view, it provides data that prolong, duplicate, or complement the primary meaning conveyed by the text, thus helping to better understand the text, context, or subtext of a document. In short, papyrologists must take these into account to have a better idea of the papyri they are studying.

For these reasons, I proposed at the 2004 International Congress of Papyrology to speak of "meaningful paleography" (paléographie signifiante); in other words, a paleography that does not simply describe the facts (in particular, to draw up typologies or evolutionary chains), but always seeks to see how these facts are indicative of what is beyond or behind signs. This namely entails the meaning of the text, but it also includes the nature and purpose of a document, the context of its writing, the personality of its writer, and, finally, the conventions regulating its drafting.[3] Here I would like to illustrate the method and the benefits of this paleography thus conceived with the particular case of documentary formats or layouts during late antiquity. However provisional this work may be, I'd like to present here some first results and a few lines of reflection.

1 Generalities

As is known, papyrus was purchased in the form of rolls, whose standard size was 3.5 to 4 meters (= 20 *kollēmata*),[4] which could be used (or "repackaged/reconditioned") in various ways to achieve the definitive document: either by cutting it into sheets ("coupons") or using it to make a codex. If the codex was a revolution in the literary domain, it remained of limited use in the documentary field,[5] however, where it was only used for private accounts,[6] public financial and tax documents (such as tax roles[7] or

---

1 Which I mean here in a broad sense: the study of scripts, writing supports, formats, and layouts.
2 Fournet 1994, and more generally Fournet 2013, 148–60.
3 Fournet 2007.
4 Skeat 1982.
5 See, in general, Gascou 1989.
6 E.g., P.Cair.Masp. 11 67138–39 (Aphrodite [541–46 CE], accounts relating to the domain of Count Ammōnios).
7 E.g., P.Aphrod.Reg. (Aphrodite [525/526 CE], tax register of the village of Aphrodite).

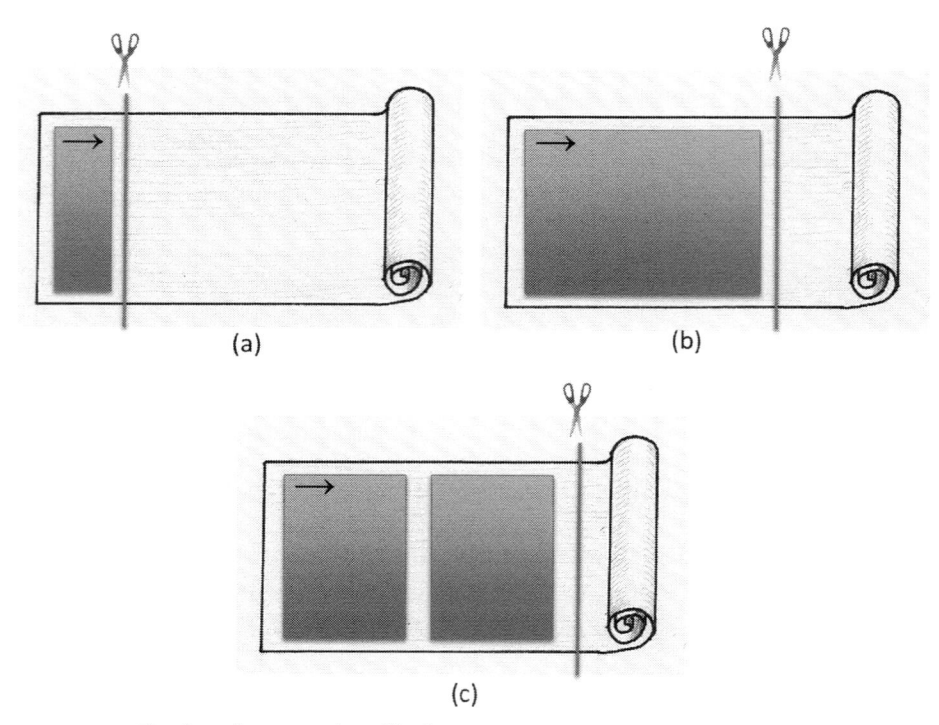

FIGURE 1.1   The three formats with perfibral writing

cadasters[8]), or to archive private documents, most often receipts[9]—that is, all types of documents for which the shape of the codex offered the utmost comfort for users by facilitating spots and repeated checks. Documents consisting of a continuous text are normally not written in codices except for archival copies.[10]

As for a single sheet of papyrus (which is the normative form for documents), it can be written either along or across the fibers (*transversa charta*). As a matter of fact, a radical change in the way of positioning the sheet

to be written occurred in the Byzantine era. During the previous period, perfibral writing far prevailed, with three distinct formats (see Fig. 1.1): a) had a single textual zone in a vertical format (higher than wide), as in P.Col. X 272 (Oxyrhynchos [242 CE], a flooded land declaration, 20 + x × 6.5 cm); b) had a single textual zone in a horizontal format (wider than high), as in SPP XX 1 (Arsinoe [83/84 CE], for the sale of catoechic land, 21 × 28.5 cm); while c) had multiple textual zones in a horizontal format (wider than tall with multiple columns), as in P.Oxy. II 237 (Oxyrhynchos [after June 27, 186 CE], Dionysia's petition to the prefect, 26 × 209.5 cm in 9 columns!).

These three formats continued to exist during the Byzantine period. An example of a) can be seen in a petition to a *riparius*, P.Cair.Masp. I 67092 (Aphrodite [528 CE], 31.5 × 12.5 cm); b) is exemplified by PSI XII 1239 (Antinooupolis [430 CE], for the sale of a house, 30.5 × 51.9 cm) and by P.Dubl. 32 (= SB I 517, Arsinoe [512 CE], for the sale of a monastery, 84.2 × 29.7 cm); while c) is exemplified by P.Cair. Masp. I 67002 (Aphrodite [566 CE], a petition to the Duke of Thebaid, 30.5 × 234.7 cm in 3 columns [see Fig. 1.9]).

A great development of the Byzantine era was the recourse to transfibral (or *transversa charta*) writing. This saw the addition of two further types of formats (Fig. 1.2), supplementing the three just outlined. The first, d) had a single textual zone in a horizontal format (wider than high, the width corresponding to the height of the roll, about 30 cm), as in the letter P.Oxy. LVI 3866 (Oxyrhynchos [VI CE?], 10 × 30 cm); while the second, e) had a single

---

8   E.g., P.Land.List I–II (Hermopolite nome [346/347 CE], land registers).

9   E.g., P.Panop. 19 (verso of P.Panop.Beatty 1–2; Panopolis [339–345 CE], tax receipts); P.Cair.Masp. III 67325 (Aphrodite [554/555–559/560 CE: see BL XII 47], tax receipts and a lease copied after accounts).

10   Exceptions are rare. I will only quote three examples from the Dioscorus archive: P.Cair.Masp. III 67325, IV recto (Aphrodite [585 CE], a lease in the midst of accounts and receipts); P.Cair. Masp. III 67341 III, recto *descr.* (Aphrodite [585 CE], a lease amid accounts); and P.Strasb. gr. inv. 1633 (ed. Fournet 2008a, 22–25; Aphrodite [587/588 CE], a lease in the midst of accounts and receipts). These are three contracts concerning fields belonging to Dioscorus's heirs (in particular his wife Sophia) whose different hands in at least two of them (P.Cair.Masp. III 67325, IV recto and 67341 III, recto) show that these are indeed original deeds that the lessors insisted on having drawn up directly in registers already containing documents relating to their family rather than having them written on separate sheets. These are atypical cases which should be taken as an indication of a personality having developed a somewhat manic predilection for the codex rather than reflecting a general trend.

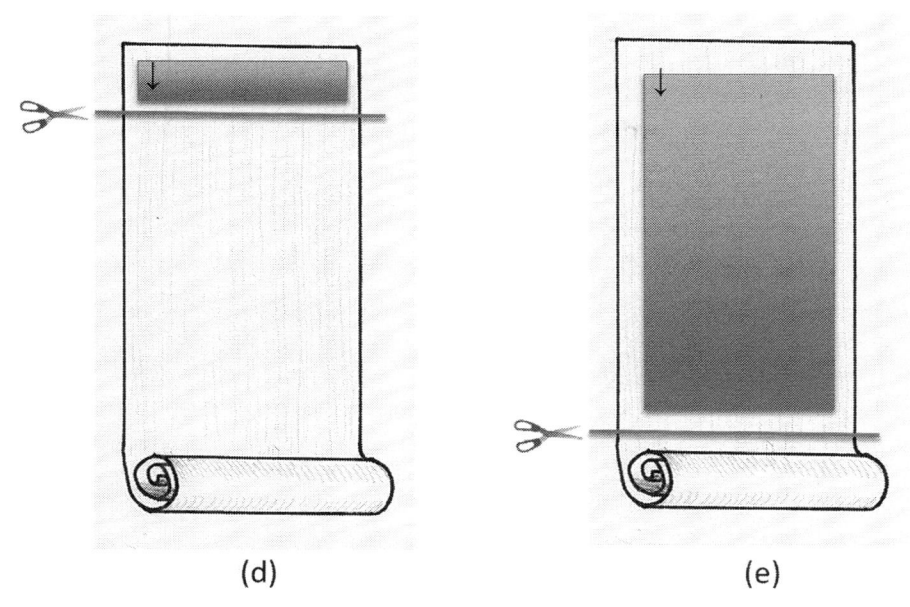

(d)   (e)

FIGURE 1.2   The two formats with transfibral writing

textual zone in a vertical format (higher than wide), as in the lease P.Hamb. I 68 (Aphrodite [548 CE], 74 × 31 cm).

The *transversa charta* writing in both formats was not strictly speaking a Byzantine innovation. In the Ptolemaic period, it was used for letters of a more formal nature, official letters[11] (e.g., P.Cair.Zen. I 59057, Syria or Palestine? [257 BCE], a letter from Zōilos to Alexandros, 12.5 × 33 cm), or for double-documents (with a *scriptura interior* and *exterior*), that is to say the so-called *syngraphai examartyroi* (e.g., P.Eleph. 1 [310 BCE], a marriage contract, 40 × 35 cm). In Roman times, it was used mainly—when wooden tablets were not employed—for a *testatio* (gr. μαρτυροποίημα), a form of double-document of Roman tradition, used for private contracts of Roman law, for declarations of illegitimate children, or for authenticated copies of public documents[12] (e.g., PSI IX 1026, Caesarea Palestine [150 CE], an authenticated copy of a petition of veterans to the governor of Judea, 36.3 × 26.5 cm). The *testatio* had given rise, in the field of legal acts, to a version adapted to papyrus, called *diplōma*, of which about twenty examples from the second century are known in the *P.Babatha* (e.g., P.Babatha 22, Province of Arabia [130 CE], sale of a harvest of dates, 28.7 × 16.2 cm) and fifteen from the third century in the P.Dura (e.g., P.Dura 26, Sachare [227 CE], sale, 30.5 × 24.7 cm), or the Euphrates papyri (P.Euphrates).

These Roman antecedents are rather marginal, however, especially in Egypt, and cannot explain the large-scale adoption of this format in the Byzantine period. In

fact, the phenomenon of *transversa charta* writing has never been the subject of a systematic study, both diachronic and synchronic. One is too often content to refer to the few lines that G. Eric Turner devoted to it in his booklet entitled *The Terms Recto and Verso: The Anatomy of the Papyrus Roll* (1974). After studying the Roman examples, he adds, "the 'vertically placed' roll never entirely disappears from view, even in the fifth century ... but re-emerges massively in the sixth." He cites as characteristic examples the papyri of Aphrodite and Syene of the sixth century but concludes that

> I must however record puzzlement as to why the "vertical" form is sometimes used, and sometimes the (previously) normal "horizontal" form, in which the writing is along the fibres and set out in columns. Both formats are in use simultaneously, and the quick survey I have made indicates no reason why one should have been preferred to the other.[13]

I'd like to show that the phenomenon is far from random; rather, it is indicative of new writing conditions.

2   The Studied Dossiers[14]

To answer questions on the extent and reasons for the widespread adoption of *transversa charta* writing, it is

---

11   See P.Mich.Zen., p. 158.
12   P.Thomas, p. 102–4.

13   Turner 1978, 47 and 49 (§ 4.12).
14   I limit my survey to the documents written in a continuous text, thereby excluding accounts, lists, and other non-syntactic texts.

necessary to identify the diachronic evolution of the phenomenon while being attentive to its synchronic diversification in terms of documentary types and provenances. For that, I will rely on several dossiers ranging from the fifth to the seventh centuries and from various provenances, each outlined below.[15] In the following I will content myself with giving the counts without the precise references to the documents, with → denoting perfibral documents and ↓ denoting transfibral (or *transversa charta*) documents.

2.1   *The Lycopolis Papyri* (*V–VI CE*)

This is a still-unpublished archive, now in the Institut de France, Paris. The majority of the texts date from the fifth century,[16] and comprise contracts (36: 34 →, 2 ↓), petitions (2 →), rent receipts (6 →), tax receipts (21: 20 ↓, 1 →), and letters (18 ↓). From this list we can see that already in the fifth century two documentary genres stand out for the use of the *transversa charta* writing: letters and tax receipts, both of which adopt the horizontal format (except when the letter is long).

2.2   *The Aphrodite Papyri* (*VI–VII CE*)[17]

These consist of two archives, that of Dioscorus (506–588 CE)[18] and that of Phoibammōn and his heirs (524–ca. 650 CE, with a good core of texts later than in the archives of Dioscorus).[19] The first, the Dioscorus archive,[20] comprises contracts (146: 99 →, 47 ↓) and private receipts (11: 7 ↓, 4 →), tax receipts (34: 23 ↓, 11 →), payment orders (5 →), governor orders (7 →), petitions (30: 23 →, 7 ↓ or ↓ / →), and letters (99: 95 ↓, 4 → or → / ↓). The second, the archive of Phoibammōn and his heirs,[21] comprises contracts (42: 34 ↓, 8 →) and rent receipts (3: 2 ↓, 1 →).

The Aphrodite papyri confirm the teachings of those from Lycopolis: the *transversa charta* writing is clearly the norm for letters and tax receipts, which adopt a horizontal

format. Petitions are almost always perfibral. But the two archives show a reversal of trend: those of Phoibammōn, generally later, show a preference for *transversa charta* writing as far as contracts are concerned, unlike those of Dioscorus, which followed the trend already observed with the more ancient papyri from Lycopolis.

2.3   *The Syene Papyri* (*VI–VII CE*)

These are found in the Patermouthis archive, whose main core ranges from 574 to 613 CE.[22] It comprises thirty-four contracts (25 ↓, 11 →).[23] These papyri confirm the tendency noted with the later Aphrodite papyri. The eleven perfibral texts are all short (between 10 and 35 + x lines), unlike the others, which are long, even very long (53–111 lines), with two exceptions: P.Lond. v 1730 and 1731 (of 30 and 46 lines[24]).

2.4   *The Petra Papyri* (*VI CE*)

These are from the archive of Flavius Theodōros, with a core of texts from the last third of the sixth century.[25] They allow us to see what the situation is outside Egypt in terms of format. They comprise the following genres: contracts, including settlements (33: 32 ↓, 1 →); tax receipts (18: 17 ↓, 1 →); requests addressed to the administration, such as the transfer of taxation, *defensio* of a sale, etc. (11 →); official letters, ordinances (4 →); and letters (2 ↓). The tendencies which we observed with the other group of texts from the same period are corroborated and even more strongly emphasized by the Petra papyri originating from the *Tertia Palaestina Salutaris*. In addition to non-official letters, contracts and tax receipts were, from that point on, all *transversa charta*,[26] while the documents sent to

---

15   I will not deal with Oxyrhynchos: Serena Causo (Ghent University) is currently devoting her PhD to the formats in the Roman and Byzantine documents from this city.

16   For a survey of this archive, see Fournet and Gascou 2008.

17   See Fournet 2008b.

18   For a list of the papyri belonging to this archive, we only have to remove the documents from the Phoibammōn archive (cited in Fournet 2016) from the list cited in Fournet 2008b.

19   See Fournet 2016, with a list of the papyri from this archive.

20   I limit myself to P.Cair.Masp. I–III and P.Lond. v except for petitions or letters (which are taken into account in an exhaustive manner). I thank Yasmine Amory for the figures concerning the letters.

21   I limited myself to P.Mich. XIII, P.Vat.Aphrod., and P.Michael.

22   www.trismegistos.org/archive/37.

23   Including two texts (P.Lond. v 1736–37) written by a non-professional. Note that P.Münch. I 2 is a contract relating to the army.

24   Note that P.Lond. v 1730 is written by a scribe who makes many mistakes and therefore does not fully master the codes of documentary writing.

25   P.Petra I–V. I do not take into account documents of indeterminate content and format (such as P.Petra IV 41, a document concerning the sale of a house, the purpose of which is unclear and whose layout in three columns is uncertain) and the documents written on a reused sheet.

26   With two exceptions: P.Petra III 20 is a receipt written along the fibers (on the picture, the fibers seem to be vertical, but it may be a false impression); P.Petra V 55, a *donatio mortis causa* (573 CE?) perfibrally written in eight columns, six of which (cols. ii–vii) repeat the same text six times, each copy in a separate column. I know no other parallel for this arrangement. The use of Latin in columns i and viii is also very strange for a legal text (even if the party is a soldier as proposed by the editor). The fact that the content of columns i to viii is identical may perhaps

authorities (there are no petitions, unlike the previous dossiers, but tax transfers or other requests) or by the authorities (official letters, ordinances) are all perfibral.[27]

3 Synthesis

Having now introduced these four dossiers, we might ask what lessons can be drawn from them in terms of late antique layout?

3.1 Letters

Transversa charta writing first developed with private letters (and incidentally tax receipts[28]) from the fifth century onwards, at a time when legal and judicial documents were perfibral. Why letters? The first explanation that can be given is of a purely material nature: the private letter being a documentary genre of variable length, practiced a priori by non-professional writers, the only format that, in theory, allows for no waste of papyrus is the *transversa charta* one.[29] Indeed, to write perfibrally, one must calibrate in advance the length of the lines according to the length of the document. Once the first line is written, the surface to be written is limited by the length of this line (= width) and the height of the roll (= height). If the text does not cover the whole sheet thus delimited, the end is left blank[30] or it can be cut off—but nothing can be done with the remaining part. If the text to be written exceeds the surface of the sheet, it can either be written in the margins (*versiculi transversi*[31]), provided that it is not too long, or added in a new column—but this is a rare format for letters[32] and can't avoid a blank space at the end of the last column and thus wasting papyrus.

On the other hand, when writing a letter *transversa charta*, the length of the lines is imposed by the height of the roll (= length) whereas the height of the document is limited only by the length of the roll; that is to say, you can write as much as you want! Once the letter is completed, the sheet is cut out of the roll. Thus, the ratio between the

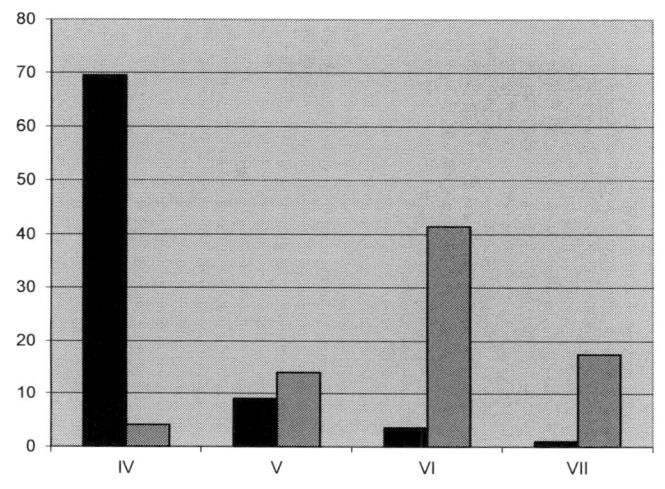

FIGURE 1.3 Perfibral (black) and *transversa charta* (light grey) letters in the P.Oxy.

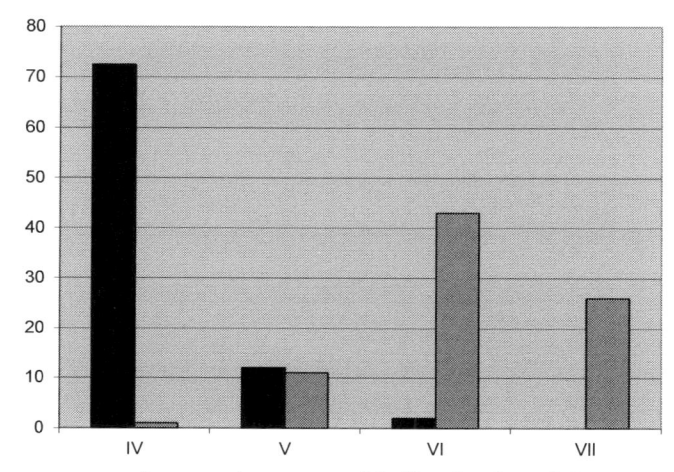

FIGURE 1.4 Letters with a prescript (black) and without (light grey) in the P.Oxy.

length of written text and the papyrus area used is the best you can hope for.

Although this explanation may have played a role, we are nevertheless entitled to wonder why *transversa charta* writing is a solution that was favored only from the fifth century onwards—a shift shown in the graph based on P.Oxy. in Figure 1.3. I would be tempted to put this change of format into a causal relationship with the change of diplomatics (i.e., of structure) experienced by this genre at exactly the same time; namely, the disappearance of the introductory formula (*praescriptum*: ὁ δεῖνα τῷ δεῖνι χαίρειν) and of the final salutation (*formula valedicendi*: ἔρρωσθαι (σε εὔχομαι))—a hypothesis that I developed elsewhere.[33] This change in structure (Fig. 1.4) is so

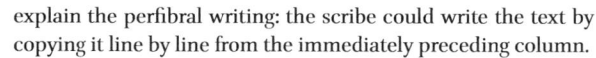

explain the perfibral writing: the scribe could write the text by copying it line by line from the immediately preceding column.

27   See already A. Arjava in P.Petra III, 1–2, and Vierros 2021.

28   Further study should examine whether the two adopt this format simultaneously or with a time-lag between them.

29   See Turner 1978, 45 (§ 4.10.2).

30   E.g., P.Flor. II 259 (Theadelphia [249–268 CE]).

31   Homann 2012.

32   E.g., P.Ammon 1 (Alexandria [348 CE?], letter of *scholasticus* Ammon to his mother, 178 lines in 6 columns, 24.5 × 77.5 cm).

33   See Fournet 2007, 354–57 and Fournet 2009, 28–32 (from which I borrow Figs. 1.3 and 1.4). In this second study, I consider the change in the format of the letter to be linked to the

perfectly synchronized with the change in format (Fig. 1.3) that it cannot be seen as mere coincidence.

In its former structure, the letter had prescript and final salutation formulas, often evidenced by *eistheseis* and *vacats*, tending to stretch the textual block vertically,

which ended with a narrow appendage accentuating this vertical arrangement (Fig. 1.5). The disappearance of the prescript and the greeting formula reduced the letter to its massive body, deprived of *eisthesis* and spacing (Fig. 1.6). The question is whether it is the change in format that reshaped the structure of the letter or the opposite. I would choose the second solution, which corresponds to an evolution of the conception of the letter, to its change of function, reflecting new rules in the late antique epistolary relationship. The letter, increasingly losing its practical mission, became a kind of conversation in which one tried to manifest one's φιλία and, if possible, one's writing talent (in other words, one's rhetorical abilities). Now the old prescript with the name of the recipient in second place, and with the infinitive χαίρειν explained by an implied λέγει (lit. "So-and-so tells someone to rejoice"), becomes incompatible with the conversation function of epistolography, with this new sociability expressed through self-depreciation and exaltation of the other; especially with the more and more sophisticated style of the letter which rejects the trivial, fixed and stereotypical elements of the traditional letter.[34]

I regard as symptomatic the reaction of an addressee of Procopius of Gaza (ca. 465–529), a certain Jerome, who reproached him for his conservatism since he was persisting in using the old prescript in the sixth century.[35] For that reason, he considers him "morbidly pretentious"! We see that the old prescript was completely out of fashion. If I am right, the change in format reflects the development of a new epistolary sensibility.

FIGURE 1.5   Typical layout of a letter
before the fifth century

FIGURE 1.6   Typical layout of a letter from the fifth century onwards

more general phenomenon of the *transversa charta* drafting of Byzantine documents. But the letter anticipated this phenomenon. We must therefore abandon this explanation and favor the one I put forward in the first study.

34   Fournet 2007, 356–57 (here translated into English).

35   Procopii Gazaei *Epistolae et declamationes*, ed. A. Garzya and R.-J. Loenertz (Studia Patristica et Byzantina 9), Ettal 1963, Letter 91 (= *Ep.* 116 ed. R. Hercher, *Epistolographi Graeci*, Paris 1873, 577–79). See Fournet 2009, 37–41.

3.2 *Legal Deeds*

From the middle of the sixth century onwards, *transversa charta* writing gained ground by becoming the increasingly common format for legal deeds (either notarized deeds or *cheirographa*). We also know that by the end of this century it had almost supplanted perfibral writing, although a precise chronology remains to be done. How do we explain this change for these kinds of documents?

It is not impossible that the demise of the habit of archiving documents in *tomoi synkollēsimoi* played a role in this phenomenon.[36] We know that in Roman times, deeds drawn up in local notarial offices (*grapheia*) were archived by being pasted together to obtain a composite roll which was deposited in the various *bibliothēkai* (public archives) and the *Katalogeion* in Alexandria. The last *tomoi synkollēsimoi* date from the middle of the fourth century, however, and thus the abandonment of this system is not the direct cause of the change in fibral orientation, which took place two centuries later. At most, the disappearance of the *tomoi synkollēsimoi*—made up of "coupons," all of the same height, perfibrally written—created the conditions favorable to the large-scale development of the *transversa charta* drafting, which other factors may have provoked more directly.

Another cause could be the notary's scribal habits. The Aphrodite papyri, for example, highlight a certain Hermauōs who left behind the most important group of leases written in a transfibral format.[37] The reason is to be sought in Hermauōs's habit of writing his documents with long lines (about 30 cm); a habit opposed to other contemporary notaries (Kyros 1, with 16 cm in the 530s, then 10 cm in the 540s; Kyros 3, with 12–14 cm; Ouiktōr 1, with 14–16 cm; and Abraam with 15–16 cm).[38] When the text of the contract is not too long, he tries to resort to a perfibral writing, resulting in a square format (e.g., P.Cair. Masp. II 67242), but for longer texts, he used *transversa charta* writing (e.g., P.Hamb. I 68). This case is particularly interesting in that it shows that the same notary could adopt the two formats on which to perform according to the length of the text.

It is ultimately the length of the text which proves to be the crucial factor in the recourse to *transversa charta* writing. On the basis not only of the Hermauōs dossier but also of all the Aphrodite notarized deeds, we can see that when the deed to be drawn up did not exceed forty-five lines (subscriptions and notarial completion included), notaries tended to favor a perfibral drafting; if it was longer, they adopted the *transversa charta* format. The perfibral drafting would actually imply, in the case of exceedingly long texts, endless lines, which could be perceived as painful to read,[39] or a layout in several columns, which was no longer in use and poses another type of problem, that of the calibration of the column width.

Moreover, the perfibral writing—as already noted about letters—requires an anticipated calibration of the space to be written and does not allow, in the case of exceedingly long texts, the addition of last-minute clauses: once the width is determined by the writing of the first line, one is condemned to fit all the text in the space delimited by the height of the roll. That discomfort is visible in certain contracts where, aware they would not have enough place to write all the text, the notary has tightened the lines approaching the end, resulting in an unattractive layout (Fig. 1.7). Conversely, *transversa charta* writing leaves infinitely more freedom: it does not require any anticipation, it allows the *ad libitum* addition of clauses, and leaves all the necessary space to the subscribers whose thick and clumsy writing sometimes requires a lot of room. It is a good compromise between legibility, freedom of writing, and the saving of papyrus.

If the "mechanical" causes of the *transversa charta* format are now clear (i.e., the need to manage the length of the text), we still have to look for the root causes of the dramatic and massive recourse to this format during the sixth century. It is indeed at this time that legal acts lengthened to an unprecedented extent, not only in Egypt, but also everywhere else. This is shown, for instance, by the Petra papyri, with the longest papyrological Greek document ever found: 8.5 meters long![40]

This lengthening can be explained anecdotally by the statuses of the individuals for whom these deeds were drawn up or by the genre of these deeds. For instance, settlements (where the least occasion for dispute must be prevented) and definitive transfers of property, such as sales, wills, or inheritance divisions (where clauses can be as numerous as the properties to bequeath or share[41]) are among the longest legal acts attested in Byzantine papyri. A notable example is P.Oxy. LXIII 4394, a 256-line acknowledgment of loan drawn up in Alexandria in

---

36   See, in general, Clarysse 2003.

37   P.Vat.Aphrod. 3 B+D (547–559 CE); P.Michael. 46 (565 CE); 54 (547–559 CE); P.Hamb. I 68 (548 CE).

38   I borrow these figures from Florence Lemaire's unfinished PhD work on the land leases of Aphrodite.

39   A disadvantage that one was ready to tolerate only when the documentary genre imposed it, as we will see. But such a constraint did not exist for legal acts.

40   P.Petra I 2 (Gaza [538 CE], an agreement concerning an inherited property).

41   For instance, P.Petra I 39 (Sadaqa [574 CE]), *dialysis* of at least 523 lines (ca. 6.5 m)!

FIGURE 1.7   P.Cair.Masp. III 67303 (Aphrodite [553 CE], cart lease written by the notary Pilatos)

499/500 CE, between, on the one hand, Flavius Ioulianos, *clarissimus tribunus, notarius sacri palatii,* and Flavius Olympiodōros, *scholasticus* and attorney at the court of the Augustal prefect, and, on the other, Flavius Maximus, a lawyer at the same court, concerning 1455 *solidi*. What an incredible length for such a trivial transaction (even if the amount is enormous)!

Yet the cause of the lengthening of the texts is, more structurally, due to the flowering of a new style aimed at prolixity, sophistication, and rhetorical effects. This was rooted in the development of a new sensibility shaped by Christianity and in a conception of temporal power which claims to draw its inspiration from God. This is not the place to dissect the tendencies of early Byzantine language used for documents,[42] but anyone who is familiar with late antique papyri knows from experience their prolixity and their tendency towards periphrasis and hypercharacterization, which results in the use of parallel or antithetic constructions, of syntagms with two or more terms of a similar meaning, arranged according to rhythmic or alliterative principles. All this does not contribute to the shortening of the documents!

This linguistic prolixity is translated into visual terms through recourse to progressively florid and dilated writing with increasingly well-spaced lines. This can be seen in P.Oxy. LXIII 4394 (Alexandria [499/500 CE]) or SB VI 9102 (Constantinople [551 CE]), two documents whose script is so dilated that each line contains no more than twenty-five letters. It is also evidenced by P.Cair.Masp. I 67019 recto (Constantinople [548/549 or 551 CE]), a petition to Justinian in which the lines are widely spaced.

3.3   *Petitions,* Epistalmata, *Reports of Judicial Proceedings, and Governors' Ordinances*

While legal acts, because of their length, were increasingly written *transversa charta,* other documents of similar length continued to be written along the fibers in a horizontal format. These could be written with very long lines, which are not always easy to follow. Among the documents with this format, one genre stands out: petitions.

Systematic research on Byzantine petitions has led me to conclude that the non-*transversa charta* format had become a norm for this genre and that in addition—albeit in a less systematic way—attempts were made to lengthen the size of the sheet by writing very long lines (Fig. 1.8).[43] The record is reached by P.Cair.Masp. I 67002 (Fig. 1.9), a petition written by Dioscorus of Aphrodite on a sheet which is nearly 2.5 meters long. Because of the length

---

42   See Zilliacus 1967.

43   See Fournet 2007, 359–60.

FIGURE 1.8   *P.Cair.Masp.* I 67006 recto (Antinoopolis [566–570], draft of a petition written
perfibrally with very long lines, 32 × 124 cm)

FIGURE 1.9   P.Cair.Masp. I 67002 (Antinoopolis [567 CE], draft of a petition written perfibrally in three columns, 30.5 × 234.7 cm)

of the lines, Dioscorus was obliged to write his texts in three columns, each with very long lines (between 70 and 85 cm). The two lines of the heading (giving the names of the addressee and the petitioner) occupy the length of the first two columns; that is, they are more than 1.5 meters long!

Another set of documents shares the same characteristics: the so-called *epistalmata* (i.e., the requests for a transfer of taxation following a property transfer). The thirty-one known *epistalmata* (ranging from 367/368 to 622 CE) are, with one exception, all written along the fibers like the petitions and show a tendency to long lines. The *epistalmata* from Egypt are written on sheets which, initially less than 25 cm wide, tend to lengthen, growing from approximately 30 cm in the second third of the sixth century to exceed 40 cm in the seventh century.

An *epistalma* from the Copenhagen collection written on a sheet that is more than 80 cm wide has by far the longest lines (Fig. 1.10). The propensity to adopt an elongated format, and thus to display the text in long lines, is even more evident in the large number of *epistalmata* from Petra and Nessana (543–570 CE), which range in width from 36 cm to more than 118 cm, with an average close to 70 cm. It is clear that from Justinian onwards, there is a general increase in the width of the sheet and the length of the lines, as we have seen with petitions.[44]

The question that arises is why this format was adopted for these two types of documents, despite it being neither very natural nor practical. The length of the lines (sometimes more than one meter) makes these documents more difficult to write, read, and use. If this format has

been adopted, it is because a constraining reason has been stronger than the search for comfort of reading or use—what might that be?

Petitions and *epistalmata* both share a common point: they are requests addressed to the authorities. One is to point out an injustice and to ask them to open a judicial investigation, the other is to point out a change of ownership and to ask them to modify the taxes that the new owner has to pay.[45] I am tempted to deduce that the non-*transversa charta* format has been adopted for *requests addressed by individuals to the authorities*.

As a matter of fact, another documentary genre, which constitutes the counterpart of the petitions, also adopts the same format: the reports of judicial proceedings (*hypomnēmata*). These are indeed always written on rolls and, because of the length of the text, are formatted in several columns, often formed of long lines (see, for instance, P.Mich. XIII 660 + 661 + SB XVI 12542, Antinoopolis [558/559 CE], written in several columns with lines of 71.5 cm).[46] One could then wonder whether this format had not specialized in the documents related to justice with the two types of documents that mark the two

---

44   See Fournet, forthcoming for the edition of the Copenhagen *epistalma* and a list of *epistalmata*.

45   Although, over time, the *epistalma* tended to resemble a legal deed by which an individual commits themself to the state, it presented itself until the end as a *request* submitted to the administration.

46   For a list of late antique reports, see Thomas 1998, 132–33, to be completed by P.Thomas, p. 217, n. 1; Gascou 2009, 149, n. 1; and Haensch 2016, 311–24 (proceedings before the civil governors). To this must be added P.Messeri 45 (590/591 or 618/619 CE), which is currently the most recent report, also perfibral. The only exception I have found in terms of fibral orientation is P.Cair.Masp. I 67131 which is a private copy: the individual who copied the original may have changed the layout for unknown reasons.

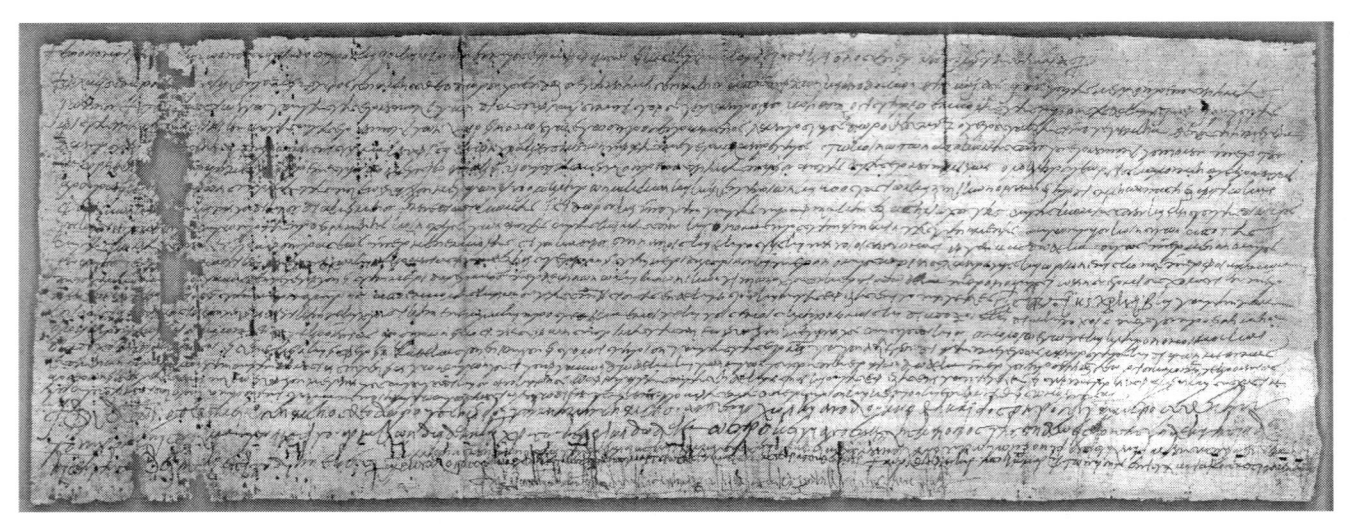

FIGURE 1.10   An *epistalma* from the Copenhagen collection (Hermopolis [622 CE], written perfibrally with long lines, 31 × 83 cm)

decisive stages in the judicial procedure; namely, the petition that initiates a judicial action and the report of proceedings that is the result with the trial and the sentence. But we have seen that this format is also used in requests of a fiscal nature (*epistalmata*).

In addition, another group of documents that goes far beyond the field of justice also adopts systematically the perfibral format with long lines in a presentation that is quite similar to the reports of proceedings: these are the governors' ordinances (*prostagmata*; Fig. 1.11). The ones that have been preserved for us most often concern matters of taxation, but there are also other decisions.[47] Most

of these *prostagmata* come from Thebaid, but the one found at Petra shows that the layout of these ordinances was not a local peculiarity but was followed by the governor's chancelleries on a large scale.

Insofar as these ordinances emanated from the governors, the very ones who, in the Byzantine period, most often heard trials and whose chancellery drew up the reports of proceedings, one would be tempted to explain the layout of the *hypomnēmata* and *prostagmata* as a specificity of the governor's administrations. But then, would there be a reason why petitions and *epistalmata* addressed to high officials adopt the same layout as those documents that emanate from high officials? One might think that, out of respect, individuals, in addressing the state, sought to formally imitate the state's practices in terms of documentary production. What is certain is that the perfibral format remained the format par excellence for administrative acts of a certain level[48] and marked with a certain formalism and that it was adopted for acts emanating from the state as much as for writings addressed to the state.

If, then, there is a formal specialization of this layout in relation to the state, the question is why. Nothing is more difficult than to answer this in the absence of ancient texts that would explicitly justify these choices. I will try anyway.

It would not be unreasonable to think that the state wanted to maintain the format employed for its acts during the Roman period: the *acta* were then recorded on

47   P.Flor. III 292 (Antinoopolis [543 CE], an ordinance of the Duke of Thebaid concerning the civil *annona* to be paid by the village of Aphrodite); P.Cair.Masp. I 67030 (Antinoopolis [546 CE], an ordinance of the *praes* of Thebaid concerning the amount of the civil *annona* to be paid by the village of Aphrodite); *P.Cair. Masp.* III 67280 (Antinoopolis [538? CE], *idem*); *P.Cair.Masp.* III 67320 = *ChLA* XLI 1193 (Antinoopolis [541 CE], an ordinance of the *praeses* of Thebaid concerning the *annona miltaris* to be paid by the village of Aphrodite); P.Erl. 55 (Antinoopolis [542 CE], an ordinance of the *praeses* of Thebaid concerning the *annona miltaris* to be paid by the village of Aphrodite); P.Cair.Masp. III 67321 (Antinoopolis [548 CE], an ordinance of the Duke of Thebaid and the *praeses* of Thebaid concerning the *annona miltaris* to be paid by the village of Aphrodite); P.Lond. V 1663 (Antinoopolis [549 CE], *idem*); SB V 8028 = *ChLA* X 464 (Antinoopolis [549 CE], an ordinance of the *praeses* of Thebaid concerning the *annona miltaris* to be paid by the village of Aphrodite); P.Laur. III 111 (Antinoopolis [VI CE], *idem*); P.Cair.Masp. I 67031 (Antinoopolis [mid-VI CE], an ordinance of the Duke of Thebaid concerning the *sportulae* required by the court officials); P.Cair.Masp. III 67281 (Antinoopolis [first quarter VI CE], an ordinance of *praeses* of Thebaid appointing Isaak as the *riparius* of Aphrodite); P.Petra V 78 (Petra? [VI CE], an ordinance of a provincial governor or a higher authority [Gascou, forthcoming]). The indictional cycle of the *prostagmata* found

in Aphrodite is often uncertain and has been discussed: see Fournet 1998, 79, n. 86.

48   I am obviously not referring to lower-level acts such as tax receipts from minor officials.

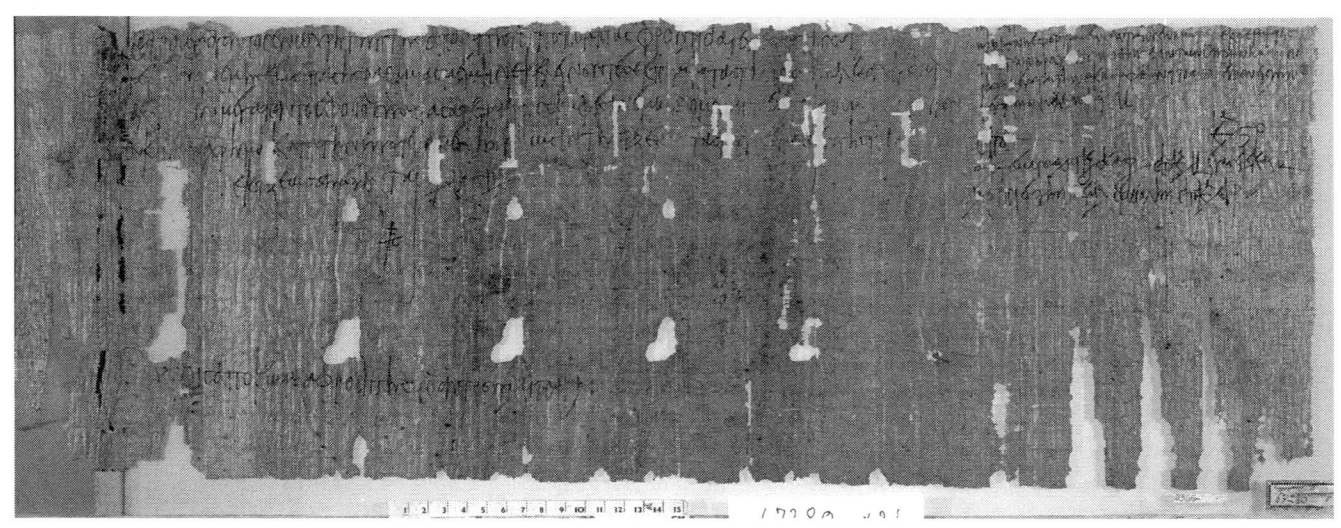

FIGURE 1.11   P.Cair.Masp. III 67280 (Antinoopolis [538? CE], an ordinance of the *praeses* of Thebaid written perfibrally in two columns, 24.4 × 67.9 cm)

rolls and the petitions it received archived in the form of composite rolls or *tomoi synkollēsimoi*. In fact, archaism or conservatism is often a feature of the administration, but one can also wonder whether this conservatism did not meet a feeling, a particular perception that one could have had of this format: in other words, it would have been reputed to have an *ēthos*, here charged with a certain formalism that could make it feel more solemn or imposing. It is difficult to get into the head of the Ancients and dangerous to seek explanations that can only be subjective, but it is possible that the long lines could be felt as strange or unusual and therefore pertaining to a more exceptional layout.

It should be noted that it was also the perfibral format that the Archbishop of Alexandria, supreme head of the Church of Egypt, continued to adopt until the end for his official letters. This was especially applied to the so-called festal letters that he regularly sent to his flock—and which, *mutatis mutandis*, were the equivalent of the governors' ordinances. This parallel is certainly not a coincidence and shows that the perfibral format was practiced by the Church as well as by the state.

Conclusions

From the sixth century onwards, we see the development of a functional opposition based on the format. Was this opposition intentional or was it a consequence of the developments at work since the fifth century? In the first case, was it the *transversa charta* format that developed in opposition to state practices (by adapting the format of legal acts to new linguistic trends) or was it the state

that maintained its old practices not only in the name of a claimed conservatism but also to distance itself from the new practices of private notaries? It is difficult to answer, but the fact is that this new situation placed in formal opposition genres that were opposed from the point of view of the procedure or the context of production.

This opposition is certainly evident in the case of the letter and the petition: while these two genres theoretically allowed an individual to address an authority, in practice the letter was reserved for a privileged few while only the petition was allowed to a private individual. Each followed different procedures (the petition was submitted in person to the authority, while the letter was sent) and specific diplomatics (the petition had a hypomnematic prescript unlike the letter). More generally, individuals communicate with each other through letters and with the state through petitions, with the opposition *transversa charta* / perfibral format corresponding to a public/ private opposition.

As we can see, the form of a document results from the combination of several factors that influence each other: 1) evidently practical considerations (such as the length of the text or the reuse of the sheet); 2) the nature and function of the text under which a particular form was conventionally assigned to a particular genre, sometimes according to opposing systems; 3) the more or less good knowledge and mastery of these conventions by each of the scribes; 4) the ever-evolving cultural trends that shape or condition the form of the text; and 5) a "feeling" whereby this or that presentation was naturally perceived in a certain way (what could be called the *ēthos* of form, a concept that is today hard to grasp and that can be better understood through cognitive psychology). We thus see that paleography is one key to understanding the psychology and cultural behaviors of the ancients in the field of written culture.

Reference List

Clarysse, Willy. 2003. "*Tomoi Synkollesimoi*." In *Ancient Archives and Archival Traditions: Concepts of Record-Keeping in the Ancient World*, edited by Maria Brosius, 344–59. Oxford Studies in Ancient Documents. Oxford: Oxford University Press.

Fournet, Jean-Luc. 1994. "L'influence des usages littéraires sur l'écriture des documents : perspectives." In *Proceedings of the 20th International Congress of Papyrologists*, edited by Adam Bülow-Jacobsen, 418–22. Copenhagen: Museum Tusculanum Press.

Fournet, Jean-Luc. 1998. "Un nouvel épithalame de Dioscore d'Aphrodité adressé à un gouverneur civil de Thébaïde." *Antiquité tardive* 6: 65–82.

Fournet, Jean-Luc. 2007. "Disposition et réalisation graphique des lettres et des pétitions protobyzantines : pour une paléographie « signifiante » des papyrus documentaires." In *Proceedings of the 24th International Congress of Papyrology*, edited by Jaakko Frösén, Tiina Purola, and Erja Salmenkivi, I, 353–67. Commentaniones Humanarum Litterarum 122:1. Helsinki: Societas Scientiarum Fennica.

Fournet, Jean-Luc. 2008a. "Archive ou archives de Dioscore? Les dernières années des « archives de Dioscore »." In *Les archives de Dioscore d'Aphrodité cent ans après leur découverte. Histoire et culture dans l'Égypte byzantine*, edited by Jean-Luc Fournet, 17–30. Études d'archéologie et d'histoire ancienne. Paris: De Boccard.

Fournet, Jean-Luc. 2008b. "Liste des papyrus édités de l'Aphrodité byzantine." In *Les archives de Dioscore d'Aphrodité cent ans après leur découverte. Histoire et culture dans l'Égypte byzantine*, edited by Jean-Luc Fournet, 307–43. Études d'archéologie et d'histoire ancienne. Paris: De Boccard.

Fournet, Jean-Luc. 2009. "Esquisse d'une anatomie de la lettre antique tardive d'après les papyrus." In *Correspondances. Documents pour l'histoire de l'Antiquité tardive*, edited by Roland Delmaire, Janine Desmulliez, and Pierre-Louis Gatier, 23–66. Collection de la Maison de l'Orient et de la Méditerranée 40, Série littéraire et philosophique 13. Lyon: Maison de l'Orient et de la Méditerranée.

Fournet, Jean-Luc. 2013. "Culture grecque et document dans l'Égypte de l'Antiquité tardive." *JJP* 43: 135–62.

Fournet, Jean-Luc. 2016. "Sur les premiers documents juridiques coptes (2): Les archives de Phoibammôn et de Kollouthos." *Études coptes XIV, Seizième journée d'études (Genève, 19–21 juin 2013)*, edited by Anne Boud'hors and Catherine Louis, 115–41. Cahiers de la Bibliothèque copte 21. Paris: De Boccard.

Fournet, Jean-Luc. Forthcoming. "Une demande de transfert d'imposition (*epistalma*) à Copenhague."

Fournet, Jean-Luc, and Jean Gascou. 2008. "Un lot d'archives inédit de Lycopolis (Égypte) à l'Académie des inscriptions et belles-lettres." *Comptes rendus des séances de l'Académie des inscriptions et belles-lettres* 153, no. 2: 1041–74.

Gascou, Jean. 1989. "Les codex documentaires égyptiens." In *Les débuts du codex. Actes de la journée d'étude (Paris, 3–4 july 1985)*, edited by Alain Blanchard, 71–101. Bibliologia 9. Turnhout: Brepols. Reproduced in Jean Gascou, *Fiscalité et société en Égypte byzantine*. Bilans de recherche 4. Paris: Association des amis du Centre d'histoire et civilisation de Byzance, 2008, 351–76.

Gascou, Jean. 2009. "Procès-verbal d'audience du juge Ammonius." *ZPE* 170: 149–55.

Gascou, Jean. Forthcoming. Review of P.Petra v. *Antiquité Tardive*.

Haensch, R. 2016. "Die Protokolle der Statthaltergerichte der spätantiken Provinzen Ägyptens." In *Recht haben und Recht bekommen im Imperium Romanum. Das Gerichtswesen der Römischen Kaiserzeit und seine dokumentarische Evidenz. Ausgewählte Beiträge einer Serie von drei Konferenzen an der Villa Vigoni in den Jahren 2010 bis 2012*, edited by Rudolf Haensch, 299–324. The JJP Supplements 24. Warsaw: University of Warsaw.

Homann, Magrit. 2012. "Eine Randerscheinung des Papyrusbriefes: der *versiculus transversus*." *APF* 58: 67–80.

Skeat, T. C. 1982. "The Length of the Standard Papyrus Roll and the Cost-Advantage of the Codex." *ZPE* 45: 169–75.

Thomas, J. David. 1998. "Ryl. IV 654: The Latin Heading." *CE* 73: 125–34.

Turner, G. Eric. 1978. *The Terms Recto and Verso: The Anatomy of the Papyrus Roll.* = Actes du XVe Congrès international de papyrologie. Brussels: Fondation égyptologique Reine Élisabeth.

Vierros, Marja. 2022. "Scribes and Other Writers in the Petra Papyri." In *Observing the Scribe at Work: Scribal Practice in the Ancient World*, edited by Rodney Ast, Malcolm Choat, Jennifer Cromwell, Julia Lougovaya, and Rachel Yuen-Collingridge, 101–15. Orientalia Lovaniensia Analecta 301. Louvain: Peeters.

Zilliacus, Henrik. 1967. *Zur Abundanz der spätgriechischen Gebrauchssprache*. Societas Scientarum Fennica, Commentationes Humanarum Litterarum 41/2. Helsinki: Helsingfors.

## CHAPTER 2

BIG & Small: The Size of Documents as a Semiotic Resource for Graeco-Roman Egypt

Marco Stroppa

Introduction

Everyday documentary texts have external characteristics that can also be seen as an expression of the socio-cultural context of writing. Among these there are the writing material, the language choice, and the document format.[1] A basic feature of the latter, and the focus of this chapter, is size. The Greek documentary papyri from Graeco-Roman Egypt cover a wide range of typologies, encompassing a span of one thousand years. The papyrus documents produced in Egypt and now kept in museums and libraries represent all sizes and it is usual for curators and others to pay attention to the size and format of a document. For instance, during work on the restoration of some papyrus fragments preserved at the Papyrological Institute of Florence, I was struck by a very small and almost complete text, which I shall return to below. This was surprising because all the other pieces in the same box were fragments of something bigger, while this piece was instead almost complete.

Before I can begin, though, it is worth briefly clarifying some points. First, in museum collections we often find fragments of papyrus which are only a part of the entire original artifact: sometimes we can reconstruct them, but it is not easy to know the original dimensions of a roll or sheet. Second, the description of an artifact as large or small is not absolute.

In light of these preliminary considerations, we might ask what are large and small papyri and how can we identify them? Furthermore, what exactly does the size of a document signify? This preliminary investigation will explore the relationship between the size of the script and the size of a document, asking whether very large and very small papyri were written for special purposes. In doing so, I will argue that the size of documents can be a semiotic resource for Graeco-Roman Egypt, particularly when that information is connected and compared with the writing material or choice of language.

1   What Is "Large"?

In order to define an artifact as "large," we can of course rely on physical data, such as height and width. Yet, by themselves this is not enough. For example, an almost complete scroll with a series of speeches by Hyperides, such as P.Lond.Lit. 132 (I–II CE), a roll more than 3 m long and about 30 cm high, is not "big"; rather, it has a "normal" size for a literary roll.[2] In addition to the dimensions of the artifact itself, we must also consider the height and width of the letters and the relationship between the size of the sheet or the roll and the letter size. Therefore, the data on the size of the script need to be combined with the data on the size of the artifact.

Following this approach, I selected three outstanding pieces, all of which can be dated exactly, are very well known, and are emblematic specimens for various reasons. The first is SB XIV 11942 (331 BCE), an order from a commander-in-chief, written *transversa charta*,[3] and measuring 35.8 × 13.4 cm. While the sheet is not large, the document is, because the height of the letters ranges from 2 to 4.1 cm and the text has only three lines:

Πευκέστου·
μὴ παραπορεύεσθαι μη-
δένα· ἱερείως τὸ οἴκημα.

Of Peukestas. No one is to pass. The chamber is that of a priest.[4]

The extraordinary dimensions of the script, which make it a large document, can also be explained by the probable function of this sheet. The order issued by Peukestas was probably intended to be posted in public and therefore had to be clearly visible, also from a certain distance. As mentioned, the text can be dated exactly as Peukestas was the distinguished Greek officer of Alexander who was

---

1   See Bentein and Amory 2019, 21–22.

2   See Johnson 2004, 141–52.

3   For the type of writing instrument used to write this particular text, see Angles 2019, 387, with an image at 398.

4   Trans. Turner 1974, 240.

Commander-in-Chief in 331 BCE. After the conquest of Egypt by the Greeks, Alexander went eastwards in search of new exploits while two of his lieutenants (the other was Balakros) stayed to manage the situation in the country: we are right at the beginning of Greek domination.

The second piece is SB I 4639 (P.Berol. inv. 11532), a letter from the prefect of Egypt, Subatianus Aquila, written in 209 CE. It measures 32 × 22 cm, with six lines of text written in letters 1.5 cm high and a subscription in smaller writing added at the bottom.[5] The content of the letter is an order issued by the supreme Roman authority in Egypt: a person sentenced to forced labor is granted release after having served his sentence. Again, we know the exact date because Subatianus Aquila was the Roman prefect of Egypt from 206 to 210 CE. During the Roman era, the prefect was the highest leader in the province and was directly responsible to the emperor for his work.

The third piece, PSI XVI 1576, is a fragment of a letter from the Patriarch of Alexandria. The measurements of the 29-line column are 24 × 21.3 cm; the height of the roll is 28.2 cm and the height of the letters 0.4 cm. It is not complete but is part of Cyril's Festal Letter no. 9, written for Easter in 421 CE: the original letter is supposed to be a 5- to 6-meter-long horizontal roll. The text, like all the other preserved festal letters on papyrus, is written in a formal book hand, the Alexandrian majuscule. This is the oldest exemplar of its kind, but five others are known with the same kind of format, the roll, which was traditionally used from the fifth to almost the eighth century.[6] Its dating is precise, as Cyril was the Patriarch of Alexandria from 412 to 444 CE: at the beginning of the fifth century, the bishop of Alexandria was not only an eminent religious authority but also assumed a prominent political role towards the whole of Egypt.

Having briefly looked these three examples, we can say that their "largeness" is associated with their "greatness." Specifically, their large format is linked to power: they are all documents coming from the highest authorities in that period. In short, we can say that size is an expression of power because the governors chose to impress the readers of a document and to give more strength to their words thanks to the document's format.[7]

Given this knowledge, we can go in search of those texts issued by the authorities that present suitable characteristics for public display, so that the written words have a more evident impact on the recipients. Of the numerous public notices produced by the Roman administration of Egypt—which ranged from its highest authority, the prefect, to local-level officials—most are copies intended for offices which were copied on sheets of a similar size to that of any other administrative document. In recent years some research has been performed and hypotheses made to identify texts posted in a public place, whose primary purpose was to be seen and read by anyone who was interested, like a sort of inscription.[8] Indeed, in Roman Egypt any text intended for public display could, in general, be defined as a πρόγραμμα: this term could indicate any type of decree, order, or notice issued by authorities of different degrees that could require widespread dissemination.[9]

For the first three centuries of Roman domination,[10] the pivotal figure in the field of public dissemination and posting was the strategus.[11] This official played a key role at nome level when texts addressed to all the inhabitants of the province (for example, a prefect's edict, with legal value throughout Egypt) or to a specific category of people (for example, an announcement containing appointments to liturgical services, which could only involve the community of a small village) had to be made known both in larger towns, such as the capital of a nome, and in the villages scattered throughout the Egyptian countryside.[12] The establishment of βουλαί in metropoleis at the beginning of the third century CE[13] does not seem to have limited the role of the strategus as a "disseminator" of the large number of official documents produced by the Roman administration. Indeed, the decrees of the same βουλαί were transmitted to local officials through the strategus's office.[14]

---

5 See Sarri 2018, 172–76 for further details, with a printed image at 173; on this papyrus, see also Conti, chapter 5 in this volume.

6 The five are P.Grenf. II 112 (577 CE), the only rotulus *transversa charta*; P.Köln V 215 (663 or 674 CE); P.Horak 3 (711 or 722 CE); BKT VI, 55–109 (713 or 719 CE); and P.Heid. IV 295 (VIII CE). See Bastianini and Cavallo 2011, 31–39 (a printed image of PSI XVI 1576 can be seen in Table I) and Stroppa 2022, 37–44.

7 Another impressive document is SB VI 9102 (548/49 CE), a 123 cm letter from the Constantinople imperial chancery to the *dux* of the Thebais (see Crisci 1996, 150; Fournet 2015, 258–59).

8 See Grossi 2016, 85–95, esp. 93–95.

9 See Stroppa 2004, 177–200.

10 For the Ptolemaic era we have P.Bingen 28 (Ptolemais Hormou? [III BCE]), administrative correspondence requiring the posting of a πρόγραμμα in each village. See P.Bingen 28, comment to line 4, for a list of documents that can be defined as προγράμματα in the Ptolemaic administration: notices of runaway slaves, notices of the sale of land by public auction, laws, convening of assemblies, and summonses to present reports.

11 See Taubenschlag 1951, 155.

12 For aspects of document transmission within Egypt, see Strassi 1993, 89–107.

13 For the introduction of βουλαί by Septimius Severus and previous town institutions, see Tacoma 2006, 118–21; Bussi 2008, 64–68.

14 See P.Oxy. XVII 2108 (259 CE), a letter from a strategus with the Senate decree attached.

As for the material features, all the προγράμματα therefore represent texts that aimed to reach the largest number of inhabitants possible in the simplest and most direct way. From a technical point of view, what devices did those in charge of dissemination use to achieve this goal? What elements were highlighted in copies intended for public display? How did the posting really take place?

To fully answer these questions, it would be necessary to analyze the original text of a notice that was created specifically to be displayed. However, although hypotheses can be formulated for some papyri (see below), there are no reliable testimonies of texts of this type, because, as I have already noted, the documentation very often consists exclusively of copies from the archives,[15] or copies probably drawn from texts posted in public places,[16] or even copies of notices that were available in the administration offices and were sent from one official to another.[17] Indeed, if you needed documents for your own interests, you had to obtain a copy of the texts posted in public: such documents, their format, layout, and other technical details, presented completely different characteristics to the specimens that were actually exhibited. Obviously, the basic criteria for attempting to identify texts of this type are the format and the size of the writing.

One interesting proposal for identifying specimens actually posted in public was presented, with due caution, with regard to P.Oxy. LI 3616 (III CE), a notice on the search for a runaway slave which has a size of 16 × 9.5 cm.[18] Two other papyri are similar to it in writing and format, and present texts that were certainly put on public display: P.Oxy. XXXIII 2664 (248–249 CE) and P.Oxy. XL 2924 (268–272 CE?). The first, P.Oxy. XXXIII 2664, reports the important provision of Marcellus and Salutaris on lightening the liturgies:[19] the size is slightly larger (25.5 × 15.2 cm) than the search notice for the runaway slave, while the writing is influenced by the Chancery style, although it is not particularly elegant.[20] The second, P.Oxy. XL 2924, is a notice by two magistrates from Oxyrhynchus,

addressed to holders of *tesserae* that they had issued: since their assignment has been completed, they are invited to collect the grain owed to them within a short time. The dimensions are similar (19 × 9.5 cm) to those of P.Oxy. LI 3616, but the writing is "not above a normal size."[21]

According to the format and writing, it cannot be said with certainty that the sheets were actually posted in public, because, for two of these three documents at least, other elements lead us to consider it unlikely. On the one hand, the slave-search notice does not carry any header that specifies the authority that issued the order; this omission is odd in a document intended to be displayed in public. On the other hand, perhaps this same omission could indicate that it was obvious which authority had issued the notice, because the document was posted in a place that made further details unnecessary, such as the office that was to be addressed directly. P.Oxy. XL 2924, on the other hand, has a header with παρά + genitive: it is likely that it may be a copy forwarded to some officials.[22]

Among the edicts of the prefect, one specimen has physical characteristics that can point to a copy that was displayed in some way: SB XII 10929 (133–137 CE).[23] In this case, in addition to the quite considerable dimensions of the artifact (30.8 × 10.2 cm) and of the writing (the largest letters are almost 1 cm high), the layout is another element in favor of the hypothesis that this sheet was posted.[24]

A further example of posted papyri from the late antique period could be P.Oxy. LXVIII 4670 verso (IV CE), whose dimensions are 15 × 13 cm—although it is not clear which kind of document it is, despite it being written in a deliberately epigraphic style. A second example, P.Oxy. LXVIII 4671 (V CE), with the drawing of a *tabula ansata* and the word Αρκαδιης is a scrap measuring 11 × 4.7 cm, with letters 1 cm high. Yet a third example, the Latin text of P.Oxy. XLI 2950 = ChLA XLVII 1414, a fragmentary dedication to the emperors Diocletian and Maximian (late III CE), also has exceptional dimensions (26 × 23 cm, and about 1 m long when complete) and, most strikingly, the letters are 3.5 cm high.

In addition to the physical features of the documents themselves, some information on the posted sheets can be obtained from a group of documents which make explicit reference to their public display: the letters of the prefects to the strategi, which specify instructions for disseminating documents issued by the prefect.[25] In some cases, it

---

15 For example, P.Flor. I 2 (265 CE), public notices from the strategus with liturgical appointments.

16 For example, PSI XIV 1406 (137–142 CE), an edict of the prefect Caius Avidius Heliodorus.

17 For example, P.Oxy. I 34 verso (127 CE), a prefect's edict about the archives.

18 P.Oxy. LI 3616, 39: "It seems not unlikely that 3616 is actually the notice posted in public, rather than a formula."

19 P.Oxy. XXXIII, 85: "The text is a *programma*, issued by the Rationalis Aegypti and his assistant. [...] What we have here is probably a local copy, for it omits the Latin subscription in 9." On the historical events, see Parsons 1967, 137–41, and Bianchi 1983, 190–93.

20 P.Oxy. XXXIII, 85: "The writing is large, bold, practised cursive of normal type: not a chancery hand."

21 See P.Oxy. XL 2924, 82.

22 See P.Oxy. XL 2924, 82.

23 See the detailed contribution by Jördens 2011, 327–56.

24 See Jördens 2011, 331–32.

25 A number of letters that the prefect—as well as other high-ranking officials—sent to the strategus, attaching a copy of the edict that he promulgated in Alexandria, are known; they contain

was specified where and how these texts were to be published. A first important aspect was the place where the notices were posted, "in the metropoleis and in the most important places of the nomes."[26]

A second indication sets out how these posters were to be written: the adjectives describing the letters (γράμματα) to be used in them are telling. In P.Oxy. VIII 1100, ll. 2–4 (206 CE), the prefect Subatianus Aquila recommends publishing his edict εὐδήλοις γράμμασι:[27] the exact words are also used in P.Oxy. XXXIV 2705, l. 10 (225 CE), while a similar formula is found in lines 12 to 13 of an inscription, SB V 8248 (= OGIS II 665), written in 48/49 CE: σαφέσι καὶ εὐσήμοις [γράμμασι]. P.Coll.Youtie I 30, l. 14 (198 CE) bears the words φανεροῖς καὶ εὐαναγνώστοις τοῖς γράμμασιν (and on the basis of this, [φανεροῖς γ]ράμμασι[ν is also integrated in P.Lips. II 145, l. 84 [189 CE]).

The terms used are quite vague and do not allow us to formulate a precise idea of the format and writing: φανερά, "clearly visible"; εὐανάγνωστα, "well legible"; σαφῆ, "safe," that is, "clear, unambiguous letters"; εὔδηλα, "manifest," that is, "not hidden"; and εὔσημα, "well marked," in the sense of "clearly visible." While four of these adjectives are in effect synonyms, the fifth, εὐανάγνωστος, refers more precisely to reading. Perhaps the only certain element that emerges from the analysis of these expressions is that the size of the letters had to be large and clear.

Having now considered examples of large documents coming from persons at the top of structures of political or religious power, I shall move on to a group of homogeneous documents which are quite different from the previous ones. In fact, they are not large at all, fitting a category of standard documents from everyday life: circus programs. Although there are very few of these papyri and, hitherto, a total of just seven have been published, they nevertheless represent an interesting category because they list the entertainment and performances that took place in the hippodromes.[28] Belonging to late antiquity (the dating is estimated to be fifth to sixth century CE, on palaeographic grounds), they are all written by different hands and present content that differs in its details, especially regarding the mention of chariot races, which is not always present. Five circus programs are from Oxyrhynchus—P.Oxy. XXXIV 2707 (VI CE); P.Oxy. LXXIX 5215 (VI CE); P.Oxy. LXXIX 5216 (V–VI CE); P.Oxy. LXXIX 5217 (VI CE); and P.Oxy. LXXIX 5218 (VI CE)—while the

provenance of the other two is unknown—P.Harrauer 56 (VI CE) and P.Bingen 128 (V–VI CE).

One of the elements these texts have in common is their large format: even though the sheets are quite damaged, this feature is clear to see (see Table 2.1 below). What is most striking is the size of the letters: the characters are at least 1 cm high and even reach 2 cm in the case of P.Oxy. LXXIX 5218. In addition to this element, the generous layout has led to speculation that the format has a special meaning. It should also be noted that in one case, P.Bingen 128, the editor expressly speaks of cardboard ("cartoncino") and the considerable thickness of the papyrus ("papiro di notevole spessore"): what does this mean? Is it a sort of more resistant and more elegant material?[29]

Although the purpose of these programs is not entirely clear, various possibilities arise when we consider their shared format and some other details, such as the fact the greeting formulas are written at a smaller scale at the bottom, below the text. For example, it is possible that the sheets were to be "handed round or pinned up,"[30] or perhaps they were copies to be displayed in public, which had to be seen and approved by a second official. They may also have been organizers' copies, allowing for various events to be "ticked off" as they were performed.[31]

Alternatively, the programs may have been distributed before an event, perhaps as invitations, and in this case the subscriptions could be a kind of greeting from the people sending them. This is the hypothesis preferred by Federico Morelli,[32] since he maintains that the circus programs were—probably—not posted in public, but rather sent to important people, like a kind of invitation, because the writing is a Chancery hand, typical of the addresses of Byzantine letters, and there are no nail holes to hang them up. Furthermore, some circus programs also have greetings to the recipient added under the main text in more informal writing, which is difficult to attribute to a public posting.

Despite these varying possibilities, what seems fairly certain is that these programs circulated among the people invited to or present at the circus at the time of the shows and therefore constituted a sort of "advertising flyer." Like the writing, the dimensions are to be counted among the elements used to draw the attention of people interested in the entertainment. In this way, we can consider them "large."

---

more or less precise instructions on how to distribute the edict itself. See Katzoff 1982, 210; a list can be found in Strassi 1993, 93–95.

26 P.Oxy. VIII 1100, 2–4.

27 P.Oxy. VIII 1100, 3.

28 See Tedeschi 2017, 241 and the texts A43, A45–47.

29 See P.Bingen 128, 523.

30 See P.Oxy. LXXIX, 182.

31 See P.Oxy. LXXIX, 182.

32 See P.Harrauer 56, 203–4.

TABLE 2.1   List of circus programs

Papyrus	Measurements in cm (n.c. = not complete)
P.Oxy. XXXIV 2707	16 × 30
P.Oxy. LXXIX 5215	12.5 × 29.7
P.Oxy. LXXIX 5216	13 × 14 (n.c.)
P.Oxy. LXXIX 5217	19.5 × 10.2 (n.c.)
P.Oxy. LXXIX 5218	11.2 × 8.4 (fr. 1; n.c.)
P.Harrauer 56	7.8 × 19 (n.c.)
P.Bingen 128	10.5 × 22.7 (n.c.)

2   What Is "Small"?

Most papyrus fragments are small only because they are fragments of larger artifacts. However, on occasion, a papyrologist may find small but complete documents. Notes, receipts, orders, and other types of documents can be short texts and therefore can have a small format. An illustrative example is a group of receipts for beer, marked with a mention of the unit "dichoron." About ten such ostraca are known and have the same structure.

Among these examples, a piece in the Archeological Museum of Florence (MAF inv. 50068), is very small, measuring 4.6 × 1.8 cm, with a thickness of 0.5 cm. It was found in Tebtynis, during the excavations by Carlo Anti in 1931, and can be dated to the second century CE.[33] The ostracon consists of two lines and is probably a short complete text. As usual, the receipt has the date with just the month and the day at the beginning (here at l. 1 Παχὼν ε̄, Pachon 5th = 30th April). The quantity, probably of beer, is found on line 2—that is, 4 dichora (δίχ(ωρα) δ)—as is clearly written in similar receipts on other ostraca. Although the names of the people involved are commonly inserted after the date and before the amount, which is always the last element of the document, this is not included here. In this case it might have been omitted because it was deemed superfluous. Texts of this kind were probably receipts for beer deliveries: 4 dichora (64 to 104 liters) seem to be the normal donkey load.[34]

Another category of documents distinguished by their small format, which could be significant, are party invitations. These might constitute a perfect case study:[35]

they comprise a group of about fifty pieces with common features, were written in the second through fourth centuries, and have been collected in recent papers. In-depth analysis has been conducted on their date, provenance, structure, and purpose: the data are available in the tables of papers published from 2016 on.[36]

A representative sample of their content is found in the text of P.Oxy. LXXV 5057 (II–III CE), column II (col. I has exactly the same text):

ἐρωτᾷ σε Ἡραῖς
δειπνῆσαι εἰς γάμους
τοῦ υἱοῦ αὐτῆς ἐν τῷ
μεγάλῳ Θοηρείῳ αὔρι-
ον ἥτις ἐστὶν κς ἀπὸ   5
ὥρας θ.

Herais asks you to dine on the occasion of the wedding of her son, in the Great Thoëreum, tomorrow, which is the 26th, from the 9th hour on.

This papyrus is a bit special because it is the only sheet containing two absolutely identical invitations: this means that the invites were prepared in "series" and subsequently cut out. For this reason, the dimensions of this object (8.4 × 4.8 cm) are exceptional. Another object shows traces of ink that could belong to the text of another party invitation, P.Oxy. LXII 4339 (maybe also SB V 7745 [II CE]).

My aim here is to investigate size, and thus because the measurements of the party invitations vary—some are larger, others smaller—I checked the measurements of all party invitations. Table 2.2 presents the data relating to the dimensions of all the documents, many of which have maintained the original dimensions. The table is arranged in increasing order of size, which is determined by the total surface area of each small sheet, which I have added to supplement the data on the height and width already available in the editions of each text. Some papyri in the lower part of the table are larger because they contain a longer and more articulated text than is standard. Thus, I have not taken them into consideration in the statistics. The last entry is an ostracon: it is separate from the others

---

33   See Stroppa, forthcoming b.

34   See Reiter 2005, 133–136; Stroppa, forthcoming a.

35   Skeat 1975, 253–54 was first to note the particular size of this category of documents; he had access to a total of twenty-nine

pieces out of the fifty-four known to date and collected in Table 2.

36   For an overview, see Pruneti 2016, 117–28 and Arzt-Grabner 2016, 508–29; for the places, see Hussein el-Mofatch 2016, 1993–2010; for new items, see Nelson, Marshall, and Gardner 2018, 207–12; for the connections between papyrological and archaeological evidence, see Alfarano and Buonfino 2022, 65–86. A party invitation that is slightly different from the others is published in Berkes 2018, 277–81.

TABLE 2.2   List of party invitations according to size[a]

Papyrus	Measurements in cm (n.c. = not complete)	Surface in cm^2
1. PSI inv. 4361	4.1 × 2.5 (n.c.)	10.5
2. SB XXII 15358 = P.Oxy. I 181 descr.	4.3 × 3.2 (n.c.)	13.76
3. P.Oxy. VI 926	4.9 × 2.9	14.21
4. P.Oxy. XII 1579	5.4 × 2.8	15.12
5. P.Oxy. XXXVI 2791	5.6 × 2.7	15.12
6. P.Oxy. XII 1484	4.9 × 3.1 (n.c.)	15.19
7. P.Oxy. XLIV 3202	4.7 × 3.3	15.51
8. P.Oxy. LXVI 4541	6.6 × 2.5	16.5
9. P.Oxy. XII 1580	6.4 × 2.6	16.64
10. P.Oxy. LXXV 5056	6.4 × 2.7	17.28
11. P.Köln VI 280	7 × 2.5 (n.c.)	17.5
12. P.Oxy. LXII 4339	7 × 2.5 (with traces of another one)	17.5
13. P.Köln I 57	4.5 × 4	18
14. P.Coll.Youtie I 51	6.4 × 3	19.2
15. P.Oxy. LXVI 4542	5.3 × 3.7	19.61
16. P.Coll.Youtie I 52	4.5 × 4.4	19.8
17. P.Oxy. VI 927	6.2 × 3.2 (on the verso)	19.84
18. P.Oxy. XII 1485	5.3 × 4	21.12
19. P.Oxy. III 524	6.4 × 3.5	22.4
20. SB XVI 12596	5 × 4.5	22.5
21. P.Oxy. XXXI 2592	5.6 × 4.2	23.52
22. SB XVI 12511	3.6 × 6.8 (n.c.; vertical)	24.48
23. P.FuadUniv. 7	5 × 5	25
24. SB XIV 11944	5 × 5 (n.c.)	25
25. P.Oslo III 157	6.6 × 3.8 (n.c.)	25.8
26. P.Oxy. XXXVI 2792	6.5 × 4	26
27. P.Fay. 132	5 × 5.3 (n.c.)	26.5
28. P.Oxy. XIV 1755	5.6 × 4.8	26.88
29. P.Oxy. I 110	6.3 × 4.4	27.72
30. P.Oxy. LII 3693	5.7 × 5.2	29.64
31. P.Oxy. LXVI 4539	8.6 × 3.5	30.1
32. SB XIV 11652	5.5 × 5.5	30.25
33. P.Oxy. I 111	8 × 4	32
34. P.Oxy. XVII 2147	7 × 4.6	32.2
35. P.Fouad 76	6.5 × 5	32.5
36. SB XVIII 13875	8.1 × 4.4	35.64
37. P.Brit.Col. inv. 1[b]	8.3 × 4.3	35.69
38. P.Heid. inv. 1639[c]	6.5 × 5.5	35.75
39. P.Oxy. IV 747	7.3 × 5.1	37.23
40. P.Yale I 85	5.7 × 6.8 (blank space under the last line)	38.76
41. P.Oxy. LXXV 5057	8.4 × 4.8 (two columns, two party invitations)	40.32
42. SB XX 14503	2.4 × 4.9 (n.c., original 6 × 7, vertical)	42
43. P.Oxy. LXVI 4540	9.1 × 4.7	42.77
44. P.Oxy. III 523	8.4 × 5.5	46.2
45. P.Oxy. XXXIII 2678	9.5 × 5.5	52.25
46. P.Oxy. XII 1487	7 × 8.3 (vertical)	58.1

TABLE 2.2   List of party invitations according to size (*cont.*)

Papyrus	Measurements in cm (n.c. = not complete)	Surface in cm²
47. PSI XV 1543	9.2 × 6.4	58.88
48. P.Oxy. LXVI 4543	11 × 6	66
49. P.Oxy. XLIX 3501	7 × 9.5 (vertical, n.c.)	*66.5*
50. P.Oxy. XII 1486	12 × 5.7	68.4
51. SB V 7745	8 × 9 (possibly two texts written one above the other?)	72
52. P.Oxy. IX 1214	8.6 × 9.6 (longer text)	82.56
53. P.Oxy. LII 3694	12.4 × 11.1 (longer text)	137.64
54. O.Medin.Madi 31	Dimensions not available	

a   Where the findings are incomplete, "n.c." is used and the cm² number is given in italics.
b   Published in Nelson, Marshall, and Gardner 2018, 207–12.
c   Published in Berkes 2018, 277–81.

FIGURE 2.1   PSI XV 1543 and PSI inv. 4361 compared

because not only the writing material but also the text is different and unique. Hence, it is doubtful that it belongs to the same category of party invitations.[37]

As can be seen from Table 2.2, the sizes range from a width of 4.1 to 12 cm and a height of 2.5 to 6.4 cm. The most common format is rectangular (e.g., P.Oxy. XXXVI 2792 [III CE], 6.5 × 4 cm), but some are square (e.g., P.Coll. Youtie I 52 [II–III CE], 4.5 × 4.4 cm). In most cases, the invitations are wider than they are long, but in a few cases it is the other way round and the format is vertical (e.g., P.Oxy. XII 1487 [IV AD], 7 × 8.3 cm). While the horizontal rectangular format can be divided into a larger and a smaller model, there are nevertheless examples of nearly all sizes in between. Two PSI (shown in Fig. 2.1), are found

at opposite ends: at the top, among the smallest, PSI inv. 4361 ([III CE] 4.1 × 2.5 cm), and at the bottom, among the largest, PSI XV 1543 ([II–III CE] 9.2 × 6.4 cm). Among the smaller papyri, a dozen have a height of less than 3 cm, but only three are less than 5 cm wide.

The smaller-sized papyri include the most recently discovered party invitation—that is, the above-mentioned PSI inv. 4361, shown in Figure 2.2—which is perhaps the smallest ever found. It was discovered together with several small fragments at the bottom of a metal box in the Papyrological Institute of Florence, where some items were starting to rust and need urgent conservation. Most of the pieces are scraps from larger rolls or sheets; for example, fragments of documents (such as the beginning of a document addressed to the praefectus castrorum, the vice prefect of the imperial command) or literary texts (such as the Iliad).

The fragment is (almost) complete; a few letters are lost because it is broken on the right, but it is easy to make out the original text and format. Measuring only 4.1 × 2.5 cm, with letters 0.2 cm high, it is tiny when compared to other party invitations. The place of provenance is likely to be Oxyrhynchus and it can be dated to the third century CE. The four-line text reads: "xx asks you to dine on the occasion of the wedding of his/her son, in the house, tomorrow, which is the 5th, from the xth hour on."[38] In the lower part, under the last line of writing, rust stains are visible due to lengthy storage in the metal box.

Even today, it is not fully understood what the real function of these little cards was. This is because they have a standard formula and yet they omit some essential details

37   The ostracon is published in Bresciani and Foraboschi 1976, 91; its text and features are discussed in P.Oxy. LII 3693, 143; Arzt-Grabner 2016, 523; Berkes 2018, 277, n. 3.

38   The complete edition will be included in a forthcoming volume of PSI.

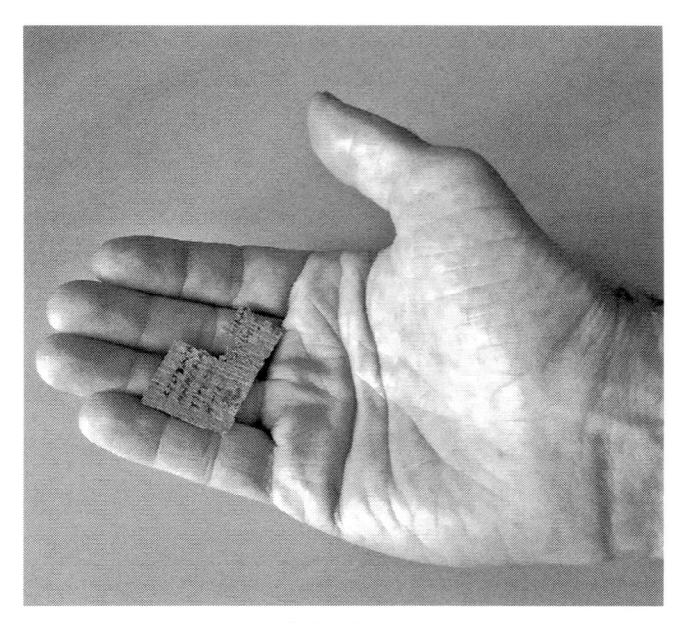

FIGURE 2.2 PSI inv. 4361 in the hand

that would allow us to consider them as invitation letters. What is certain is that they were delivered by someone who added information orally and also that they served as a reminder, as can be seen from the specification "tomorrow, which is day x."[39] Various hypotheses have been reconstructed as to aspects of their use, including that their format may have had a particular meaning.[40]

Returning to our central question, though, why were these cards so small? I would argue it is because party invitations were made for a private purpose and individual use and are tiny sheets that can be held in the hand and thus easily carried or hidden. It is tempting to hypothesize that they could have been a sort of entrance ticket, to check who could enter a party.[41] We can also imagine that they had an affective value, because they remembered feasts, happy and fun-filled moments. They could have been a tangible sign of participation in an event and could have been kept in memory of it. Even today, we often keep the entrance tickets to concerts or sports matches that have a particular meaning for us.

A less attractive hypothesis is that such collections of sheets were preserved to be shown and exhibited as a distinctive sign of a more affluent class:[42] as is clear from the detailed analyses of their dimensions, they are not eye-catching documents that could attract the attention of people looking at them. Even the largest specimens in

the category were not made for this purpose; the writing itself is often rapid and shoddy, which shows that the artifacts are objects made for practical use rather than with aesthetic intentions. For this reason, the format and writing can reveal information concerning status and social relations, as Ulrich Wilcken and Theodore C. Skeat had already guessed,[43] but they belong to a more intimate and restricted area, perhaps to the family sphere, rather than to more extensive forms of social bonds.

A second object that could be easily held in the hand is P.Messeri 33 (IV AD). It is a small document (when folded) containing a list of a decania (probably the names of soldiers). Measuring 5.5 × 25 cm, it is a tall and thin sheet, with a clear list of thirty-three mostly Semitic names under the heading "decania of Theodorus," which is stated at the top (ll. 1–2, δεκανία | Θεοδώρου).

The clue to discovering how small it could have been is the fact that the papyrus was folded horizontally and vertically, meaning it could have been reduced to an object measuring about 3 × 3 cm. It is evident that the sheet has been folded several times (see Fig. 2.3): first, in two horizontally, halfway between lines 19 and 20, where a fracture is visible (see the middle arrow in Fig. 2.3). In addition, six other horizontal fold lines are evident; these are 3 to 3.5 cm apart, both above and below the central fold, and because they are less marked they were probably made later (see the other arrows in Fig. 2.3). Finally, there is a fairly marked vertical fold perpendicular to the writing axis, roughly in the center of the sheet, about 3 cm from the left edge (see the vertical arrows in Fig. 2.3). It therefore appears that the sheet was folded three times horizontally, in half each time; finally, it was folded once vertically, reducing it to about 3 × 3 cm and thus rendering it containable in a very small space.

It is not completely clear who the listed people were and the purpose for which this list was made. Due to both the number (33) and the presence of Greek, Roman, and Semitic names, some of which are rarely seen in other ancient texts, as well as the absence of Egyptian names, it is possible to assume that they were soldiers in service in Egypt, belonging to auxilia (perhaps knights?).[44] The document does not seem to be an official one, like others of a military nature,[45] but it could have been a sheet for personal use by some army commander. It is worth noting,

39   For more on the practice of delivering an oral message by the bearer of the letter see Amory 2022, 237–241.

40   See the summary in Berkes 2018, 277–78.

41   See Berkes 2018, 278.

42   See, in particular, Skeat 1975, 253–54; Berkes 2018, 278.

43   See Wilcken 1912, 419; Skeat 1975, 253–54.

44   See P.Messeri 33, 186–94.

45   For papyri with similar lists of soldiers, found in Nubia, see Łajtar, Płóciennik, and Derda 2015, 47–57. For examples of official military documents, see the rosters from Dura Europos (Rom.Mil.Rec. 1–4).

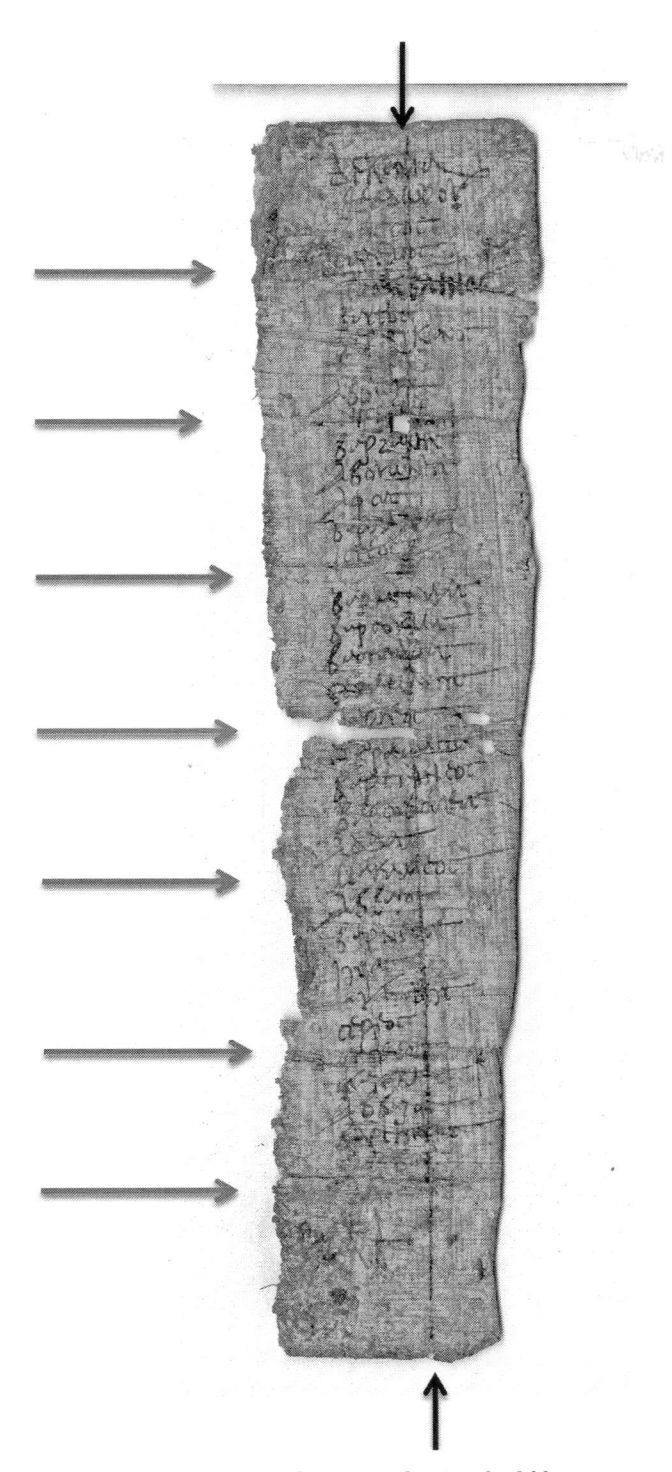

FIGURE 2.3 P.Messeri 33 with arrows indicating the folds

for example, that the small size of the folded sheet meant it could have been hidden in a very small pocket.

Conclusions

By analyzing some examples of particularly large and particularly small documents, and above all through the analysis of data offered by categories of documents from everyday life with similar, extraordinary dimensions, I have tried to illustrate the reasons leading to the choice of a specific size of document format. In general, a large format was used to underline official power and for stronger communication, while a small format was appropriate for expressing private feelings and personal needs, thanks to the possibility of keeping small documents among personal items, and in some way protected and hidden. In short, then, the size of documents can be a semiotic resource for Graeco-Roman Egypt, particularly when data on size are connected and compared with content and other data about the writing material or choice of language.

Reference List

Alfarano, Stefania, and Alberto Buonfino. 2022. "Architettura della convivialità nell'Egitto romano e tardoantico: le evidenze papirologiche." In *Proceedings of the 29th International Congress of Papyrology. Lecce, 28 July–3 August 2019, I–II*, edited by Mario Capasso, Paola Davoli, and Natascia Pellé, 65–86. Lecce: Centro di Studi Papirologici dell'Università del Salento.

Amory, Yasmine. 2022. "When the Letter Speaks Up: Living and Lifeless Letters." In *DocuMentality: New Approaches to Written Documents in Imperial Life and Literature*, edited by Jacqueline Arthur-Montagne, Scott Digiulio, and Inger Kuin, 233–249. Berlin: De Gruyter.

Angles, Pierre-Luc. 2019. "Le grec tracé avec un pinceau comme méthode d'identification des scripteurs bilettrés: généalogie, limites, redéfinition du critère." In *Proceedings of the 28th International Congress of Papyrology, Barcelona 2016*, edited by Alberto Nodar and Sofía Torallas Tovar, 382–98. Barcelona: Universitat Pompeu Fabra.

Arzt-Grabner, Peter. 2016. "Why Did Early Christ Groups Still Attend Idol Meals?" *Early Christianity* 7: 508–29.

Bastianini, Guido, and Guglielmo Cavallo. 2011. "Un nuovo frammento di lettera festale (PSI inv. 3779)." In *I papiri letterari cristiani. Atti del convegno internazionale di studi in memoria di Mario Naldini*, edited by Guido Bastianini and Angelo Casanova, 31–45. Florence: Istituto Papirologico "G. Vitelli."

Bentein, Klaas, and Yasmine Amory. 2019. "Everyday Writing in Graeco-Roman and Late Antique Egypt: Outline of a New Research Programme." *COMSt Bulletin* 5, no. 1: 17–27.

Berkes, Lajos. 2018. "An Unusual Party Invitation from Graeco-Roman Egypt." In *Across the Mediterranean—Along the Nile*, edited by Tamás A. Bács, Ádám Bollók, and Tivadar Vida, 277–81. Budapest: Archaeolingua.

Bianchi, Angelo. 1983. "Aspetti della politica economico-fiscale di Filippo l'Arabo." *Aegyptus* 63: 185–98.

Bresciani, Edda, and Daniele Foraboschi. 1976. *Rapporto preliminare delle campagne di scavo 1968 e 1969. Ostraka e papiri greci da Medinet Madi nelle campagne 1968 e 1969.* Milan: Cisalpino.

Bussi, Silvia. 2008. *Le élites locali nella provincia d'Egitto di prima età imperiale.* Milan: Cisalpino.

Crisci, Edoardo. 1996. *Scrivere greco fuori d'Egitto: ricerche sui manoscritti greco-orientali di origine non egiziana dal IV secolo a.C. all'VIII d.C.* Florence: Gonnelli.

Fournet, Jean-Luc. 2015. "Des villageois en quête de lettres officielles : le cas des pétitionnaires d'Aphrodité (Égypte, VIe s. ap. J.-C.)." In *Official Epistolography and the Language(s) of Power*, edited by Stephan Procházka, Lucian Reinfandt, and Sven Tost, 255–66. Vienna: Verlag der Österreichischen Akademie der Wissenschaften.

Grossi, Marco. 2016. "ΕΓΡΑΨΕΝ ΔΕ ΚΑΙ ΤΙΤΛΟΝ Ο ΠΙΛΑΤΟΣ (Gv 19,19). Verso una nuova definizione di iscrizione." *ZPE* 197: 85–95.

Hussein el-Mofatch, Rasha. 2016. "Where Is the Party?" In *Proceedings of the 27th International Congress of Papyrology Warsaw, 29 July–3 August 2013*, edited by Tomasz Derda, Adam Łajtar, and Jakub Urbanik, 1993–2010. Warsaw: University of Warsaw.

Johnson, William A. 2004. *Bookrolls and Scribes in Oxyrhynchus.* Toronto: University of Toronto Press.

Jördens, Andrea. 2011. "Eine kaiserliche Konstitution zu den Rechtsprechungskompetenzen der Statthalter." *Chiron* 41: 327–56.

Katzoff, Ranon. 1982. "Prefectural Edicts and Letters." *ZPE* 48: 209–17.

Łajtar, Adam, Tomasz Płóciennik, and Tomasz Derda. 2015. "Three Lists of Soldiers on Papyrus Found in Qasr Ibrim." In *Ad fines imperii Romani. Studia Thaddaeo Sarnowski septuagenario ab amicis, collegis discipulisque dedicata*, edited by Agnieszka Tomas, 47–57. Warsaw: University of Warsaw.

Nelson, Max, C. W. Marshall, and Chelsea A. M. Gardner. 2018. "P.Brit.Col. Inv. 1 and Invitations to Sarapis Dinners." *ZPE* 205: 207–12.

Parsons, Peter J. 1967. "Philippus Arabs and Egypt." *JRS* 57: 137–41.

Pruneti, Paola. 2016. "Alcune considerazioni sui bigliettini d'invito." *Analecta Papyrologica* 28: 117–28.

Reiter, Fabian. 2005. "Symposia in Tebtynis." In *Tebtynis und Soknopaiu Nesos: Leben im römerzeitlichen Fajum, Akten des Internationalen Symposions vom 11 bis 13 Dezember 2003 in Sommerhausen bei Würzburg*, edited by Sandra Lippert and Maren Schentuleit, 131–40. Wiesbaden: Harrassowitz.

Sarri, Antonia. 2018. *Material Aspects of Letter Writing in the Graeco-Roman World.* Berlin: De Gruyter.

Skeat, Theodore Cressy. 1975. "Another Dinner-Invitation from Oxyrhynchus (P. Lond. Inv. 3078)." *JEA* 61: 251–54.

Strassi, Silvia. 1993. "Problemi relativi alla diffusione delle disposizioni amministrative nell'Egitto romano." *ZPE* 96: 89–107.

Stroppa, Marco. 2004. "Il termine πρόγραμμα nella documentazione dell'Egitto romano." *Aegyptus* 84: 177–200.

Stroppa, Marco. 2022. "Lettere festali su papiro." In *Comunicazioni dell'Istituto Papirologico «G.Vitelli» 14*, edited by Simona Russo, 37–49. Florence: Firenze University Press.

Stroppa, Marco. Forthcoming a. "Grandi sorprese in piccoli reperti del Museo Archeologico di Firenze." In *Comunicazioni dell'Istituto Papirologico «G.Vitelli» 15*. Florence: Firenze University Press.

Stroppa, Marco. Forthcoming b. "Receipt." In *Tebtynis in the Italian Collections (1): The Objects from the Tebtynis Excavations in the Florence Egyptian Museum*, edited by Giorgia Cafici and Giulia Deotto. Padua: Padua University Press.

Tacoma, Laurens E. 2006. *Fragile Hierarchies: The Urban Elites of Third-Century Roman Egypt.* Leiden: Brill.

Taubenschlag, Rafal. 1951. "Les publications officielles du stratège dans l'Egypte gréco-romaine." *JJP* 5: 155–60.

Tedeschi, Gennaro. 2017. *Spettacoli e trattenimenti dal IV secolo a.C. all'età tardo-antica secondo i documenti epigrafici e papiracei.* Trieste: Edizioni Università di Trieste.

Turner, Eric G. 1974. "A Commander-in-Chief's Order from Saqqâra." *JEA* 60: 239–42.

Wilcken, Ulrich. 1912. *Grundzüge und Chrestomathie der Papyruskunde. Erster Band: Historischer Teil. Erste Hälfte, Grundzüge.* Leipzig: Teubner.

## CHAPTER 3

Notes on Ostraca and Scribal Practice

Sofía Torallas Tovar

It is now becoming something of a trend to pay attention to *The Use of Ostraca in Antiquity*, to borrow the title of a recent text, edited by Julia Lougovaya and Clementina Caputo.[*,1] The studies in that volume join other recent editions and research projects in opening new ways of looking at a widespread medium and scribal practice, with specific characteristics and use. In this way it stands in contrast to the earliest publications, where little analysis was performed on the materiality, the chosen medium, and the scribal practice of the texts the ostraca bear.[2] Until recently, ostraca were generally considered a low-cost solution to the lack of papyrus, or an opportunity medium.

This recent shift in focus has also been attended by the growing number of ostraca available for study. Roger Bagnall called attention to the ostraca finds in archaeological excavations throughout the twentieth century, observing that a growing interest translated into growing numbers of these written sherds being rescued from excavations.[3] During the "papyrus rage," expeditions to Oxyrhynchus and other sites may have overlooked ostraca, but comparatively recent excavations have unearthed massive quantities, and interest in their archaeological context has given them an enhanced value. As Lougovaya notes, "this avalanche of ostraca finds and publications, both existing and expected, affects our overall view of preferences for writing supports and even of the function of writing in general."[4]

In this chapter, I would like to add some notes on scribal practice on ostraca to these recent discussions. In doing so I will suggest some possible avenues of analysis of the material. Beginning with the choice of pottery, I will then look at several text types, including tax receipts, lists and accounts, letters, and "series." With a view to better understanding the choices and practices of scribes and the constraints placed by the nature of the ostraca, I will also offer a comparison with scribal practice on other mediums.

1 Choice of Pottery

About one third of the documents we have received from Egypt are written on pottery or stone ostraca.[5] Many of these show signs of having been written by professional or at least skillful scribes. We should probably imagine that a skilled scribe produced documents on both papyrus and ostraca, and even on wood, and the skills the scribes learned were applied to the production of documents on all these media.

Turning to the choice to produce documents on pottery, two aspects are relevant. One, why pottery (and not papyrus or wood), has been discussed by Lougovaya.[6] She presents three cases for the use of ostraca (Trimithis, Oxyrhynchus, and Philadelphia), analyzing their use in the context of the availability of other writing media, especially papyrus. Lougovaya concludes that in these cases, the choice of ostraca was due to convenience and cost.

The second aspect regards the choice of specific pottery. Did scribes discriminate between types of pottery and are there clear trends in the choices of specific sherds and shapes? Caputo[7] has recently demonstrated that

---

* This paper builds upon previous work, like that of Lougovaya 2018 and Caputo 2018, 2019a, and 2020, among other interesting observations on scribal use and ostraca, and my own observations on the as-yet-unpublished ostraca from the excavations of the Swiss Institute of Archaeology in Aswan (see Hepa and Torallas Tovar, 2022 for a first edition of these ostraca, and von Pilgrim et al. 2019 for a description). I am aware of the need to hold and observe ostraca to understand their shapes and formats; however, I wrote this paper during the 2020 pandemic without access to anything but print and digital images. I am very grateful to my colleagues Clementina Caputo (Milan), Korshi Dosoo (Würzburg), Mariola Hepa (Cairo), Julia Lougovaya (Heidelberg), and Raquel Martín (Madrid), for their extremely useful comments and additions to this paper.

1 Caputo and Lougovaya 2020.
2 Discussed in Caputo 2019a, 2019b.
3 Bagnall 2011, 120–24.
4 Lougovaya 2018, 52. See also Davoli 2020.

5 Bagnall 2011, 119–20 gives comparative numbers of papyri and ostraca by town or site. Numbers also vary according to the type of document. For ostraca in general, see Maltomini 2012–13; for ostraca in the north of Africa, see Ast 2016; for recently excavated ostraca in Ephesus, see Biagetti and Sänger 2019.
6 Lougovaya 2018. Hélène Cuvigny (2003, 265–67) reached somewhat similar conclusions in her analysis of the ostraca finds in comparison to the absence of papyri and the presence of other organic material found at the same site.
7 Caputo 2020; see also Caputo and Cowey 2018.

the serial production of certain documents, such as tax receipts, tags, and labels (in trade) could not depend on the casual finding of sherds adequate in size and shape for the recording of these documents. Most probably, scribes had large sherds or even whole discarded pots which they conveniently cut and tailored to meet scribal needs.[8] Mechanical cutting by a practiced scribe probably produced similarly shaped and sized sherds. Although the variation in quality and shape might be noticeable, there is some regularity observed in the patterns when one looks at certain documents of a precise period and place.[9] These sherds were definitely cut before being written on and the pottery used to create them was often locally produced, used, and discarded.

Recent analysis has shown that there was a trend to use specific kinds of vessels more than others,[10] and one may imagine that experience led scribes to choose those pots or jars with specific qualities which made inscription easier and more durable. This might include a surface that was smooth yet porous enough to receive the ink and not smudge it;[11] a color light enough to offer a good contrast with the ink; and a shape offering a surface flat enough, or with a slight curve, that would make the document readable, transportable, and archivable. These choices played a role in the presence of local or imported pottery for the ostraca.[12]

Other important aspects of the use of ostraca include whether the concave or convex side of the sherd was employed. The external, convex side was most frequently used,[13] explained by the fact the convex side is generally smoother than the concave one. The use of the "verso," the concave side, was subject to the type of vessel used; for instance, the relatively common pitched jars could, of course, only be inscribed on the vessel's exterior.[14] The concave side is generally used as a continuation of the text on the convex side, or simply reused for a different document. There are of course exceptions to this tendency; for example, the case of O.Kellis 145 (TM 74674 [294 CE]),[15] a contract written on the concave side, and O.Sarga 27 (TM 89513 [V–VII CE]).[16] In opistographic documents on ostraca, the direction of the text is normally the same on both sides.[17]

2 Document Production

There are many material aspects involved in the production of documents. On the one hand, there are material constraints on the written production, starting with the scribe's posture. The manner in which a scribe held the ostracon when writing it can explain, for example, blank margins. Conversely, a lack of margins can indicate the posture adopted for the production of the text. The scribe could be standing, holding the ostracon on their left- or right-hand side, depending on their laterality, or sitting and supporting the ostracon on their knee or a firm surface,[18] thus allowing all margins to be covered with writing. Different documents can bear witness to different practices: a list or inventory is more likely to have been written and checked while standing and a tax receipt or a letter could have been produced at a desk or by a sitting

---

8   Also, Peña 2007, 162 includes a brief discussion on casual shapes and tailored shapes in ostraca.

9   For example, the regularity of the shapes of small tags—triangular with the inverted triangle shape—as presented in Caputo 2020.

10 Caputo 2016, 2020; Barba Colmenero 2021; Hope 2004, 7–10; Bavay and Delattre 2013.

11 Nikos Litinas (2008, 1) observes that the Abu Mina ostraca did not use local pottery; rather, documents used imported pottery that was of higher quality and less porous.

12 María Jesús Albarrán Martínez (2016) proved that the Palau Ribes ostraca were produced with local pottery, typical of middle Egypt (Bawit), a fact that was confirmed by the text's content. Cromwell 2020, 220–21 covers the curious use of pharaonic pottery for Arabic tax receipts; Adam Bülow-Jacobsen (in Cuvigny 2012, 297) also talks about choice when noting that scribes chose non-pitched jars for longer letters that were written opisthographically. Choice also plays a role for magical texts. The magical handbooks often indicate the kind of ostracon required for specific procedures; see Martín Hernández and Torallas Tovar 2014 and Lougovaya 2020a. Raffaella Cribiore 2001, 35 describes a young student choosing an ostracon adequate for the size or extension of the writing exercises for school.

13 Caputo and Cowey 2018 give the proportions for their case studies, including whether the use of the verso is a continuation or, in a few cases, a second use. However, Aramaic ostraca present a different situation. Folmer 2020, 159 indicates that the concave side was preferred to avoid the ribbed surface of the convex side.

14 Bülow-Jacobsen in Cuvigny 2012, 297.

15 Worp 2004, 128–29. See Hope 2004, 6 on the use of convex and concave sides.

16 Lougovaya (2020b) has recently established that the text of this division table written on the rim of a bowl started on the concave side and continued on the convex.

17 As an exception to this, for example, O.Did. 393 (end I CE), features writing oriented differently on both sides.

18 A firm surface is less likely than the knee or forearm, since the curved shape of ostraca makes it very difficult to hold it still on a table. Litinas (2008, 1) states that the Abu Mina ostraca were always written on the convex side, because, as he explains, they were supported on the scribe's knee. In the revisions of this article, Clementina Caputo generously shared her views on document production and scribal practice gathered over her decade-long experience on ostraca. Her observations, which I hope she will soon publish, support the argument I am making.

scribe. On the other hand, the experience of a scribe in producing specific types of documents on papyrus can influence the practice when producing documents on ostracon.[19]

Some of the most basic constraints, however, are those determined by the characteristics of an ostracon's surface. Writing on ostraca generally runs along the curve, and thus along the throwing lines of the vessel.[20] This seems natural and compares with writing along the fibers of the papyrus, as it is easier to write along the lines, using them as a guide. However, there are many documents, especially smaller pieces, where the texts are written across the throwing lines,[21] and it does remain difficult to systematize the tendencies.

Three documents dating to the second century CE, that are from Mons Claudianus and are written by the same scribe, present different choices.[22] The first, O.Claud. II 260 (TM 29680), has a squarish shape and is written horizontally, by which I mean that the slightly longer axis of the piece is horizontal. The text is written across the throwing lines of the vessel, on the convex side. The second, O.Claud. II 261 (TM 29681), presents a trapezoidal shape, with the longer side on top. The text is written along the throwing lines, starting on the longer side and ending on the shorter side, with lines progressively diminishing in length. The third document by the same scribe, O.Claud. II 262 (TM 29682), is an irregular pentagon, written across the throwing lines. These examples prove that a single scribe can employ different practices. The general trend, however, is that the writing follows the throwing lines[23] and the convex side is used far more frequently than the concave side of the ostracon.

Turning to the distribution of the text on the surface of the ostracon and whether this corresponds to the page setup of documents on papyrus, there is evidently a clear distinction in the production of these different media and the documents they respectively bore. Papyrus was produced industrially in a specific manner, cut in a certain way, had a regular size and shape, and the use of the side with horizontal and the one with vertical fibers of papyrus is easier to trace. Pottery, on the other hand, was produced for a different purpose and repurposed for writing after being discarded. However, repurposing did give some kind of uniformity to the sherds. The cutting was not merely casual.[24] The direction of the writing across or along the throwing lines, or the choice of a concave or convex surface for the text have some order and rationale.

3   Case Studies by Genre

Having established these key points regarding the choice of pottery and document production, it is worthwhile to attempt a comparative analysis by document genre. Recent studies on the format of letters, petitions, and other documents can serve as a model for the study of these aspects in ostraca document production.[25] I am aware that a comparative analysis by document genre requires the autoptic examination of a large corpus of documents to find trends and assumed regularities in their production. However, I think it is useful to begin with a few case studies on specific document types that might identify trends which an exhaustive study of a larger corpus can then confirm or disprove. The case studies I present here are drawn from the available edited ostraca with images in print or online, and from my own experience in the Swiss Institute excavations in Aswan.[26] I offer it as a *prolegomenon* to a more exhaustive analysis of a larger corpus of ostraca, perhaps organized chronologically, and compare it to the formats of equivalent documents on papyrus, applied to my study of the Aswan ostraca.

In the tables below I present the approximate figures for documents distributed by genre and language taken from the Trismegistos database. The cut by language is not indicative of chronology, since from the fourth century CE, Coptic and Greek were contemporary. The figures are approximate and do not correspond to a verifiable reality, since the documents included in the database are those that have been not only found or excavated but edited. This corresponds to a very small percentage of those currently in museums and collections, which often remain unpublished for a long time due to their state of

---

19   This principle is not necessarily always true. Some tax collectors might not have ever written on papyrus but became skilled at producing tax receipts on ostracon.

20   This is observed by Colin Hope (2004, 6–7), in O. Kellis.

21   Here I understand the curvature of the ostracon as if it were a cylinder, with a curved and a straight axis. This is the case for many tax receipts written on the necks of amphoras, for example, or simply smaller documents written on a curved ostracon, with the curvature running vertically.

22   Three letters from Maximus to Alexas (Bingen et al. 1997, 91–94).

23   Caputo and Cowey 2018 gives the proportions of ostraca written along or across the throwing lines in two case studies. Writing along the lines is invariably more frequent. Below I will refer to the ridges in later pottery and how they mark the direction of writing, though exceptions also exist.

24   See the above reference to Caputo 2020.

25   E.g., Fournet 2009, 2019.

26   I understand it is often difficult to establish the direction of the pot, curvature, etc. from images. I have chosen examples in which I felt more confident about the shape of the ostraca or the editors had produced a careful description.

TABLE 3.1   Percentages of documents by genre and language on different media

Greek	papyrus	ostracon	wood	total
letters	9249 (9.14%)	2426 (20.75%)	11 (0.09%)	11686
tax receipts	5774 (34.2%)	11086 (65.6%)	21 (0.12%)	16881
accounts	1251 (93%)	93 (6.9%)	0	1344
contracts	7550 (98.5%)	88 (1.14%)	20 (0.26%)	7658
Coptic	papyrus	ostracon	wood	total
letters	1813 (32.8%)	3690 (66.9%)	9 (0.16%)	5512
tax receipts	111 (12%)	807 (87.9%)	0	918
accounts	212 (50.9%)	197 (47.3%)	7 (1.68%)	416
contracts	626 (67%)	305 (32.6%)	3 (0.32%)	934

preservation or scholarly availability. However, certain trends can be observed that are sufficiently indicative.

The first noteworthy observation is that the genre of tax receipts was generally produced in greater proportion on ostracon, both in Greek and Coptic, while in the epistolary genre the trend is reversed in Greek, but not in Coptic, where there is a greater use of ostracon. It is also to be noted that almost all of the attested contracts were produced on papyrus, although the tendency is somewhat moderated in the examples we have in Coptic. This could be a chronological trend, and it could be argued that the ostracon became a more popular medium in Coptic times. Third, accounts, despite not being an officialized document in the way contracts could be, tended to be produced on papyrus, at least in the Greek examples.

3.1   *Tax Receipts*

Tax receipts had already been singled out in the early observations of papyrus editors for their use of a different type of pottery than other documents.[27] I will refer here specifically to a kind of first and second-century tax receipt. Tax receipts from Aswan and Thebes present a variety of typologies. One of the widely occurring formats is that where the texts are written on the top part of an ostracon. There are examples that are rectangular (wider than tall), round, and square, as well as smaller pieces written on the full surface.

In the examples on ostracon we have from the first and second centuries CE, one observes some tendency toward horizontal shapes, often polygonal, with the text written across the throwing lines and mostly in the upper half of the ostracon. This can be seen, for example, in O.Eleph.DAIK 16 (TM 24197), 32 (TM 24212, see Fig. 3.3),

40 (TM 24220), or 42 (TM 24222); O.Bankes 14 (TM 699487), 17 (TM 699490), or 21 (TM 699494); as well in in several unpublished tax receipts from the Swiss Institute excavations. The photographs below present three tax receipts from the beginning and middle of the second century CE, all of which present the setup described above, with two on papyrus (Figs. 3.1–3.2) and one on ostracon (Fig. 3.3).

Tax receipts on papyrus, like those on ostracon, do not present a strict typology.[28] Nevertheless, we can find a tendency to a rectangular or square ticket with the text written on the upper half and a wider lower margin. This was perhaps left for additional annotations, the signatures of tax collectors (often found on the ostraca),[29] or even a seal, as in the Berlin example.[30] Additionally, having the upper part written, while leaving the lower part blank could be due to the archival method; that is, the documents were nested onto each other, leaving the upper part visible, and consultation was easier when the text was written on the top half.[31]

Finally, I include below, by way of example, the text of O.Eleph.DAIK 32 (see Fig. 3.3) in which a second hand has added a *postscriptum*.

27   See Caputo 2019a, 95–96, which refers to the case studied by Bavay and Delattre 2013.

28   There are examples of vertical longer documents like P.Oxy. XXXIV 2717 (TM 16590 [III CE]) or P.Oxy. XLVIII 3392 (TM 22488 [IV CE]), as well as combined tax receipts upon one single sheet of papyrus, like P.Monts.Roca IV 72 (TM 219247 [IV CE]).

29   Signatures: for example O.Eleph.DAIK 71 (TM 24246 [131 CE]), with a signature Σωκρατ|ίων σεσημίομαι (l. σεσημείωμαι) by a second hand, which is also an indication of the scribal process in the production of these documents.

30   Two further examples from the Berlin collection are SB XII 10907 (P.Berol. inv. 13308; TM 14352 [120 CE]) and SB XII 10915 (P.Berol. inv. 13311; TM 14361 [154 CE]), both from Soknopaiou Nesos.

31   Already suggested in Peña 2007, 162–63. This archival practice would also explain the preference for the convex side.

FIGURE 3.1 BGU III 718 ([103 CE], tax receipt, ca. 6 × 9 cm)
© STAATLICHE MUSEEN ZU BERLIN, ÄGYPTISCHES
MUSEUM UND PAPYRUSSAMMLUNG. PHOTO: SANDRA
STEISS, P 7882

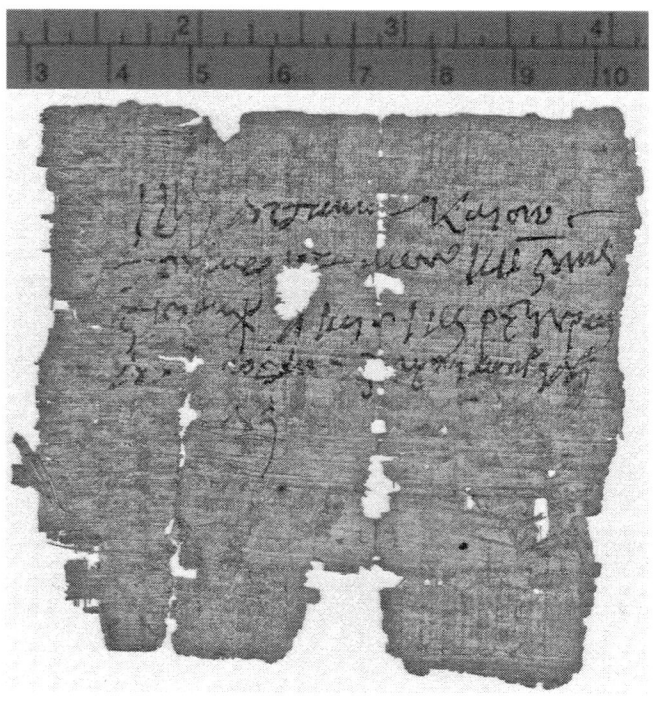

FIGURE 3.2 P.Oxy. LXXV 5053 ([149 CE], pig tax receipt, ca. 7 × 7 cm)
COURTESY OF THE EGYPT EXPLORATION SOCIETY
AND THE UNIVERSITY OF OXFORD IMAGING PAPYRI
PROJECT

No. 32

FIGURE 3.3 O.Eleph.DAIK 32 (TM 24212
[156 CE], poll tax receipt,
8 × 7.5 cm)
© DAI CAIRO

O.Eleph.DAIK 32

> Στλάκιος μισθ(ωτὴς) ἱερᾶς πύλ(ης) Σοήνης.
> διέγρ(αψεν) Πατσίβτις Πετορζμήθ(ιος)
> μητ(ρὸς) Σενπελαίας ὑ(πὲρ) λαο(γραφίας) ιθ
>   (ἔτους)
> δραχ(μὰς) δεκαεπτὰ ὀβολ(ὸν) (γίνεται)
> (δραχμαὶ) ιζ (ὀβολὸς). (ἔτους) ιθ
> Ἀντωνίνου Καίσαρος τοῦ κυρίου   5

(*M2) Μεσορὴ ι. *Διονυσόδωρος διὰ Σερή-
> νου ἀδελφοῦ ἔσχον δραχ(μὰς) δεκαεπτὰ ὀβολ(όν)
> (γίνεται) (δραχμαὶ) ιζ (ὀβολός).

This comparison of similar documents on ostracon and papyrus exemplifies a methodology that I believe deserves to be followed through in future studies. With a more systematic and exhaustive analysis of tax receipts across the centuries, it may be possible to establish a typology, on both papyrus and ostracon. An interesting case would be the identification of receipts produced by the same scribe on different media.

3.2 Lists and Accounts

A still-unpublished document from Aswan called my attention to the scribal practice used for inventories and lists.[32] This document dates to the second century CE and is an inventory list or account of goods sent up-river to the military camps to the south of Aswan, with payments listed in columns as is customary (Fig. 3.4). The

---

32 For the Aswan ostraca, see Torallas Tovar in von Pilgrim et al. 2019, on this ostracon see 38. This list bears the inventory number 12-2-70-9/14, found in 2013 in Area 2, together with other documents that point to the Roman Army stationed in Aswan.

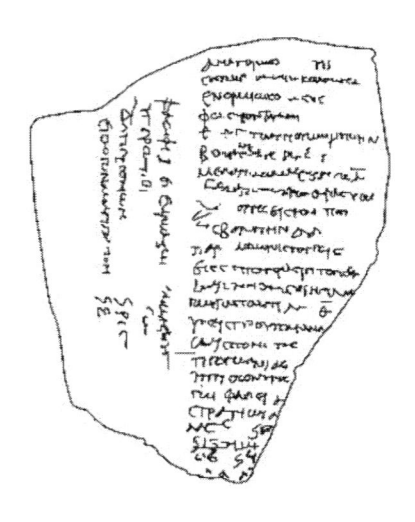

FIGURE 3.4 O.Syene Swiss s/n with drawing by Raquel Martín Hernández
© SWISS INSTITUTE CAIRO

reconstruction of the fragments gives a document with an irregular shape, close overall dimensions of width and height (19 × 15 cm), writing in a regular elegant hand, and a column to the right that leaves a margin to the left of about one third of the width of the document, which was later filled with more entries of the account. The scribe could have held the sherd in his left hand while inscribing it with his right, before rotating it ninety degrees to the left to continue the list on the left margin holding the sherd by the top margin of the first column inscribed. This is just a hypothetically reconstructed scribal action, but it is reasonable to think that a list and an inventory are produced in a more dynamic situation than a document produced at a desk by a sitting scribe. Interestingly, many documents with lists and inventories present wide margins that can be explained by the fact that the sherd was held while being written or checked.[33]

Lists among the ostraca from Mons Claudianus[34] often feature a somewhat wider margin, when compared, for example, to letters. O.Claud. I 115 (TM 24127 [early II CE]) is a list of workers, with a title in *ekthesis* and a list placed on the left-hand half of the ostracon (perhaps held by a left-handed scribe?). O.Claud. I 83 (TM 24095 [early II CE]), however, features an ample left-hand margin as does 90 (TM 24102 [early II CE]), which also features slash markings on the left of the names.

In short, it is difficult to systematize the production of lists, which present many irregularities since they are not a formalized genre. Nevertheless, one might argue that their production required the scribe to adopt a different posture to that employed when writing a document at a desk. Thus, it is possible that the scribe's posture might have some impact on the use of margins.

33   Cf. a register of wheat issued for the production of bread, Philadelphia BGU VII 1552 from the end of the third / beginning of the second century BCE, with a wider right-hand margin, perhaps held by a left-handed scribe (image in Lougovaya 2018,

56). Perhaps a similar situation can explain the large left-hand margin in BGU VII 1544, discussed in Lougovaya 2018, 60 (with image).

34   Bingen et al. 1992.

3.3 Letters[35]

Letters on papyrus are the least formalized of all documents, both from the point of view of the language and their material or visual qualities. Letters are written by scribes at all levels of literacy, with greater or lesser writing skills. Letters can be formal and long, using greeting and farewell formulas, or just short notes or memoranda devoid even of greetings. Letters can be spontaneous and casual, or official and formulaic, with a specific page setup.

Jean-Luc Fournet has studied the evolution of the format and production of late antique letters.[36] His analysis, of course, is based on letters on papyrus. In his exhaustive investigation of both the textuality and the materiality of letters, he observes a progressive literalization of letters from the second century CE on. There is also a shift in the material format of the letters, from vertical to horizontal, a shift that would be finalized in the sixth or seventh century CE. My question here, then, is whether a similar study can be undertaken on letters on ostraca; that is, whether the scribal practice observed on papyrus documents finds a parallel in documents written on other supports or media.

Like letters on papyrus, those on ostraca present enormous variation, due in part to different levels of literacy and to the nature of the messages sent.[37] Ostraca do not generally carry long documents. However, there are a few examples of large sherds, up to 30 cm in height, with letters of twenty to thirty lines. These texts might have been the final letter, or a draft to be copied onto papyrus and kept for archival purposes.[38] In any case, some of these letters present a formalized aspect, in terms of handwriting and the use of the surface of the ostracon. Even if the surface of the sherd is curved and sometimes has cumbersome shapes, the formal page setup of a letter, as it appears on a papyrus, maps onto it nicely.

I present below three examples of longer letters from the Didymos ostraca, all dating from the end of the first century to the beginning of the second century CE and written by different scribes.[39] The text is skillfully written on an ostracon with a wing-like shape in the first case

FIGURE 3.5   O.Did. 339 (TM 144902)
PHOTO BY ADAM BÜLOW-JACOBSEN

(Fig. 3.5), on a somewhat rectangular sherd in the second (Fig. 3.6),[40] while the third letter is broken but shows the page setup clearly (Fig. 3.7). In all cases the scribes have respected a top and left-hand margin, visible also in other, slightly later, letters from the same site.[41] The right-hand side, however, does not feature a margin, as the line ends reach closely to the edge. The greeting formula is clearly highlighted and often begins in *ekthesis*, while the body of the letter is followed by a *vacat* before the closing farewell formula is inserted. A comparison with a second-century letter on papyrus (Fig. 3.8) from the Oxyrhynchus papyri shows how the scribes mapped the original structure and page setup of a letter onto the challenging surface of the ostracon as best as they could.

In order to illustrate the features described above, I include below the text of O.Did. 339 (TM 144902). The first line of the greeting formula and of the body of the text are in *ekthesis* and the first letter is slightly larger in

---

35   For a recent excellent study of the materiality of letters in antiquity, see Sarri 2018.

36   Fournet 2009.

37   For a reconstruction of the methods of letter sending see, e.g., Bülow-Jacobsen in Cuvigny 2012, 136.

38   For an example of a draft, see O.Did. 29 (TM 144596 [236 CE]) in Cuvigny 2012, 89–96, esp. 91, a large sherd (29 × 19 cm) containing a letter. The opening greeting formula in four lines appears in what is now the left-hand margin, while the text continues at ninety degrees. The scribe seems to have started writing on that side, and then turned the sherd ninety degrees and continued copying.

39   See Cuvigny 2011, 2012. For more examples of the ostraca from the same region, see Cuvigny 2005.

40   Bülow-Jacobsen in Cuvigny 2012.

41   See, for example O.Did. 406 (Fig. 3.8), in which the left-hand margin has been used for a final postscriptum at ninety degrees to the main text.

FIGURE 3.6 O.Did. 343 (TM 78790)
PHOTO BY ADAM BÜLOW-JACOBSEN

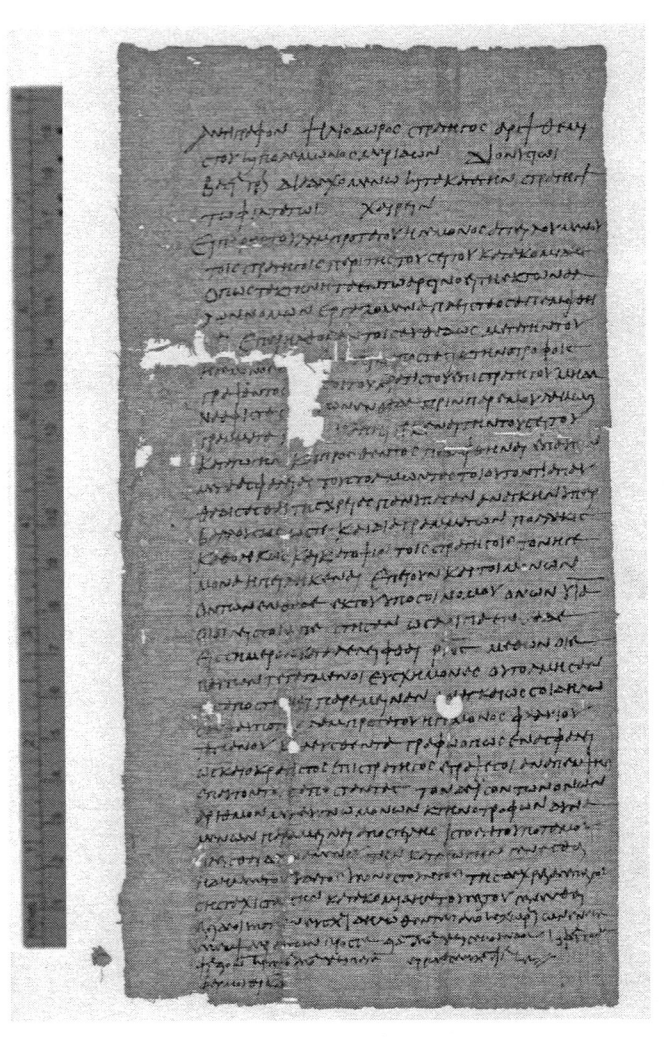

FIGURE 3.7 P.Oxy. XVIII 2182 (TM 12608)
PHOTO COURTESY OF THE EGYPT EXPLORATION
SOCIETY AND THE UNIVERSITY OF OXFORD IMAGING
PAPYRI PROJECT

size and with word spacing. There is some extra interlinear space after the greeting formula and a *vacat* before the farewell greeting.

Γάιος Ἀντώνιος   Λογγίνωι
Κρίσπῳ τῷ ἀδελφῷ χαίρειν·
ἀπέσταλκά σοι χίλωμα τὸ σὸν διὰ
Δώρου ἱππέος καὶ ζεύγη ἄρτου τρία,
καὶ οὐκ ἀντέγραψάς μοι. εἰ ἐκομίσου,   5
ἀντίγραψόν μοι. καὶ ἀπέσταλκάς
μοι ἐπιστολὴν ἣν οὐχ εὗρον διελ-
θεῖν, καὶ εἰ ἤκουκας περὶ σουπ-
κεσόρων ἀκριβέστατα, γράψον
μοι. μὴ οὖν ἄλλως ποήσεις, ἄδελ-   10
φέ μου. ἀσπάζου τοὺς ἐκεῖ
πάντες κατ' ὄνομα.

ἔρρωσο.   ια.

1 l. Λογγίνωι ‖ 4 l. ἱππέως ‖ 10 l. ποιήσῃς ‖ 12. l. πάντας

The *postscriptum* or continuation of a letter, when the whole surface is full, is regularly written on the left-hand margin, which is wider than the right-hand one, which is, in fact, often non-existent.[42] The third ostracon letter (Fig. 3.8) is an example of this, as is the unpublished document from Aswan mentioned in the previous section.[43]

42   Although there are letters that continue on the verso (concave side) or even on a second or further ostraca. For this see below.

43   The still unpublished correspondence of Akkas and Chairas from Area 88 in Aswan gives a small case study of certain scribal practices that I have not observed in other ostraca letters. This small archive was found in the dump material inside a building after its abandonment in Area 88 and is composed of at least seven letters, all written by Akkas and addressed to Chairas, in the same hand. Akkas's spelling is most often correct, and he has a nice, regular cursive hand. Through these seven examples, the style and scribal practice of Akkas can be traced. Namely, he always uses the same expressions for salutation and farewell, and seems to finish his letters, after the farewell, with *postscripta*,

εἴ τις ἔχι πρᾶγμα πρὸς αὐτὴν 25
ὅδε Λογγεινᾶς ἀναβαί-
νει, ὁ δεκουρίων, πρὸς
αὐτὸν ἕξουσι[ν.]

..[...].εὺς ['Ρο]υστίχῳ
τῷ [τι]μειωτ[άτ]ῳ πλ(εῖστα)
χ(αίρειν)· εὔχομαί σε ὑγιαίνειν.
γεινώσκειν σε θέλω τὴν γυ-
ναῖκα μου παραδεδω-   5
κέναι σοι αὐτὴν ἵνα ἀπο-
καταστήσῃς ἐν πραισει-
δίῳ Ἀφροδί{δ}\τ/ης ὅρους.
ἣν ἐάν τις ὑβρίσῃ πά-
λι ἐμοὶ ἀποκαταστή-   10
σεις, ἔχοντός μου πρὸ⟨ς⟩
σὲ ὥστε μὴ [ἐ]ξεῖναι αὐ-
τῇ κοιμᾶσθα[ι] ἐκτὸς σοῦ
πρός τινα. ἂν δὲ ἔχῃ
πρᾶγμα ἐκεῖ, ὃ μὴ δύν-   15
ηται εὐλυτωθῆναι πα-
ραδέξῃ αὐτὰ ἕως ἔλθῃ
ὁ κεντυρίων. εἶτα γὰρ,
ἐὰν γένηται, ἔξω πρὸς σέ·
σοὶ γὰρ τὰ ἐμὰ πάντα ἐ-   20
πίστευσα καὶ ἀποδώσεις
μοι τὴν παρακαταθήκην.
    ἀσπάζου Ἀγκυρᾶν καὶ Εὔβιν.
    (M2) ἔρρωσσο

2 l. [τι]μιωτ[άτ]ῳ ‖ 3–4 l. γι|νώσκειν ‖ 7–8 l. πραισι|δίῳ ‖ 17 corr.
ex αυτο, l. αὐτὸ ‖ 23 l. Εὔβιον ‖ 24 l. ἔρρωσο ‖ 25 l. ἔχει ‖ 26 l. ὧδε

FIGURE 3.8 O.Did. 406 (TM 144967)
PHOTO BY ADAM BÜLOW-JACOBSEN

To illustrate one of the possibilities of marginal script, I copy below the text of O.Did. 406 (TM 144967, fig. 3.8) from the beginning of the second century CE. It shows a *vacat* after the greeting formula, which probably started in *ekthesis*, and at the end, before the farewell, there is a substantial space. The first line of the body of the letter was probably in *ekthesis*, but the condition of the ostracon does not allow us to confirm this, nor the first line of the greeting formula.

Shorter letters from the Didymos ostraca, dating to the first century CE, are, however, horizontal, often featuring a vertical curvature; that is, they are normally written across the throwing lines. These texts and documents look very similar to horizontal receipts.[44] Textually, they are more succinct than the longer letters, have a shorter farewell formula, do not include salutations nor special greetings, and have a clear direct message. Examples of these types of messages are O.Claud. I 145 (TM 24157), 147 (TM 29813), 148 (TM 24159), 159 (TM 24167) or O.Did. 327 (TM 144890), 328 (TM 144891), 370 (TM 144931), and 371 (TM 144932). To give an idea of the type of short message found on horizontal letters, I copy below the texts of O.Did. 328 and 370 (also see Figs. 3.9 and 3.10).

For the fifth century CE, when the shift from vertical to horizontal letters on papyrus had taken place, we have some examples of horizontally written letters on ostraca, but the situation is not clear. At this point, a change in the type of pottery used for ostraca had a clear constraint on the production of writing. After the fourth century CE,

---

often over two lines, placed in the margins. He invariably writes the salutations and farewell at the bottom of the ostracon, then turns the ostracon around and continues writing the extra lines of the *postscriptum* at one hundred and eighty degrees to the main text in the top margin and continues in the left-hand margin. On Area 88, see Müller in von Pilgrim et al. 2015, 16–19. On the ostraca, see Torallas Tovar in von Pilgrim et al. 2019, 34–36.

44 This made me think of the fact that we use A4 for longer letters, and A6 (horizontally), or even smaller cards, when we want to send a short thank you note, or a message of that kind.

Ἀλβούκιος Παύλῳ καὶ Σενπρωνίῳ
χαίρειν · δέξε δέσμην ἀσπαρά-
γου καὶ δύο ῥαφάνους. καὶ περὶ
τοῦ πιπεριδίου γράψεις μοι εἰ ἔχεις,
πόσον καὶ πόσου, καὶ Ἀννίῳ ἐρεῖς   5
ἵνα μοι τὴν φάσιν πέμψῃ. ια
    ἔρρωσθε.

1 l. Σεμπρωνίῳ || 2 corr. ex χαιραιν || 2 l. δέξαι

FIGURE 3.9   O.Did. 328. (TM 144891 [end I CE])
            PHOTO BY ADAM BÜLOW-JACOBSEN

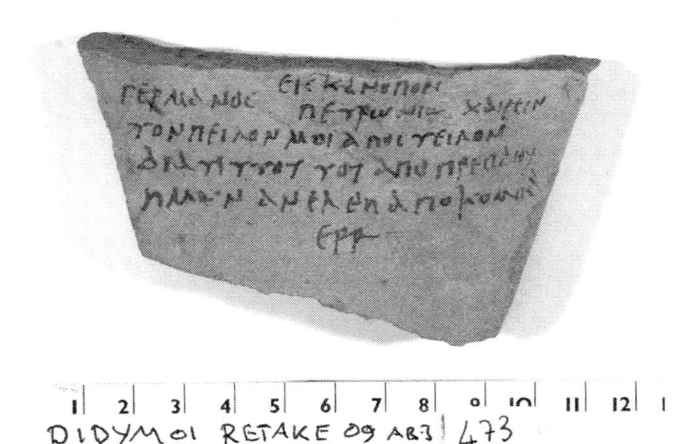

εἰς Κάνοπον
Γερμανὸς   Πετρωνίῳ   χαίρειν·
τὸν πεῖλόν μοι ἀπόστειλον
διὰ Τίττου τοῦ ἀπὸ πρεσιδίου
ἡμῶν ἂν ἔλθῃ ἀπὸ Κομπασι.   5
    ἔρρ(ωσο) λ.

3 l. πῖλον || 4. l. πραισιδίου

FIGURE 3.10   O.Did. 370 (TM 144931 [end of I CE])
             PHOTO BY ADAM BÜLOW-JACOBSEN

amphorae present a ridged surface, instead of the smooth surface of previous centuries.[45] This type of surface has an immediate effect and poses a new limitation on the format of the documents written on it. The lines of writing must follow the ridges in order to be readable, and thus, the direction in which the sherd is inscribed was largely imposed on the scribe. That said, there are always exceptions to most of the characteristics described for the use of ostraca. For example O.Eleph.DAIK 319 (TM 38594), a sixth- or seventh-century account of money, is written at approximately forty-five degrees to the ridges on the surface of the ostracon, which are, it must be said, not very pronounced, and thus do not interfere much with the legibility of the text.[46]

Looking at the ostraca from the Frange archive, for example, there are a number of documents written on amphora belly sherds with a ridged surface. For example, in O.Frange 208 (TM 219752 [VIII CE]; Fig. 3.11), the text follows the ridges of the amphora, while the margins present a quite capricious shape. O.Frange 217 (TM 219761 [VIII CE]; Fig. 3.12) is the shoulder of the LRA 7 amphora, where the ridges are also followed in a quite interesting shape. Another example of a text following the accidents of the shapes of the sherd is O.Frange 342 (TM 219881 [VIII CE]; Fig. 3.13).[47]

45   Amphorae with ribbed surfaces existed in Roman times from the first to second century CE (type Amphora AE 3); however, the ribbing was not yet as pronounced as in later late antique amphorae and the rim design is of course different. Strongly pronounced ribbing started in the fourth century CE (Dixneuf 2011).

46   OBawit IFAO 28 (TM 80156 [VII–VIII CE]) is one more example. Other examples in the Oxyrhynchus Racing archive (TM Archive 343) are the receipts of Kyriakos the wine-seller,

mentioned in Lougovaya 2018, 55. She claims that there is a tendency to use the ostraca vertically, allegedly for ease of holding when inscribing, but there are multiple examples where a horizontal orientation was preferred, so I would argue that the explanation should be different.

47   Boud'hors and Heurtel 2010.

FIGURE 3.11   O.Frange 208 (TM 219752)
WITH PERMISSION OF THE
MISSION ARCHÉOLOGIQUE BELGE
DANS LA NÉCROPOLE THEBAINE

FIGURE 3.12   O.Frange 217 (TM 219761)
WITH PERMISSION OF THE MISSION
ARCHÉOLOGIQUE BELGE DANS LA NÉCROPOLE
THEBAINE

FIGURE 3.13   O.Frange 342 (TM 219881)
WITH PERMISSION OF THE MISSION
ARCHÉOLOGIQUE BELGE DANS LA NÉCROPOLE
THEBAINE

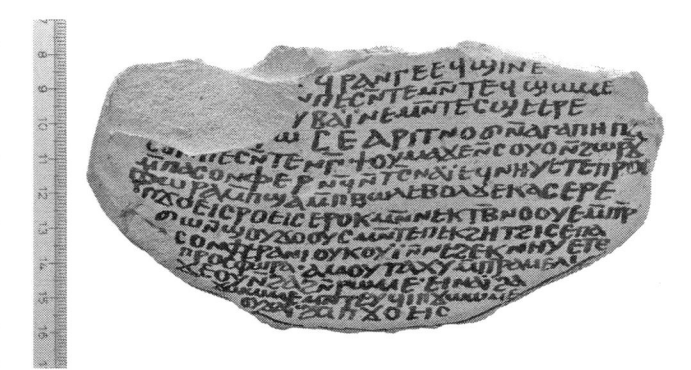

FIGURE 3.14   O. Frange 68 (TM 140990).
WITH PERMISSION OF THE MISSION
ARCHÉOLOGIQUE BELGE DANS LA NÉCROPOLE
THEBAINE

In other Frange documents, the flat surface of the stone slabs allowed more flexibility in the choice of page setup, and thus some examples seem closer to a contemporary letter. Figure 3.14 shows O.Frange 68 (TM 140990 [VIII CE]), which is compared to Figure 3.15, a papyrus letter, P.Mon. Epiph. 431 (TM 86966 [VII CE]),[48] featuring a horizontal format. From the same monastery and time, O.Mon.Epiph. 380 (TM 86913 [VI–VII CE]; Fig. 3.16) uses a vertical format for a letter, probably because of the constraints mentioned above.

These examples are just a first approach to the typology of letters on ostraca as compared to the analogues on papyrus. It is perhaps as risky as the comparison of

---

48   Crum and Evelyn-White, 1926, 263, no. 431. Cf. the documents and letters on ridged pottery ostraca in the archive of Frange, O.Mon.Epiph. 380 (TM 86913 [VII CE]).

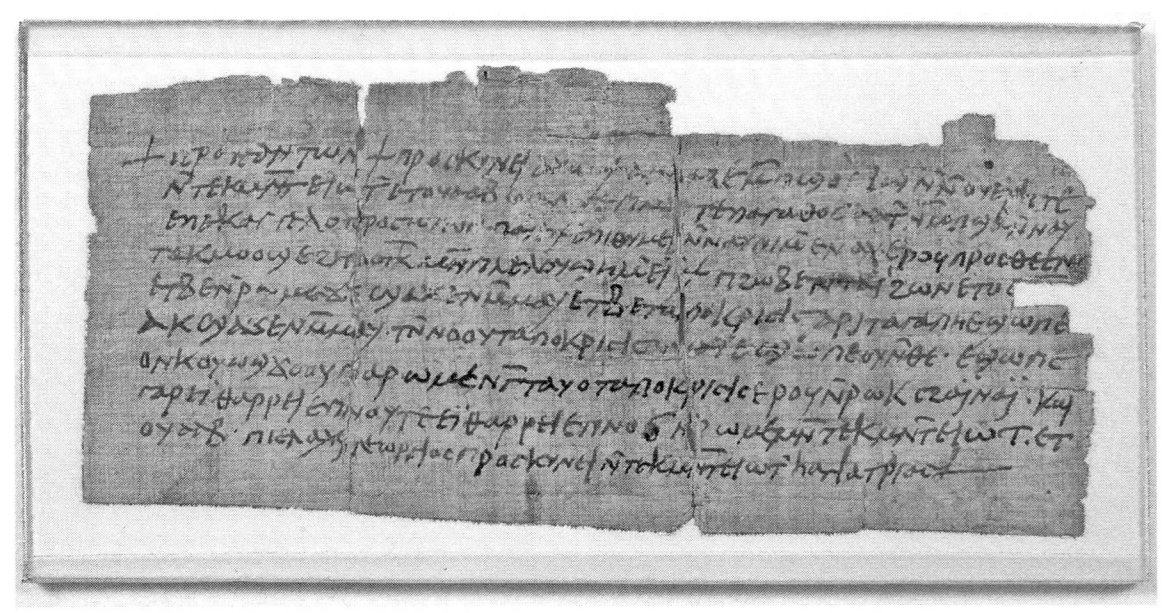

FIGURE 3.15   P.Mon.Epiph. 431 (TM 86966 [VI–VII CE], papyrus fragment of a letter from Victor to Psan)
METROPOLITAN MUSEUM, NEW YORK: PUBLIC DOMAIN

FIGURE 3.16   O.Mon.Epiph. 380 (TM 86913 [VI–VII CE], letter from
Pesynthius to Peter)
METROPOLITAN MUSEUM, NEW YORK: PUBLIC
DOMAIN

ostracon and papyrus tax receipts, since it is difficult to read the mind of the scribe.

3.4   Series of Ostraca

I will finish with a reference to the use of "series" of ostraca for the production of documents. In cases of longer and shorter series, the ostraca were either numbered or presented a catchword for interconnection. Francesca Maltomini has already referred to an "extreme" example, ODN 100–188 (150–225 CE), a set of eighty-nine bilingual ostraca (mainly Demotic with some passages in Greek) with an account of a long legal dispute.[49] The ostraca are numbered.[50] Also from Narmouthis, two second or third-century Demotic petitions are written across four and seven ostraca respectively.[51] To the documentary examples of this practice, we may add O.Did. 376 (TM 144937 [ca. 110 CE]), a letter written on two ostraca, using a catchword to connect both texts. Other letters from the same site seem to be incomplete, perhaps because they were written on more than one ostracon or because they were originally written that way. Among documentary texts, there are some further examples for Coptic ostraca

49   Maltomini 2012–13.
50   See Menchetti 2005; Bresciani, Giannotti, and Menchetti 2009, 56, 60–3, nos. 11–18; Caputo 2019a, 98–99.
51   O.Narm. Dem. III 155–157 + P.Narm. 2006 15 (TM 91501, 91502, 91503, 128999 [198–206 CE]), belonging to Phatres son of Horminos; OMM 272, 206, 1504, 758 + 1518, 1507 + two unnumbered ostraca (TM 91501, 91502, 91503, 128999 [198–206 CE]), belonging to Horos, perhaps Phatres' brother (see Bresciani, Giannoti, and Menchetti 2009, 79–80).

in the Frange archive and a few more unsure examples mentioned by Walter Crum.[52]

This phenomenon is also attested in liturgy for ostraca and for papyrus sheets.[53] We have an interesting example in magical texts too:[54] O.BYU Mag. 1–3 (VII–VIII CE), a series of three pottery ostraca that contains a single erotic procedure on their convex sides.[55] Two series of Greek ostraca from the Theban region contain sequential or nearly sequential verses of biblical texts.[56]

4 Conclusion

I have tried to put together some ideas or avenues of research to understand scribal practice on ostracon, beyond reducing it to a method adapted to the irregularity of the medium. It is already a trend in recent publications and editions of ostraca to include observations on the sherds' materiality, their shape, the direction of the throwing lines, and the use of one or both sides. These observations by editors, archaeologists, and ceramologists, along with advances in imaging, have changed the perception we had of documents on ostraca. It seems to me absolutely clear that the collaboration between papyrologists or editors of texts, and specialists in pottery and archaeologists is the right and only path for these types of research projects.

My main purpose was to explore the production of documents of the same kind and genre across media. While I artificially gave priority to papyrus documents over ostraca or other media in scribal production, perhaps we should instead try to understand the situation differently. The comparison of some tax receipts on papyrus and ostracon, along with some second-century letters on papyrus and ostracon, seems to suggest a pre-existing model in the mind of the scribe. However, it is difficult to say which came first. As Raffaella Cribiore points out, ostraca were a pervasive medium for education, and even skillful scribes must have learned and practiced writing on pottery sherds and stone slabs, as well as wooden waxed tablets.[57] How were these models for the page setup of a letter or a tax-receipt then created? Were they intended to be performed on a papyrus sheet or a waxed tablet, or a pottery sherd? As I already pointed out above, a practiced tax-collector, who produced hundreds of exemplars on ostracon, might have never written a single receipt on a papyrus, but do so daily on ostraca, confirming and establishing a model. Further research on scribal practice on ostraca will require, as I noted, exhaustive examination of a large corpus and specific case studies, as well as collaboration between specialists on pottery and specialists on texts. I believe there is an exciting future for these kinds of studies.

Reference List

Albarrán Martínez, María Jesús. 2016. "The Coptic Ostraca of the Palau-Ribes Collection: New Perspectives and Edition." In *Coptic Society, Literature and Religion from Late Antique to Modern Times*, edited by Paola Buzi, Alberto Camplani, and Federico Contardi, 1301–15. Orientalia Lovaniensia Analecta 247. Leuven: Peeters.

Ast, Rodney. 2016. "Latin Ostraca from Vandal North Africa." In *Mélanges Jean Gascou: Textes et études papyrologiques*, edited by Jean Gascou, Jean-Luc Fournet, and Arietta Papaconstantinou, 7–32. Paris: Association des Amis du Centre d'Histoire et Civilisation de Byzance.

Ast, Rodney, and Roger S. Bagnall, eds. 2016. *Amheida III: Ostraka from Trimithis, Vol. 2: Greek Texts from 2008–2013 Seasons.* New York: ISAW.

Bagnall, Roger S. 2011. *Everyday Writing in Graeco-Roman Egypt.* Berkeley: University of California Press.

Barba Colmenero, Vicente. 2021. "La Cerámica Bizantina del sur de Egipto. El Monasterio Copto de Qubbet El-Hawa en Asuán." PhD diss., University of Jaén.

Bavay, Laurent, and Alain Delattre. 2013. "La céramique des reçus de taxe thébaines du VIIIe siècle." *CE* 88: 379–84.

Biagetti, Claudio, and Patrick Sänger. 2019. "Ostraka e iscrizioni su ceramica da Efeso tardo-antica. Per un corpus dei frammenti." *Axon. Iscrizioni storiche greche* 3, no. 2: 67–86.

Bingen, Jean, Adam Bülow-Jacobsen, Walter E. H. Cockle, Hélène Cuvigny, Lene Rubinstein, and François Kaiswer. 1992. *Mons Claudianus: Ostraca graeca et latina.* Documents de Fouilles 29. Cairo: Institut Français d'Archéologie Orientale.

---

52 O.Frange 255 + 256 (TM 219797 + 219798 [VIII CE]); O.Crum 84 (TM 82975 [VI–VII CE]) and O.Crum 401 (TM 83292 [VI–VIII CE]); although the matching ostraca of these latter two texts are unknown, Crum (1902, 15) notes (for no. 84), "this text appears incomplete; the document must therefore have occupied more than one ostracon." Cf. also O.Crum 465 (TM 83354 [VI–VII CE]), a list of household items which seems to have belonged to a series too.

53 See Mihálykó 2019, 166–67 on series of ostraca in liturgy; 163–64 for series of sheets!

54 See Dosoo and Torallas Tovar, 2022.

55 Blumell and Dosoo 2018. See also Dosoo and Torallas Tovar, 2022, on series in magical formularies.

56 These are O.Petr. Mus. 4–7 (TM 68817 [V–VII CE]), containing selections from Acts 2:22–19:9; see also O.Petr. Mus. 13–16 (TM 61646 [V CE]), containing selections from 1 John 2:12–4:21.

57 Cribiore 2001, 151.

Bingen, Jean, Adam Bülow-Jacobsen, Walter E. H. Cockle, Hélène Cuvigny, François Kayser, and W. Van Rengen. 1997. *Mons Claudianus: Ostraca graeca et latina. II.* Documents de Fouilles 3, nos. 191–416. Cairo: Institut Français d'Archéologie Orientale.

Blumell, Lincoln H., and Korshi Dosoo. 2018. "Horus, Isis, and the Dark-Eyed Beauty: A Series of Magical Ostraca in the Brigham Young University Collection." *APF* 64, no. 1: 199–259.

Bresciani, Edda, et al. 2010. *Narmouthis 2006: Documents et objets découverts à Medinet Madi en 2006* Pisa: Plus-Pisa University Press.

Bresciani, Edda, Sara Giannotti, and Angiolo Menchetti. 2009. "Ostraka demotici e bilingui da Nar-muthis: testi miscellanei." *EVO* 32: 39–59.

Boud'hors, Anne, and Chantal Heurtel. 2010. *Les ostraca coptes de la TT29: Autour du moine Frangé*, 2 vols. Études d'archéologie thébaine 3. Brussels: CReA-Patrimoine.

Caputo, Clementina. 2016. "Ceramic Fabrics and Shapes." In Ast and Bagnall, *Amheida III*, 62–88.

Caputo, Clementina. 2018. "Gli ostraka e l'importanza del supporto scrittorio: evoluzione delle metodologie di studio." In *Polymatheia. Studi classici offerti a Mario Capasso*, edited by Paola Davoli and Natascia Pellé, 677–701. Lecce: Pensa Multimedia.

Caputo, Clementina. 2019a. "Looking at the Material: One Hundred Years of Studying Ostraca from Egypt." In *Antike Texte und ihre Materialität: Alltägliche Präsenz, mediale Semantik, literarische Reflexion*, edited by Cornelia Ritter-Schmalz and Raphael Schwitter, 93–117. Materiale Textkulturen 27. Berlin: De Gruyter.

Caputo, Clementina. 2019b. "Dati preliminari derivanti dallo studio degli ostraca di Berlino (O. Dime) da Soknopaiou Nesos." In *Proceedings of the 28th International Congress of Papyrology (Barcelona 2016)*, edited by Alberto Nodar and Sofia Torallas Tovar, 534–539. Barcelona: Publicacions de l'Abadia de Montserrat, Universitat Pompeu Fabra.

Caputo, Clementina. 2020. "Pottery Sherds for Writing: An Overview of the Practice." In Caputo and Lougovaya, *Using Ostraca*, 31–58.

Caputo, Clementina, and James M. S. Cowey. 2018. "Ceramic Supports and Their Relation to Texts in Two Groups of Ostraca from the Fayum." In *The Materiality of Texts from Ancient Egypt: New Approaches to the Study of Textual Material from the Early Pharaonic to the Late Antique Period*, edited by Francisca A. J. Hoogendijk and Steffie van Gompel, 62–75. Papyrologica Lugduno-Batava 35. Leiden: Brill.

Caputo, Clementina, and Julia Lougovaya. 2020. *Using Ostraca in the Ancient World: New Discoveries and Methodologies*. Berlin: De Gruyter.

Cribiore, Raffaella. 2001. *Gymnastics of the Mind: Greek Education in Hellenistic and Roman Egypt*. Princeton, NJ: Princeton University Press.

Cromwell, Jennifer. 2020. "'Forgive Me, Because I Could Not Find Papyrus': The Use and Distribution of Ostraca in Late Antique Western Thebes." In Caputo and Lougovaya 2020, 209–33.

Crum, Walter E. 1902. *Coptic Ostraca from the Collections of the Egypt Exploration Fund, the Cairo Museum and Others*. London: Offices of the Egypt Exploration Fund.

Crum, Walter E., and Hugh G. Evelyn-White. 1926. *The Monastery of Epiphanius at Thebes: Vol. II*. New York: The Metropolitan Museum of Art.

Cuvigny, Hélène. 2003. *La route de Myos Hormos. L'armée romaine dans le désert Oriental d'Égypte*. 2 vols. Praesidia du désert de Bérénice I–II, Fouilles de l'Ifao 48/1–2. Cairo: Institut français d'archéologie orientale.

Cuvigny, Hélène. 2005. *Ostraca de Krokodilô. La correspondance militaire et sa circulation, (O. Krok. 1–151)*. Praesidia du désert de Bérénice II, Fouilles de l'Ifao 51. Cairo: Institut français d'archéologie orientale.

Cuvigny, Hélène, ed. 2011. *Didymoi. Une garnison romaine dans le désert Oriental d'Égypte): Vol. I, Les fouilles et les matériels*. Praesidia du désert de Bérénice IV. Fouilles de l'Ifao 64. Cairo: Institut français d'archéologie orientale.

Cuvigny, Hélène, ed. 2012. *Didymoi. Une garnison romaine dans le desert Oriental d'Égypte: Vol. II, Les Textes*. Praesidia du désert de Bérénice IV, Fouilles de l'Ifao 67. Cairo: Institut français d'archéologie orientale.

Davoli, Paola. 2020. "Papyri and Ostraca as Archaeological Objects: The Importance of Context." In Caputo and Lougovaya 2020, 11–29.

Dixneuf, Delphine. 2011. *Amphores égyptiennes. Production, typologie, contenu et diffusion (III siècle avant J.-C.-IXe siècle après J.-C.)*. Études Alexandrines 22. Alexandria: Centre d'etudes Alexandrines.

Dosoo, Korshi, and Sofía Torallas Tovar. 2022. "Roll vs. Codex: the Format of the Magical Handbook." In *The Greek and Demotic Magical Handbooks: Libraries, Books and Recipes*, edited by Christopher Faraone and Sofía Torallas Tovar, 64–120. Ann Arbor: University of Michigan Press.

Folmer, Margaretha. 2020. "Hi Aḥuṭab: Aramaic Letter Ostraca from Elephantine." In Caputo and Lougovaya 2020, 145–64.

Fournet, Jean-Luc. 2009. "Esquisse d'une anatomie de la lettre antique tardive d'après les papyrus." In *Correspondances. Documents pour l'histoire de l'Antiquité tardive. Actes du colloque international, université Charles-de-Gaulle-Lille 3, 20–22 novembre 2003*, edited by Roland Delmaire, Janine Desmulliez, and Pierre-Louis Gatier, 23–66. Lyon: Maison de l'Orient et de la Méditerranée Jean Pouilloux.

Fournet, Jean-Luc. 2019. "Anatomie d'un genre en mutation: la pétition de l'Antiquité tardive." In *Proceedings of the 28th Congress of Papyrology (Barcelona, 1–6 August 2016)*, edited by Alberto Nodar and Sofía Torallas Tovar, 654–63. Barcelona: Publicacions de l'Abadia de Montserrat.

Hepa, Mariola, and Sofía Torallas Tovar. 2022. "On the Southern Frontier: Latin Ostraca from Aswan." In *Uniformity and Regionalism in Latin Writing Culture in the First Millennium of the Common Era*, 61-78, edited by Rodney Ast, Tino Licht and Julia Lougovaya. Wiesbaden: Harrasowitz Verlag.

Hope, Colin A. 2004. "The Ostraka and the Archaeology of Ismant el-Kharab." In *Greek Ostraca from Kellis: O. Kellis, Nos. 1–293*, edited by Klaas A. Worp, 5–28. Dakhleh Oasis Project, Monograph 13. Oxford: Oxbow.

Litinas, Nikos. 2008. *Greek Ostraka from Abu Mina*. Berlin: De Gruyter.

Lougovaya, Julia. 2018. "Writing on Ostraca: Considerations of Material Aspects." In *The Materiality of Texts from Ancient Egypt: New Approaches to the Study of Textual Material from the Early Pharaonic to the Late Antique Period*, edited by Francisca A. J. Hoogendijk and Steffie M. T. van Gompel, 52–61. Leiden: Brill.

Lougovaya, Julia. 2020a. "Greek Literary Ostraca Revisited: Using Ostraca in the Ancient World." In Caputo and Lougovaya 2020, 109–41.

Lougovaya, Julia. 2020b. "Reedition of a Division Table Preserved on Tableware." *ZPE* 216: 240–42.

Maltomini, Francesca. 2012–13. "Greek Ostraca: An Overview." *Manuscript Cultures* 5: 33–41.

Martin Hernández, Raquel, and Sofía Torallas Tovar. 2014. "The Use of the Ostracon in Magical Practice in Late Antique Egypt." *SMSR* 80, no. 2: 780–800.

Menchetti, Angiolo. 2005. *Ostraka demotici e bilingui da Narmuthis III (ODN 100–188)*. Bibliotecadi Studi egittologici 5. Pisa: ETS.

Mihálykó, Ágnes. 2019. *The Christian Liturgical Papyri: An Introduction*. Tübingen: Mohr Siebeck.

Peña, John Theodore. 2007. *Roman Pottery in the Archaeological Record*. Cambridge: Cambridge University Press.

Sarri, Antonia. 2018. *Material Aspects of Letter Writing in the Graeco-Roman World*. Berlin: De Gruyter.

von Pilgrim, Cornelius, Marcel Marée, and Wolfgang Müller. 2015. "Report on the 15th Season of the Joint Swiss-Egyptian Mission in Syene / Old Aswan (2014/2015)." http://www.swissinst.ch/downloads/Swiss%20Institute%202014_2015.pdf.

von Pilgrim, Cornelius, Mariola Hepa, Jan Novacek, Kristina Novacek-Scheelen, Wolfgang Müller, and Sofía Torallas Tovar. 2019. "Report on the Eighteenth Season of the Joint Swiss-Egyptian Mission in Syene / Old Aswan (2017/2018)." https://swissinst.ch/downloads/Report%20Swiss_Egyptian%20Mission%20ASWAN%202018.pdf.

Worp, Klaas A. 2004. *Greek Ostraca from Kellis: O. Kellis, Nos. 1–293*. Dakhleh Oasis Project, Monograph 13. Oxford: Oxbow.

## CHAPTER 4

Visual Signs of Deference in Late Antique Greek Letters on Papyrus

Yasmine Amory

Introduction*

Letters on papyrus have been thoroughly examined and investigated in the last century, from the beginnings of the discipline to today. However, while many studies have focused on the typology, format, linguistic features, and epistolary clichés of this documentary genre, its paleographical aspects have so far received less attention. This reflects a general and consolidated trend in papyrology, whereby researchers have always paid more attention to the text and the content of a document than its context. Things have recently started to change, however, and paleography has begun to be considered less and less as a mere auxiliary tool—used primarily to date documentary papyri that do not contain explicit internal evidence of their chronology—in favor of a new approach.

The concept of "paléographie signifiante" was first introduced in 2007 by Jean-Luc Fournet with the aim of rehabilitating paleography by pointing out its semiotic value.[1] Concurrently with this redemption of paleography in papyrology, the same process was taking place in social semiotics; more specifically, within research on multi-modality. This meant that the visual-graphological aspect, hitherto labeled and confined to consideration as a para-linguistic element,[2] was finally starting to be considered a valid semiotic resource.

In the paper "Towards a Semiotic of Typography," published in 2006, Theo van Leeuwen proposed a classification of distinctive features of modern typography used for "explicitly 'semioticizing' typography, for *making*

something meaningful that was not previously regarded as semiotic."[3] Weight, expansion, slope, curvature, connectivity, orientation, and regularity are the main features the scholar identified, and they can be used to express different interpersonal meanings. For example, increased weight gives salience to a part or an entire sentence, vertical orientation can express aspiration and elevation, while regularity usually serves to improve legibility. Since these categories are conceived in the modern use of fonts and typography, they are strictly linked to printed or digital documents and are therefore unlikely to be adopted for the study of ancient documents as they are. Nevertheless, when approaching the study of a text—whether a papyrus, an inscription, or a manuscript—we should keep in mind that the visual and graphic aspects of a document are not merely secondary elements but help to convey a certain message.[4] After all, these aspects constitute the first impact of the text on the receiver and denote or enhance some characteristics of the document even before reading.

Paleographical and material aspects might immediately reveal the purpose of a document to its reader. Moreover, they might change according to the function of the text and its recipient. A draft of a petition appears different from its official version, in the same way as a letter would have different characteristics depending on its addressee. A request to a superior would include more refined and formal grammatical constructions than a message to a friend,[5] since this kind of request would need to be softened by different rhetorical strategies to convey politeness and to ingratiate itself with the addressee.

The question, then, is can these features also be identified on a visual level? And would the register of deference also be visible on the graphic and visual level, representing

---

* A preliminary version of this paper was presented at the conference "Novel Perspectives on Communication Practices in Antiquity: Towards a Social-Semiotic Approach" (Ghent, October 3–5, 2019) and benefitted from the discussion that followed. In particular, I would like to thank Floris Bernard, Jean-Luc Fournet, and Martti Leiwo for their suggestions and comments, as well as Korshi Dosoo for improving my English. The research for this chapter was conducted within the ERC Starting Grant project EVWRIT ('Everyday writing in Graeco-Roman and Late Antique Egypt. A socio-semiotic study of communicative variation', PI Klaas Bentein), a project which has received funding from the European Research Council under the Horizon 2020 research and innovation programme (Grant Agreement No. 756487).

1 See Fournet 2007.
2 See, e.g., Liebert and Metten 2012, 6.

3 van Leeuwen 2006, 147. On the relationship of typography to linguistics, see also Walker 2001, 2–11.
4 The importance of the study of textual materiality in papyrology has been recently underlined in Hoogendijk and van Gompel 2018 and Sarri 2018; for the close correlation between text and material support in epigrams, see Floridi 2018 and Nobili 2018; more generally, for a study on the materiality of inscribed texts in classical antiquity, see Petrovic, Petrovic, and Thomas 2019.
5 For the late antique period, see Koskenniemi 1956, 54–154 and Papathomas 2007, 497–512; for requests in private letters, see the second section in Koroli 2016.

---

an additional way of mitigating the illocutionary act of the request? I will investigate these questions by taking into consideration late antique letters on papyrus written from subordinates to superiors, arguing that deference could be expressed through elaborate graphic elements, both on a macro and micro level.

1 Toward a "Visual Politeness Theory"

The concept of politeness in linguistics is by now well-known and has been applied to ancient languages and specific corpora of ancient documents.[6] However, the classic approach, both in modern and ancient languages, is solidly linked to verbal communication and rarely deals with non-verbal elements. With a few exceptions, the visual and the graphic aspect is not taken into consideration.

As one exception in modern languages, Dániel Z. Kádár has analyzed Chinese written deferential and rude communication and, focusing on Chinese wedding invitations, showed that graphic arrangements were made to elevate the addressees and denigrate the senders.[7] The size of the characters which are used for the names of the parents of the young couple were therefore smaller than the characters that refer to the addressees. Other elements that are used to convey a deferential semiotic message are the position of the elements (the names of the parents are written in the lower part of the card, while the names of the addressees are on the upper part) and the use of boldface (used to elevate, while non-boldface is used to denigrate). In another modern example, Klaas-Hinrich Ehlers discussed how spatial structure in German letters of the nineteenth and twentieth centuries could be orchestrated to show different degrees of respect for the addressee.[8] In this case, the message of deference was transmitted by the dimensions of the areas of blank space, the format and material of the letter, and by capitalizing terms of address.

Turning to ancient documents, Fournet has recently noted that a system of graphic oppositions was used in late antique petitions, whereby the *inscriptio*, which carries the name of the authority to whom the petition is addressed, is sometimes written in a more elegant handwriting than the rest of the document.[9] The use of a *rhétorique graphique* glorifies the addressee through the choice of more elaborated, elevated, and stylized writing.

In this way it provides a visual contribution to the deferential rhetoric of the text.

Having established these precedents, I would like to attempt to apply this novel approach to documentary letters. I have chosen to focus on the late antique period, since research in documentary epistolography has thus far mainly focused on the earlier Greco-Roman period.[10] Moreover, the letter underwent relevant and drastic changes, both material and linguistic, in late antiquity and thereby offers a challenging framework for a historical socio-semiotic perspective.

2 A Graphic Perspective of Deference in Late Antique Letters

While the Greco-Roman letter is characterized by a vertical format with a defined layout for the prescript, the main message, and the *formula valedicendi*, where all the elements can be easily identified on first glimpse,[11] the late antique letter evolved into a horizontal and narrow strip and lost the prescript and final greetings.[12] The dynamic structure of the Greco-Roman letter becomes frozen as a static block of text, which complicates any possible attempt at visual interpretation. However, it is still possible to individuate, on a macro and micro level, some visual refinements that are employed to please the addressee. Below, I will address these aspects as they apply to the prescript, the body of the letter, and the address.

2.1 *The Prescript*
Letters at the outset of the late antique period still sometimes present the Greco-Roman prescript, even when already adopting the typical horizontal format of their time. This hybrid form is not very common, however, and for this reason I will not linger on it. Nevertheless, its use shows an attention to the indication of the epistolary correspondents by visual disposition and use of space, as in P.Herm. 17, from Lykopolis and probably dating to the end of the fourth century CE. In this example, the first line is dedicated to the prescript, reading: τῷ κυρίῳ μου θεωσεβῆ (l. θεοσεβεῖ) Ἄπα Ἰωάνην (l. Ἰωάννῃ) Λεῦχις Μαλαμος (l. Μαλάμου). As a sign of respect, the addressee's name

---

6   See Poccetti 2014 for some general bibliography and Dickey 2016 for an application of four linguistic politeness theories (Brown and Levinson, Watts, Terkourafi, and Hall) in Cicero's letters.

7   See Kádár 2011.

8   See Ehlers 2004.

9   See Fournet 2019, 572–75.

10   This trend is still ongoing, since the last exhaustive monograph on ancient letters covers only the Greco–Roman world from 500 BCE to 300 CE (Sarri 2018).

11   See Sarri 2018, 114–24.

12   On the evolution of the structure of the letter and its social implications, see Fournet 2009.

comes first,[13] and his relevance is visually enhanced through the use of *vacat* before and after the name.[14]

In a similar way, the scribe of SB XIV 11882 (unknown provenance [IV–V CE?]) visually delimits the prescript from the rest of the letter with a larger interlinear space between these two sections. The prescript occupies the first two lines: the first is dedicated to all sorts of honorific appellations for the addressee, while the second contains the names of the correspondents. The addressee's name is in *eisthesis* and a large *vacat* stands between the addressee's and sender's names. The layout visually differentiates the elements, consecrating an entire line to the honorific epithets of the addressee, and helps confer a deferent value to the addressee along with the text.

Even though it dates to the late sixth century CE, it is worth mentioning P.Rain.Cent. 125 (Memphis [19 August 575]), since deference is here conveyed through a means other than the spatial disposition of the elements; namely, the difference in graphic style. The first line of the document (see Fig. 4.1), which contains the name of the addressee and his honorific predicate, is written in an upright and more elevated handwriting, while the rest of the text—even the second line, which is still part of the prescript and specifies the title of the addressee—is written in cursive handwriting.[15] This graphic opposition is surely functional within the different parts of the message,[16] but the fact that only the addressee's name is visually differentiated from the rest suggests that this visual choice was mainly made to elevate the addressee.

Though less striking, a similar procedure might be observed in Chr.Wilck. 23 (= BGU IV 1035; Arsinoites) from the first half of the fifth century CE. Its first line,

FIGURE 4.1   Detail of P.Rain.Cent. 125, ll. 1–3
© AUSTRIAN NATIONAL LIBRARY, PAPYRUS COLLECTION

containing the first part of the prescript, is in an upright style, while the rest of the prescript and the body of the letter are written in a more sloping hand. We will see later how the same graphic differentiation is usually employed on the verso for the address.

2.2   *The Body of the Letter*

From the fifth century CE, letters are usually limited to the *sôma*; that is, the main body of the text. The written part appears as a single block of text, leaving limited freedom to the scribe to play with the layout. However, professional writers could adapt their handwriting to the addressee and prefer a more formal, regular, and legible style for official communication as a sign of respect to the addressee and to assure the reception of the message.

The Greek correspondence of Dioscorus of Aphrodite, to whom belongs the richest papyrological archive from late antiquity, offers clear evidence of what has been defined as the "functional use of handwriting."[17] Dioscorus's handwriting changes and evolves according to the purpose and the addressee of the letter.[18] This means that a personal draft would be written in a chaotic and careless way, as for example P.Berol. inv. 25721 (VI CE), where the handwriting is extremely ligatured, the size of the characters is completely irregular, and the extended hastas of the letters often exceed the upper or lower lines. In contrast, his letters to high officials demonstrate regularity and legibility. Such is the case for P.Cair.Masp. I 67069 (VI CE), which is written with a polished cursive handwriting and a remarkable attention to perfect balance between the text and the material. The interlinear space is regular throughout the document and the hastas of the letters rarely reach other lines.

Yet Dioscorus's attention to the visual aspect goes even further. Some of his autographs do not in fact present the traditional Byzantine cursive, but show a distinctive "sloping majuscule," a majuscule with cursive tendencies. This can be seen in the letter SB XX 14241 (ca. 566–567 CE), in

13   The inversion of the correspondents' names in the traditional prescript is to be observed from the third century CE and is related to a development of politeness in private relationships, as stated by Fournet 2009, 43: "cette évolution tient à l'exacerbation bien connue des rapports hiérarchiques et à leur expression de plus en plus envahissante, mais elle doit aussi beaucoup au développement d'une politesse qui touche la sphère privée. S'affirme, même entre égaux, une forme de sociabilité qui se construit dans l'exaltation de l'autre et la dépréciation de soi, dont la conjugaison donne lieu à tout un vocabulaire, une phraséologie et une rhétorique qui imprègnent le style des correspondances privées."

14   This procedure is not typical for late antiquity but can already be found in letters from the Zenon archive.

15   See also the comment to the first line of the text by the editor Pieter J. Sijpesteijn: "diese Zeile ist, wohl von derselben Hand, aber mit größeren und schmäleren Buchstaben geschrieben. Wir finden das den öfteren in der Adresse (vgl. z. B. P.Oxy. XVI 1830, 1–2)."

16   For the use of different styles for different elements, see the preliminary analysis on contracts by Fournet in P.Worp, 245–49.

17   Luiselli 2008, 690.

18   I thoroughly examined this aspect in Amory 2018, 61–65.

which Dioscorus is seeking justice after having endured an abuse of power from the ex-*diadôtes* Kollouthos. Lucio Del Corso has remarked that Dioscorus adopted this particular style for certain public documents when he wanted to increase the legibility of the text.[19] The request is therefore related to the clarity of the message and is strengthened through the praise of the addressee. This is why individuals, though literate and perfectly able to pen letters themselves, might choose to turn to a professional writer if they needed to send messages to officials in high positions.[20]

We should note, however, that the attention to graphic features in relation to the reader is not a feature exclusive to the late antique period. Already in the Zenon archive, papyri addressed to higher spheres displayed a more formal handwriting.[21] Raffaele Luiselli has pointed out how correspondence between officials in the highest posts demonstrate an outstanding "chancery style," while communication to lower-level officials is expressed with less formal hands.[22] As for the Arab period, H. Idris Bell observed that "official letters addressed to single officials and not intended for publication were written in the current hand (a flowing, sloping type of script); official letters addressed to a multiplicity of persons and intended or adopted for public exhibition were written in the minuscule hand."[23]

The legibility of the document is therefore one of the main means employed by the scribe as a sign of respect to the recipient and is, without doubt, the first feature a reader would notice on receiving a message. André Bataille already noted in 1954 that the legibility of the handwriting is directly proportional to the respect the writer owes to the addressee. In this way, he distinguished a deferent style (the so-called *mode déférent*) for requests or complaints, where the writer adopts a highly legible style to honor the addressee, usually a superior.[24] More recently, Gabriella Messeri and Rosario Pintaudi have identified, using the term *scritture di rispetto*, hybrid writing styles used for documents such as petitions and requests to authorities, which share some graphic characteristics with literary handwriting (such as fluidity, high legibility, and elegance).[25] They have also remarked that the visual aspect of the text and the elegance of a hand are more careful in accordance with the higher social importance of the addressee.

Legibility is mainly expressed by regularity, and as outlined above, a professional writer was aware of this fact. The wooden tablet SB IV 7433 (= P.Ross.Georg. V 30; Panopolis [449/450 or 464/465 CE]) offers an example of the importance of the visual aspect of the message. The material aspects of the document suggest an educational context, and the content confirms this assumption. The same administrative letter has in fact been copied five times by a skillful and professional hand with little lexical variation and few grammatical uncertainties. The editor thought the piece was a writing exercise for someone practicing the Chancery style,[26] but it has recently been suggested that the document belongs to a more professional milieu.[27] The bureaucrat-to-be was probably practicing his formal handwriting for administrative correspondence, improving his fluidity and regularity.

Literary sources also give us a glimpse of the importance of a regular writing style,[28] as clearly expressed in *Letter* 334 by Basil to a calligraphist:

Ὀρθὰ γράφε καὶ χρῶ τοῖς στίχοις ὀρθῶς· καὶ μήτε αἰω-
ρείσθω πρὸς ὕψος ἡ χεὶρ μήτε φερέσθω κατὰ κρημνῶν.
μηδὲ βιάζου τὸν κάλαμον λοξὰ βαδίζειν, ὥσπερ τὸν παρ'
Αἰσώπῳ καρκίνον· ἀλλ' εὐθὺ χώρει, ὥσπερ ἐπὶ στάθμης
βαδίζων τεκτονικῆς, ἣ πανταχοῦ φυλάττει τὸ ἴσον καὶ πᾶν
ἀναιρεῖ τὸ ἀνώμαλον. τὸ γὰρ λοξὸν ἀπρεπές, τὸ δὲ εὐθὺ

---

19 See Del Corso 2008, 108–9.

20 Author of more than one hundred letters, Philokles asked a professional scribe to write O.Did. 390 (Didymoi [ca. 125–40 CE]). See the introduction of the text by Adam Bülow-Jacobsen: "this is the only letter sent by Philokles which is not in his own hand. He may have felt that his Greek was not good enough for the complex message he wanted to convey, or perhaps that his handwriting was not nice enough for an important client." Antonia Sarri also remarked that Abinnaeus, who probably penned the letter P.Abinn. 43 himself (Philadelphia? [ca. 348–351 CE]), preferred to employ a professional writer for the petition P.Abinn. 1 (Philadelphia? [341/342 CE]); see Sarri 2018, 126.

21 See Bagnall and Cribiore 2006, 42.

22 Luiselli 2008, 690.

23 See Bell 1945, 79. On the use of different scripts in the Arabic period, see also the striking introduction by Federico Morelli to CPR XXII, 7–10.

24 See Bataille 1954, 77–78.

25 See Messeri and Pintaudi 1998, 47.

26 See Zereteli 1928 (with a picture of the text on p. 121) and also Ulrich Wilcken in APF 9, 1930, 251, n. XXI.

27 See the comment by Hermann Harrauer and Pieter J. Sijpesteijn in P.Rain.Unterricht., 96–97, as well as Fournet 2009, 60.

28 Thought to date from the tenth century, another passage from a letter in the codex Patmius 706, fol. 228ᵛ shows the admiration of the addressee for the visual aspect of the letter he just received: θαυμάζειν δὲ οὐ παυόμεθα τὸ ἐκτύπωμα καὶ τὴν ἐν αὐτοῖς τῶν γραμμάτων εὐμετρίαν καὶ τὴν ἰσότητα, ἥτις πρὸς γνῶσιν ἠρέθι(σε) κ(ρεί)ττονα καὶ τῆς μουσικῆς ἠνάγκασεν εὐγλοττίας τρυφᾶν, "et je ne cesse pas d'admirer l'écriture ainsi que l'élégance et l'égalité des caractères de la lettre, ce qui me pousse à l'étudier de plus près et me force à jouir de l'hamornieuse beauté de la langue" (trans. Karlsson 1962, see 98 and 97–99 for more details on this text).

τερπνὸν τοῖς ὁρῶσιν, οὐκ ἐῶν ἀνανεύειν καὶ κατανεύειν, ὥσπερ τὰ κηλώνεια, τοὺς ὀφθαλμοὺς τῶν ἀναγινωσκόντων. ὁποῖόν τι κἀμοὶ συμβέβηκε τοῖς γράμμασιν ἐντυχόντι τοῖς σοῖς. τῶν γὰρ στίχων κειμένων κλιμακηδόν, ἡνίκα ἔδει μεταβαίνειν ἐφ᾽ ἕτερον ἀφ᾽ ἑτέρου, ἀνάγκη ἦν ἐξορθοῦν πρὸς τὸ τέλος τοῦ προσιόντος. ἐν ᾧ μηδαμοῦ φαινομένης τῆς ἀκολουθίας, ἀνατρέχειν ἔδει πάλιν καὶ τὴν τάξιν ἐπιζητεῖν, ἀναποδίζοντα καὶ παρεπόμενον τῷ αὔλακι, καθάπερ τὸν Θησέα τῷ μίτῳ τῆς Ἀριάδνης φασί. γράφε τοίνυν ὀρθῶς, καὶ μὴ πλάνα τὸν νοῦν τῷ πλαγίῳ καὶ λοξῷ τῶν γραφομένων.

Write straight and keep straight to your lines; and let the hand neither mount upwards nor slide downhill. Do not force the pen to travel slantwise, like the Crab in Aesop; but proceed straight ahead, as if travelling along a carpenter's rule, which everywhere preserves the even course and eliminates all irregularity. For that which is slantwise is unbecoming, but that which is straight is a joy to those who see it, not permitting the eyes of those who read to bob up and down like well-sweeps. Something of the sort has happened to me when reading your writing. For since your lines rest ladderwise, when I had to pass from one to another I was obliged to lift my eyes to reach the beginning of the next line. And then when no sequence was evident at that point, I had to run back again and seek the order, retracing my steps and "following the furrow," just as they say Theseus followed the thread of Ariadne. Therefore write straight and do not confuse our mind by your oblique and slanting writing.[29]

Similarly, a legible and regularly written message helps to clearly convey the request. It is simultaneously a symbol of the writer's straightforward intentions and a sign of respect to the addressee, since a clear writing style would save the reader time, something that would be appreciated, especially if the recipient were a high official.

Besides the graphic style of a text, other signs of deference can be revealed on a micro level. The *scriptum continuum* being the norm at this time, a small *vacat* could at times be used to separate part of the text in much the same way as modern punctuation signs are employed, especially by experienced writers. In particular, a little space is often left before the main request of the sender, with the aim of stressing the request and preparing the reader to pay attention to the demand.[30] The *vacat* is also used to mark an aside and highlight its polite meaning, as in P.Oxy. XVI 1859 (VI–VII CE)[31] or in CPR XXX 17 (Hermopolites [ca. 643–644 CE]),[32] and CPR XXX 20 (Hermopolites [ca. 643–644 CE]).[33]

Finally, even if most late antique letters lack a final clause and greeting formula, letters to superiors often end by a simple and respectful δέσποτα, which refers to the addressee of a letter.[34] Eleanor Dickey has already investigated the politeness value of this form of address, which was probably influenced by Christian epistolography, in which δεσπότης was considered a term of great respect, mainly used for a person who had authority over the sender.[35] If, in the fourth century CE, the vocative was used "in private letters to social superiors and men of whom the writer is making requests and/or whom he is treating with notable respect," in the fifth through seventh centuries the author could find "no occurrences of the address in letters to actual relatives, subordinates, or people to whom the writer is clearly not expressing deference."[36]

This stated, I would like to see whether these assumptions are also supported visually. In many cases, a small *vacat* is employed to differentiate the body of the letter from the final δέσποτα in order to visually enhance the vocative.[37] The placement of different symbols could also be used for the same goal: two crosses are placed before and right after it in P.Oxy. LIX 4008, 5 (VI–VII CE) and in CPR XIX 30, 4 (unknown provenance [VIII CE]), while

---

29   Trans. Deferrari 1934, 283–85, with tiny alterations.

30   E.g., in P.Cair.Masp. I 67064, 15 (Aphrodite [538–547/548 CE]), date suggested in Fournet 2008, 315; P.Stras. IV 279, 5 (Aphrodite [VI CE]), provenance confirmed by Amory 2018, I, 50–53; SB IV 7438, 11 (Constantinople [ca. 551 CE]); P.Fouad. I 88, 4 (Aphrodite [VI CE]); P.Giss. I 57, 5 (Oxyrhynchus [VI–VII CE]); PSI XIII 1345, 11 (Apollonopolis [second half VII CE]), for the provenance and the date, see BL IV, 91 and BL VIII, 410.

31   Small *vacat* delimitate ἐὰν ἔστι δυνατόν in the request at the beginning of the letter: † παρακαλῶ τὸν ἐμὸν ἀγαθὸν δεσπότην ἐάν ἐστι δυνατὸν κελεῦσαι κτλ.

32   εἰ χρεία γένηται is delimitated by two *vacat* in the following sentence (ll. 8–9): εἰ δὲ βαρέως ἔχει τὴν αἴτησίν μου δέξασθαι γράψῃ μοι καὶ αἰτ[ῶ τὸν περίβλ(επτον)] | χαρτουλά(ριον) καὶ εἰ χρεία γένηται τὸν ἐνδοξότατον ἰλλού(στριον) [.

33   In this document, the *vacat* is placed before the request (ll. 9–11: *vac.* παρακαλῶ | οὖν τοὺς θεοφυλά(κτους) ὑμᾶς κελεῦσαι τοῦτον ἀπολυθ\ῆναι/ | ἕως ὅτε ἔλθη ὁ ἄλλος) and before the final referential greetings (ll. 12–13: *vac.* τοὺς πόδας τῶν | θεοφυλά(κτων) ὑμῶν κατασπάζομαι ἄχρι θέας.†).

34   See Luiselli 2008, 707 and Papathomas 2007, 507.

35   See Dickey 2001.

36   Both quotations are from Dickey 2001, 4.

37   As in CPR XXV 11, 7 (Hermopolis? [VI CE]); P.Fouad. I 88, 13 (Aphrodite [VI CE]); P.Fouad. I 89, 11 (Aphrodite [VI CE]); PSI III 237, 14 (Oxyrhynchus [V–VI CE]).

two oblique strokes are placed before and after κύριέ μου δέσποτα πάτηρ (l. πάτερ) in P.Haun. II 25, 7 (unknown provenance [IV–V CE]). The more complex vocative address is here found after the opening greetings, and not at the end of the message. Therefore, the two strokes help identify and underline the deferent address form.

Sometimes, δέσποτα is written larger than the rest of the text (P.Giss. I 57, 9 [Oxyrhynchus, VI–VII CE]) or in a more extended form (P.Oxy. XVI 1834, 8 [late V–early VI CE], where it is used in combination with a preceding vacat). Alternatively, it is even placed below the body of the letter in the center of the line (SB XXVI 16351, 9; Hermopolites? [IV CE]). Of course, a scribe could also combine two or more of these elements: using both a vacat and differentiation in size (P.Cair.Masp. I 67068, 14; Aphrodite [VI CE]) or both placement and style (e.g., Chr.Wilck. 23 = BGU IV 1035, 19; Arsinoites [first half V CE], where † δέσποτά μου κύριε comes below the body after a large vacat, in a more elevated and polished handwriting). Here the deferent meaning of the vocative was also conveyed in a range of visual and graphic ways.

2.3 The Address

I will now discuss the address on the back, although I should perhaps have discussed it earlier, given the address was the first element that the recipient of the message would see upon the delivery of the letter. Once the message was written, the letter was rolled up, folded, tied, and sealed. The scribe would then write the address, usually on one line, and give it to the letter carrier, who, most of the time, was someone who happened to be going in the right direction, since there was no public postal service.[38] We should then expect that the address contains specific indications for the messenger, and sêmasiai are indeed sometimes given on the verso of letters, but, considering the number of letters preserved, only exceptionally.

The epistolary address generally contains the names of the correspondents, with the name of the addressee on the left and that of the sender on the right. The addressee section contains the name, and may include their teknonym, and is usually enriched with elaborate honorific predicates and adjectives, while the sender section is always limited to the name and teknonym—sometimes, the name is only followed by the term doulos to stress the inferior position of the sender.[39] This is visually translated

by a long line mostly dedicated to the addressee, where the sender's name is limited to a small section on the extreme right corner.[40] The addressee element can also take up all of the first line; in this case, the information regarding the sender is written below it on the right.[41] The two sections can also be visually separated by a small vacat,[42] the locus sigilli, or a cross preceding the sender's name.

If the position of the elements already gives an idea of the deferential mode of the sender, the address is also characterized by refined, elegant, elevated, and narrow handwriting, similar to that of the official Chancery. This makes reading them quite complex, even leaving aside the fact that most honorific predicates are highly abbreviated. This can be seen in P.Oxy. XVI 1860 (VI–VII CE) in Figure 4.2, which reads: [† δ]εσπό(τη) ἐμῷ τὰ πά(ντα) περιβλέ(πτῳ) πά(σης) τιμῆ(ς) (καὶ) προ(σκυνήσεως) ἀξίῳ γνη(σίῳ) φίλῳ (καὶ) ἀδελφῷ Γεωργίῳ κόμε(τι) χαρτουλαριυ (l. χαρτουλαρίῳ) καὶ διοικ(η)τ(ῇ) † Μηνᾶς σὺν θ(εῷ) | † ἔκδι-κ(ος) Κυνο[π]ο[λ(ίτου).

Since it is highly improbable that a non-professional letter carrier could read such an address, one may assume that its style was entirely conceived as a sign of deference. This is confirmed by the same letter: the teknonym of the sender Menas is in fact written in rather clumsy small capitals, as a sign of denigration. Though this last element may have been added later, other letters present similar stylistic differentiation in their treatment of the two correspondents, in which the more elaborate style only affects the addressee's part.[43] This confirms the supposition that the Chancery style was at that time seen as a distinctive feature for titles and headers of important acts.[44] Thus,

FIGURE 4.2 Detail of the verso of P.Oxy. XVI 1860, ll. 16–17
© ARCHIVES PHOTOGRAPHIQUES INTERNATIONALES
DE PAPYROLOGY

---

38   On the choice of a messenger and their functions, see Head 2009, 283–98, though this study is limited to the P.Oxy. corpus.

39   E.g., P.Fouad I 89, 12–13 (Aphrodite [VI CE]): σὺν Θ(ε)ῷ. τῷ ἐμῷ ἀγαθῷ δεσπότ(η), μετὰ τ(ὸ)ν Θ(εό)ν, προεστ(ῶτι), † Ψοῖος, ἐλά-χ(ιστος) | δοῦλος. For the concept of the sender as a "slave" of the

addressee, under the influence of Christianity, see Papathomas 2007, 509.

40   E.g., P.Oxy. XVI 1857 (VI–VII CE).

41   E.g., P.Neph. 1 (Alexandria [IV CE]), date proposed in BL IX, 173; PSI VII 742 (unknown provenance [V–VI CE]); and SB XVI 12573 (Arsinoites [mid-VI CE]).

42   E.g., P.Cair.Masp. I 67066 (Aphrodite [VI CE]) and P.Oxy. I 123 (III–IV CE).

43   P.Oxy. XVI 1841 (VI CE) and SB XVIII 13111 (provenance unknown [V–VI CE]). From the Arab period, see also P.Oxy. XVI 1862 (ca. 624 CE?), on the date, see BL VIII, 250.

44   See Messeri and Pintaudi 1998, 49: "la scrittura della cancelleria centrale con tutte le sue peculiarità divenne, sul

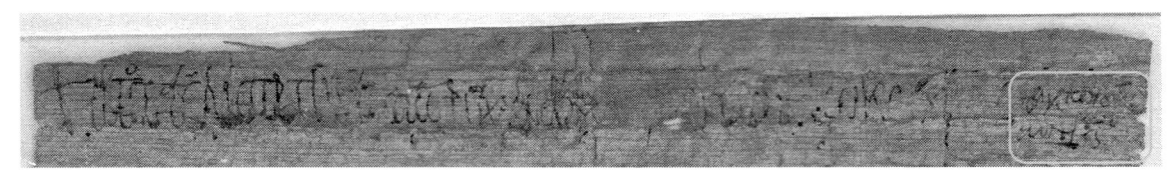

FIGURE 4.3 Detail of the address of P.Oxy. XVI 1845. The sender's part is circled in light grey
© ARCHIVES PHOTOGRAPHIQUES INTERNATIONALES DE PAPYROLOGIE

FIGURE 4.4 Detail of the address of P.Oxy. XVI 1859, line 8: † τῷ ἐμῷ ἀγαθῷ δεσπό(τῃ) τῷ ἐνδοξο(τάτῳ) ἰλλ(ο)υ(στρίῳ) (καὶ) ἀντιγε(ούχῳ) † Μηνᾶς χαρτ(ουλάριος) ὑμέ(τερος) δο[ῦλ(ος)]
© ARCHIVES PHOTOGRAPHIQUES INTERNATIONALES DE PAPYROLOGIE

the adoption of this style for the addressee was a sign of deference from the sender.[45]

In other letters, the name and/or the details of the sender are written in smaller characters.[46] One example can be seen in P.Oxy. XVI 1845 (VI–VII CE), where the sender's details (ll. 6–7: Βίκτωρ σὺν θ(εῷ) | ἀντιγε(ούχος)) are compressed in the extreme right margin of the document (see Fig. 4.3). The sender's name and details are sometimes more constricted, however, while the addressee element is extended and expansive, as in P.Oxy. XVI 1859 (VI–VII CE; see Fig. 4.4).

In summary, senders could therefore use several different techniques to express deference: positioning, size, expansion, and style. Furthermore, although often neglected by papyrologists, the address in late antique letters was an important element of the letter.[47] It constituted the first element seen by the addressee, and the sender paid attention to its visual features to be as deferential as possible and predispose the addressee to the request.

3 A Graphic Education

The similarity and repetition of these visual signs in different archives and dossiers might suggest the possibility of a graphic education at school, along the same lines as the classic grammatical and rhetorical education. However, ancient epistolary handbooks do not contain any indications of this kind.[48] The only, exceptional, suggestions on the visual or graphic aspects to be adopted in letters are preserved in Julius Victor's rhetoric handbook (IV CE), which instructs that one should pen a letter to one's closest friends by oneself, or if that is not possible, at least add an autograph postscript.[49] The practice of adding a personal subscription at the end of the text written by a professional scribe is common in documentary letters.[50] It can also be identified in literary letters: after having dictated his letters to a secretary, Libanius personally added the final greetings (Ep. 1123).

The recommendation of Julius Victor is probably linked to the fact that the letter was traditionally seen as a substitute for the sender.[51] As an "icon of the soul" (εἰκὼν τῆς ψυχῆς),[52] the letter had to create the illusion of the sender's presence. Although this could be achieved by imitating the style of the sender and employing elements of everyday speech, as suggested in different epistolary

---

versante documentario, la scrittura distintiva da usare per titoli e intestazioni di atti importanti."

45　Sarri (2018, 123–24) noted that the elongated style made its first appearance in the external address of letters from the late first or early second century CE, and that "this special ornamental feature is part of the overall tendency towards greater ornamentation of the script [...]. This ornamental address was intended to flatter the addressee, while the name of the sender, if included, was written in ordinary, smaller letterforms."

46　See also P.Oxy. XVI 1862.

47　Morelli suggests that we consider the address as a real part of the letter and supposes that it was perceived as equivalent to the final greetings of the Greco-Roman letter; see Morelli 2010, 90–91.

48　For an overview of ancient epistolary manuals and their contents, see Poster 2007.

49　Julius Victor, Ars Rhetorica (De Epistolis) 448.10–11, p. 106 Giomini and Celentano, Observabant veteres carissimis sua manu scribere vel plurimum subscribere, "As a rule, the ancients wrote in their own hands to those closest to them, or at least frequently appended a post-script" (trans. Malherbe 1988, 65).

50　See Sarri 2018, 125–91.

51　On this topic, see Koskenniemi 1956, 38–42.

52　On this concept, see Karlsson 1962, 94–98 and Littlewood 1976, 216. See also Tomadakis 1969, 113–16, for references to this topos in Byzantine literary epistolography.

treatises,[53] the graphic elements played an important role in this too. If senders penned the letter themselves, this detail would more easily bring together the epistolary correspondents, as the addressee would recognize the sender's handwriting at the very opening of the message, and this would contribute to reducing the physical distance between them.

Letters sometimes contain explanations from the sender justifying why the latter could not pen the letter, showing the sender's concern that the addressee might be offended by this and receive it as an act of impoliteness. To personally write messages to friends was conceived as an act of courtesy and respect, especially in a literate milieu, since it would mean that the senders had dedicated some of their time to their correspondent.[54] Numerous letters by the Roman elite are accompanied by excuses when the sender had to turn to a secretary and dictate the message.[55] In papyri, a similar situation is to be found in P.Oxy. XVI 1860 (VI–VII CE). Its sender, Menas, is also the author of P.Oxy. XVI 1858 and 1859, which were probably written by Menas himself, unlike P.Oxy. XVI 1860, for which he apologizes at the end of the letter at lines 13 to 14: σύγ-\γ/νωθι δέ, δέσποτα, ἐπιδὴ (l. ἐπειδὴ) ὁ δοῦλός σου ὁ ἐμὸς ὑὸς (l. υἱός) ἔγραψα (l. ἔγραψε) τὴν παροῦσαν | ἐπιστολὴν ταύτην, "and forgive me, master, that your servant my son wrote this present letter."

The illusion of the presence of the sender[56] is therefore constructed through the style of the message, which should resemble an oral conversation and should avoid ornate rhetorical figures. This was achieved through the use of specific lexical expressions, such as ὡς παρών, "as if I were there,"[57] and through the sender's own handwriting. Declarations such as δόξομεν γὰρ διὰ | [τῶν γ]ραμμάτων ἀλλήλους ὁρᾶν, "we shall have the impression, through our letters, of seeing one another face to face" (P.Oxy. XLII 3067, 12–13 [III CE]), found in a private letter from Achillion to Hieracapollon, might also include a tangible expectation—the wish to see an autograph missive—in addition to its more figurative sense. If these considerations are correct, it is tempting to see in the famous *synkrisis* of the letter P.Oxy. XXXI 2603, 3–25 (IV CE), in which the reality of the writer's affection for the sender is compared to the reality of the objects reflected by a mirror, an allusion to the fact that the letter itself serves as a mirror of the writer's affection.[58] This is confirmed by literary sources and is clearly depicted in a passage of a letter by John Crysostom to the deacon Theodotus (Arabissos, summer 406).[59]

As for letters to superiors, ancient epistolary manuals only affirm that they might not be droll,[60] and the definition of a requesting letter is anything but tautological, if we value Pseudo-Libanius' statement.[61] Nevertheless, writing exercises on papyri seem to suggest that a visual education

---

53 For example, Pseudo Libanius, *Epist.Charact.* 2.10–11, p. 27 Foerster, ἐρεῖ δέ τις ἐν αὐτῇ ὥσπερ παρών τις πρὸς παρόντα, "one will speak in it as though one were in the company of the absent person" (trans. Malherbe 1988, 67); Demetrius, *Eloc.* 227.1–3, p. 64 Chiron, πλεῖστον δὲ ἐχέτω τὸ ἠθικὸν ἡ ἐπιστολή, ὥσπερ καὶ ὁ διάλογος· σχεδὸν γὰρ εἰκόνα ἕκαστος τῆς ἑαυτοῦ ψυχῆς γράφει τὴν ἐπιστολήν, "the letter, like the dialogue, should abound in glimpses of character. It may be said that everybody reveals his own soul in his letter" (trans. Malherbe 1988, 19); Gregory of Nazianzus, *Ep.* 51, 4.18–23, p. 67 Gallay, περὶ δὲ σαφηνείας ἐκεῖνο γνώριμον, ὅτι χρὴ φεύγοντα τὸ λογοειδές, ὅσον ἐνδέχεται, μᾶλλον εἰς τὸ λαλικὸν ἀποκλίνειν· καί, ἵν' εἴπω συντόμως, αὕτη τῶν ἐπιστολῶν ἀρίστη καὶ κάλλιστα ἔχουσα, ἢ ἂν καὶ τὸν ἰδιώτην πείθῃ καὶ τὸν πεπαιδευμένον, τὸν μέν, ὡς κατὰ τοὺς πολλοὺς οὖσα, τὸν δέ, ὡς ὑπὲρ τοὺς πολλούς, καὶ ᾗ αὐτόθεν γνώριμος, "as to clarity, everyone knows that one should avoid prose-like style so far as possible, and rather incline towards the conversational. To put it briefly, the best and most beautifully written letter is the one that is persuasive to the uneducated and educated alike, appearing to the former as written on the popular level, and to the latter as above the level, a letter which furthermore is understood at once" (trans. Malherbe 1988, 59).

54 For the use of *autographia* to please the addressee in John Chrysostom's correspondence, see Bady 2014, 170–72.

55 See Sarri 2018, 127, for references in Cicero's letters, and Freisenbruch 2007, 252, for references in Fronto and Marcus Aurelius's correspondence.

56 See Karlsson 1962, 34–37, on the theme of the "illusion de la présence" in Byzantine epistolography.

57 See, e.g., SB XVI 12980, 1 (unknown provenance [end of VI to beginning of VII CE]): † διὰ τοῦ παρόντος ἡμετέρου γράμματος πλεῖστα ὡς παρὼν προσκυνῶ καὶ ἀσπάζομαι τὴν ὑμετέραν θεοφιλ(εστάτην) ἀδελφότητα, "through this present letter of mine I greatly embrace and greet Your Brotherhood most beloved of God as if I were there."

58 On this letter, see Harrop 1962 and Fournet (2013) 2015, *passim*.

59 *Letter* 68 (PG 52.645–646): Μετὰ μὲν τὸ τὴν προτέραν ἀναγνῶναι ἐπιστολήν, ἐδεξάμην καὶ δευτέραν, ἐν μιᾷ ἀμφοτέρας ἡμέρᾳ, καὶ σφόδρα ἥσθην. Εἶχε γάρ τι πλέον ἡ δευτέρα, οὐχὶ ῥήματα σὰ μόνον, ἀλλὰ καὶ γράμματα σὰ ἡμῖν ἐπιδεικνῦσα· ὃ καὶ προσθήκην ἡμῖν πεποίηκεν ἡδονῆς, ὅτι μὴ τῆς ψυχῆς σου μόνον τῆς θερμῆς καὶ γνησίας, ἀλλὰ καὶ τῆς δεξιᾶς μετὰ δαψιλείας τὴν εἰκόνα ἐθεασάμεθα, "After having read the first letter, I received a second one, both on the same day, and I was very much delighted. The second one had something more: it showed us not only your words, but also your handwriting. What gave us additional pleasure is that we did not only see the icon of your warm and honest soul, but also the icon of your hand." For other examples in literary letters, see Karlsson 1962, 95–96.

60 Julius Victor, *Ars Rhetorica* (*De Epistolis*) 448.35, p. 105 Giomini and Celentano, *Epistola, si superiori scribas, ne iocularis sit,* "a letter written to a superior should not be droll" (trans. Malherbe 1988, 65).

61 *Epist.Charact.* 6.15–16, p. 29 Foerster, Παρακλητικὴ δι' ἧς ἀξιοῦμέν τινα διά τι πρᾶγμα, "the requesting letter is that in which we make

might have somehow taken place. P.Rain.Unterricht 77 (Hermopolites [v/vi ce]), for example, presents on both of its faces two hands which write an epistolary address several times. The first is ligatured, confident, and sloping, while the other is more hesitant and upright. The student is copying the line written by the teacher and is certainly practicing the elaborate formalisms of a late antique epistolary address, but one may assume that the training was not only formulaic, but also graphic. The editor's comment seems to confirm this assumption: the verso of the papyrus contains the same formula as the recto, with a small linguistic variation,[62] as well as a graphic variation concerning the shape of the beginning cross (the staurogram with a curved appendix on the recto, ⳨, is replaced with a simple cross, †, on the verso). Moreover, it is clear that the student is trying to practice and imitate the teacher, since the large, left-leaning *delta* of the verso (l. 7) adapts its shape to a more elegant and right-leaning *delta* on the recto (l. 3), as the student comes closer to imitating the teacher's handwriting.

Even more evident is the case of P.Rain.Unterricht. 79 (unknown provenance [vi–vii ce]), where the scribe is improving the fluidity of certain abbreviations and addressee formulae over and over again. Big, ample, and elegant Φλϛ, the abbreviation standing for Φλ(αουίῳ), are subsequently repeated all around the papyrus; their shape and size suggest that the scribe was practicing the style of the prescript of official documents. At the same time, he was training his fluidity in epistolary addresses with more extended formulae, as variations of Φλ(αουίῳ) Ἀπίωνι τῷ μεγαλοπρ(επεστάτῳ) are written in a sloping, cursive handwriting in the bottom-right corner. Even if the manuals do not leave graphic indications, letters and writing exercises suggest that the visual aspect of a document was indeed valued and used to express deference.

Conclusions

To conclude, even if there is almost no mention of any kind of visual and graphic norms in ancient epistolary manuals, writing exercises show that there might have been some awareness of the visual disposition of a text and of its semiotic possibilities. Different elements and techniques were used to express deference on a visual level, and the choice of writing style was essential: a professional scribe would use their most regular and legible handwriting for the body of the letter, focusing on the clarity of the message and request, and a very elaborate style for the address, where clarity was markedly put aside in favor of magnificence in honor of the addressee. This play of oppositions would act on a general level (*sôma* vs. address), but also on an internal level, as, in the address, the name of the sender could be visually differentiated from the addressee element. Senders would write their names in a more modest style or in smaller and compressed characters to humble themselves and elevate the addressee. Size was therefore also a tool used to trigger a semiotic message, along with space and the disposition of the graphic elements. As a result, the graphic representation could affect how a text was read, interpreted, and understood by the recipient. In other words, getting somebody to do something was not only a choice of lexical and grammatical constructions, but also of visual strategies. In short, deference could be expressed through elaborate graphic elements, both on a macro and micro level.

All of these elements help to define a graphic perspective on the most common document in antiquity, the letter, and may hopefully form the basis for a "visual politeness theory" for ancient documents. In the long run, it would be profitable and engaging to examine whether other languages in use in Egypt applied any visual techniques to praise the recipient of a document, and, in the event those techniques are similar to those used in Greek texts, to investigate the possibility of language contacts on a graphic level. The results of this study could also benefit from a comparison with letters between equals or with letters from superiors to subordinates, who might have used visual signs to affirm their authority or even to belittle their subalterns.

Reference List

Papyri are cited according to J. F. Oates et al., 2001, *Checklist of Editions of Greek, Latin, Demotic, and Coptic Papyri, Ostraca and Tablets*, suppl. 9 of *basp*, 5th ed. An up-to-date version is available online at http://papyri.info/docs/checklist.

Amory, Yasmine. 2018. "Communiquer par écrit dans l'Égypte de l'Antiquité tardive: les lettres grecques des archives de Dioscore d'Aphrodité." PhD diss., École Pratique des Hautes Études.

Bady, Guillaume. 2014. "'Des lettres comme des flocons de neige'? Le fait épistolaire dans la *Correspondance d'exil* de Jean Chrysostome." In *La lettre gréco-latine, un genre littéraire?*, edited by Jean Schneider, 165–87. Collection de la

---

a request of someone in consequence of something important" (trans. Malherbe 1988, 69).

62   τῷ δεσπότῃ μου τὰ πάντα [instead of τῷ δεσπότῃ μου τῷ (l. τῷ) τὰ [πάντα.

Maison de l'Orient et de la Méditerranée 52, Litt. 19. Lyon: Maison de l'Orient et de la Méditerranée.

Bagnall, Roger S., and Raffaella Cribiore. 2006. *Women's Letters from Ancient Egypt, 300 BC–AD 800*. Ann Arbor: University of Michigan Press.

Bataille, André. 1954. *Pour une terminologie en paléographie grecque*. Paris: C. Klincksiek.

Bell, Harold Idris. 1945. "An Official Circular Letter of the Arab Period." *JEA* 31: 75–84.

Deferrari, Roy J. (trans.). 1934. *Basil. Letters 249–368. On Greek Literature*. Cambridge, MA: Harvard University Press.

Del Corso, Lucio. 2008. "Le scritture di Dioscoro." In Fournet 2006, 89–116.

Dickey, Emily. 2001. "Kyrie, ΔΕΣΠΟΤΑ, Domine: Greek Politeness in the Roman Empire." *JHS* 121: 1–11.

Dickey, Emily. 2016. "Politeness in Ancient Rome: Can It Help Us Evaluate Modern Politeness Theories?" *Journal of Politeness Research* 12, no. 2: 197–220.

Ehlers, Klaas-Hinrich. 2004. "Raumverhalten auf dem Papier. Der Untergang eines komplexen Zeichensystems dargestellt an Briefstellern des 19. und des 20. Jahrhunderts." *Zeitschrift für germanistische Linguistik* 32: 1–31.

Floridi, Lucia. 2018. "Αὐδὴ τεχνήεσσα λίθου. Intermedialità e intervisualità nell'epigramma greco." *Segno e testo* 16: 25–54.

Fournet, Jean-Luc, ed. 2006. *Les archives de Dioscore d'Aphrodité cent ans après leur découverte*. Études d'archéologie et d'histoire ancienne. Paris: De Boccard.

Fournet, Jean-Luc. 2007. "Disposition et réalisation graphique des lettres et des petition protobyzantines: pour une paléographie 'signifiante' des papyrus documentaires." In *Proceedings of the 24th International Congress of Papyrology*, edited by Jaakko Frösen, Tiina Purola, and Erja Salmenkivi, 353–67. Helsinki: Societas Scientarum Fennica.

Fournet, Jean-Luc. 2008. "Liste des papyrus édités de l'Aphrodité byzantine." In Fournet 2006, 307–44.

Fournet, Jean-Luc. 2009. "Esquisse d'une anatomie de la lettre antique tardive d'après les papyrus." In *Correspondances: documents pour l'histoire de l'Antiquité tardive*, edited by Roland Delmaire, Janine Desmulliez, and Pierre-Louis Gautier, 23–66. Collection de la Maison d'Orient et de la Méditerranée 40, Série littéraire et philosophique 13. Lyon: Maison de l'Orient et de la Méditerranée.

Fournet, Jean-Luc. (2013) 2015. "Culture grecque et document dans l'Égypte de l'Antiquité tardive." *JJP* 43: 135–62.

Fournet, Jean-Luc. 2019. "Anatomie d'un genre en mutation: la petition de l'Antiquité tardive." In *Proceedings of the 28th International Congress of Papyrology (Barcelona August 1st–6th, 2016)*, edited by Alberto Nodar and Sofía Torallas Tovas, 571–90. Barcelona: Publicacions de l'Abadia de Montserrat, Universitat Pompeu Fabra.

Freisenbruch, Annelise. 2007. "Back to Fronto: Doctor and Patient in his Correspondence with an Emperor." In *Ancient Letters: Classical and Late Antique Epistolography*, edited by Ruth Morello and Andrew D. Morrison, 235–56. Oxford: Oxford University Press.

Harrop, J. H. 1962. "A Christian Letter of Commendation." *JEA* 48: 132–40.

Head, Peter M. 2009. "Named Letter-Carriers among the Oxyrhynchus Papyri." *Journal for the Study of the New Testament* 31, no. 3: 279–99.

Hoogendijk, Francisca A. J., and Steffie M. T. van Gompel, eds. 2018. *The Materiality of Ancient Texts from Ancient Egypt: New Approaches to the Study of Textual Material from the Early Pharaonic to the Late Antique Period*. P.L.Bat. 35. Leiden: Brill.

Kádár, Dániel Z. 2011. "A Graphic-Semiotic Analysis of the Chinese Multimodal Elevation and Denigration Phenomenon." *US-China Foreign Language*: 美中外語 9, no. 2: 77–88.

Karlsson, Gustav. 1962. *Idéologie et ceremonial dans l'épistolographie byzantine. Textes du Xᵉ siècle analysés et commentés*. Uppsala: Almqvist and Wiksell.

Koroli, Aikaterini. 2016. *Το αίτημα στις ελληνικές ιδιωτικές επιστολές σε παπύρους και όστρακα. Από την εποχή του Αυγούστου έως το τέλος της αρχαιότητας*. Athens: Institoúto tou Vivlíou-Kardamítsa.

Koskenniemi, Heikki. 1956. *Studien zur Idee und Phraseologie des griechischen Briefes bis 400 n. Chr.* Helsinki: Suomalainen Kirjall, Kirj.

van Leeuwen, Theo. 2006. "Towards a Semiotics of Typography." *Information Design Journal + Document Design* 14, no. 2: 139–55.

Liebert, Wolf-Andreas, and Thomas Metten. 2012. "Multimodal Text." In *The Encyclopedia of Applied Linguistics*, vol. 7, edited by Carol A. Chapelle. New York: Wiley-Blackwell. https://onlinelibrary.wiley.com/doi/abs/10.1002/9781405198431.wbeal0816.

Littlewood, Anthony R. 1976. "An 'Ikon of the Soul': The Byzantine Letter." *Visible Language* 10, no. 3: 197–226.

Luiselli, Raffaele. 2008. "Greek Letters on Papyrus First to Eight Centuries: A Survey." In *Documentary Letters from the Middle East: The Evidence in Greek, Coptic South Arabian, Pehlevi and Arabic (1st–15th c. CE)*, edited by Eva M. Grob and Andreas Kaplony, 677–737. Asiatische Studien, 62. Bern: Peter Lang.

Malherbe, Abraham J. 1988. *Ancient Epistolary Theorists*. Sources for Biblical Study 19. Atlanta: Scholars Press.

Messeri, Gabriella, and Rosario Pintaudi. 1998. "Documenti e scritture." In *Scrivere libri e documenti nel mondo antico*, edited by Guglielmo Cavallo, Edoardo Crisci, Gabriella Messeri, and Rosario Pintaudi, 39–54. Papyrologica Florentina 30. Florence: Gonnelli.

Morelli, Federico. 2010. "Der Briefschreiber an der Arbeit: Aus der Praxis der Epistolographie." In *Stimmen aus dem Wüstensand. Briefkultur im griechisch-römischen Ägypten,* edited by Claudia Kreuzsaler, Bernhard Palme, and Angelika Zdiarsky, 85–91. Nilus 17. Vienna: Phoibos Verlag.

Nobili, Cecilia. 2018. "Εἰκὼν λαλοῦσα. Testo, immagine e memoria intervisuale nell'epigramma greco arcaico." *Segno e testo* 16: 1–24.

Papathomas, Amphilochios. 2007. "Höflichkeit und Servilität in den Papyrusbriefen der ausgehenden Antike." In *Akten des 23. Papyrologenkongresses*, edited by Bernhard Palme, 497–512. Vienna: Verlag der Österreichischen Akademie der Wissenschaften.

Petrovic, Andrej, Ivana Petrovic, and Edmund Thomas, eds. 2019. *The Materiality of Text Placement, Perception, and Presence of Inscribed Texts in Classical Antiquity*. Brill Studies in Greek and Roman Epigraphy 11. Leiden: Brill.

Poccetti, Paolo. 2014. "Politeness/Courtesy Expressions." In *Encyclopedia of Ancient Greek Language and Linguistics*, edited by Georgios K. Giannakis, vol. 3, 113–14. Leiden: Brill.

Poster, Carol. 2007. "A Conversation Halved: Epistolary Theory in Graeco-Roman Antiquity." In *Letter-Writing Manuals and Instruction from Antiquity to the Present*, edited by Carol Poster and Linda C. Mitchell, 21–51. Columbia: University of South Carolina Press.

Sarri, Antonia. 2018. *Material Aspects of Letter Writing in the Graeco-Roman World. 500 BC–AD 300*. Materiale Textkulturen 12. Berlin: De Gruyter.

Tomadakis, Nikolaos. 1969. *Βυζαντινὴ ἐπιστολογραφία: Εἰσαγωγὴ εἰς τὴν Βυζαντινὴν φιλολογίαν*, vol. 3. Athens: typ. Myrtídīs, Mīnás.

Walker, Sue. 2001. *Typography and Language in Everyday Life: Prescriptions and Practices*. Language in Social Life Series. Harlow: Longman.

Zereteli, Gregor. 1928. "Eine griechische Holztafel des V Jahrh. in der Sammlung der Ermitage." *Aegyptus* 9: 113–28.

## CHAPTER 5

The Spread and Persistence of Roman Features in Some Greek Papyrus Letters of the High Chancery

Eleonora Angela Conti

Introduction

P.Oxy. L 3577 (January 28, 342 CE)[1] is an original letter from the chancery of the *praeses Augustamnicae*, edited by John R. Rea. This text provides a clear example of one type of official letter from the high Roman chancery, whose typology has distinct characteristics in terms of the format, the styles of handwriting, the use of the Latin and Greek languages, and the specific position of the date and sender's greetings. The combination of these features, born in the Roman diplomatic context, had the function of guaranteeing the authenticity of the document and, at the same time, underlining the official nature of the authority that issued the letter.

The purpose of this contribution is to collect all the specimens characterized by these peculiar features together in order to highlight the spread of this Latin practice in documents written in Greek. I will show how a set of formal elements can become essential to identify the social status of the sender, when unknown, and the level of formality of the letter itself. In so doing, I will also demonstrate that these formal characteristics are extremely significant and can be considered semiotic elements defining the official nature of the letter and its origin from the high chancery.

1 The Typology, as Seen in P.Oxy. L 3577

To begin, since not all the samples collected are intact, it is necessary to show the features occurring in the aforementioned P.Oxy. L 3577, which is exemplary since it is an original and is complete. For the sake of clarity, I have chosen to separate these features into three groups. The first feature is the format: the sheet is cut from a roll and written along the fibers and since the document is almost intact,[2] the original, very large, dimensions (27.5 × 24.5 cm) are preserved. The second feature is the handwritings, at least three hands: 1) the hand who wrote the heading and the body of the letter in Chancery style; 2) the hand, probably of the sender, who wrote the farewell formula; and 3) the hand who wrote the date in Latin with a different ink. The third and final feature is the sheet's formal aspects: 1) the position of the sender's farewell formula is very close to the text of the letter, 2) Latin is used for the date, and 3) the date is separated into two parts so that the consular year is in the lower margin,[3] whilst the day, month, and place where the letter was written, preceded by the word *dat*(*a*),[4] "issued," are in the left margin.[5]

These features combine with two important content data. First, the identity of the sender, the *praeses Augustamnicae*, who was the highest Roman officer when late antique Egypt was split into provinces,[6] and second, the content, which concerns important financial issues. The *praeses Augustamnicae* addresses himself to Aetius and Dioscorus, leading citizens of Oxyrhynchus, concerning the proper collection of the *chrysargyron*, a tax on traders. The pair had collected tax from persons who should not have been liable, so the governor orders them to return the contributions which had been levied improperly and collect what was due from the persons who were legally liable.

Rea compares P.Oxy. L 3577 with the famous letter of the prefect Subatianus Aquila, P.Berol. 11532 (December 27, 209 CE),[7] which represents an illustrious antecedent of the same type of document, even though there are obviously many differences, explainable by the fact about 130 years

---

1 = ChLA XLVII 1421 = CEL III 225 quater = TM 15398; BL VIII, 272; XI, 170; XII, 151.

2 See P.Oxy. L 3577 introd., 194.

3 See P.Oxy. L 3577, l. 9: *d*(*ominis*) *n*(*ostris*) *Const*[*ant*]*io Aug*(*usto*) *ter et Constante Aug*(*usto*) *iterum co*(*n*)*s*(*ulibus*).

4 On the possibility of expanding this *dat* into *data* or *datum* see Iovine 2019, 164–66, n. 18: in the cases analyzed here, it should always mean *epistula*, so *data* seems to be the correct solution.

5 See P.Oxy. L 3577 left margin, opposite ll. 4–6: *dat*(*a*) |*v Kal*(*endas*) *Febr*(*uarias*) |*Heracl*(*eopoli*). At first Rea had speculated that the two parts of the date in the lower and the left margin were written by two different hands (see P.Oxy. XLIII 3129 introd.), however, despite some doubts, in P.Oxy. L 3577 Rea seems to have changed his mind and instead believes the hand to be the same (see P.Oxy. L 3577 introd., 195). See also Sarri 2018, 174–75, n. 613.

6 See Kruse 2019, 133–38.

7 = SB I 4639. For a bibliography on this text, which is still under discussion, see https://berlpap.smb.museum/00467.

had passed between them. However, it is necessary to compare the two specimens from not only a palaeographic but also a diplomatic point of view. To begin with their most immediate similarities, the format is nearly the same in the two samples, with P.Berol. 11532 measuring 28.3 by 22 cm and P.Oxy. L 3577 27.5 by 24.5 cm. In both documents we can see at least three hands: one person wrote the main text, somebody else wrote the farewell formula, and another person still the date.[8] In both cases the writing of the main text is very clear, formal, and issued from the high chancery.

Among the most obvious differences, the older specimen can certainly be reported to display a more hieratic style and greater formal care, while P.Oxy. L 3577 is characterized by a slighter and certainly less systematic modular contrast. The letter *alpha*, in fact, is frequently much smaller than the other letters, but sometimes this difference is almost imperceptible, while in the Berlin document this letter is always small and positioned high on the line. It is certainly surprising to observe the hatching of the letter *omicron*, an oval-shaped form with a tip at the bottom, which appears absolutely identical in both papyri.[9]

In the letter of Subatianus Aquila we can see the greetings written by the hand of the prefect himself in the same position as the greetings of the *praes* in P.Oxy. L 3577. This farewell formula certainly had the function of marking the end of the letter, thereby guaranteeing the authenticity of the document issued by the authority; moreover, its position, so close to the text of the letter, was intended to prevent possibly unauthorized additions. I will hereafter refer to this as "the authenticity position."

The older document has been countersigned by someone: in the lower margin of P.Berol. 11532, before the date, we read Μαυρικιανὸς Μήνιος ἀνέγνων, while the other one has no note that it was checked by a member of the *officium*. Both documents have the date with the indication of the year in the lower margin, but in P.Berol. 11532 the year is indicated in Greek and in the Greek manner, with the regnal year and the titulature, while in P.Oxy. L 3577 we find the consular year in Latin—in other words, following the Roman way of dating. Last, in P.Berol. 11532

there seems to be no trace of the part of the date in the left margin. In P.Berol. 11532, the same Μαυρικιανὸς Μήνιος who checked the document also completed the date by adding the month and the day, Τῦβι νεομηνία, after the regnal year and titulature.

The presence of the date in a letter, in particular in an official letter, is obviously not a singular fact in itself,[10] however, it is remarkable that in P.Oxy. L 3577 the date is written in Latin, separated into two parts, and that one of these also contains the indication of the place where the letter was written. Rea calls this very peculiar part of the date the "*dat(a)* clause" and I will refer to it by this name. This Roman use probably had the function of a trademark, a sort of label affixed to guarantee the authenticity and the official nature of the document.[11] It can be assumed that the date written in Latin had the function of highlighting the official status of the document and the authority of the sender. Therefore, as Rea suggests, these two marginal dockets in Latin had the same function as the countersignature and the date added by Mauricianus Menios.

2   Letters Demonstrating the Pattern

The pattern of the Roman administration evident in P.Oxy. L 3577 is also found in a group of letters originally collected by Rea,[12] and here improved with some other samples. Table 5.1 details this list of texts, which I will study here, including their features that are known to date. For the sake of clarity, I chose to investigate only those cases in which all the features occurred or, if the papyrus is partially preserved, they can at least be reconstructed with some certainty: that is, the format, the handwritings, and the formal aspects, in particular the consular year in the lower margin and the expression *dat(a)* in the left margin.[13]

As we will see from the documents in which it occurs, this pattern is attested above all in the fourth century CE, but traces of it are found as far back as the second century as well as in documents from the fifth century, both in letters written in Greek and, obviously, in Latin. Furthermore, it is not exclusive to Egypt as it is found in a third-century

---

8   The number of hands that wrote the text of P.Berol. 11532 has long been under discussion; however, for the purposes of our investigation, it does not matter whether there are handshifts or simply changes of *ductus*: see Sarri 2018, 172–74. Indeed, the use of different handwriting probably had the purpose of visually highlighting the sections of the letter.

9   The only exception seems to be the *omicron* of χρυσίον in P.Oxy. L 3577, l. 6, which is rounder in form and clearly smaller because of its position at the end of the line.

10   See Sarri 2018, 121–22.

11   On the origins of this format and on its evolution in the Middle Ages, see Tjäder 1973 and Iovine 2019, 196–206.

12   See P.Oxy. L 3577 introd., 192–195.

13   A list collecting all the documents, including as-yet unpublished ones, in which the expression *data* or *datum* also occurs in other positions can be found in Iovine 2019, 157–230.

TABLE 5.1   Letters with the Roman administration pattern

Pap.	Date	Place of discovery	Place of origin	Main text language
P.Dura 56	208 CE	Dura	?	Latin
P.Oxy. XLIII 3129	335 CE	Oxyrhynchus	Alexandria	Greek
P.Oxy. LV 3793	340 CE	Oxyrhynchus	?	Greek
P.Oxy. LV 3794	340 CE	Oxyrhynchus	Alexandria	Greek
P.Oxy. L 3577	342 CE	Oxyrhynchus	Herakleopolis	Greek
P.Oxy. L 3579	341–343 CE	Oxyrhynchus	Pelusium	Greek
P.Abinn. 2	344 CE	?	?	Latin
P.Oxy. LXIII 4369	345 CE	Oxyrhynchus	?	Greek
ChLA XI 472	347 CE	?	?	Greek
ChLA V 285	357 CE	?	?	Greek
ChLA XLIII 1248	395, 396, 401 CE	?	Psobthis?	Latin
P.Sijp. 23	396 CE	Herakleopolis	?	Greek
P.Mich. XVIII 794	ex. V CE	?	Herakleopolis	Greek

document, P.Dura 56, which will be analyzed later, from another area of the Roman Empire, the Middle East.

The task, then, is to analyze how the features highlighted so far recur in the letters listed above and how they combine with the content and status of the sender. Trying to respect the chronological order, I will first analyze the most complete letter before turning to the more fragmented ones. In doing so I will show how the presence of some of these characteristics can play an essential role in the identification and comprehension of the text.

P.Oxy. XLIII 3129 (335 CE),[14] again edited by Rea, is a letter by the prefect Flavius Philagrius who instructs the strategus of the Oxyrhynchite nome to investigate the facts stated in a petition that had been sent to him. We can observe at first glance that the format is different: while the previous P.Oxy. L 3577 is very large, this is smaller, at 13.5 by 25 cm. Furthermore, the Chancery style used here is more fluid and freer.

On the other hand, we can see the same features in P.Oxy. XLIII 3129 as in P.Oxy. L 3577. First, there are three handshifts: one person wrote the letter in Chancery style; in the authenticity position, the prefect himself probably wrote the ἔρρωσο in a smaller cursive; then, a third hand wrote the date. Second, the date is in Latin and split into two parts: the consular year is in the lower margin[15] and

the day, month, and place where the letter was written are in the left margin, preceded by the expression *dat(a)*.[16]

Another example is P.Oxy. L 3579 (341–343 CE),[17] an unfortunately much-damaged papyrus. This is a letter from the chancery of the *praeses Augustamnicae*, Flavius Iulius Ausonius, to Aetius, the same leading citizen of Oxyrhynchus as the recipient of P.Oxy. L 3577, instructing him to take appropriate action if he found that the facts submitted in a petition to the *praeses* by an inhabitant of Oxyrhynchus were true. The date of the letter is partly lost, but we can date the document by the *praeses* Ausonius, who was in charge from 341 to 343 CE. Here too, despite the poor condition of the papyrus, we can make some observations. First, the format is smaller (15 × 26 cm) and the Chancery style less formal, like in the previous P.Oxy. XLIII 3129. Second, the other features recur in a similar way as in P.Oxy. L 3577 and P.Oxy. XLIII 3129. Third, we can identify three different hands; the farewell formula of the *praeses*, despite being partially lost, is in the authenticity position,[18] and, even though the traces left are very scanty, it is clear that the date is in Latin and separated into two parts, with the *dat(a)* clause in the left margin and the consular year in the lower margin.[19]

---

14   = ChLA XLVII 1419 = CEL III 224 bisi = TM 16008; BL VIII, 266; IX, 200; XI, 167; XII, 149.

15   See P.Oxy. XLIII 3129, ll. 10–11: *Iulio Consta]ntio u(iro) c(larissimo) pat[r]icio |fratre d(omini) n(ostri)* [– – –].

16   See P.Oxy. XLIII 3129 ms: *dat(a)* |[– – –] ... *Kal(endas)* |[– – –] *Octobr(es)* |[– – –] *l( )*. Only the *l* is visible in the name of the place of issue, so it could be *Alexandria* or *Herakleopolis*: see P.Oxy. XLIII 3129, margin.

17   = ChLA XLVII 1422 = CEL III 225 quinquies = TM 15400; BL VIII, 272; XI, 170.

18   See P.Oxy. L 3579, l. 12.

19   See P.Oxy. L 3579, ll. 13 and 14–17 nn.

Rea suggests that there were probably two standard formats: a larger one used for "grander documents," like P.Berol. 11532 and P.Oxy. L 3577, and a smaller one for routine messages, like P.Oxy. XLIII 3129 and P.Oxy. L 3579.[20] As we have noted, even the Chancery style in which they are written shows differences: the smaller examples show more freedom in the forms of the letters and in the use of ligatures than the larger documents. "This seems to suit the suggestion," Rea writes, "that the formats are indications of the degree of importance attached to the cases."[21]

In summary, the larger format and more formal Chancery style are accompanied by more important content; namely, issues of a broader scope not concerning individual matters. P.Oxy. L 3577, in fact, concerns an important financial matter. Otherwise, the narrower format and freer handwriting, nevertheless still adhering to the Chancery style, are applied to routine administrative documents: both P.Oxy. XLIII 3129 and P.Oxy. L 3579 are covering letters sent by high officials with copies of documents, requiring action or consideration from the local officials.

Two further examples, P.Oxy. LV 3793[22] and 3794[23] (340 CE), were joined together as a dossier. Both are addressed to the *curator* of the Oxyrhynchite nome and relate to the same topic; that is, the supply of craftsmen for government works. The name of the sender has been lost in the first letter, but from the content it is clear he is a military man, a subordinate of the *dux Aegypti*,[24] instructed to check all the military forts in the province. Having found that the walls of the fort of Psobthis needed to be decorated, he wrote to the *curator* of the Oxyrhynchite nome to ask him to send a craftsman there. The second letter is sent by the same person as P.Oxy. XLIII 3129, the prefect Flavius Philagrius, and is addressed not only to the *curator* but also to other officers, such as the "syndic," the *exactor*, the "overseer of the peace," and the principal councilors of the city. Although a lot of text has been lost, the issue dealt with seems to be wider: the supply of craftsmen to the pretorian prefects.

P.Oxy. LV 3793 is missing the left margin and the first part of each line, while P.Oxy. LV 3794, on the right, in the best-preserved part, has lost about twelve letters per line,[25] along with the whole right margin. In addition, it must be considered that the two texts have been joined by overlapping the right edge of P.Oxy. LV 3793 with the left edge of P.Oxy. LV 3794. On this occasion, the two texts may have been trimmed along the upper and lower margins. The preserved height, 25.5 cm, may not be original: for P.Oxy. LV 3794 especially, the bottom margin seems too short.[26] The surviving width of P.Oxy. LV 3794 is about 28 cm and, given what is missing on the right, it follows that the dimensions were much larger than the two examples of larger formats seen thus far. Nevertheless, the surviving width of P.Oxy. LV 3793, about 21 cm, leads one to believe that this is a specimen of a larger format too, although in comparison with P.Oxy. LV 3794 it is narrower.

The difference in the type of script used in the two letters clearly reflects the difference in content just stated. The main hand of P.Oxy. LV 3793 is less formal: Rea defines this script as a "fluent, but unpretentious official cursive," while P.Oxy. LV 3794 is written in a very formal Chancery style, closer to the script of P.Oxy. L 3577. Therefore, in the case of these two samples, the most relevant aspect is not the format—because we have seen that they are both wide—but the type of Chancery style: fluid in P.Oxy. LV 3793, which expresses a precise order, and more formal in P.Oxy. LV 3794, which deals with a broader topic.

As in the other examples seen thus far, we can observe three hands in P.Oxy. LV 3793 too, whilst there are two hands in P.Oxy. LV 3794 because of the loss of the farewell formula. At least one more hand can be recognized in both specimens. This is probably the hand of some employee in the curator's office who inserted a notation about the receipt of the letter in the upper margin.[27]

In the lower margin of P.Oxy. LV 3793 we read, in Latin, the indication of the consular year, while the *dat(a)* clause has been lost along with the left margin. It is also extremely interesting that the sender's greeting in the authenticity position is in Latin, which supports the hypothesis that he is a military man.[28] In P.Oxy. LV 3794 the traces of the *dat(a)* clause are preserved in the left margin, partially covered by the overlapping right margin of P. Oxy. LV 3793; the part relating to the consular year is completely lost.

---

20   See P.Oxy. L 3577, introd., 193.

21   "It seems to make no difference to the format that 3129 comes from the chancery of a prefect at a time when Egypt was a single province, while 3577 and 3579 come from a *praeses* of *Augustamnica*": see again Rea P.Oxy. L 3577 introd., 193.

22   = ChLA XLVII 1426 = CEL I 225 bis = TM 22517.

23   = ChLA XLVII 1427 = CEL I 225 ter = TM 22518.

24   See P.Oxy. LV 3793–94, introd., 63.

25   See P.Oxy. LV 3794, ll. 2–6.

26   If it is correct that the lower margin of P.Oxy. LV 3794 has been trimmed and, therefore, was originally wider, the part of the date with the consular year could have been found in the cutaway part of the margin. Moreover, since it was a dossier, the indication of the year was probably unnecessary, because already given in P. Oxy. LV 3793.

27   It is possible that the hands of these notations in P.Oxy. LV 3793 and P.Oxy. LV 3794 are different: see P.Oxy. LV 3793, l. 1 n. and P.Oxy. LV 3794, l. 1 n.

28   See P.Oxy. LV 3793, introd., 63 and ll. 2 n. and 15–17 n.

Another almost complete example of this type of official letter is P.Sijp. 23 (396 CE).[29] This papyrus contains a letter of the *praeses Arcadiae* to the administration of the Neilopolites nome. The *praeses* orders that receipts from *nautai* (χειρογραφίαι ναυτῶν) should not be accepted without the authentication of cιτομέτραι, otherwise the punishment will be death. The format is the larger one (37.5 × 27 cm) and we can identify three hands: the first wrote the main text in good Chancery style, the second wrote the farewell formula in the authenticity position,[30] and the third wrote the consular year in Latin in the lower margin. Even though—judging from the image of this papyrus available online[31]—the ink would seem to be very faded, therefore making it very difficult to read, in the left margin it possible to make out some traces of ink not recognized in the *ed.pr.*: these could be remains of the *dat(a)* clause.[32]

This official format also occurs in Latin letters from Egypt. P.Abinn. 2 (344 CE)[33] is a letter from the chancery of the *dux Aegypti*, Valacius, who is sending Abinnaeus a notice of dismissal from the command of his *ala*. The format is the larger one (38 × 25 cm), but this time it is written across the fibers. The three changes of hand that occur in the specimens written in Greek are observed in the Latin document too: one hand wrote the body of the letter; another the greetings of the sender, in the same position that guarantees the authenticity of the document; and a third hand wrote the date. The *dat(a)* clause is lost with the left margin, but the consular year is preserved in the lower margin.

Another example in Latin is ChLA XLIII 1248 II (396 CE),[34] the second document belonging to a *tomos sunkollesimos* made with the aim of documenting the career of a Roman soldier. The letters of the dossier are specifically labelled as copies[35] and seem to be mainly in the same hand: they are all addressed to a prefect of a fort, *praefectus castri*, in a place called Psoftis or Psofthis. ChLA XLIII 1248 II is sent by the *comes Aegypti* Flavius Pulcher[36] and the *dat(a)* clause is written in its left margin.[37] The

absence of the consular date at the foot is probably due to the fact the document is a copy.

As has already been noted, we also have one other exemplar in Latin, found outside Egypt, in Dura Europos, and dated one century earlier than the documents analyzed thus far. This is P.Dura 56 (208 CE),[38] which contains the remains of a *tomos sunkollesimos* composed of three letters: they concern the *probatio* and the assignment of horses to cavalrymen of the Palmyrene cohort by the governor of Syria Coele, Marius Maximus. In two of these letters, B and C, we can already see our key features, even though the state of the documents is extremely fragmentary. In particular, we can observe two hands: one for the main text and another for the date. In both documents the farewell formula and the consular year are lost, but the *dat(a)* clauses in the left margins are preserved.[39]

Extremely significant in demonstrating the antiquity of this pattern of official documents is P.Oxy. XX 2265[40] (120–3 CE):[41] an order of the prefect Haterius Nepos to the strategi of Upper Egypt concerning the collection of the *vicesima libertatis*, a tax upon the manumission of slaves. The letter is written in an official hand on the *verso* of the papyrus. Since it is a copy, there is no trace of handshifts, but the document is written entirely by the same hand. Furthermore, in the left margin we read in Greek:[42]

$$
\begin{aligned}
&[\dot{\epsilon}]\delta\acuteο\theta\eta &&5\\
&[\pi]\rho\grave{ο}\ \tau\rho[\epsilon]\iota\text{-}\\
&[\hat{\omega}]\nu\ \nu\omega\text{-}\\
&[\nu]\hat{\omega}\nu\ \text{'O-}\\
&[\kappa]\tau\omega\beta\rhoί\text{-}\\
&[\omega]\nu &&10
\end{aligned}
$$

As has already been observed, this is the exact Greek translation of the *dat(a)* clause placed in the left margin: [ἐ]δόθη is indeed the Greek equivalent of the Latin *data*, "issued." This must be the date of issue from the prefect's chancery. There is no trace of the part containing the indication of the year, which must have been at the bottom. It is difficult to say whether it was lost or never transcribed, because, as we have already seen, this can happen in copies of letters like ChLA XLIII 1248. In any case, we cannot rule out that in the office of the Oxyrhynchite strategus, the employee who transcribed the prefect's letter on the back of his papyrus sheet translated the Latin date into

---

29   = CPL 230 = ChLA XLIII 1249 = P.Vindob. L 9 = TM 70039.

30   See P.Sijp. 23, l. 9: ἔρρω[c]θαι.

31   See http://data.onb.ac.at/rep/102151A7.

32   See Iovine 2018, who recognizes the letter "d" of the word *dat(a)*.

33   = CEL I 227 = CPL 264 = ChLA I 8 = Chrest.Wilck 464 = P.Gen. I 45 = TM 10021.

34   = CPR V 13 + P.Rain.Cent. 165. See Rea 1984, 79–88.

35   We can read *exemplum* in the lower margin of ChLA XLIII 1248 I and II.

36   See CPR V 13, l. 18 and Rea 1984, 82–83, 86.

37   See ChLA XLIII 1248 II, ms: *dat(a) |xv Kal(endas) Maias |Alex(andriae)*.

38   = ChLA VI 311 = Rom.Mil.Rec. 99 = CPL 330 = CEL I 179; BL X, 65.

39   See P.Dura 56 B, ms: *dat(a) |iiii Idus Mai(as) |Hieropo(li)*; P.Dura 56 C, ms: *dat(a) |xvi Kal(endas) [S]ept(embres) |Antiochia*.

40   TM 17201. See Van Minnen and Worp 2009, 20.

41   See BL VI, 106–7; Bastianini 1975, 284 and Werner, 205–6.

42   See BL VI, 107.

Greek and only transcribed the necessary information—namely, the day, the month, and the place where the letter was written—probably considering the indication of the year superfluous.

P.Oxy. XX 2265 is important because it testifies the antiquity of this practice. If the use of marginal dockets was already established in the second century, one might then wonder why they are not present in P.Berol. 11532, which is the only surviving original prefectorial letter from the pre-Diocletian period.[43] Indeed, as we have seen, P.Berol. 11532 has the same format, highly formal Chancery style, and authentication of the sender as the specimens analyzed here. Nevertheless, the *dat(a)* clause is absent and the indication of the year is given in Greek and in the Greek way with the titulature, despite being in the lower margin. The month and the day, written in Greek in the lower margin, were entered by the hand that made the revision. It is possible that the *dat(a)* clause in the left margin was then lost—we know that the left margin has been reinforced with a strip of parchment.

This explanation notwithstanding, the problem of indicating the year remains. It is possible that before the fourth century CE not all letters issued by the prefect were written following the Roman practice; hence, P.Oxy. XX 2265 could attest an isolated example. Indeed, the finds are almost entirely concentrated in the fourth century, when this custom must have been consolidated in Egypt. Alternatively, it could be argued that P.Berol. 11532 does not use the Roman pattern because, although it contains an order from the prefect to the strategus, it is a document that concerns a single individual; specifically, it is an order for release, while the documents analyzed thus far, albeit with some differences,[44] concern more complex matters.

At this point it is appropriate to show how the data analyzed herein function as official marks and can help identify the sender or the content. In P.Oxy. LXIII 4369 (345 CE),[45] the sender instructs the receivers of a monetary tax to deliver the money to the *praefectus annonae Alexandriae*.[46] The top and bottom edges are partially preserved, but the beginnings of the lines are lost, so we do not know the name of the sender. The three hands are clearly visible, in addition to further corrections.[47] The main text of the letter is written in a very formal Chancery style. The autograph subscription giving the greetings of

the sender, in Greek, is preserved in the authenticity position, as is the consular year in Latin in the lower margin, whilst we have lost the *dat(a)* clause. The format is probably the larger one, since the width of the partially preserved sheet is 27 cm. In this case the sender's name has been lost, but as Rea, the *editor princeps*, notes, this set of formal data alone should suggest that the sender was "an official in a high government post, quite probably a *praeses Augustamnicae*."[48]

ChLA XI 472 (347 CE) retains the final part of a letter: in the *ed.pr.* it is called "Acte indéterminé," but if the corrections proposed below are right, it is plausible it is an official letter of the type investigated here. The letter is missing the upper part, but the other three sides are preserved. The *dat(a)* clause is lost, but in the lower margin we can read the consular year in Latin. The script of the main text is in a careful Chancery-style hand, and the width of the sheet, 32.5 cm, suggests that it is a letter in the larger format. At line 7 the editors transcribe δευτέροις ϲε μεθοδεύϲω γράμμαϲιν ....[...] ., but the traces visible after γράμμαϲιν are written with a different *ductus* and pen; in addition, there is no letter after the gap because the trace is actually part of the descending stroke of the last letter in the upper line (l. 6). From the image available online, other traces of the same type can be seen immediately below those in line 7, and thus the transcription should be:

δευτέροις ϲε μεθοδεύϲω γράμμαϲιν.......[7
   (vac.)   ......

They are, therefore, the sender's greetings written on two lines and attached, as usual, to the body of the letter in the authenticity position. Unfortunately, at this point the text is very damaged, but the traces seem to be Latin letters; maybe we could read:

δευτέροις ϲε μεθοδεύϲω γράμμαϲιν ọptọ ḅẹn[ẹ]   7
   (vac.)   ṿạḷẹạṣ

It would therefore be a situation similar to that found in P.Oxy. LV 3793, whose authenticity position contains the greetings, written in Latin, sent by a high Roman officer by order of the *dux Aegypti*. The presence of the greetings in Latin would also place the letter in a military context.

ChLA V 285 (357 CE)[49] is part of a letter,[50] probably found in Egypt, but its provenance is unknown, because

---

43   See Haensch 2000, 261 and Sarri 2018, 172.

44   See what has been said above about the different format and different level of formality in the Chancery style used in P.Oxy. XLIII 3129, P.Oxy. L 3579, P.Oxy. LV 3793, and P.Oxy. LV 3794.

45   = ChLA XLVII 1429 = CEL III 228 bis = TM 22132; BL XI, 173.

46   See P.Oxy. LXIII 4369, introd., 51–2.

47   On whether it is actually another hand or just a change of style see Rea, P.Oxy. LXIII 4369, l. 3 n.

48   See also P.Oxy. LXIII 4369, l. 1 n., where Rea suggests that he could be the *praeses Augustamnicae* Flavius Olympios.

49   = TM 69891; BL VIII, p. 83.

50   The *ed. pr.* says that "il s'agit d'une proclamation officielle, peut-être sous forme de lettre."

the papyrus was purchased.[51] This papyrus is complete at the top and at the bottom, but part of the text is lost both on the right and on the left. The greetings written in Greek by the sender are visible in the authenticity position, and the consular year in Latin is in the lower margin. The preserved dimensions are 26.4 by 11.2 cm, and since the width is not the original size, this suggests it had the larger format. The sender appears to be someone called Proclos, who does not seem to be known so far from the documentation in our possession, but, as we have seen, he must certainly be either a high Roman officer[52] or an official writing by order of a high Roman officer, as was the case in P.Oxy. LV 3793.

We also have a sample from the fifth century with this same Roman pattern: P.Mich. XVIII 794[53] (ex. V CE).[54] This is a letter from the *praeses Arcadiae* who addressed officials at the metropolis of Oxyrhynchus, the *ekdikos*—that is, the *defensor civitatis*—and the *riparii*, to compel a certain Dionysos, acting *logistes* of the city, to dispatch garlands for the public market at Herakleopolis, probably for the New Year's Day celebrations. The bottom of the papyrus is broken and therefore the farewell formula and the indication of the consular year have been lost. In the left margin we read the *dat(a)* clause in Latin. We recognize a hand who wrote the main text in a "large, pretentious, and practiced script," a "more severe and more rapid version" of the Chancery style,[55] then a hand who wrote the *dat(a)* clause in the left margin in a fast Latin cursive. Here we can observe a further formal element compared to those analyzed thus far: the letter has a header at the top, written in a different hand, containing the address, indicating the sender and recipients.[56]

Conclusion

To conclude, these formal characteristics of this Roman pattern can be considered semiotic elements defining the official nature of the letter and its origin from the high chancery of the governor, the prefect, the *praeses*, the *comes*, or the *dux*. Furthermore, the presence of different hands combined with the format and the style can help us recognize whether a letter is original; although, when it comes to copies not all these features are preserved.[57] Finally, the presence of these formal features can therefore be extremely significant in understanding the status of the sender and the importance of the content.Of the letter even when it is not preserved.

Reference List

Bastianini, Guido. 1975. "Lista dei prefetti d'Egitto dal 30ª al 299ᴾ." *ZPE* 17: 263–328.

Haensch, Rudolf. 2000. "Le rôle des officiales de l'administration provinciale dans le processus de décision." *CCG* 11: 259–76.

Iovine, Giulio. 2018. "Korr.Tyche 870: A Dating Formula ad latus in P.Sijp. 23." *Tyche* 33: 239–40.

Iovine, Giulio. 2019. "*Data epistula*: Later Additions of Latin Dating Formulae in Latin and Greek Papyri and Ostraka from the First to the Sixth Centuries AD." *Manuscripta* 63, no. 2: 157–230.

Kruse, Thomas. 2019. "The Branches of Roman and Byzantine Government and the Role of Cities, the Church, and Elite Groups." In *A Companion to Greco-Roman and Late Antique Egypt*, edited by Katelijn Vandorpe, 119–38. Hoboken: Wiley Blackwell.

Rea, John R. 1984. "A Cavalryman's Career, A.D. 384(?)–401." *ZPE* 56: 79–88.

Sarri, Antonia. 2018. *Material Aspects of Letter Writing in the Graeco-Roman World. c. 500 BC–c. AD 300*. Berlin: De Gruyter.

Tjäder, Jan-Olof. 1973. "*Et ad latus*. Il posto della datazione e della indicazione del luogo negli scritti della cancelleria imperiale e nelle largizioni di enfiteusi degli arcivescovi ravennati." *Studi Romagnoli* 24: 91–124.

Van Minnen, Peter, and Klaas Worp. 2009. "A Latin Manumission Tax Tablet in Los Angeles." *BASP* 46: 15–22.

Werner, Eck. 1977. "Zur Erhebung der Erbschafts- und Freilassungssteuer in Ägypten im 2. Jahrh. n.Chr." *ZPE* 27: 201–209.

---

51   On papyri.info it is said that ChLA V 285 was written in Jerusalem, but it is a misunderstanding of what is written in the *ed. pr.* In fact, the edition says that, regarding the origin of the fragment, reference should be made to what has been said about the previous ChLA V 284, which is almost two centuries older. About ChLA V 284 the *ed.pr.* says: "Acheté à Londres en 1925 (lot III de la collection Nahman), provenance précise inconnue. Ecrit à Jerusalem en AD 188 d'après les l. 1 et 2, peut-être apporté en Egypte par un vétéran." It is clear, therefore, that Jerusalem is the place where ChLA V 284 was written, but this is not the case for ChLA V 285.

52   Given the date of the document, 357 CE, we can say that a *praefectus Aegypti*, a *praeses Augustamnicae*, and a *praeses Thebaidis* coexisted at that time: see Kruse 2019, 135.

53   TM 35625; BL XI, 135; XII, 126; XIII, 141.

54   See CPR XXIV, l. 71 and P.Oxy. LXVIII 4696, l. 4 n.

55   See Ann E. Hanson in P.Mich. XVIII 794 introd., 306.

56   See P.Mich. XVIII 794, ll. 1–3 and BL XI, 135.

57   See ChLA XLIII 1248 and P.Oxy. XX 2265.

## CHAPTER 6

Applied Category Analysis for Interpreting a List in the Late Antique Documentary Tradition: Some Preliminary Considerations

Antonella Ghignoli

Introduction*

From the third to the eighth century CE some historical phenomena can be studied in continuity.[1] Documentary practice is certainly one of these. The basic textual frame of "Barbarian" documents is recognizable as part of a Roman "discourse." This fact is fundamental evidence for the derivation of the early medieval documentary practice in the West from the late Roman world.[2] At the same time, however, this fact constitutes the main obstacle to our understanding the process of derivation in all its aspects.[3]

This paper will not follow long-term developments of specific documentary typologies. Rather, it is concerned with a mode of written communication connected to a particular need that emerges as a constant in the whole documentary tradition of the period, regardless of questions concerning the *longue durée*: the need to represent a sequence of "things" within the written records produced for pragmatic purposes by bureaucrats, official scribes, notaries, and individuals.[4] The paper attempts to reflect on the possibility of framing significant features in the "practice of writing a list" within the rich transmission of documentary papyri of late Roman and Byzantine Egypt. The aim is to assemble a minimal number of critical elements useful for comparative analysis of similar practices

attested in the very poor transmission of documentary sources in the late Roman and post-Roman West. The specific goal is to interpret a sixth-century Latin documentary papyrus; a fragmentary list recently added to the group of Italian papyri edited by Jan Olof Tjäder.

1   List, Inventory, and the Others

The terms "list," "catalogue," "table," and "index" are currently used as scientific terminology in fields ranging from information science to lexicography and computational linguistics. The same can be said for the words "catalogue" and "inventory," which are employed respectively in the fields of library science and archival science as technical terms. The specificity of all these terms in each field, however, is somehow based on the meaning they have in everyday language.

In Italian both the words "elenco" and "lista" imply the idea of a certain intrinsic order meaning a series of items (words, objects, etc.).[5] The same idea is implied in the definition of "Verzeichnis" and "Liste" in German,[6] whereas in French the term "liste" seems to convey the idea of an order, but with regard to the external written structure of the series of names or things rather than to the internal one, because the items are "le plus souvent inscrits l'un au-dessous de l'autre."[7] According to the *Oxford English Dictionary* (*OED*), a "list" is "a catalogue or roll consisting of a row or series of names, figures, words, or the like. In early use, esp. a catalogue of the names of persons engaged in the same duties or connected with the same

---

*   The research on which this paper is based is part of the ERC-2017-Advanced Grant project NOTAE ("Notae: not a written word but graphic symbols," PI Antonella Ghignoli), which has received funding from the European Research Council under the Horizon 2020 research and innovation programme (Grant agreement No. 786572).

1   The period is defined by two overlapping terms: late antiquity and the early Middle Ages. On the one hand, for medievalists the early Middle Ages refers nowadays to the period from the fourth/fifth to tenth century CE. On the other hand, the current model of a "long" late antiquity covers the period from the third to the eighth century CE, though there is still a strong debate about the periodization. For more details and bibliography see Cameron 2015, 4. For the notion of "continuity" see Wickham 2005, 12–14.

2   A classic remains Steinacker (1927) 1977. Fundamental surveys are Classen 1977a and 1977b.

3   On this question, see Ghignoli 2009, Ghignoli and Bougard 2011, and Rio 2009.

4   For reflection on the "need" to write a list, the starting point remains Goody 1977.

5   See the entries for "elenco" and "lista" in Istituto Treccani-Enciclopedia Italiana, Vocabolario online: <http://www.treccani.it/vocabolario/elenco/>, <http://www.treccani.it/vocabolario/lista/>, accessed on 08.18.2020. Also see the entry for "indice": <http://www.treccani.it/vocabolario/indice/>, accessed on 08.18.20.

6   See the entries for "Verzeichnis" and "Liste" in Duden Wörtebuch online: <https://www.duden.de/rechtschreibung/Verzeichnis>, <https://www.duden.de/rechtschreibung/Liste>, accessed on 08.18.20.

7   See the entry for "liste" in Larousse Langue Française online: <https://www.larousse.fr/dictionnaires/francais/liste/47418#definition>, accessed on 08.18.20.

object," whereas a "catalogue" is "a list, register, or complete enumeration, and in this simple sense now obsolete or archaic."[8] The Italian term "catalogo" means a list is not only systematic, but also ordered ("genericamente, elenco ordinato e sistematico di più oggetti della stessa specie").[9]

As for the other terms, in English the concept of order is apparently implied in the definition of a "table," which is, according to the *OED*, "a systematic arrangement of numbers, words, symbols, etc., in a definite and compact form so as to show clearly some set of facts or relations, esp. an arrangement in rows and columns, typically occupying a single page or sheet."[10] Turning to "inventory," the first and proper meaning of the word in English is related to the semantic area of inheritance law, from which it derives its figurative meaning of "a detailed account" and thus its use as a synonym of "list, catalogue."[11] In contrast, in Italian, "inventario" is a written list in which all the objects *in a given place* and *at a given time* are systematically and accurately described.[12] The next term, "register," primarily refers in both Italian and English to a "book or a volume in which important items of information of a particular kind are regularly and accurately recorded and a collection of entries so created."[13] Finally, an "index" in English is "an alphabetical list, placed usually at the end of a book, of the names, subjects, etc. occurring in it,"[14] with the word "indice" in Italian having the same meaning.[15]

When dealing with the large number of late antique documentary papyri, "list" and "inventory" (more rarely catalogue, register, or index) are the words usually employed to describe and classify any text consisting of a sequence of words or groups of words that are written next to each other and not (or not necessarily) connected to each other syntactically.[16] Many such texts survive from late antiquity and the early Middle Ages. The choice of an appropriate modern term to define them is possible only when we can define or guess at the circumstances of creation of the document and at its function with a certain degree of plausibility. It is often impossible a priori to establish the origin and the function of a list. Indeed, even when it is theoretically possible, it is not easy.

The issue of the choice of a modern word might arise, on the other hand, by translating ancient terms present in the text of a documentary papyrus whenever the context and the experience of the papyrologist suggest that they mean a written text structured (more or less) as a sequence of items. Also in this circumstance, the choice of a definition from the range of different modern terms available, as we have seen, depends on our understanding of the nature and function of the document cited in the papyrus. Searching the English definitions mentioned above in the Trismegistos (TM) database of words in Greek papyrological texts is an interesting experiment that illustrates this sort of hermeneutic circle at work.[17]

In late antique and early medieval documentary sources, the items more frequently listed (separately or in combination) are personal names, place names, role

---

8   See <https://www.oed.com>, accessed on 10.06.20, for the entry "List, noun 6," and "Catalogue," which notes that catalogue in the simple sense of complete enumeration is considered "obsolete or archaic."

9   See the entry for "catalogo" in Istituto Treccani-Enciclopedia Italiana, Vocabolario online: <http://www.treccani.it/vocabolario/catalogo>, accessed on 08.18.20. The same meaning is in German: see the entry for "Katalog" in Duden Wörtebuch online: <https://www.duden.de/rechtschreibung/Katalog>, accessed on 08.18.20. The Italian "ruolo" (from the French "role," derived from late Latin rŏtŭlus; i.e., "rotolo") has the specialized meaning of a systematic and ordered list of persons belonging to the same organization: <http://www.treccani.it/vocabolario/ruolo/>, accessed on 08.18.20.

10   See the entry "Table, II. 14. A," *OED*, accessed on 10.06.20.

11   See, respectively, the entries "Inventory 1" and "Inventory 2.a," *OED*, accessed on 10.06.20.

12   See the entry for "inventario" in Istituto Treccani-Enciclopedia Italiana, Vocabolario online: <http://www.treccani.it/vocabolario/inventario/>, accessed on 18.08.20. Apparently, the meaning of the French "inventaire" and the German "Inventar" is more specialized and connected to property and inheritance: <https://www.larousse.fr/dictionnaires/francais/inventaire/> and <https://www.duden.de/suchen/dudenonline/Inventar>, accessed on 08.18.20.

13   See the entry "register 1.1.a," *OED*, accessed on 10.06.20; the noun is considered obsolete in the meaning of "catalogue." For comparison see the entry "registro" in <https://www.treccani.it/vocabolario/registro/>, accessed on 06.10.20.

14   See the entry for "Index 5.b," *OED*, accessed on 10.06.20.

15   See the entry for "indice," <https://www.treccani.it/vocabolario/indice/>, accessed on 10.06.20.

16   The French terms "liste" or "catalogue," however, are preferable as "archilèxemes," at least in French, in order to describe the lists transmitted within ancient literary texts: Loriol 2020, 22.

17   This database is a "new addition to the Trismegistos universe" in cooperation with Alek Keersmaekers; for further information about coverage and accuracy see <https://www.trismegistos.org/words/about.php>, accessed on 08.20.2020. Results of a search performed on 08.22.20 state that "list" is a translation of: διαγραφή (which can be translated also as "payment and certificate"), γραφή (also translated as "catalogue" and "return"), ἀπαιτήσιμον (as "list of lands subject to dues"), παραδοχή (also translated as "collection"), βρέβιον (also translated as "inventory" and as *brevis*, in Latin), ἀναγράφιον (also translated as "index"), μεταλόγιον (as "secondary list"), and σύγγραφος (as "inscribed list"). "Inventory" is a translation of βρέβιον (also translated as "list") and σκευογραφία. "Catalogue" is a translation of κατάλογος (also translated as "enrolment" or "register") and γραφή (also translated as "list").

names, names of objects and animals, and numerals expressing dates or amounts of something (money, goods, or livestock). In some cases, the list item consists of a phrase or phrases, given without verbal elements in the vast majority of cases. This happens when a scribe has to list, for instance, books, documents, or textiles. We have good reason to think that the word order was designed in a way considered adequate for the purpose. Since the purpose of a list is often the unknown factor in criticism, on which the criticism itself depends, the textual structure of the item in a written sequence arranged as a "list" has the value of a primary source.

2   The Part and the Whole

P.Lips. I 123 (TM 22445) is a sort of collaborative text. What we observe on the recto of the papyrus is a stratification of three texts arranged one below the other in a unique column, written by three different hands (in at least two different times) for a total of twenty-two lines.[18] It starts as a sort of "cover letter" accompanying the delivery of four official journals, and ends up becoming the proof of the delivery itself. In the first text (*anagraphê*)—the "cover letter"[19]—the provenance, nature, and purpose are clearly stated, and Philiskos, *strategos* of Mendes, is expressly declared the sender of some official journals that are to be stored in the record-office of the Alexandria city district Patrika. It closes with the date April 10, 136 CE, which is written in final position (hand 1: ll. 1–14).

The second text is a statement by the person who materially brought the journals from the office of the *strategos* to the Patrika archive. It is presumably an autograph. It has no dating formula. We can guess that it was written immediately upon delivery (hand 2: ll. 15–16). The third text is the acknowledgment of receipt. Written in the Patrika archive in the name of the *bibliophylax* (the keeper of the archive, Markos Ulpios Phainippos Tryphonianos), it attests that the four rolls entered the archive on April 15, 136 CE (hand 3: ll. 17–22.). A horizontal line was drawn, probably by the same hand three, under line 22 and part of line 21, in order to frame—and therefore to close—the final text.[20] In the empty space below the line, the number

of rolls was written again by hand three at a distance of 6 cm.

The former "cover letter" was returned to the sender as proof of delivery for preservation in his archive. This can be deduced by analyzing the structure of the short text written on the verso, where someone (hand 4) summarized the document.[21] The dorsal note is a sequence of three elements: 1) a definition of the document ("Receipt of the keeper of the archive in the Patrika"); 2) the timespan covered by the journals delivered as a whole ("from Hadrianus 21 to Phamenoth 4"—i.e., December 18, 135—February 28, 136 CE); and 3) the number of the delivered rolls ("in 4 rolls"). The key element is the first: it evidently shows that the note was written from the point of view of the former "sender" of the cover letter. In conclusion, the dorsal note communicates the information needed to manage that written record effectively in the archive of the *strategos* Philiskos, who can therefore be considered the final recipient of the papyrus.[22]

The papyrus, which Ludwig Mitteis classified as "Aktenablieferung an das Archiv,"[23] is included in a recent anthology of documents concerning law and legal practice in Egypt with the title "List of journals followed by endorsements."[24] A list is actually present (in the first text), which contains a section that serves to communicate the material transferred from Mendes to Patrika and is structured as a short list. The list starts after the phrase εἰσὶ δέ near the end of line 5, immediately after the presentation of the sender and the nature of the document (παρὰ Φιλίσκου στρατηγοῦ Μενδ[ησί]υ ἀναγραφὴ ὑπομνηματισμῶν κ[ατ]αχωρισθέντων εἰς τὴν ἐν Πα[τ]ρ[ικο]ῖς βιβλιοθήκην τοῦ εἰκοστοῦ ἔτους Ἁδ[ριαν]οῦ Καίσαρος τοῦ Κυρίου: ll. 1–5),[25] and it ends at line 12, before the dating formula (ll. 13–14). It consists of four "items" (ll. 5–11) plus a summation (l. 12). The four items each have two elements. The first element offers precise chronological information and is structured in the format "from … to" (ἀπὸ … ἕως), with the addition of the conjunction "and" (καὶ) before the

---

18   Digital image available at <http://papyri-leipzig.dl.uni-leipzig.de/receive/UBLPapyri_schrift_00001230>, accessed on 10.29.2020. German translation: Scholl 2000, 9. English translation: Kruse 2014, 83.

19   The best translation of the term *anagraphê* is in German, *Versandnachweis*; Scholl 2000, 9.

20   This is done to prevent additions; the x-shaped signs drawn by hand 3 at the end of lines 11, 12, and 14 have the same function

(Scholl 2000, 11). The horizontal line is indicated as "Schnörkel" in the *editio princeps* (Mitteis 1906, 335). The horizontal line is indicated as "*monogr.*" in the *Duke Databank of Documentary Papyri* (*DDbDP*): <http://www.papyri.info/ddbdp/p.lips;1;123/>, accessed on 10.29.2020.

21   Scholl 2000, 12. In the *editio princeps* this text is attributed to hand 3: Mitteis 1906, 335.

22   See also Scholl 2000, 12.

23   Mitteis 1906, 334.

24   Kruse 2014, 82–83, where *anagraphê* is translated as "list" (see above, note 18).

25   Here and below the text follows the transcription in *DDbDP*: <http://www.papyri.info/ddbdp/p.lips;1;123/>, accessed on 10.29.2020.

second, third, and fourth items in a manner equivalent to the modern semi-colon. The second element indicates the precise number of rolls in each instance. The summation that concludes this list at line 12 indicates the total number of rolls in question, viz. four or one roll for each "journal":

Καίσαρος τοῦ Κυρίου. εἰσὶ δέ· ἀπὸ κα   5
Ἀδριανοῦ ἕως Τῦβι κα τόμ(ος) α,
καὶ ἀπὸ κβ Τῦβι ἕως Μεχεὶρ ε τόμ(ος) α,
καὶ ἀπὸ ϛ Μεχεὶρ ἕως κα τοῦ αὐτοῦ
μηνὸς τόμο[ς] α
καὶ ἀπὸ κβ Μεχεὶρ ἕως ι Φαρμοῦθι   10
τόμος α
γ(ίνεται) [ὁμοῦ] τόμοι δ.

The fact that the second item starts and ends on the same single line (l. 7) is apparently random. The list is communicated without the need for an arrangement different from that of the previous portion of text (ll. 1–5). It might perhaps be explained by assuming that the list was not the core item for the scribe of the first text and that he knew in advance that the main function of that papyrus sheet was to receive acknowledgement of both delivery and receipt (second and third texts) and that its final destination as a completed document would be the same as its origin.

Another sample of a "list" transmitted without breaking the "normal" text alignment in the writing frame is BGU 2 610 (TM 69916 [140 CE]), a Latin document.[26] The list begins at line two, since line one contains the dating formula and the word ue[terani], which introduces the series of names of veterans residing in Alexandria. The names are written one after another on the same line. The text has blank spaces which separate one item from the next. Since all of the text is a pure sequence of names (apart from the first line), we cannot exclude the possibility that the blank space here performs its usual function as a marker of major pauses within a paragraph.[27]

P.Sakaon 1 (TM 13025 [February 27, 310 CE])[28] is a fiscal declaration from Theadelpheia (Batn el-Harit) that is preserved intact, dated, and written in Greek with the subscription of the author in Latin. Within the text of the declaration (an apographé), there is a portion indicating the personal names of the taxpayers and the tax amounts. This portion is arranged in tabular format in the modern sense of the term: the writing lines from 7 to 15 are actual rows; that is, horizontal sections in which various

information relating to the same person is organized so that all elements of the same kind (for different persons) are aligned in the same column. The tabular format gives this portion of the document—and only in this case—a "visual" dimension which is lacking in the samples mentioned above. There is no reason to think that the tabular format was not deliberately designed for this purpose. In other words, it is clear that the textual scheme of the table was applied for its functionality, as it was a well-known practice used in the administrative and fiscal sphere. Let us imagine for a moment that all the text of P.Sakaon 1 around the central portion containing the table had been lost, it would still not be difficult to recognize it as a fragment of a fiscal declaration of the fourth century CE, for the content of the items is fairly clear and whole documents of this typology are preserved for the period.

The same cannot be said for P.Vindob L8 (395–401 CE), at least while it was separated from P.Vindob. L 125 (395–401 CE). The real nature of the whole papyrus (P.Vindob L8+125), probably originating from Arsinoites (Fayum), which we now cite as ChLA XLIII 1248 (TM 12866), is that of "a short liber epistularum"[29] set up by the Roman soldier Sarapio after his discharge from the army, so as to collect the copies (exempla) of three letters issued by the higher competent authorities attesting his career steps and therefore his veteran status. The third letter deals with the dismissal of a group of matriculae, among whom figures the decurio Sarapio. In this case, too, the tabular format seems to effectively serve the purpose of communicating the relevant case information. It is arranged in a careful manner with four columns (role, name, reason for dismissal, and salary) and eleven rows (one for each soldier). The first row contains the name of Sarapio, as decurio, according to the role indicated in the first column, who was discharged because of colicus (third column) and his XVIII stipendia (fourth column).[30]

There is no reason to think that the texts of this dossier are not relatively exact transcriptions of the original letters received by Sarapio.[31] This also holds true for their layout, especially at crucial points such as that in Letter III, where the list of soldiers discharged is announced (l. 10: et sunt). Therefore, it seems reasonable to suppose that what we now see at that point of the copy was the same in the original letter. Moreover, we can assume that point in the original letter contained, in all likelihood, an

---

26   Digital image: <https://berlpap.smb.museum/02208/>, accessed on 11.02.2020.

27   Parkes 1992, 10.

28   P.Strasb. Gr. 1 42; facsmile in ChLA XIX 685.

29   The illuminating definition of this piece is from Iovine 2019, 185.

30   Digital image: <http://data.onb.ac.at/rep/10206713>, accessed on 10.29.2020.

31   On this point see also the considerations in Iovine 2019, 187 n. 82.

appropriate excerpt from the official military rolls where discharges were recorded in tables.

A table can be read in several directions, following one's own index finger or a stick: in vertical fashion (from top to bottom and *vice versa*) and horizontally (not necessarily from left to right). On occasion, multidirectional reading generates several different lists within the same textual structure, and these lists can number as many as the columns and rows. For instance, one may scroll the third column of the excerpt of the table of discharged soldiers copied in Letter III and then read a list of diseases or impediments to the status of the Roman soldier: *colicus, debilis, senex, aegrotus, senex, ut supra, colicus, debilis, senex, ut supra, ut supra* (ll. 11–21).[32] The fact that the phrase *ut supra* replaces an item is noteworthy, for it directs the reader's eye upwards within the same column and to the item written on the line above.

One can easily assume that the use of tables is connected with highly organized milieux such as the fiscal or military administration of the Roman State. For instance, the military administration's use of "single-column tables" (in other words, lists in the modern sense of the term, where each line corresponds to one item, and each item is written in a vertical series, one below the other) seems frequent in documentary practice. The new edition of the Latin papyri from Dura-Europos offered by Robert Marichal in four volumes of the *Chartae Latinae Antiquiores* represents a model in studying similar forms of written records.[33] It includes a long introduction which provides a masterly survey of palaeographical and diplomatic aspects of the military roles (*ruoli* in Italian) as documents in the form of lists. Specific graphic signs (points, lines), layout (in most cases designed in single long columns), and the dynamics of written registration (the writing of the main text—i.e., the items in a column; writing additions or corrections, inserted later into the series of lists) are significant features, because they served the pragmatic purposes for which this particular type of document was created. Specific signs and layout were conceived to manage the written lists. This global punctuation system on the one hand represents the document's "grammar of use."[34] On the other hand, it is constitutive of the document itself.

These observations notwithstanding, further, critical comparative analysis of all the evidence is needed and a survey of this topic as a whole remains to be done.[35] Moreover, the relationship between the external form and formulae of the *laterculi* and the form of list of the documents produced by the military administration is a topic currently being discussed by epigraphers. It seems likely that the *laterculi* somehow reflect the form of the documents produced by the Roman military bureaucracy.[36]

3　　Documents, Fragments, Lists

Nearly all preserved documentary papyri are fragments of rolls or codices. Rarely can we read a document as an original whole. The impact and variable extension of this loss of text differs according to the material support on which the text was written (papyrus, parchment, wood, or stone) and the type of medium used to transmit the document (roll or codex, single sheet, single piece of stone/slate, bound tablets, etc.). The writing material and type of support employed make a fragment "different." Whereas writing material is evident, the medium must be inferred, and this makes it even harder to identify the lost original form of a document that is now preserved as a fragment showing only a sequence of words.

The definition of a fragment as a list/inventory/catalogue is given in the first instance on the basis of the internal organization of the surviving text as a sequence of elements, so that it is normal and inevitable to classify it as a "list" in the context of an edition. In the context of research and study, however, we need to verify at the outset that what in a fragment appears to be a list really does represent a type of document distinct from the others (letters, contracts, etc.) and therefore that it ought to be classified as such. This procedure might cause distortion on several levels. It might do so specifically as regards the possibility of hypothesizing an original whole (i.e., the real typology of that document which has survived in fragmentary condition) and in general as regards the possibility of investigating the existence, uses, and circulation of textual patterns that arguably originated in particular

---

32　It could be worth comparing the structure of this kind of list with that of the "listes nominatives des malades" mentioned in Ricciardetto 2016, 678 n. 3, even though they are written on ostraca in Greek.

33　ChLA VI–IX, published 1975–77. For the importance of the Dura papyri in the history of Latin script, see Zamponi 2021.

34　In using this expression, I am extending the concept of "the grammar of legibility," introduced by Malcom Parkes (1992, 20) to the palaeography of the Latin medieval manuscripts.

35　Salati 2020, consisting of a global critical analysis of the military documents from Egypt in comparison with the documents from Dura and other proveniences, represents, however, a recent, real step forward on this topic.

36　See, in particular, Cenati et al. 2017. The word *laterculum* was used to mean "list" from the fourth century CE onwards, mainly in the military milieu. It is adopted, as is well known, by the editors of the *CIL* to indicate those Latin epigraphic monuments erected by soldiers (*praetoriani* and *urbaniciani*) on the occasion of their discharge.

spheres of documentary practice, where the list (whether arranged in tables or single columns, on a roll or codex) might instead be properly considered a peculiar form of written communication.

The more documents that are preserved relatively intact (with portions of text arranged as lists or tables), the more feasible it will be to classify the lists in fragments. Increasingly well-studied areas and documentary typologies will greatly facilitate our interpretation of them. This is a well-known basic rule of the critical method.

The current state of knowledge of official archives and registration in Roman Egypt and related written records containing a list such as *anagraphê*, for instance, allows us to make judgements about the nature of a list preserved in a fragment in many cases.[37] As regards lists of books, the work of Rosa Otranto is an excellent starting point in terms of both theoretical questions and criticism, since she deals with the uncertainty regarding the distinction between bibliographical lists and library catalogues and provides the edition of nineteen "lists of books" attested in the papyrological sources.[38] The results of the research of Jean Gascou on documentary codices and tax-accounting in Egypt form the essential basis for both investigation in that field and source-criticism.[39] Thanks to this basis, for example, Arietta Papaconstantinou has been able to identify an opisthograph papyrus fragment, datable to the early sixth century CE and containing texts arranged in tabular format (rows and columns), as page recto/verso of a documentary codex devoted to the registration of tax receipts.[40]

Nevertheless, a significant quantity of fragments will continue to maintain the appearance of pure and simple lists or inventories for a variety of reasons: unknown provenance of the papyrus, no significant elements allowing the papyrus to be dated with relative precision (i.e., within at least two centuries), no significant papyrological data, and no significant textual elements that could make it possible to guess the medium and context of its origin. In such cases we can detect and describe significant "external features,"[41] thereby contributing to a minimal evidential basis for future investigation. This opens the possibility, for scholars dealing with problematic fragments, to engage in critical comparison and historical argumentation, even at minimal levels. This helps to identify among the "large but heterogeneous group of *private notes, lists, and memoranda*"[42] those "lists" that in some way have a formal appearance.

4 Attempts at Analysis

In actual practice, there are not many elements available for such analysis. Some have already been illustrated indirectly above: the arrangement of text on the papyrus sheet; alignment; punctuation marks in the sense of any kind of graphic signs employed both to organize the writing of the items within the writing frame and to manage the list later, at the moment of its possible use; the presence and position of possible graphic Christian symbols; handwriting, in terms of ascertaining whether the hand is individual or Chancery/bureaucratic and whether the writing is cursive or accurate/calligraphic;[43] and the presence of a sort of "title" or definition as *incipit* of the text, which is perhaps the only internal element useful for a comparison.

On occasion, for instance, the presence of graphic Christian symbols is omitted from editions. For example, in the edition of P.Vindob. G 20737 (CPR 7 28; TM 35937)—a "Bevölkerungsliste" dated to the sixth to seventh century from Hermopolis, arranged in one column in which each line corresponds to each item of the list— we learn that the sequence is opened by a staurogram only thanks to the printed reproduction.[44] By contrast, the editors of the short collection called "O Kyrios lists" note of one—P. Vindob. G 19611 (SB 16 12745; TM 34888 [V–VI CE]), which probably originated from Arsinoites (Fayum)—that the "Chrismon am Anfang und am Ende stellen sicher, dass die Liste vollständig ist."[45] It is a noteworthy remark, because it is based on the assumption that a graphic Christian symbol—it is not a *chrismon* but a stylized staurogram—may also have a distinctive function, as a punctuation sign, in a short text of five lines. This assumption is entirely reasonable, but it still has to be proved by collecting similar cases and comparing related

37 Steinacker (1927) 1977, 31–41; Montevecchi 2008, 199–201; Kruse 2014, 62–82.

38 Otranto 2000.

39 Gascou 1989.

40 Papaconstantinou 1994.

41 According to the terminology of palaeography and diplomatics, which have traditionally been concerned only with Latin texts on papyrus and parchment of the Latin West (Roman and post-Roman) and Greek texts from Byzantium. What is meant here as "external features" overlaps with the concept of the "visual-graphological mode" of a text, and in particular with

that of the "typography," introduced as a critical tool in the ERC research project EVWRIT; see Bentein and Amory 2019, 21.

42 Palme 2009, 363; original emphasis.

43 That is, in terms of an evaluation of significant common criteria both in the Greek and Latin documentary tradition of the period; see Cavallo 2009.

44 Zilliacus et al. 1979, 119–21, image 21.

45 Rom and Harrauer 1983, 111.

practices. For example, a similar graphic symbol appears as the *incipit* in the fragment of the verso page of the documentary codex already mentioned above; the same function is noted *en passant* by the editor also in this case.[46]

A further instance of the presence of Christian graphic symbols in a list is offered by a fragment of unknown provenance, but probably from Byzantine Egypt, which dates to the sixth century CE. Preserved at the National Museum of Antiquities in Leiden in the von Scherling collection, it has been published as a "List of documents," with the editor noting it is "apparently the beginning of a list of letters."[47] The beginning is marked by a splendidly drawn staurogram (Fig. 6.1), but what is also noteworthy is the well-arranged alignment of the verbal items of the list (note, in particular, the point on line four from which the scribe starts to write the text, which belongs to the second item of the list) and the position in *ekthesis* of the first word of each item, Χ(ει)ρ(όγραφον); it is expressed in the monogrammatic abbreviation *chi-rho* and as such it seems to perform here too the distinctive (and thus punctuative) function of being the initial sign of an item.[48] Another interesting feature should be noted: the presence of a sort of title/definition (although incomplete here) which serves to communicate the list: Γνῶσ(ις) γραμμά-τ(ων) γε . [.

The practice of introducing a list with a definition/title, preceded by a staurogram, is also attested in the "O-Kyrios" lists already mentioned. For instance, in SPP 20 259, from Egypt (TM 36635 [VI CE])—γνῶσ(ις) μοναδίον[49]—and in SPP 20 248, from Egypt (TM 38811 [VII CE]), with the lapidary title: Γνῶσ(ις). The question posed by the editors makes sense: "Ist irrtümlich die Angabe, worüber eine Liste erstellt ist, ausgefallen?"[50]

FIGURE 6.1   RMO Inv. no. F 1948/3.5
IMAGE COURTESY OF THE RIJKSMUSEUM VAN
OUDHEDEN, LEIDEN, THE NETHERLANDS

Gnosis, isolated as "lapidarer Titel" or followed by a genitive as specification of the listed objects, seems to have a parallel in the Latin word *notitia* (from *notus*, derived from *nosco*, thus from archaic *gnosco*), which is attested both followed by the genitive (*notitia testium* for instance, in the documentary practice of late antique Ravenna)[51] or followed by *de* and the ablative. *Notitia* emerges in scattered but significant Western documentary sources of the same period (VI–VIII CE) as a text header, in which it is clear that the list is the core of the written record and that the function of the whole document is the written communication of a series of "things."[52] In the Italian papyri, too, the term *brevis*, which is mainly use to indicate an official return,[53] can bear the meaning of "list," perhaps because reports often contained information organized in lists or in tables.[54] The same practice continued into the

46   Papaconstantinou 1994, 94: "La premiere colonne comporte, sous la croix incipitale, une serie de chiffres (10, 14, 15, 16), en ordre croissant."

47   Worp 2013, 37–38.

48   A survey on the use of the monogram *chi-rho* in the meaning of *cheirographon* is being prepared by Anna Monte within the research activities of the ERC-2017-AdG project NOTAE.

49   Note that in this fragment, a hand (probably the same hand responsible for the list) traced a line ending with a thick point on the left side of the sheet, near the start point of each writing line corresponding to each item of the list. These could be signs drawn when writing the list (such as punctuations marks) or, more likely, when reading and using the list (for example, as marks in a verification procedure). A digital image of the list is available at <http://data.onb.ac.at/rec/RZ00001785>, accessed on 04.21.22.

50   Rom and Harrauer 1983, 113. A digital image of the list is available at <http://data.onb.ac.at/rec/RZ00001775>, accessed on 11.01.2020.

51   On this "Zeugenverzeichnis, (*notitia testium*), wahrscheinlich nachjustinianisch," see Tjäder 1955, 276–77.

52   With regard to the papyri from Italy, see Tjäder 1955, 406 (*Kommentar n. 7* to the word *notitia* in P.Ital. 1 2, l. 16).

53   Jones 1964, 405. See also Di Paola 2000.

54   In fact, Tjäder translates *brevis* both as *Verzeichnis* and *Spezifikation* depending on the case.

eighth century CE in Lombard Italy.[55] All the same, the word βρέβιον in the meaning of "list" or "inventory" also appears in documentary papyri from Egypt ranging from the fourth to the seventh century CE;[56] in particular, βρέβιον sometimes appears as a title at the beginning of a text with the form of a list.[57]

According to an unforgettable observation by Marc Bloch, "il n'est pas de connaissance véritable sans un certain clavier de comparaison. À condition, il est vrai, que le rapprochement porte sur des réalités à la fois diverse et pourtant apparentées."[58] Every palaeographer knows that the writing material and form of medium play a role in determining the external features of a text as well as the purpose for which the text was created. Thus, critical comparison in terms of long-term practices within the written documentary culture means simultaneously taking into account the possible persistence of past practices and graphic solutions as well as the contemporary functions and constraints of writing materials and medium on a macrohistorical level.

The Lombard *breve de moniminas* (ChLA XXVI 808 [763–769 CE]) is written on a sheet of parchment (49.2 × 24/16.9 cm), broken in the lower part with a loss of text. It preserves 62 lines, and the items of the list, which begins at line 2, are written one after another on the same line, with punctuation marks (point and colon) and sometimes little blank spaces separating one item from the next. The point of interest is not this external feature, but the phrasing *Breve de moniminas que reddidet Teuspert Ghittie Dei ancille...*, which serves to introduce the list of ninety-nine documents and some valuables written on the following lines and represents, at the same time, the definition of this document (which is basically a return) in its entirety.

Thus, it makes clear the persistence in the background of the late antique *brevis* and the same communicative function performed by it, although transformed through widespread and intensive use in a different socio-economic context in which documentary texts are now written on a single sheet of a valuable material (parchment).[59]

A critical comparison in terms of external features between the Lombard *breve de moniminas* and late antique lists presenting, in appearance, similar solutions must lead to the conclusion that the choice of arrangement of the sequence of items on the same line in the Lombard *breve* was conditioned by the writing material and by what the use of parchment represented in terms of expense in late eighth-century Lombard Italy. The same writing material, on the other hand, did not prevent the arrangement of accounting records, lists of rents and incomes, and the like in a series of one-column tables on the same parchment sheet at the royal monastery of St. Martin of Tours in Merovingian France in the second half of the seventh century CE.[60] It makes sense to compare, in terms of external features, this practice and that used in the fiscal or military sphere of the late Roman state.

5   P.Vic.: A New Latin Documentary Papyrus Containing a List

Not included among the Latin documentary papyri from Italy edited by Jan Olof Tjäder, this papyrus was (re)discovered in 2001 in a drawer of the Civic Museums of Vicenza. Announced to the scientific community some years later,[61] it was presented and discussed for the first time at a conference in Seville.[62] The fragment is currently housed at the Istituto papirologico "Girolamo Vitelli" in Florence, where it has been restored and is waiting to be returned to the Museums of Vicenza. An edition of the papyrus and commentary are forthcoming in a publication authored by myself, Teresa De Robertis, and Stefano Zamponi, which will be published in the editorial series of the Istituto Vitelli.

The size of the papyrus fragment is 24.5 × 30.0 cm, with this current width possibly not be so different from the original. The papyrus is badly damaged, in particular on the left and right edges, and the lower edge seems to have been cut clean. Moreover, there are three holes in the

---

55   A famous example is that of ChLA XXVI 808, the *Breve de moniminas* (*monimen/munimen* is attested in the meaning of a valid legal document in the Italian papyri: P.Ital. 2 31, col. iii, l. 8 [540 CE]), which contains a list of ninety-nine documents and some valuables written on parchment between March 763 and July 769 in Pisa for (or on behalf of) the Lombard bishop Domnucianus. For new insights and a fresh approach to this text in terms of commentary and critical edition, see Ghignoli 2004, 38–69. Further comments about this *breve* can be found in Brown et al. 2013, 1, 234, 241, 248, 263, 275, however these are based on false elements provided by the previous editions of Luigi Schiaparelli and Jan Olof Tjäder.

56   The term appears with this meaning at least twelve times, according to the results of a query in TM (made on 05.24.20). For more details about the percentage of *gnôsis* and *brevium* attested, see Clarysse 2020, 114.

57   For instance: P.Herm. 23 (TM 33475 [IV CE], a list of food products), CPR IX 68 (TM 35335 [V CE], a list of expenses), and SB XVIII 13266 (TM 36293 [VI–VII CE], a list of accounts).

58   Bloch 2020, 92.

59   On the use of parchment from the eighth century CE in Lombard Italy see Internullo 2019a, 540.

60   Some seventh to eighth-century examples are ChLA XVIII 659 and ChLA XLVII 1404, 1405.

61   De Robertis 2004, 232, n. 32.

62   De Robertis, Ghignoli, and Zamponi 2018.

middle of the sheet, and many fibers have been removed on the upper side. There are twenty-two lines of text written across the fibers preserved, but the first two of these are almost completely illegible. There is no visible *kollēsis* and the verso is blank.

The Latin text is written in a fluent "nouvelle écriture commune" according to the definition of Jean Mallon; that is, it is written in the script commonly known as later Roman cursive. On palaeographic grounds, it dates to the sixth century CE, and certainly to a period not later than the seventh decade of the century. The mention of *curial(es) Panhormitani* at line 17 it is not sufficient to prove the Sicilian provenance of the papyrus, but it does demonstrate its Italian provenance and confirms the impression gained from palaeographical analysis.

The fragment contains the final part of a list arranged in one column, wherein each writing line corresponds to one item in the list. The list consists of twenty-two items, with each containing the summary of the content of a document or a description of documentary material. It is clear that the list was originally designed to be composed of two different sections from two elements: the presence (or the absence) of a numeral at the beginning of the text string of the item and the textual structure of the item.

In the first section, which includes the first twenty lines corresponding to the first twenty items, there is a numeral in sequential order at the beginning of each line; it is followed by a blank space before the beginning of the text of the item, which consists of the summary (more or less detailed) of a written documentary record. The last item of this part is marked by the numeral "xxv" (l. 20). Since twenty lines are preserved and marked by legible or illegible numerals, we can be certain that the upper part of the fragment contained at least a further five lines containing the first five items of this section of the list.

The second section can be observed in the last two lines corresponding to the last two items (ll. 21–22). There is no numeral at the beginning, but an evident blank space, so that the beginning of the text of the first item falls almost exactly under the starting point of the text of the last item of the first section placed on the line above. The same happens for the second and last item. The result is that the items of the second section are perfectly aligned with the ones placed above belonging to the first section. An elegant and distinctive (in terms of size) initial letter *f* of the first word marks the beginning of the two final items (Fig. 6.2).

In both instances the text consists of the vague description (or so it seems) of "documentary" material. The transcription of the last three lines (ll. 20–22) preserved in the fragment reads as follows:

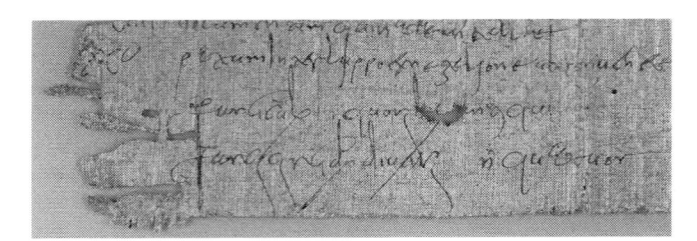

FIGURE 6.2   P. Vic., showing the initial part of lines 20–22
IMAGE COURTESY OF TERESA DE ROBERTIS,
ANTONELLA GHIGNOLI, AND STEFANO ZAMPONI

xxv pactum inter Luppo et Negelione ubi conuenet eis ut fratres ement
    Fascicul(us) in quo s(unt) br(eues) antiqui
    Fasc(iculi) scid(arum) diuers(arum) n(umero) quattuor[63]

xxv Agreement between Lupus and Negelio, in order to buy as brothers.
    A bundle, in which are old returns;
    bundles of diverse official drafts: four, in total.[64]

As we have seen, investigating texts that appear to have the form of a list involves some peculiar difficulties in addition to the usual ones encountered in editing documentary papyri. The original context, the function, and (sometimes) the content itself are nearly always a matter of guesswork. The hands that wrote them nearly always remain unknown, and the same can be said about their recipients and the purposes for which those texts were created. This is true even in the case of documentary papyri from Graeco-Roman and late antique Egypt, where it is easier to suggest institutional or personal contexts despite (or thanks to) the fact that the evidence consists of thousands of fragments. Therefore, in this research context it is possible to investigate texts preserved in the form of lists,

---

63   The reading of the first word of the last line is *fascc* with a sign of abbreviation for each letter *c*; it can be interpreted as a suspension with a double final consonant, marked by a double sign of abbreviation, meaning the plural of the word: *fasc(iculi)*. It is possible to read the second *c* with sign as an independent abbreviated word: *c(um)*; in this case the transcription would be *fasc-(iculi) c(um) scid(is) diuers(is)*.

64   The linguistic features of the late Latin attested in the fragment may justify other translations (in particular for l. 20): these are all discussed in the forthcoming publication on P.Vic. announced above. According to my interpretation, the clearly visible *vacat* on line 22 between *diuers(arum)/diuers(is)* and *n(umero)* performs the function of communicating that *quattuor* is the total amount of all the bundles mentioned in the second section of the list (ll. 21–22), and not of the *fasc(iculi)* mentioned only at line 22.

also taking into account the external elements illustrated above.

The situation is completely different for the late antique West, where the number of documentary papyri is extremely limited. Among the fifty-nine Latin documentary papyri of Italy edited by Tjäder, only seven fragments contain a list: P.Ital. 1 1 (TM 114798 [September 445–September 446 CE]), P.Ital. 2 47–48 (TM 114845 [first half VI CE, certainly after 510]), P.Ital. 1 3 (TM 382974 [mid-VI CE]), P. Ital. 1 8 (TM 114801 [July 564 CE]), P.Ital. 1 2 (TM 382976 [November 565–August 570 CE]), P. Ital. 2 50, 1 (TM 383097 [590–604 CE]), and P.Ital. 2 53 (TM 783442 [second half VIII CE]).[65]

P. Ital. 1 1, P.Ital. 1 2, and P.Ital. 1 3 do not offer a comparative basis from which to understand P.Vic., because their "lists" are basically in tabular format. In all three cases fiscal matters and the management of landed properties are involved, directly or indirectly, and in all three cases it is very likely that the scribe (i.e., the scribe of the original text in the event they are transmitted in copy) took the "tables" from a "register" that was produced and held either by offices or by a private landowner and existed in the form of a roll or codex.[66] Thus they must

be approached via a critical comparison with the use of tables and similar schemes attested in the documentary papyri from Egypt and somehow related to the various Roman administrative milieux.

Another example, P. Ital. 1 8, does not help, because it is an official *gesta municipalia* protocol, which does not preserve the original layout of one *breue* and two *notitiae* (copied respectively at col. ii, ll. 4–10, col. ii, ll. 11–14, and col. ii, l. 14–col. iii, l. 3) inserted in it with a *chartula plenariae securitatis*. Nor does P. Ital. 2 50, 1 help either. A beautiful example of the continuity of the list in *notitia*-shape mentioned above, it is a list of holy oils brought from the tombs of martyrs in Rome to the Lombard queen Theodelinda in Monza by a certain Johannes in the time of pope Gregory the Great. The text is written on a single papyrus sheet (32.0 × 24.5 cm). After the "title" written on the first long line announcing the list (*Notitia de olea sanctorum martyrum, qui Romae in corpore requiescunt, id est*), the list is arranged in a two-column table. The left-hand column contains a copy of the text of the labels attached to the ampules (i.e., the authentication of the relics); written on single small pieces of papyrus, some are even preserved in the original. The right-hand column contains the list of the corresponding names of the martyrs to whose tombs the oils belonged. Between the two columns there is a long line representing perhaps a stylized spray of vine. Under the last item of the right-hand column containing the list of names, there is a final short declaration, which represents a kind of dated subscription: *Quas olea sancta temporibus domni Gregorii pape adduxit Iohannis indignus et peccator domnae Theodelindae reginae de Roma.*

Only P.Ital. 2 47–48 and P.Ital. 2 53 present a structure similar to that of P.Vic. in two important aspects. In all three the list is arranged in one column, with each item written one below the other in a single writing line. The writing line is relatively long as regards the width of the papyrus sheet, because items consist of relatively long text strings.

P.Ital. 2 53 cannot tell us any more than that, however, because it is a fragment in which only four very

---

65   Here I differ slightly from Internullo 2019b, 657 regarding the selected evidence and the idea that "inventories and lists" can be *a priori* classified as a distinct "type of document" outside the peculiar context of an edition.

66   P.Ital. 1 1 (one sheet, fragment) contains the copy of three letters issued by Lauricius, *praepositus sacri cubiculi*, about his private asset in Sicily (a *commonitorium* and two letters of recommendation) and a list (ll. 57–83) compiled in a two-column table (names of *fundi* and *massae*; payments to be due) not perfectly arranged, probably because the copyist disregarded the original alignment of the model. The reason for the creation of this dossier is unclear. According to Tjäder, it is likely that it was created immediately after the original letters, and therefore the date of the papyrus lies somewhere between September 445 and September 446. Tjäder judged only a final annotation (ll. 81–85) to be original and not the result of a copy: see Tjäder 1955, 169–73. P.Ital. 1 2 (one sheet, fragment) contains a copy of a *gesta municipalia* protocol about a debate held before the *exarchus* of Ravenna between November 565 and August 570, about the *patrimonium* that once belonged to the Arian church of Ravenna and was later donated to the Catholic church by the emperor Justinian; lines 1 to 13 contain the final part of a well-arranged two-column table (containing the names of the properties, related incomes, and the final amounts due in taxes). It is certainly the final part of a series of tables, according to the declaration made by Honorius, the accounts officer of the *scrinium suburbicarium et canonum*, reported in the following lines, who declares, with regard to the tables, that he had presented *notitias: Secundum iussionem praecelse potestatis vestrae ostidimus notitias superius positas* (l. 16). Tjäder's translation of the passage is "die oben stehenden Tabellen" (1955, 183). The fragment is evidently a copy written by a notary of the Church of Ravenna not long after the original protocol: Tjäder 1955, 181. P.Ital. 1 3 is

a fragment of a papyrus roll on which the text was written in ten columns along the fibers (perhaps an original *gesta* protocol); only two columns are preserved. Each contains a multi-column table in which are recorded rents in produce and in money related to landed properties. In the second column, the table alternates with a short text written on the line. For commentary, see Tjäder 1955, 185–87. For the purpose of this investigation, the most striking features are the disordered way in which the tables are arranged and the number of mistakes and corrections made by the scribe when writing the items, as though he were copying data arranged in a way that was too complicated for him to transcribe.

badly damaged lines (the beginning of each is lost) are preserved, and because this list's four items are descriptions of ecclesiastical textiles that probably belonged to a church in Northern Italy.[67] P. Ital. 2 47–48, instead, is helpful in investigating P.Vic., but only because forty-two of the forty-four preserved items are summaries of the content of documents. We can compare the structure of the summary in both cases in order to frame a possibly widespread use in summarizing documentary records. As a result, it is possible to identify constants or variables by comparing syntax and terminology and taking into account the stage of documentary Latin in the sixth century CE. For example:

> P.Vic., l. 18: *XXIII Cauti<o> greca ad nome(n) Theopinti solid[o]r(um) decem et septem*
>
> P. Ital. 2 47–48, A, l. 27: *Cautio greca Pauli facta ad nomen Petri solidorum numero C[...] Venanti[o] consule*

P. Ital. 2 47–48 consists of two different papyrus fragments (A and B) preserved in two different places. They were not originally contiguous, but probably belonged to the same roll, according to the masterly commentary of Tjäder.[68] This papyrus is a very problematic source. In his edition, Tjäder entitled the document "Inventar eines Archivs," but in his dense commentary he explained that "es sich kaum um ein ordentliches Inventar handeln kann."[69] The original context, function, and nature of this text remain unsolved, for the two lists preserved in the two different fragments are very different from each other as regards the type of documents they summarize.[70] Perhaps only one fact is certain: the documents listed in the two different fragments seem somehow connected to the administrative activity (understood in a broad sense and in terms of both incoming and outgoing documents) either of the *arcarius* of the *praefectus praetorio per Italiam* or of his officials. Any other confident characterization of P.Ital. 2 47–48 is based on a superficial reading of the sources.[71]

Comparing the textual structure of the items of P.Vic. and P.Ital. 2 47–48 is important, but not sufficient for the main issue that both sources raise. How was the text string of each item written? Was it composed by the lists' scribes (or, more probably, by the person dictating) by reading the documents to be listed and summarized, or was it composed by copying the docket already attached to the documents or the dorsal note written on the verso? This is not a philological issue, pure and simple. It is a question of our being able to capture the viewpoint of the "author" of these microtexts, and consequently to suggest a provenance for the documents listed, in order to form a hypothesis about the provenance and the destination of the list itself.

The Italian documentary papyri did not preserve any dorsal notes on the verso, and this can be explained by the fact that none is preserved in its entirety.[72] The only Latin examples we have are preserved in the *Tablettes Albertini*, where Latin dorsal notes summarize the Latin acts contained on the polyptych's interior surfaces,[73] so that a comparison with the structure of these texts is possible. Dorsal notes are well attested, instead, in the documentary tradition of late Roman Egypt, and what we learn from an analysis of their scribe's "point of view" (as we have briefly seen, for example, above with the dorsal note of P.Lips. I 123) is decisive in the same way as (or, perhaps, more decisive than) the notes on the *Tablettes*.

The first section of the list in P.Vic. is characterized, as we have seen, by the presence of a numeral at the beginning of each line. Both fragments (A and B) of P.Ital. 2 47–48 are damaged on the left side, where 2 cm of papyrus is missing.[74] All the same, it is unlikely that this space was sufficient to host both the necessary free area before the beginning of the writing and the space for a numeral, which must have consisted of more than one alphabetic character. Therefore, this feature of P.Vic. represents a hapax within the Western late antique documentary tradition in the Latin language.

It is necessary to ascertain whether numbered lists comparable with P.Vic. are preserved among Greek papyri fragments from late Roman Egypt, and the examination of the sources is still ongoing. Nevertheless, from the lists preserved in that documentary tradition we learn that if a list serves as a written step in procedures employed by a

---

67   Already published by Tjäder (P.Ital. 2 53) and by Bruckner (ChLA I 1b), the papyrus has been recently edited again and commented by Internullo 2020, 252–57.

68   Tjäder 1982, 186–90.

69   Tjäder 1982, 188.

70   And given the fact that in each list fragment there is one item that is not the summary of a document but the description of "found objects," though containing written records: P.Ital. 2 47–48 A, l. 12, *chartarium ... quod ... inibi inventum est*; P.Ital. 2 47–48 B, l. 11, *cista in qua invente sunt*; Tjäder 1982, 188.

71   Everett 2013, 75: "A glimpse at the fragments of Ravenna's praetorian prefect's archive—or more precisely, an archival index."

72   Only two dorsal notes are preserved (in P.Ital. 2 35 and P.Ital. 2 37). Containing few legible words, they are both unpublished; Internullo 2019, 544, n. 42.

73   For example, T. Alb. 7 (tablet 14a): *instrumentum Uictorini Nugualis de dibersas loca*. On the function of the dorsal notes in the Albertini Tablets, see Conant 2004, 215.

74   Tjäder 1982, 186.

particularly well-organized milieu, then it is more likely to include as a final item an indication of the amount of the listed objects. In view of this, the series of numerals in the first section of P.Vic. is an economical system to successfully communicate an amount without adding a further line to the list.

Last of all, another external feature of P.Vic. has not yet been mentioned but is equally characteristic and important: the presence of two Christian graphic symbols. The first staurogram is drawn at the end of line 20, containing the last item of the first section of the list. It is written in ligature with the final letter *t* of the final word of the item, *ement*. The second is drawn at the end of line 22 containing the last item preserved of the second section of the list. Also in this case, the graphic symbol is written in ligature with the final letter *r* of the final word of the item, *quattuor* (Figs. 6.3 and 6.4).

Thanks to the evidence of the documentary papyri of late Roman Egypt, which attest the use of such graphic symbols as signs to mark the beginning and/or the end of a textual unit,[75] we can assume the same function for the staurograms of P.Vic., and we can conclude that what we have called the "first" and "second" sections of the list were both actually considered by the scribe as "completed" and therefore "closed" parts of the text. Along the lower edge of the fragment there are the remains of a lost written line: two visible small traces, both probably traces of a vertical stroke. The first trace is placed almost at the beginning of the edge, exactly corresponding with the letter "v" of the numeral "xxv" above, on the third-to-last line of the fragment. The second trace is placed under the letter "a" of the word "quattuor" in the last line of the fragment (Fig. 6.4). This means that the list preserved in P.Vic. is a part of a whole.

What kind of document it was, where, when, how, and why it was written are entirely matters of guesswork, for now. To address this, only an extensive and complex commentary can provide the necessary basis, with a painstaking exposition of clues and arguments. The forthcoming edition of the papyrus and commentary mentioned above will therefore supplement the initial findings offered here.

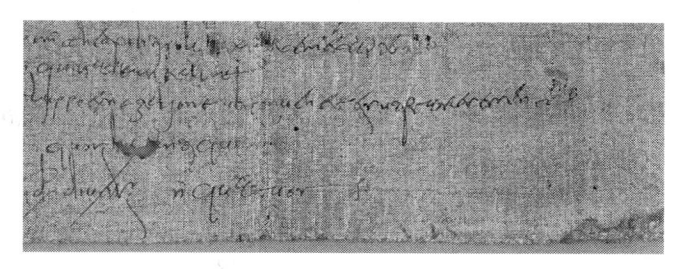

FIGURE 6.3 P. Vic., showing the final part of lines 20–22
IMAGE COURTESY OF TERESA DE ROBERTIS,
ANTONELLA GHIGNOLI, AND STEFANO ZAMPONI

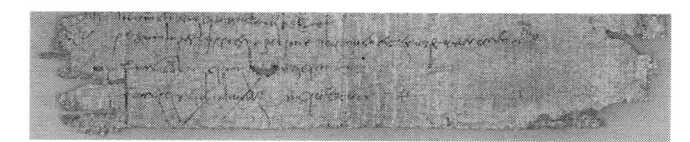

FIGURE 6.4 P. Vic., showing the last three lines (ll. 20–22)
IMAGE COURTESY OF TERESA DE ROBERTIS,
ANTONELLA GHIGNOLI, AND STEFANO ZAMPONI

Reference List

Amory, Yasmine. 2023. "Usi intratestuali dei simboli cristiani nei papiri documentari di epoca bizantina ed araba." In *Segni, sogni, materie e scrittura dall'Egitto tardoantico all'Europa carolingia*, edited by Antonella Ghignoli, Maria Boccuzzi, Anna Monte, and Nina Sietis, in press. Rome: Edizioni di Storia e Letteratura.

Bentein, Klaas, and Yasmine Amory. 2019. "Everyday Writing in Graeco-Roman and Late Antique Egypt: Outline of a New Research Programme." *Comparative Oriental Manuscript Studies Bulletin* 5, no. 1: 17–28.

Bloch, Marc. 2020. *Apologie pour l'histoire ou Métier d'historien*. Annotated edition by Étienne Bloch. Malakoff: Dunod.

Brown, Warren C., Marios Costambeys, Matthew Innes, and Adam J. Kosto, eds. 2013. *Documentary Culture and the Laity in the Early Middle Ages*. Cambridge: Cambridge University Press.

Cameron, Averil. 2015. "Christian Conversion in Late Antiquity: Some Issues." In *Conversion in Late Antiquity: Christianity, Islam and Beyond. Papers from the Andrew W. Mellon Foundation Sawyer Seminar, University of Oxford, 2009–2010*, edited by Arietta Papaconstantinou, Neil McLynn, and Daniel L. Schwartz, 3–21. Farnham: Ashgate.

Carlig, Nathan. 2020. "Les symboles chrétiens dans les papyrus littéraires et documentaires grecs: forme, disposition et fonction (IIIe–VIIe/VIIIe siècles)." In *Signes dans les textes. Continuités et ruptures des pratiques scribales en Égypte pharaonique, gréco-romaine et byzantines. Actes du colloque international di Liège (2–4 Juin 2016)*, edited by Nathan Carlig, Guillaume Lescuyere, Aurore Motte, and Nathalie Sojic,

---

75 On lists, see, for example, the case of P. Vindob. G 19611 mentioned above. For a short overview, see Carlig 2020; for a more detailed study on specific Greek documents, see Amory 2023. Investigating these kinds of graphic symbols in the *longue durée* and in a wider documentary context than that of the Egyptian papyri represents one of the objectives of the ERC project NOTAE.

271–81. Collection Papyrologica Leodiensia, 9. Liège: Presses universitaires de Liège.

Cavallo, Guglielmo. 2009. "Greek and Latin Writing in the Papyri." In *The Oxford Handbook of Papyrology*, edited by Roger S. Bagnall, 101–48. Oxford: Oxford University Press.

Cenati, Chiara, Giorgio Crimi, Silvia De Martini, and Davide Redaelli. 2017. "Laterculi praetorianorum *rivisti e corretti*," poster presented at the 15th International Congress of Greek and Latin Epigraphy: Languages—Culture of Writing—Identities in Antiquity, Vienna, August 28–September 1, 2017, available at <https://www.academia.edu/43166132/Laterculi _praetorianorum_rivisti_e_corretti_Poster_presented_at _the_XVth_International_Congress_of_Greek_and_Latin _Epigraphy_Languages_Culture_of_Writing_Identities_in _Antiquity_Vienna_28th_August_1st_September_2017_>.

Clarysse, Willy. 2020. "Headers for Lists and Accounts in Ancient Documents and in Modern Editions." In *Accounts and Bookkeeping in the Ancient World*, edited by Andrea Jördens and Uri Yftach, 109–21. Philippika, 55/2. Wiesbaden: Harrassovitz.

Classen, Peter. 1977a. *Kaiserreskript und Königsurkunden*. Thessaloniki: Kentron byzantinon ereunon.

Classen, Peter. 1977b. "Fortleben und Wandel spätrömischen Urkundenwesens im Frühmittelalter." In *Recht und Schrift im Mittelalter*, edited by Peter Classen, 13–54. Sigmaringen: Thorbecke.

Conant, Jonathan P. 2004. "Literacy and Private Documentation in Vandal North Africa: The Case of the Albertini Tablets." In *Vandals, Romans, and Berbers: New Perspectives on Late Antique North Africa*, edited by Andrew H. Merrills, 199–224. Aldershot: Ashgate.

De Robertis, Teresa. 2004. "La scrittura romana." *Archiv für Diplomatik* 50: 221–46.

De Robertis, Teresa, Antonella Ghignoli, and Stefano Zamponi. 2018. "Un nuovo papiro latino del VI secolo." In *De la herencia romana a la procesal castellana. Diez siglos de cursividad. Actas del IV Encuentro Internacional del Seminario permanente "Escrituras cursivas,"* edited by Carmen Del Camino Martínez, 11–28. Seville: Editorial Universidad de Sevilla.

Di Paola, Lucietta. 2000. "Sull'uso dei breves nell'amministrazione romana tardoantica." In *Il Tardoantico alle soglie del Duemila. Diritto, religione, società*, edited by Giuliana Lanata, 189–204. Pisa: ETS.

Everett, Nicholas. 2013. "Lay Documents and Archives in Early Medieval Spain and Italy, c. 400–700." In *Documentary Culture and the Laity in the Early Middle Ages*, edited by Warren C. Brown, Marios Costambeys, Matthew Innes, and Adam J. Kosto, 63–94. Cambridge: Cambridge University Press.

Gascou, Jean. 1989. "Les codices documentaires égyptiens." In *Les débuts du codex*, edited by Alain Blanchard, 71–101. Bibliologia, 9. Turnhout: Brepols.

Ghignoli, Antonella. 2004. "Su due famosi documenti pisani dell'VIII secolo." *Bullettino dell'Istituto storico italiano per il medio evo* 106, no. 2: 1–69.

Ghignoli, Antonella. 2009. "Koinè, influenze, importazioni transalpine nella documentazione 'privata' dei secoli VII–VIII: lo stato dell'arte." In *Le Alpi porta d'Europa. Scritture, uomini, idee da Giustiniano al Barbarossa*, edited by Laura Pani and Cesare Scalon, 83–110. Spoleto: CISAM.

Ghignoli, Antonella, and François Bougard. 2011. "Elementi romani nei documenti longobardi?" In *L'héritage byzantin en Italie (VIIIe–XIIe siècle). I. La fabrique documentaire*, edited by Jean-Marie Martin, Annick Peters-Custot, and Vivien Prigent, 241–301. Rome: École française de Rome.

Goody, Jack. 1977. *The Domestication of the Savage Mind*. Cambridge: Cambridge University Press.

Internullo, Dario. 2019a. "Du papyrus au parchemin. Les origines médiévales de la mémoire archivistique en Europe occidentale." *Annales. Histoire, Sciences Sociales* 74, nos. 3/4: 523–57.

Internullo, Dario. 2019b. "Latin Documents Written on Papyrus in the Late Antique and Early Medieval West (5th–11th century): An Overview." In *Proceedings of the 28th Congress of Papyrology, Barcelona 1–6 August 2016*, edited by Alberto Nodar and Sofía Torallas Tovar, 654–63. Barcelona: Publicacions de l'Abadia de Montserrat.

Internullo, Dario. 2020. "58. Inventory of Church Textiles (P. Bas. inv. 1 C+B verso)." In *Papyri of the University Library of Basel (P.Bas. II)*, edited by Sabine Hübner, W. Graham Claytor, Isabelle Marthot-Santaniello, and Martin Müller, 252–57. Berlin: De Gruyter.

Iovine, Giulio. 2019. "*Data epistula*: Later Additions of Latin Dating Formulae in Latin and Greek Papyri and Ostraka from the First to the Sixth Centuries AD." *Manuscripta: A Journal for Manuscript Research* 63, no. 2: 157–230.

Kruse, Thomas. 2014. "Archives and Registration in Roman Egypt." In *Law and Legal Practice in Egypt from Alexander to the Arab Conquest*, edited by James G. Keenan, Joseph Gilbert Manning, and Uri Yiftach-Firanko, 62–83. Cambridge: Cambridge University Press.

Jones, Arnold Hugh Martin. 1964. *The Later Roman Empire 284–602: A Social Economic and Administrative Survey*. Norman: University of Oklahoma Press.

Loriol, Romain. 2020. "La liste comme forme-savoir. Ou comment lire une liste antique?" In *Penser en listes dans le mondes grec et romain*, edited by Marie Ledentu and Romain Loriol, 15–48. Pessac: Ausonius.

Mitteis, Ludwig. 1906. *Griechiesche Urkunden der Papyrussamlung zu Leipzig*, vol. 1. Leipzig: Teubner.

Montevecchi, Orsolina. 2008. *La papirologia*. Milan: Vita e Pensiero.

Otranto, Rosa. 2000. *Antiche liste di libri su papiro*. Rome: Edizioni di Storia e Letteratura.

Palme, Bernhard. 2009. "The Range of Documentary Texts: Types and Categories." In *The Oxford Handbook of Papyrology*, edited by Roger S. Bagnall, 358–94. Oxford: Oxford University Press.

Papaconstantinou, Arietta. 1994. "Conversions monétaires byzantines. P. Vindob. G. 1265." *Tyche* 9: 93–98.

Parkes, Malcom Beckwith. 1992. *Pause and Effect: An Introduction to the History of Punctuation in the West*. Aldershot: Scolar Press.

Ricciardetto, Antonio. 2016. "Inventaire et typologie des listes grecques et latines de produits pharmaceutiques." In *Proceedings of the 27th International Congress of Papyrology, Warsaw 29 July–3 August 2013*, edited by Tomasz Derda, Adam Lajtar, and Jakub Urbanik, 677–98. The Journal of Juristic Papyrology, supplement, 28. Warsaw: Faculty of Law and Administration, University of Warsaw.

Rio, Alice. 2009. *Legal Practice and the Written Word in the Early Middle Ages: Frankish Formulae, c. 500–1000*. Cambridge: Cambridge University Press.

Rom, Brigitte, and Hermann Harrauer. 1983. "'Ο ΚΥΡΙΟΣ-Listen auf Papyrus." *Aegyptus* 63, n. 12: 111–15.

Salati, Ornella. 2020. *Scrivere documenti nell'esercito romno. L'evidenza dei papiri latini d'Egitto tra I e III d. C.* Philippika, 139. Wiesbaden: Harrassowitz Verlag.

Scholl, Reinhold. 2000. "Ein «Bibliotheksdirektor» und seine «Bibliothekare». Ein «Geschäftsgang» aus dem römischen Ägypten." In *Von Alexandrien nach Leipzig. Erschließung von Papyri und Handschriften in der Universitätsbibliothek*, edited by Reinhold Scholl, Günther Wartenberg, and Gerhard Karpp, 7–12. Schriften aus der Universitätsbibliothek Leipzig, 5. Leipzig: Universitätsbibliothek Leipzig.

Steinacker, Harold. (1927) 1977. *Die antiken Grundlagen der frühmittelalterichen Privaturkunden*. Leipzig: Teubner. Reprint, Hildesheim: Olms.

Tjäder, Jan-Olof. 1955. *Die nichtliterarischen lateinischen Papyri Italiens aus der Zeit 445–700. I. Papyri 1–28*. Lund: C. W. K. Gleerup.

Tjäder, Jan-Olof. 1982. *Die nichtliterarischen lateinischen Papyri Italiens aus der Zeit 445–700. II. Papyri 29–59*. Stockholm: Paul Åströms Förlag.

Wickham, Chris. 2005. *Framing the Early Middle Ages: Europe and the Mediterranean 400–800*. Oxford: Oxford University Press.

Worp, Klaas. 2013. "Greek von Scherling Papyri in Leiden." *BASP* 50: 15–38.

Zamponi, Stefano. 2021. "I papiri di Dura Europos nella storia della scrittura latina." In *Scribes and Presentation of Texts (from Antiquity to ca. 1550): Proceedings of the 20th Colloquium of the Comité International de Paléographie latine*, edited by Barbara A. Shailor and Consuelo W. Dutschke, 29–43. Bibliologia, 65. Turnhout: Brepols.

Zilliacus, Henrik, Jaakko Frösén, Paavo Hohti, Jorma Kaimio, and Maarit Kaimio, eds. 1979. *Corpus papyrorum Raineri archeducis Austriae VII. Griechische Texte IV*. Vienna: Brüder Hollinek.

PART 2

A Multi-Modal Approach to Ancient Sources

∴

The Textualization of Women's Letters from Roman Egypt: Analyzing Historical Framing Practices from a Multi-Modal Point of View

Klaas Bentein

Introduction*

The status and role of women in antiquity, as well as the social construction of gender, has become an expanding field of study since the 1970s, not only in classics, but also in related fields such as ancient history, archeology, and art history.[1] As most of our textual evidence originates from Egypt, particular attention has been paid to the position of women there. Studies have focused on places[2] and periods[3] that are specific to Egypt, but at the same time findings from Egypt have also been included in studies of women's relationship to broader societal topics, such as women and the law,[4] women as widows,[5] women and motherhood,[6] women and Christianity,[7] and women and education,[8] among others.

Scholars have also dedicated considerable energy to making available the textual corpora that we have: important sourcebooks were published by Mary Lefkowitz and Maureen Fant,[9] Jane Rowlandson,[10] and Roger Bagnall and Raffaella Cribiore.[11] In this chapter, I will engage in particular with Bagnall and Cribiore, a publication that goes beyond the traditional sourcebook in the sense that the authors also offer a concise commentary on the linguistic, paleographical, and material characteristics of each text, in order to compensate for the relatively little we know about the context of writing.[12] The book thus offers an important stepping stone for research into the *textualization* of women's letters; that is, the study of how consciousness and thought materialize into text.[13] Research of this type has a long tradition when it comes to literary texts with an oral background, such as the Homeric epics or the New Testament, but in the area of documentary culture has attracted relatively little attention so far.[14]

Bagnall and Cribiore most explicitly address questions of textualization in the introduction to their volume, where they make an argument for using late medieval letters as comparative evidence to alleviate the lack of context one is confronted with in Greco-Roman and late antique women's letters. They do not engage with modern scholarship in fields such as linguistics, semiotics, and communication theory, however, and *vice versa*, modern scholarship in these fields has hardly paid any attention to our subject. In this chapter, I want to argue that the consideration of insights and concepts developed in these fields has the potential to substantially enrich ongoing discussions. One concept I want to focus on is that of "framing."[15] Social semioticians such as Gunther Kress view *semiosis* (that which I referred to as consciousness and thought above) as an ongoing, endless activity, which can be materialized and actualized in particular social situations through texts belonging to various generic types ("textualized"). Frames in this context refer to "the formal semiotic resources which separate one semiotic entity

---

*   The research for this chapter was conducted within the ERC Starting Grant project EVWRIT ('Everyday writing in Graeco-Roman and Late Antique Egypt. A socio-semiotic study of communicative variation', PI Klaas Bentein), a project which has received funding from the European Research Council under the Horizon 2020 research and innovation programme (Grant Agreement No. 756487).

1   See, e.g., McClure 2001, 3; James and Dillon 2012, 1.

2   See, e.g., Wilfong 2002.

3   See, e.g., Pomeroy 1984 (Hellenistic); Salmenkivi 2017 (Roman); Fournet 2012 (late antique).

4   See, e.g., Arjava 1996.

5   See, e.g., Krause 1995.

6   See, e.g., Nifosi 2019.

7   See, e.g., Krawiec 2002.

8   See, e.g., Haines-Eitzen 2000.

9   Lefkowitz and Fant [1982] 2016.

10   Rowlandson 1998.

11   Bagnall and Cribiore 2006 (also see the expanded online edition from 2008).

12   Bagnall and Cribiore 2006, 25.

13   Ready 2019 distinguishes "textualization" from "entextualization," the latter referring to how an instance of discourse is made detachable from its original, local context (e.g., how the Homeric epics took shape, independently from medial considerations).

14   Scholarly attention has mostly focused on scribes and dictation. See, e.g., Verhoogt 2009; Evans 2012; Halla-aho 2018.

15   The notion "frame" has had a long history in a broad range of fields, including philosophy, psychology, sociology, artificial intelligence, narratology, and linguistics, without there being a "unified frame theory with specific terms and definitions" (Bednarek 2005, 688). Space does not permit extensive discussion here. For a good introduction, see, e.g., MacLachlan and Reid 1994.

from its environment "pre-frame" or from other semiotic entities";[16] by doing so, they provide unity and coherence to what is framed, and guide and enable interpretation by the reader.[17]

This chapter is structured as follows: after more extensively discussing the concept of framing and its relationship to central terms such as "textualization" and "literacy/orality" (§ 1), I present different types of framing practices in women's letters (§ 2), distinguishing between documents with "maximal" vs. "minimal" discourse planning. Rather than maintaining a strict separation between these two types, I argue that they are best viewed in terms of a continuum (§ 3). I conclude the chapter by discussing the relationship between textualization and social context (§ 4), drawing attention to differences in communicative functions. Rather than analyzing the entire corpus of women's letters, I focus on texts from the Roman period (I–III CE), the period from which most of our letters stem.[18]

1 Textualization and Discourse Planning

Previous scholarship has suggested that written texts could come about in a variety of ways in antiquity. For example, situating the composition and writing of St. Paul's letters in the broader context of first-century letter writing, Ernest Richards suggested that secretaries could take on various roles, including that of transcriber, contributor, or composer.[19] A similar conception underlies Bagnall and Cribiore's work, where three main scenarios are suggested for the coming into being of women's letters:[20] 1) a woman could provide a scribe with general directions on the matter she wanted to communicate, not participating in the writing event herself; 2) a woman could dictate a letter to a professional scribe or member of the family, adding the final salutation and perhaps also the date herself; and

3) when she had an education, was able to write with a certain ease, and thought the circumstances justified it, a woman might decide to write the letter herself.

Bagnall and Cribiore's approach is explicitly oriented towards the medial process of committing thought/ speech to paper (*Verschriftung*), focusing as it does on who did the writing. The (complementary) approach that I want to develop in this chapter is instead focused more on the conceptual mechanisms that make a document a *text* (*Verschriftlichung*).[21] This means closely investigating the linguistic and typographic[22] features that characterize those texts, and more generally looking at the different types of textuality that are attested.

An interesting starting point in regard to those different types of textuality is the ever-growing scholarship on orality and literacy: whereas previously orality was strictly related to the medium of communication, more recently scholars have argued for a distinction between "medial" and "conceptual" orality. Particularly well-known in this regard is the work of Peter Koch and Wulf Oesterreicher, who consider conceptual orality in terms of a continuum, ranging from informal/oral on the one hand to formal/ literate on the other. They characterize these two poles (known as "Sprache der Nähe" and "Sprache der Distanz" respectively) in terms of an open-ended set of emotive and situational dichotomies, such as private vs. public, dialogue vs. monologue, spontaneity vs. reflection, and involvement vs. detachment.[23] In what follows, I would like to add depth and breadth to the discussion, by suggesting 1) that conceptual orality and literacy need not be limited to language (§ 1.1), and 2) that types of discourse are best studied by taking into account relevant communicative functions, categories, and levels (§§ 1.2–3).

1.1 Extending Conceptions of Orality and Literacy

A conceptual distinction between orality and literacy need not be confined to language: other semiotic resources[24] ("codes") also form an inherent part of textuality, and can, therefore, be included in the discussion. This seems to be recognized by Koch and Oesterreicher, who place text types on a horizontal continuum ranging from "Konzeption gesprochen" to "Konzeption geschrieben," also acknowledging that these two types can be further

---

16 Kress 2010, 149.

17 Compare the physical frames around paintings.

18 There are about 170 Greek letters from this period. Some of the letters discussed here were not included in Bagnall and Cribiore 2006, or the 2008 online edition of that volume: new letters have been edited since then, and some letters also seem to have been overlooked. Not included in the present study are letters where it is uncertain whether the sender is female, either because of the state of preservation (e.g., Ἰσιδώρα in SB VI 9165 [1–50 CE]) or the status of the name as male or female (e.g., Αὐνῆν in P.Louvre I 67, l. 2 [275–299 CE]). Also not included are party invitations by women (e.g., P.Coll.Youtie I 52 [II–III CE]), which are rather short and stereotypical.

19 Richards 2004, 56–67.

20 Cf. Huebner 2018, 165.

21 For *Verschriftung* and *Verschriftlichung*, see, e.g., Oesterreicher 1993.

22 I use "typography" here in a broad sense (and following Sue Walker) "to refer to the visual organization of written language in whatever way it is produced" (2001, 2).

23 See, e.g., Oesterreicher 1993, 269–70; Koch and Oesterreicher 2007, 351.

24 For the notion of "semiotic resource," see, e.g., Kress 2010, 5–8.

classified as having either a graphic code or phonic code.[25] In an earlier discussion, Oesterreicher had already noted that the written production of so-called "Schreibnovizen" clearly illustrates the conceptual continuum of graphic realization:

> Wenn wir uns für einen Augenblick einmal allein dem konzeptionellen Kontinuum in graphischer Realisierung zuwenden, so zeigt uns die Textproduktion der sogenannten Schreibnovizen, also ungeübter oder ungebildeter Schreiber, mit großer Klarheit, in welchen Punkten von ihnen die Möglichkeiten der Schriftkommunikation nicht genutzt werden (können). In ihren Texten erfüllen sie nicht oder nur mangehalft die Anforderungen einer distanzsprachlichen Schriftkommunikation.[26]

Such a continuum approach towards the graphic code fits in nicely with paleographical observations regarding documentary sources from antiquity. Bagnall and Cribiore, for example, recognize three types of handwriting, called "documentary" (rapid, ligatured), "secretarial" (legible, well-spaced), and "personal" (lack of expertise).[27] They argue that these three types form a continuum, ranging from very experienced to very inexperienced. A similar argument was made by Alan Mugridge,[28] who assigns Greek handwriting from the fourth century BCE to the fourth century CE to two spectra, one of *writing* ("book" hand vs. "documentary" hand) and one of *writers* ("professional" vs. "non-professional"). With regard to the latter, he notes that "it would seem fair to posit a spectrum between the most regular work of a professional scribe and the most irregular work of an ordinary writer."[29]

Oesterreicher relates graphic properties to the notion of "Sprache der Distanz"; for example, when he refers to "die anforderungen einer distanzsprachlichen schriftkommunikation." Since I find this terminology somewhat vague and ambiguous, especially when it comes to typographic properties, I will refer to *planned* vs. *unplanned* discourse instead, following an earlier proposal by Elinor Ochs.[30] In her formulation, planned discourse "has been thought out and organized (designed) prior to its expression," whereas unplanned discourse "lacks forethought and organizational preparation."[31] Ochs explicitly notes that

the distinction should be thought of as a continuum, and that "most of the discourse we encounter in the course of day-to-day communications falls at neither extreme. We usually find ourselves producing and listening to language that is relatively unplanned or relatively planned."[32]

1.2 Communicative Functions and Systems

As Ochs notes, it would be somewhat simplistic to refer to planned vs. unplanned discourse without further qualification, as "to characterize a discourse simply as planned or unplanned underrates the social behavior carried out and the breadth of planning demanded in particular situations."[33] Ochs therefore proposes to refine her observations by distinguishing between two categories, called the "referential" function of language (the use of language to refer and to predicate), and the "non-referential" function of language.

A similar argument has been made in Systemic Functional Linguistics, where it is claimed that language serves three major functions: ideational (construing our experience of the world and our consciousness; e.g., "pen" = instrument for writing), textual (organizing discourse and creating continuity and flow in texts; e.g., "I love music, so I will go to the festival," with *so* indicating a consequential relationship between two clauses), and interpersonal (enacting personal and social relations; e.g., "I might go," with *might* indicating the probability of realization). Social semioticians have argued that the same three functions are relevant for other semiotic resources, too. A groundbreaking study in this regard was Kress and Theo van Leeuwen's *Reading Images: The Grammar of Visual Design*,[34] a book that intended to set out a "grammar" of the meaning-making possibilities available in visual-based communicative artifacts. Kress and van Leeuwen did so by discussing the systems of choice available for each of these three functions, recognizing, for example, for the textual function, the systems of "information value," "salience," and "framing."

Whereas earlier studies viewed framing as specific to visual communication, more recent scholarship has come to realize that framing is essential to meaning making in all *modes*, not only linguistic but also visual. This extension of the concept is explicitly recognized by van Leeuwen when he writes that "in *Reading Images* (1996), Gunther Kress and I discussed framing as something specific to visual communication. Since then it has become

25   Koch and Oesterreicher 2007, 349.
26   Oesterreicher 1993, 280.
27   Bagnall and Cribiore 2006, 42–45.
28   Mugridge 2010.
29   Mugridge 2010, 580.
30   Ochs 1979.
31   Ochs 1979, 55.

32   Ochs 1979, 55.
33   Ochs 1979, 56.
34   Kress and van Leeuwen 1996.

clear to us that framing is a multimodal principle."[35] Fuller discussion of framing has been taken up by Kress in particular,[36] who underscores the importance of framing for meaning making in general. As noted in the introduction to this chapter, Kress relates framing to the materialization of semiosis, text representing "the focal formal unit of social-semiotic punctuation." Kress has raised a number of important issues in this regard, such as the extension of the concept of "intertextuality," the trade-off between semiotic resources in textualization, the specific kinds of textual framings that exist (at the level of the text and below), and the historical development of frames and framings, among others.

1.3   *Levels of Discourse*

Apart from relating planned and unplanned discourse to communicative functions and categories (such as the textual function and framing), it is also beneficial to relate it to distinct communicative levels. As is generally acknowledged, discourse does not come as an undivided whole: it is built up from smaller "building blocks" ("segments" or "chunks"), which together make up a coherent whole.[37] There is no consensus as to what the smallest building blocks look like, and how they are related to each other. In their discussion on the function of conjunctions, for example, Stanley Porter and Matthew O'Donnell, basing themselves on the Systemic Functional model, recognize at the smallest discourse level the conjoining of words, moving from there to the conjoining of word groups, clauses, clause complexes, paragraphs, and discourses.[38] Michel Buijs, on the other hand, in his discussion of clause combining in narrative, only recognizes three hierarchical levels, called the "development unit," "build up unit," and paragraph.[39]

Another problem surrounding discourse segmentation is the fact that it has often been seen as a purely linguistic phenomenon. As Anna Bonifazi and David Elmer recognize, however, "discourse marking is an inherently multi-modal activity, involving linguistic, para-linguistic, and extra-linguistic features."[40] The means by which discourse boundaries are created may reinforce each other, but this is not necessarily the case: as Bonifazi and Elmer again note, "they can often be at odds, creating expressive

tensions that complicate efforts to describe a single, unambiguous organizational scheme."[41]

When it comes to Ancient Greek, studies have mostly focused on prosody. Much less work has been done in the visual domain, for which we can turn to recent studies in multimodality, which have started to analyze compatibilities and mismatches between semiotic resources, language and typography in particular, and have also made an effort to distinguish relevant typographic units. Paul Thibault, for example, has proposed a "graphological" rank scale, on a par with a linguistic rank scale, distinguishing between as many as eight different levels.[42] For our present purposes, I will limit myself to distinguishing between three levels for both language and typography: units at each of these levels can be seen as a type of "framing,"[43] with their own framing features, as summarized in Table 7.1.

At the micro-level, the smallest linguistic unit of analysis (at least in this chapter) is the clause, whose relevant framing features include subordinating and coordinating conjunctions (particles). Typographically speaking, the relevant unit of analysis is not the clause but the line: framing features include word-splitting at the end of the line, line fillers, and the enlargement of letters. At the meso-level, thematic units are relevant and can be indicated by coordinating conjunctions, or by certain formulaic phrases. Corresponding to these thematic units from a typographical point of view are lay-out units; that is, the visual clustering of lines. Lay-out units are distinguishable by a number of typographical features, such as the use of blank spaces, alignment, and lectional signs. At the macro-level, we can recognize generic parts such as the "opening," "body," or "closing" of letters as the relevant unit of analysis. Such generic parts are typically introduced by formulaic phrases.

Corresponding to these generic parts from a typographical point of view are lay-out parts, the largest type of visual clustering below the level of the text as a whole. The features that effect such clustering are partly similar to those that indicate lay-out units. As can be seen in Table 7.1, I have also included "text" in its entirety under the macro-level: one could argue that formulaic phrases (especially initial ones) do not simply introduce a generic

---

35   van Leeuwen 2005, 14.
36   E.g., Kress 2000; 2004, 122–39; 2010, 149–54.
37   See, e.g., Ronald Langacker (2001), who proposes the notion of a "current discourse space," which is continually updated as expressions are encountered.
38   Porter and O'Donnell 2007, 8–9.
39   Buijs 2005, 139.
40   Bonifazi and Elmer 2012, 91.

41   Bonifazi and Elmer 2012, 91.
42   Thibault 2007.
43   I follow Wolf 2006 in restricting the term "frame" to abstract, conceptual entities (that is, elements of thought), and "framings" to the codings of those abstract entities. This is in contrast to Kress (2004, 122), who argues that frames can be both concrete and material (such as a full stop or semicolon) and intangible (such as social and cultural frames).

TABLE 7.1 Multi-modal discourse segmentation

	Language	Framing features	Typography	Framing features
Micro-level framing	Clause/sentence	E.g., particles, subordinating conjunctions	Line	E.g., line fillers, word splitting, enlargement of letters
Meso-level framing	Thematic unit	E.g., particles, formulaic phrases	Lay-out unit	E.g., blank space, alignment, lectional signs
Macro-level framing	Generic part	E.g., formulaic phrases	Lay-out part	E.g., blank space, alignment, lectional signs, indentation
	Text	E.g., formulaic phrases	Page	E.g., margins, material substrate

part, but also indicate that a document belongs to a generic type. The typographic equivalent would be the page, which is framed by elements such as the margins or the material substrate (a potsherd framing in a different way than a papyrus).[44]

Finally, although this proposed scheme covers many features, both linguistic and typographical,[45] it leaves out others, such as handwriting, lexical choice, and orthographic and morphological "correctness." Such features may be considered conceptually different for two reasons. First, they are more concerned with quality of execution than with the way thought is organized and are therefore less narrowly related to framing. Second, they concern levels of writing below the ones that are considered here, such as the grapheme, morpheme, and word.

2 Discourse Planning in Women's Letters

Having now established the analytical framework for multi-modal discourse segmentation, I can combine it with usage evidence drawn from our corpus. In the following, I will look first at maximal (§ 2.1) and then at minimal discourse planning (§ 2.2), considering the micro-level, meso-level, and macro-level for each, with further divisions in terms of language and typography.

2.1 *Maximal Discourse Planning*
2.1.1 The Micro-Level
Language. Asyndeton is avoided, and clauses/sentences are explicitly related through the use of various

particles,[46] particularly καί and δέ (additive relations), γάρ and οὖν (causal relations), and ἀλλά (adversative relations). Combinations of particles, well known from Classical Greek, are not unattested: they include καὶ γάρ, λοιπὸν οὖν, and διὸ οὖν, as well correlative particles such as οὔτε … οὔτε, μήτε … μήτε, and μέν … δέ. In a limited number of letters, rhetorically heavier combinations can be found, such as οὐ μόνον … ἀλλὰ καί (e.g., P.Ryl. II 243, ll. 4–5 [II CE]), πρῶτον μέν … ἔπειτα (e.g., P.Oxy. IX 1217, ll. 4–5 [III CE]), and τοίνυν (e.g., P.Flor. III 332, l. 14 [113–120 CE]).

Writers can integrate clauses more narrowly by opting for clause complexing[47] (adverbial subordination and complementation), rather than clause combining. The highest degree of clausal integration[48] in this regard is achieved through non-finite strategies: so, for example, conjunct participles are used rather than combining finite verbs, as in καλῶς οὖν ποιήσαντες | δότε (P.Oxy. I 116, ll. 5–6 [II CE]) "please give," or ἔρρωσο ἀσπαζόμενός μου λείαν τὰ | τέκνα (P.Princ. II 67, ll. 5–6 [I–II CE]) "farewell, greeting my children warmly" (trans. Bagnall and Cribiore). In a couple of letters, a series of conjunct participles is connected with the main verb, as in διὸ ἐρωτηθεὶς ἐκλαβὼν | ἀντίγραφον καὶ βαλὼν εἰς ἀγγῖον (l. ἀγγεῖον) | σφράγι[σ]ον (P.Gen. II 1, 74, ll. 8–10 [139–145 CE]) "therefore please take

---

44 See Torallas Tovar, this volume.
45 These features are discussed in Bagnall and Cribiore 2006.
46 My use of the term "particle" includes what some scholars call a "conjunction."
47 The terminology is that of Christian Matthiessen (2002), who distinguishes between clause combining (co-ordination), clause complexing (adverbial subordination/complementation), and clause embedding (relativization). I will not further go into clause embedding for reasons of space.
48 On degrees of clausal integration, see, e.g., Chafe 1985; Matthiessen 2002.

a copy, seal it and deposit it in a jar," where the imperative σφράγι[σ]ον is preceded by three aorist participles, the temporal order of which does not seem to be entirely straightforward.[49] A high degree of clausal integration can also be achieved through non-finite complementation: for example, writers sometimes use the polite καλῶς ποιέω as a complement-taking verb, rather than as a conjunct participle, as in καλῶς | πυήσις (l. ποιήσεις) τοῖς ἀναδιδουντί (l. ἀναδιδοῦσί) συ (l. σοι) ταῦτά μου τὰ γράμματα δοῦνε (l. δοῦναι) (P.Oxy. XIV 1773, ll. 16–18 [III CE]) "please give the people who deliver to you this letter of mine" (trans. Bagnall and Cribiore) or καλῶς οὖν ποιήσεις μείνας παρὰ σοί (PSI IX 1042, ll. 6–7 [III CE]) "please stay where you are" (trans. Bagnall and Cribiore).

Such non-finite complementation strategies are employed quite frequently, the nominative/accusative with infinitive in particular, after verb classes such as manipulative verbs (ἀναγκάζω, ἐπιτρέπω, ποιέω, etc.), verbs of communication (γράφω, ἐρωτάω, λέγω, etc.), and psychological verbs (δοκέω, θέλω, οἴομαι, etc.), rather than the combination of a complementizer and a finite verb, such as ὅτι with the indicative or ἵνα with the subjunctive. The situation is different when it comes to adverbial subordination, where the use of an adverbial subordinator and a finite verb is more standard and reflects the broad range of adverbial relations that may hold between a subordinate and a main clause. A broad range of such patterns can be found in the areas of causality (e.g., ἐπεί, ἐπειδή, ἐπείπερ, ὅτι, ὡς with the indicative), condition (e.g., εἰ/ἐάν with the indicative/subjunctive/optative), and purpose (e.g., ἵνα, ὅπως with the subjunctive). It is interesting to note, however, that in the areas of time, cause, and purpose, writers sometimes use the substantivized infinitive as an alternative to finite subordination patterns, as in διὰ τὸ μὴ βλέπεσθαί σε ὑπ' ἐμοῦ (P.Oxy. XLII 3059, l. 4 [II CE]) "because you are not being seen by me."[50]

Typography. At the micro-level, explicit attention is paid to the main typographic unit, the line, its ending in particular. Writers often attempt to reduce the space between the last letter of the line and the right margin, and thus to end the line in a more "harmonious" way,[51] by using line fillers. Such line fillers usually appear as

FIGURE 7.1   Line fillers in P.Mert. II 82, ll. 15–19

extensions of the final stroke of the last letter,[52] in particular letters such as *alpha*, *sigma*, *tau*, and *upsilon*. An example can be seen in Figure 7.1, where *alpha* has been extended three times in five lines.[53]

When it comes to the beginning of the line, initial letters are aligned vertically. Occasionally, however, writers make an attempt to mark the beginning of the line by enlarging letters: this can be seen in documents such as P.Gen. II 1 74 (139–145 CE) and SB VI 9120 (ca. 31–64 CE).[54] A similar practice can sometimes be found at the end of the line, though less consistently. In P.Giss. Apoll. 8 (115 CE), for example, the final *nu* seems to be written in a larger size (especially on lines 11, 12, and 14).[55]

In other documents, rather than (or in combination with) extending or enlarging letters, space is reduced by writing until the right edge of the document and, if necessary, splitting words over two lines. Word splitting occurs rather frequently in a number of documents,[56] such as P.Oxy. LXXV 5062 (III CE), with fifteen word splits in thirty-eight lines;[57] P.Oxy. VI 930 (II–III CE), with thirteen word splits in twenty-eight lines; P.Oxy. XIV 1773 (III CE), with seventeen word splits in thirty-nine lines; P.Mert. II 81 (II CE), with seventeen word splits in forty-two lines, and P.Flor. III 332 (ca. 113–120 CE), with eleven word splits in twenty-six lines. Whereas in these letters one word split occurs on average every 2.5 lines, other writers seem to avoid word splitting. Several letters in our corpus only

---

49   The genitive absolute construction is also attested in our corpus. See, e.g., P.Oxy. XXXIII 2680, ll. 3–4 (I–III CE); P.Flor. III 332, l. 8 (113–120 CE); P.Oxy. XIV 1773, ll. 9–10 (III CE).

50   For similar examples, see, e.g., SB VI 9026, ll. 4–5 (II CE); P.Ryl. II 232, l. 3 (II CE); P.Oxy. XXXIII 2680, l. 23 (II–III CE); P.Oxy. X 1295, l. 4 (II–III CE).

51   Cf. Bagnall and Cribiore 2006, 343.

52   Occasionally, strokes are introduced that are separate from the last letter, as in P.Oxy. XXXVI 2789 (242–299 CE), a document containing two letters from a certain Cleopatra, where lines 8 (the last line of the first letter) and 11 (the third line of the second letter) end in a separate stroke.

53   For similar examples, see SB VI 9271 (I–II CE); SB XIV 12024 (II CE); P.Mert. II 81 (II CE).

54   Other examples include P.Ryl. II 243 (II CE); P.Oxy. XII 1581 (II CE); P.Oxy. LXXV 5062 (III CE).

55   On the enlargement of individual letters, compare Sarri 2018, 118–20.

56   Word splitting/syllabification has not received a lot of scholarly attention (but see now Depauw, this volume). Some observations can be found in the standard grammars.

57   Line counts do not include the address on the verso side.

have one or two word splits, and some (usually shorter letters) even have none, including P.Oxy. IX 1217 (III CE) and PSI IX 1080 (III CE?).

As is well-known, literary and non-literary documents from our period were written in *scriptio continua* (that is, without modern word, clause, and sentence division), so that the line, rather than the sentence, served as the main unit of visual perception.[58] Although it is sometimes said that *scriptio continua* had no punctuation, this must be qualified. William Johnson, for example, notes that it is not true that ancient books lacked punctuation; rather, their punctuation system was much less elaborated (and less systematic), and mostly focused on major points of division, such as the marking of periods or changes between speakers in drama and dialogue, for instance.[59] Scholars of non-literary sources have observed an increasing tendency to adopt diacritical signs (accents, breathings, punctuation marks) in letters and petitions starting from the fourth century CE,[60] a tendency which is also reflected in women's letters from this period.[61]

Even before the late antique period, a number of diacritical signs appear in non-literary papyri, such as the *diaeresis* to separate vowels, and the *apostrophe* and *diastole* to separate syllables and words.[62] In several letters from our corpus, too, *diaeresis* is used,[63] both in its proper, "organic" use,[64] to separate vowels that do not belong together, and in its "inorganic" use, to mark an initial vowel. In P.Mert. II 83 (175–199 CE), for example, *diaeresis* occurs fourteen times in twenty-five lines, always with ι and υ, often to disambiguate vowels between and inside words, as in καὶ ὑφειρηκέναι (ϋφειρηκεναι papyrus; l. 6) or ὁ υἱός (ϋϊοσ papyrus; l. 15). Interestingly, however, *diaeresis* is also used four times with ἵνα, only once to disambiguate between vowels (l. 10). In the other three cases, *diaeresis* marks the start of the function word, and thus also of the subordinate clause.

Blank spaces were also used as a lay-out device.[65] Again, this mostly seems to have been the case for macro-level framing purposes. Eric Turner refers to the use of blank spaces to separate a lemma from a comment, to close a period, or to indicate a change of speaker in dramatic

FIGURE 7.2 Word spaces in P.Hamb. II 192, ll. 9–14 (III CE)
© STAATS- UND UNIVERSITÄTSBIBLIOTHEK
HAMBURG (GR. 404)

texts.[66] Interestingly, there are several documents in our corpus which make use of blank spaces at the micro-level: in P.Hamb. II 192 (III CE), for example, each new sentence of the body is preceded by a significant space (ll. 9, 14, 17, 23, 25; see Fig. 7.2). The same can be observed in P.Oxy. XII 1581 (II CE), where each of the three new sentences in the part of the body that is completely preserved is preceded by a space. In PSI IX 1080 (III CE), blank spaces are placed between almost every word (and sentence); in a number of cases, clauses/sentences are separated by a horizontal line extending from the final stroke of the final letter of the previous clause/sentence (ll. 4, 7, 10).[67]

2.1.2 The Meso-Level

Language. Generally speaking, the meso-level is less heavily marked than the micro- or macro-level. A number of linguistic features are used to distinguish between thematic units in the body. Most notable in this regard is the alternation between καί and δέ, indicating thematic continuity vs. discontinuity in the Classical period.[68] Whereas such pragmatic distinctions were breaking down in the post-classical period, in the lower registers in particular, some writers still made use of them. Thus, for example P.Oxy. X 1291 (30 CE) contains two thematic units (ll. 3–8, bread; ll. 8–12, going to Alexandria), which are separated by δέ. Similarly, SB XVI 12589 (II CE) has three thematic units (ll. 4–5, you are well; ll. 5–13, message for Par ...?; l. 14, additional request), the last two of which are introduced by δέ. Inside the second (and longest) thematic unit,

58   See, e.g., Turner 1987, 7.
59   Johnson 2011.
60   See, e.g., Fournet 1994; 2009, 36.
61   See, e.g., SB XVIII 13612 (IV CE); SB XVIII 13762 (550–599 CE).
62   See Turner 1987, 10–11, and more recently Fournet 2020.
63   The use of the apostrophe is less common in our corpus: see, e.g., BGU VII 1680, l. 8 (III CE).
64   The terminology is Eric Turner's (1987, 10).
65   Turner 1987, 8.

66   Raffaele Luiselli (2008, 688), however, notes that "epistolary texts of documentary character admit blank spaces between words more frequently than literary manuscripts."
67   On this practice, compare Turner 1987, 8.
68   See, e.g., Bakker (1993) for δέ as a boundary marker. As Buijs (2005, 137–38) notes, thematic discontinuity typically co-occurs with a break in one or more coherence strands, such as a change of participants (referential coherence), time period (temporal coherence), location (locational coherence), or type of event, such as background vs. foreground (action-event coherence).

καί and δέ are used to indicate lower level continuity vs. discontinuity.[69]

In some letters, the use of δέ is over-extended, at least in comparison to Classical usage: in PSI IX 1080 (III CE), for example, δέ is used six times[70] in just twelve lines, even when there is very little thematic change. In the body of this text, the two main thematic units (ll. 3–7, a new house; ll. 8–11, Bolphius), are separated not just by δέ, but additionally by the introductory formula εἰδέναι σε θέλω, "I want you to know," which is more often used at the beginning of the body (sometimes with γινώσκειν instead of εἰδέναι).[71] The shorter form of this formula, the imperative γεινώσκετε (l. γινώσκετε), "know," appears in the middle of the body of another document from our corpus, P.Mich. VIII 507, ll. 8–9 (ca. 107–185 CE).

Typography. There is relatively little evidence for typographic framing at the meso-level:[72] one could argue that the introduction of blank spaces between sentences[73] is in fact a feature of framing at the meso- rather than micro-level, since letters from our corpus are often relatively short, and the introduction of two or three significant blank spaces can already give the suggestion of a meso-level structure. An interesting letter from this perspective is P.Mert. II 83 (175–199 CE), where three significant spaces split up the main lay-out part of the text.

Another type of meso-level typographic framing can be found in letters where the opening and/or closing greetings are not placed on a separate line, but rather belong to the main lay-out part of the text, being slightly separated through the use of a vertical blank space. An interesting example is P.Princ. II 67 (I–II CE), a short letter from Theanô to her husband Dionysius, which starts with the usual opening greeting on lines one and two. Whereas some care has been taken to insert blank spaces between the major constituents of this greeting, the body of the letter continues on line 2, right after χαίρειν, and the repeated closing greeting (ἔρρωσο … πάλιν ἔρρωσο) is not visually separated either: only the date on line 6 is slightly separated visually through a blank vertical space.[74]

What happens more often is that the initial and final lay-out parts are internally structured. P.Oxy. X 1291 (30 CE), for example, has three lay-out parts, two of which seem to be internally structured above the sentence-level: the main lay-out part consists of the body, which also has on its last line (l. 12) the closing greeting ἔρρω(σο), which is visually separated through a vertical blank space (*vacat*). The final lay-out part consists of the date, which is placed on two separate lines (one for the year, one for the month), with a *paragraphos* between. Whereas the first part of the date has the regular alignment, the second part is aligned to the right, which underscores typographic structuring at the meso-level.

2.1.3 The Macro-Level

Language. In documentary genres such as letters, petitions, and contracts, macro-level framing is done through a set of formulaic phrases.[75] Such formulaic phrases not only set apart the opening and closing from its body, but also signal to the reader the genre to which a text belongs: in petitions, for example, a different closing greeting is used than in letters (διευτύχει vs. ἔρρωσο). This is not to say that generic parts are always framed in the same way, as writers could, for example, add intensifiers or forms of address, as well combining formulaic phrases, omitting them, or using shorter variants.[76]

Apart from the name of the initiator, addressee, and opening greeting, the opening part may also include a health wish and *proskynêma* formula.[77] An elaborate, eight-line opening can be found, for example, in P.Oxy. XIV 1758 (II CE).[78] Similarly, in the closing the farewell greeting can be accompanied by elements such as a health wish, salutations, and the date. In P.Flor. III 332, ll. 15–21 (ca. 113–120 CE), for example, the farewell greeting is preceded by a health wish and a personal request that the addressee write about his health.

Sometimes, writers attempt to introduce some originality in the closing. In P.Princ. II 67, ll. 5–6 (I–II CE), for example, the writer integrated the farewell greeting and salutations more closely than usual by using a participle for the salutations, but then felt obliged to formally close the letter by using another farewell greeting, accompanied by the date: ἔρρωσο ἀσπαζόμενός μου λείαν | τὰ τέκνα. πάλιν ἔρρωσο. Φαρμοῦθι κϛ´ "Farewell, greeting my children warmly; again—farewell. Pharmouthi 26" [trans. Bagnall and Cribiore].

---

69 For similar examples, see P.Oxy. XIV 1758 (II CE); P.Oxy. XLII 3059 (II CE); PSI IX 1042 (III CE); PSI IX 1080 (III CE).

70 Or seven times, if we assume that the uncertain reading of lines 9 to 10 (ἔπεμψά σοι δετριον [….]) includes a form of δέ.

71 See, e.g., SB VI 9120, l. 3 (ca. 31–64 CE); P.Oxy. XIV 1773, ll. 5–6 (III CE); BGU VII 1680, l. 3 (III CE).

72 Compare Luiselli 2008, 689.

73 As noted in § 2.1.1.

74 Compare SB XX 15180 (ca. 150 CE); P.Oxy. XXXVI 2789 (242–299 CE); BGU VII 1680 (III CE).

75 See, e.g., Nachtergaele 2015, with references.

76 See Luiselli 2008; Nachtergaele 2015.

77 Luiselli (2008, 700) considers these elements to be part of the body, rather than opening, but does not adequately distinguish between linguistic and typographic framing.

78 For other texts with both a *proskynêma* formula and health wish, see P.Mert.2.82 (175–199 CE); SB XXII 15453 (II CE).

Typography. Writers not only linguistically separated the opening and closing of the letter, but also visually set apart an initial and final part that is distinct from its main lay-out part. Such visual structuring is absent from the earliest, Ptolemaic letters: the practice seems to have been adopted in formal letter writing first, and then adopted in informal writing, too.[79] In most cases, linguistic and typographical structure do not entirely correspond: since it would be difficult to visually highlight some of the (very) long openings and closings, writers usually only set apart the most important parts; that is, the opening and closing greetings.

The initial lay-out part in particular, usually consisting of one or two lines (known as the "prescript"),[80] is typographically set apart through a variety of techniques:[81] it may have wider horizontal and vertical spacing (e.g., P.Mert. II 82 [175–199 CE]; P.Hamb. II 192 [III CE]); it may be separated from the main lay-out part by a line space (e.g., P.Oxy. IX 1217 [III CE]); it may have a different alignment than the main lay-out part, such as both lines or the second line being centered (e.g., P.Flor. III 332 [ca. 113–120 CE]); its first or second line may be indented (*eisthesis*) or outdented (*ekthesis*) (e.g., Chr.Wilck. 499 [II CE]; P.Giss.Apoll. 15 [113–120 CE]); or its first or last letter may be enlarged (e.g., P.Col. VIII 212 [49 CE]; P.Ryl. II 243 [II CE]). Less often, the initial lay-out part is separated from the main lay-out part through a lectional sign such as the *paragraphos* (e.g., P.Mich. VIII 507 [ca. 107–185 CE]). Whereas some letters are limited to one or two of these typographic techniques, often several are used at the same time.

Most of these typographic techniques can also be used to distinguish the final lay-out part, even though it is usually somewhat less elaborate: it may be separated from the main part through a line space (e.g., P.Giss.Apoll. 15 [113–120 CE]); it may be differently aligned from the main text, mostly in the center or on the right (e.g., P.Hamb. II 192 [III CE]); or it may be indented (e.g., P.Mert. II 82 [175–199 CE]; P.Oxy. X 1295 [II–III CE]). Rather than being written very spaciously, the final lay-out part is sometimes set apart from the main lay-out part through the use of more narrow horizontal and vertical spacing (e.g., P.Giss.Apoll. 1 [ca. 115–117 CE]).

At the macro-level, written text is of course in its entirety framed by the material substrate, which can be vertically or horizontally oriented, thus providing different types of frames.[82] Another element worth drawing attention to are margins: as we have seen, the right margin tends to be rather small, but a substantial amount of blank space is often left on top and at the left, with one document displaying an upper margin of 2.8 cm (P.Col. VIII 212 [49 CE]), and another a left margin of 4 cm (P.Giss. Apoll. 1 [ca. 115–117 CE]). Even more striking is the amount of space that is left at the bottom: there are several documents with more than 5 cm of blank space (e.g., P.Col. VIII 212 [49 CE]; PSI IX 1042 [III CE]) and one with more than 8 cm (P.Mich. VIII 507 [ca. 107–185 CE]).[83] The substantial amount of space that is left blank in such documents not only functions as a typographic framing device at the macro-level, but at the same time signals towards the receiver that the initiator is sending a well-planned message.[84]

Whereas the sort of macro-level framing discussed here obviously works best with papyrus as a substrate, there are a couple of ostraca in our corpus of women's letters in which similar principles are adopted.[85] A good example is SB VI 9271 (I–II CE), a rectangular-shaped ostracon with a substantial left and especially upper margin (1.95 cm), which sets apart the initial lay-out part from the main lay-out part through indentation.[86] It also places the closing greeting on a separate line (in a smaller letter size).

2.2   *Minimal Discourse Planning*
To some extent, minimal discourse planning represents a *contradictio in terminis*, since without planning and framing, there can be no written communication. Writers cannot get their message across without adopting the form of clauses, for example. In what follows, I outline what a minimal amount of linguistic and typographic framing at the three different levels looks like.

79   Antonia Sarri (2018, 114) notes that the layout and palaeography of letters started being more sophisticated "from about the end of the first century BC and the early years of the first century AD."

80   For an initial lay-out part with three lines, see P.Oxy. LXXV 5062 (III CE).

81   See Sarri 2018, 114–20.

82   Most letters have vertical orientation (that is, they are longer than wide), but not always: see, e.g., P.Oxy. I 115 (II CE); BGU VII 1680 (III CE); P.Oxy. IX 1217 (III CE). For further discussion about changes in writing direction and orientation, see Fournet 2007, 2009; Sarri 2018, 87–113.

83   I have calculated as the lower margin the space below the final part of the letter (typically the closing greeting). The lower margin would be even larger if counting from the bottom of the main part of the letter.

84   Alternatively, though, when too much blank space was left at the bottom, it could have been taken as an indication that the scribe could not calibrate the message very well.

85   Also see Torallas Tovar, this volume.

86   Compare O.Did. 427 (125–140 CE).

2.2.1 The Micro-Level

Language. At the micro-level, writers use a much less wide-ranging variety of particles: additive καί is most frequently used, not only to connect clauses, but also sentences. In P.Koeln. I 56, ll. 3–9 (I CE), for example, the letter body consists of clauses and sentences that are connected through καί: γινώσκιν (l. γινώσκειν) σε θέλω, ὅτι δεκαταῖοι ἐπτάκαμεν (l. ἐφθάκαμεν) εἰς τὴν μητρόπο- | λιν‖ν‖· καὶ εὐθέως ἀνέβην πρὸς | τὴν ἀδελφήν σου· καὶ εἰθὺς (l. εὐθὺς) | ἔγραψά σοι, ὅτι ἀπρόσκοπός ἴμιν (l. ἤμην) καὶ ἐσώθημεν τῶν θηῶν (l. θεῶν) | θελόντων, "I want you to know that it is ten days that we came first to the metropolis and I went straightaway to your sister and right away I wrote to you that I am free from harm and we were saved with the gods' will" [trans. Bagnall and Cribiore]. The next four lines with the salutations contain five more instances of καί and are followed by a request that is again structured through καί.

Perhaps in an attempt to limit the use of καί, other writers keep repeating the same particle to connect clauses and sentences. In SB III 6264, ll. 8–19 (II CE), for example, the causal particle γάρ is used multiple times in an additive sense, a relatively uncommon usage:[87] ἀνερχόμενος δὲ ἔδωκά σοι κερμάτιον, | ὅτι δέξασα τὰ | σιτάρια ἐν αὐτῷ | γὰρ τῷ μηνὶ [οὐ]χ εὗρον δῶναί (l. δοῦναί) σ[οι]. | οὐδέν σε γὰρ | ὑποστέλλομε (l. ὑποστέλλομαι), | πάντα σοι γὰρ | πιστεύω, ἡ γὰρ | γυνή σου λέγι (l. λέγει) κτλ. "when you came up, I gave you small coins because I received some grain; but this month I could not find (anything) to give you. I am keeping nothing back from you because I trust you in everything. Your wife says etc." [trans. Bagnall and Cribiore]

Even more common in our corpus is the complete absence of particles, particularly when it comes to relating sentences. In some letters, particles are almost entirely absent, as for example in SB V 7572 (104 CE): in this entire letter, καί is used three times at the beginning of a sentence, but most often there is no sentence connection at all.[88] Even between clauses, particles are sometimes omitted, as in πρό|λαβε οὖν τὴν ἄλω ἵν' εὐθέως ἀπο|λάβῃς ἐκλείσῃς (P.Sel.Warga. 12, ll. 7–9 [II CE]) "take the threshing floor beforehand so that you may take and lock it up immediately" (trans. Bagnall and Cribiore). The use of asyndeton also extends to subordinating relations, particularly complementation with verbs of communication and manipulative verbs, as in κα|λῶς οὖν πυήσεις (l. ποιήσεις) ἐπ' ὀνόμα|τος Σαραπίωνο[ς] μονος (l. μόνου) | καταχωρη[ση]ς (l. καταχωρίσῃς) [τα]ῦτα (l. [τα]ῦτα) (P.Giss. 97, ll. 7–10 [II CE]) "you will do well to register these things in the name of Sarapion only" or εἶπον αὐτῷ πένψον (l. πέμψον) τὸν | παῖδα (O.Did. 360, ll. 11–12 [ca. 88–96 CE]) "say to him: send the child." With verbs of communication, one also frequently finds the use of ὅτι in its "recitative" function, without adaptation of personal references/pronouns, tense, and mood.[89]

Typography. Not a lot of attention is paid to line endings. There is often considerable variation between the lines, with some running to the right edge of the document, and others leaving a considerable amount of space, which is not filled by line fillers. Examples of letters with such variability include P.Mert. II 63 (57 CE; Fig. 7.3), P.Mich. III 202 (105 CE), P.Oxf. 19 (208 CE), and PSI XIV 1418 (III CE). In such documents, we often see other alignment problems, too: writers struggle to vertically align the initial letter of each new line,[90] and they have problems keeping text horizontally level, resulting in what Bagnall and Cribiore refer to as "wavering lines."[91]

Due to a lack of planning, writers sometimes had to resort to a smaller letter size towards the end of the line, or to decrease spaces between letters. Alternatively, we see that these writers sometimes placed one or more final letters above the line. In BGU I 261 (105 CE), for example, shown here in Figure 7.4, the writer had to place the final *nu* of χαίρειν (l. 2) above the line, which forms a remarkable contrast with the amount of attention that this central word receives in documents with maximal discourse planning.[92]

More often, writers resorted to word splitting: several documents in our corpus contain a high number of word splits, such as BGU I 261 (105 CE), with nineteen word splits in thirty-four lines; BGU III 827 (II–III CE), with twenty word splits in thirty lines; and SB XX 14132 (I CE), with eighteen word splits in forty-two lines. Whereas word splitting is not absent from maximally planned documents, it is interesting to note that syllabification seems to play less of a role for word splitting decisions. For example, the writer of SB XX 14132 (I CE) splits right after the first letter of the word on multiple occasions, resulting in word splits such as ε|[ὔ]χωμέ (ll. 4–5), κ|[αί (ll. 6–7), σ|α[ν] δαλι (ll. 32–33), and σ|ου (ll. 39–40). The same writer also splits before the last letter of words: twice we find γὰ|[ρ (ll. 11, 19).[93]

---

87   See Bentein 2016, 92–95.

88   For similar examples, see P.Bad. II 35 (87 CE); O.Did. 360 (88–96 CE); P.Col. VIII 215 (ca. 100 CE); BGU III 827 (II–III CE).

89   For some examples, see SB XIV 11585, ll. 9–11 (59 CE); P.Bad. II 35, ll. 10–12 (87 CE); BGU II 602, ll. 5–6 (II CE).

90   See, e.g., P.Mich. III 202 (105 CE).

91   See, e.g., BGU II 380 (III CE).

92   The same can be seen in SB V 7572, l. 10 (104 CE) with the final *nu* of τόν (l. 10) written above the line.

93   For similar examples, see O.Did. 360, ll. 6–7 (ca. 88–96 CE); P.Leid.Inst. 42, ll. 5–6 (II CE); P.Tebt. II 413, ll. 9–10 (175–199 CE).

FIGURE 7.3 Variable line endings in P.Mert. II 63, ll. 2–7 (57 CE)

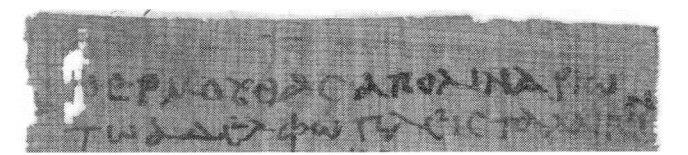

FIGURE 7.4 Opening of BGU I 261, ll. 1–2 (105 CE)

2.2.2 The Meso-Level

Language. Because writers tend to overuse the same particle (καί in particular), distinctions between thematic units are often not clearly highlighted. An amusing example can be found in SB V 7572 (104 CE): Thermouthas starts the body of her letter (ll. 2–8) by informing the addressee, her mother, about goods that have been received, and also requesting she sends goods. Surprisingly, right before the greetings in line nine, Thermouthas mentions the fact that she is seven months pregnant: κὲ (l. καὶ) αἰπτάμηνον (l. ἑπτάμηνον) εἰμῖν (l. ἡμῖν) ἄρτι "we have just been seven months pregnant" [trans. Bagnall and Cribiore]. Rather than drawing attention to this presumably significant fact through the use of a formula (γινώσκε) or a particle such as δέ, Thermouthas employs καί, effecting for the modern reader a parallel between the goods and the seven-month-old fetus. Somewhat more discourse planning can be found in SB XIV 11585 (59 CE), a document which deals with three different topics related to Lucius's return home. Each of these topics is introduced by περί (l. 3, περὶ τοῦ σάκκου αὐτοῦ τοῦ παχέως "about his smock of coarse sackcloth"; l. 8, περὶ τῶν μισθῶν τῶν πυμένον (l. ποιμένων) "about the shepherds' wages"; l. 14, περὶ τῆς ἄμης "about the shovel"), but the different topics themselves are connected through καί.

Apart from thematic breaks being less well indicated, the thematic structure is also much more chaotic. Statements are less clearly grouped in thematic units, as can be seen in P.Col. VIII 215 (ca. 100 CE), a letter with two broad topics, the health of the recipient and that of a young girl who has been ill on the one hand, and the sending and buying of goods on the other. Statements related to these topics occur in a very disordered fashion, with references to the young girl in lines 8–12, 17–20, 21–24, and 28–31 being interrupted with other news and requests. Another noticeable tendency is for afterthoughts related to the text's main body to occur right before or after the closing greeting. In P.Koeln. I 56 (I CE), for example, Diodora informs Valerius Maximus that she has arrived in an unspecified nome capital. She then sends salutations to various people (ll. 9–12), but instead of closing the letter she afterwards returns to the topic of her travels, noting that she will sail down to Valerius as soon as she has finished her business in the nome capital (ll. 12–15). Only then follow the date and closing greeting.

Generic parts other than the body also often give a rather chaotic impression. In P.Col. VIII 215 (ca. 100 CE), for example, Apollonous sends salutations to a broad range of people (ll. 31–33), then closes the letter with the farewell greeting ἔρρωσ(ο), only to remember that she had more people to salute (l. 34: ἐπισκοπούμε (l. ἐπισκοποῦμαι) Ἡρᾶν ⟦.⟧ καὶ τὰ τέκνα αὐτῆς "I send regards to Hera and her children"), followed by the date. The same can be seen in O.Did. 451 (ca. 176–210 CE), where we have salutations in lines 14 to 17, then a closing greeting (ll. 17–19), more salutations (ll. 20–22), and a second closing greeting (ll. 23–24). An even more striking example is found in P.Oxy. I 114 (II–III CE), where the writer closes the letter with salutations, a farewell greeting, and then puts another name belonging to the salutations right after the farewell greeting: ἄσπασαι πολλὰ Ἀίαν καὶ Εὐτυχίαν | ἐρρῶσθαί [σ]ε [ε]ὔχομαι. καὶ Ἀλεξάνδραν (ll. 16–17) "many salutations to Aia and Eutychia. Farewell. And (salutations to) Alexandra."

Typography. Lay-out parts are not structured in different lay-out units through the use of blank spaces, or lectional signs, for example. This is not to say that there is no visual structuring, but it is unintended: through a lack of space (and planning), writers are often forced to continue writing in places which in maximally planned documents remain blank, such as the margins or verso. Several documents in our corpus have writing in the margins,[94] ranging from one or two lines (e.g., P.Petaus. 29, l. 15 [II CE]; P.Giss.Apoll. 5, ll. 31–32 [113–120 CE]) to five lines (P.Col. VIII 215, ll. 30–34 [ca. 100 CE]); in the latter case, marginal writing includes a part of the body, salutations, final greetings, and the date. P.Col. VIII 215 is interesting not only for the length of what is written in the margins, but also for the fact that writing is found in the right, rather than the

---

94   For further discussion, see Homann 2012.

left margin, as is common practice.[95] Ostraca, too, often have writing in the margins: an interesting example is SB XXII 15453 (II CE), a document which not only has writing in the left margin, but also in the upper margin (written upside down).[96]

Alternatively, some writers continue writing on the back of the document, which is usually reserved for the address. For example, having concluded her letter with salutations and a farewell greeting, the writer of O.Did. 451 (ca. 176–210 CE) extended the closing section by adding more salutations and another greeting on the concave side of the ostracon. Other writers use both the margins and the verso to gain as much space as possible: in BGU IV 1097 (41–67 CE), for example, the writer puts a first part of the closing (the date) in the margin, and then continues with the salutations as well as the address on the verso side.

2.2.3 The Macro-Level

Language. As we have seen above in 2.1.3, writers of maximally planned documents make an explicit effort to embed the body of the letter in an opening and a closing. Much less embedding can be found in minimally planned documents, especially in the closing.[97] Quite a few letters in our corpus, for example, end with the salutations, without an explicit closing formula. BGU II 385 (II–III CE) simply ends with καὶ ἀσπάζομαι | τὴν μητέρα μου καὶ τοὺς ἀδελφούς μου καὶ Σεμπρῶνιν | καὶ τοὺς παρ' αὐτοῦ "and I greet my mother and my brothers and Sempronius and his people" [trans. Bagnall and Cribiore].[98] Other letters end, somewhat unusually, with a health wish (P.Oxy.Hels. 45, ll. 15–16 [I CE]) or *proskynêma* formula (P.Leid.Inst. 42, ll. 26–27 [II CE]). Still other letters do not have a closing at all (not even salutations): this can be seen, among others, in P.Oxf. 19 (208 CE) and SB XIV 11580 (175–299 CE). Contrary to the closing greeting, the opening greeting is usually maintained: occasionally, however, only the name of the initiator and addressee are mentioned, without χαίρειν, as in BGU III 801 (II CE), Νεῖλος (l. Νείλῳ) τῷ ἀδελφῷ | παρὰ Τασουχαρίου, "to Neilos her brother, from Tasoucharion."

Openings and closings often have a somewhat unusual appearance, which can be related to lesser experience with writing (and framing). In BGU II 380 (ll. 23–25

[III CE]), for example, we find two sets of openings and closings: Hegelochus is addressed first by his mother, and then very briefly by his son: Αὐρήλιος Πτο|λεμινο τῷ πατρεὶ (l. πατρὶ) χαίριν (l. χαίρειν) πεῖ|σον Διονύσιον χα[ί]ρειν τέχν(ον) (l. τέκν(ον)) "Aurelius Ptoleminos to his father, greetings. Persuade Dionysios. Farewell, child (?)."[99] Here it is noteworthy that χαίρειν is used both for the opening and closing greeting, contrary to common practice.

Problems with framing at the micro- and meso-level may also contribute to the unusual outlook of some openings and closings. So, for example, letter writers tend to integrate different elements of the opening or closing section more narrowly than is usually done: they may either place them within one sentence, as in ἔρροσο (l. ἔρρωσο), πρὸ πάντων σατοῦ (l. σαυτοῦ) ἐπιμελοῦ, ἵνα ὑγ[ιαί]νῃς (P.Bad. II 35, l. 26 [87 CE]), "above all, take care of yourself so that you may be well,"[100] or explicitly connect sentences with a particle, as in Ταρεμ.αι Χαιρημῶν (l. Χαιρήμονι) τῷ πατρὶ πλ|εῖστα χαίρειν. καὶ πρὸ μὲν πάντων | εὔχομέ (l. εὔχομαί) σαι (l. σε) ὑγιαίνειν κτλ. (SB V 8027, ll. 1–3 [II–III CE]), "Tarem ... to Chairemon her father, very many greetings and before everything I pray for your health" [trans. Bagnall and Cribiore].[101]

Typography. As Bagnall and Cribiore note,[102] the use of typographic frames at the macro-level was quite popular in informal letters, too, even in those written by less-educated people. Nevertheless, there are quite a few letters in our corpus that do not visually distinguish a main lay-out part from an initial and final part: this includes documents such as BGU I 261 (105 CE), P.Tebt. II 413 (175–199 CE), and BGU II 385 (II–III CE). Other documents in our corpus display more of an effort towards typographic structuring, but only distinguish two lay-out parts, rather than three. Several letters visually separate the final lay-out part of the letter from its main part, employing some of the typographic techniques outlined above in 2.1.3. In P.Mich. III 202 (105 CE), for example, no effort is made to separate the opening of the letter from the body, but the two constituent parts of the closing—that is, the farewell greeting and the date—are each placed on a new line, with different degrees of indentation. Similarly, in BGU III 827 (II–III CE), no effort is made to separate the opening from the rest of the text, but there is a considerable space between the salutations and the final line (in a second hand), with the farewell greeting and date.

---

95 Homann (2012, 69–70) notes that there are only five texts in the entire papyrological corpus with writing in the right margin.

96 Compare P.Tebt. II 414 (II CE).

97 This foreshadows later developments of the epistolary frame in late antiquity, on which see, e.g., Fournet 2009.

98 For similar examples, see O.Did. 386 (120–125 CE); P.Tebt. II 413 (175–199 CE); SB XXII 15453 (II CE); SB V 8027 (II–III CE).

99 It is unclear why Hegelochus is first addressed as "father" and then as "child" (τέκν(ον)).

100 Compare P.Mert. II 82, ll. 22–23 (175–199 CE).

101 For a combination of both, see P.Mich. VIII 464, ll. 21–24 (99 CE).

102 Bagnall and Cribiore 2006, 46.

FIGURE 7.5 BGU II 602, ll. 1–3 (III CE)
© STAATLICHE MUSEEN ZU BERLIN, ÄGYPTISCHES
MUSEUM UND PAPYRUSSAMMLUNG (P 6699)

Other letters do the contrary, and only highlight the initial lay-out part: in BGU II 380 (III CE), for example, the (clearly inexperienced) writer makes an explicit effort to separate the opening greeting from the rest of the letter, setting apart and centering χαίρειν on the second line. The same writer makes no effort, however, to visually distinguish the end of the letter, which is remarkable, given that we are dealing here with a double letter, in which the receiver is not only addressed by his mother but also by his son.[103] Another example is BGU II 602 (II CE): as can be seen in Figure 7.5, the names of the initiator and addressee are highlighted by slightly outdenting the first line and leaving a substantial part of the line blank. The rest of the opening, however, is placed on the second line together with the remainder of the text—πλεῖτα (l. πλεῖ⟨σ⟩τα) χαίριν (l. χαίρειν). πρὸ μὲν πάντων κτλ.—separated only by a small *vacat*.

As noted in 2.1.3 above, margins work as a macro-level framing device. Blank space is less substantial in minimally planned documents, however, since writers are often in need of additional writing space, and therefore use the margins (even the top and right margin) as well as the verso. Even without additional writing appearing there, some of the documents in our corpus display minimal margins: an overall small document such as P.Koeln. I 56 (I CE), which measures 11.5 by 10.4 cm, for example, has no right margin, and only tiny left, top, and lower margins. The same can be seen in larger documents, too: SB V 7572 (104 CE), for example, which has an overall size of 23 by 14.4 cm, has a small upper margin, but virtually no left, right, or lower margins. The absence of margins is even more striking in documents written on ostracon:[104] often, writers left no blank spaces at all, as can be seen in O.Did. 360 (88–96 CE) and O.Did. 451 (176–210 CE).[105]

Whereas writers usually employed new sheets that were blank on both sides,[106] in one case, P.Oxf.19 (208 CE),

a person used the lower margin of a document that had become obsolete (a receipt),[107] to write a short letter. As Bagnall and Cribiore note,[108] an attempt had first been made to wash out the previous text, but this was given up, and the sheet was simply turned, with the lower margin now on top.

3 Discourse Planning as a Continuum

In the previous section I discussed features of maximal and minimal discourse planning; however, in doing so, I may have created the wrongful impression that all documents in our corpus can be categorized as either maximally or minimally planned, or that the documents that were mentioned to illustrate a specific feature display maximal or minimal planning across the board. In reality, maximal and minimal discourse planning are best viewed in terms of a continuum, with exemplary ("prototypical") instances of each category at each end.

It is not uncommon to find documents in our corpus that are not completely homogeneous when it comes to discourse planning:[109] at first sight, for example, PSI XIV 1418 (III CE) demonstrates little discourse planning, especially from a typographic point of view, with variable line alignment, no clear visual distinction of the opening, and small left and upper margins. From a linguistic point of view, however, the letter shows much more attention to discourse planning: the writer makes frequent use of the particle δέ, as well as subordinating conjunctions such as ἐάν and ὅπως; the letter body is divided into thematic units through the repetition of the formula γινώσκειν σε θέλω (ll. 17–18), which is also used to introduce the body of the text (ll. 8–9); and there is much attention given to the opening of the letter (consisting of no fewer than seven lines), with an opening greeting, a health wish, and a *proskynêma* formula. The separation of the opening from the body is not only supported by the use of the formula γινώσκειν σε θέλω, but also by a subtle *paragraphos*.

Documents that are less straightforward to classify as maximal or minimal discourse planning may not only display different degrees of attention to the two main semiotic resources that are involved (language and typography), but also to the three different levels of discourse planning (micro, meso, and macro). That the linguistic

103 Other double letters make more of an effort towards visual structure: see, e.g., SB XX 14132 (I CE); P.Leid.Inst. 42 (II CE).

104 On ostraca, see Torallas Tovar, this volume.

105 For an ostracon with a tiny left and bottom margin, see O.Did. 386 (120–125 CE).

106 See Luiselli 2008, 686.

107 The receipt was published as P.Oxf. 9 (208 CE?).

108 Bagnall and Cribiore 2006, 35.

109 To complicate matters further, writers do not always maintain the same amount of attention to framing throughout their letters. I will not go further into this here.

characteristics of a document are not always completely homogeneous has been observed by a number of other scholars, too. Patrick James,[110] for example, has noted that one and the same letter writer may display different levels of proficiency in the areas of orthography and syntax, and Hilla Halla-aho[111] has suggested that even in one and the same area it may be possible to identify different registers occurring next to each other (standard letter phrases being combined with colloquial syntax, for example). Less attention has been paid to divergences between semiotic resources, in part perhaps because of a lack of an adequate conceptual apparatus. Such questions have started to be addressed in scholarship on multimodality under the heading of "intersemiotic complementarity,"[112] however, with the primary focus on how visual and verbal meanings can complement each other.

When it comes to intersemiotic complementarity in the corpus of women's letters, Bagnall and Cribiore have drawn attention to the fact that there is a group of documents with more systematic divergences between the two major semiotic resources involved, in the sense that there is significantly more attention to typography than there is to language.[113] Bagnall and Cribiore interpret this as a sign of dictation, with an experienced writer penning literally what a female initiator is saying, while at the same time paying attention to typography (in other words, a scribe adopting a mixed approach towards textualization). Quite often, in such letters the closing greeting is in a second hand (the hand of the initiator herself),[114] or is first written by the scribe and then repeated in a second hand.[115] Space does not permit me to fully explore the nature and extent of these divergences in the corpus of women's letters, and the papyrological corpus more generally speaking, so I will limit myself to commenting on three sample documents, with the intention of assessing, in a preliminary fashion, systematic divergences across the two semiotic resources (and three levels).

The first document I want to discuss here, P.Mich. III 221 (297 CE; Fig. 7.6), is a letter from Ploutogenia to her mother Heliodora, which is of a relatively large size (25.9 × 12.5 cm). Typographically speaking, this is one of the most elegantly written documents in our corpus: it was written in Alexandria by a professional scribe familiar

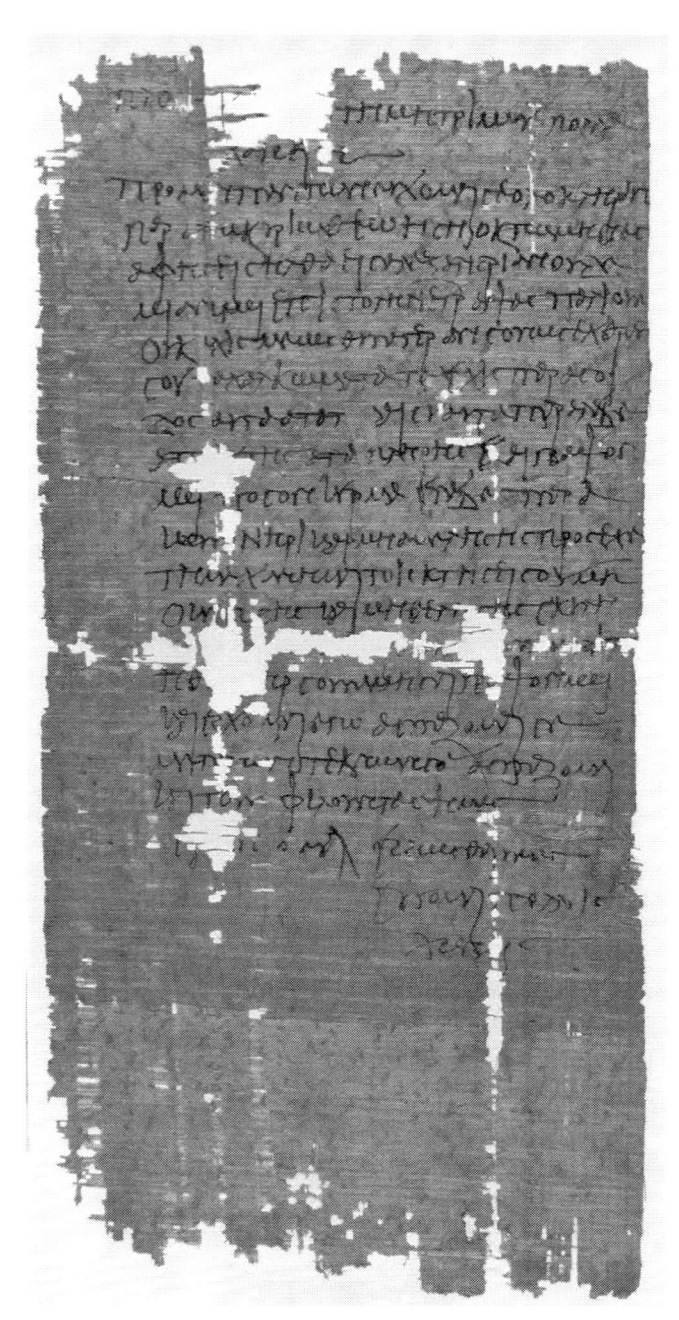

FIGURE 7.6   P.Mich. III 221 (ca. 297 AD)
© UNIVERSITY OF MICHIGAN PAPYRUS COLLECTION (P.MICH.INV. 1362)

with the Chancery style,[116] as indicated by the upright, elongated letters. The disposition of the letter is well thought through, with a significant left margin (ranging from 1.4 to 2.6 cm) and especially lower margin (ca. 7 cm). Particularly noteworthy are the well elaborated initial and final lay-out parts: the former is highlighted through horizontal and vertical spacing, with χαίρειν as the only word on the second line, while the latter, consisting of the long

---

110   James 2014, 14.
111   Halla-aho 2010, 172.
112   See, e.g., Royce 2007.
113   This is particularly true for syntax and lexis, less so for orthography and morphology (Halla-aho 2018). The question is less relevant for framing, so I will not go further into it here.
114   See Halla-aho 2018, 228.
115   On double farewell greetings, see Sarri 2018, 184–88.

116   See Bagnall and Cribiore 2006, 294.

closing greeting ἐρρῶσθαι ὑμᾶς | εὔχομαι πολλοῖς | χρόνοις (ll. 20–22), "I wish you well for many years," is equally well elaborated: it is right aligned, with the first letter of each new line (twice *epsilon*) enlarged,[117] and the last letter of each elongated (three times *sigma*).

Explicit attention has also been paid to framing at the micro-level: lines either run until the right edge of the document, or line fillers are used (with letters such as *alpha*, *epsilon*, and *sigma*). The scribe avoids word splitting, with only one word split in lines 14 to 15 (σκυλῆ|ν[αι]). The first letter of each new line seems to be slightly enlarged; given the considerable amount of attention paid to visual appearance, it is noteworthy that the initial letters are not placed on a perfectly straight vertical line, but rather form a curve.

In contrast, typographic framing at the meso-level seems to play a less important role: there is a blank space before the beginning of the salutations (ἀσπάζομαί σε, l. 17), but there are other blank spaces which seem to be less relevant (after μίαν μοι on l. 6, after οὐκ on l. 7). From a linguistic point of view, the letter is much less elaborated: it is well framed at the macro-level, with long opening and closing sections, consisting respectively of an opening greeting and health wish, and salutations and a long closing greeting. At the micro-level, however, the text mostly consists of short commands that are connected asyndetically or through the use of καί. Thus, for example, lines 10 to 15: καὶ γράψον | μοι πόσον κέρμα ἔλαβες παρὰ | Κουπινῆρι καὶ μὴ ἀμελήσῃς. πρόσεχε | τῇ μεχανῇ (l. μηχανῇ) καὶ τοῖς κτήσεί (l. κτήσί) σου, μὴ | ὀκνήσῃς καὶ μὴ θελήσῃς σκυλῆ|ν[αι] "and write to me how much money you got from Koupineris, and do not neglect it. Attend to the irrigation wheel and to your cattle; do not hesitate and do not wish to trouble" [trans. Bagnall and Cribiore]. As Bagnall and Cribiore observe, "the scribe took down what this woman told him without much reworking."[118] Apart from the elaborate opening and closing sections, the text does contain an instance of δέ thematically separating lines 15 to 17 from the rest of the body.

Our next document, P.Mich. VIII 514 (Fig. 7.7), shows a lot of similarities with the first: this, too, is a letter from a daughter to her mother (Isidora to Sarapias), of even larger size (ca. 36 × 12 cm), also written in third-century Alexandria. Visually speaking, this letter gives a somewhat less elegant impression than P.Mich. III 221: it was written by a "proficient and elegant hand,"[119] but in a much less

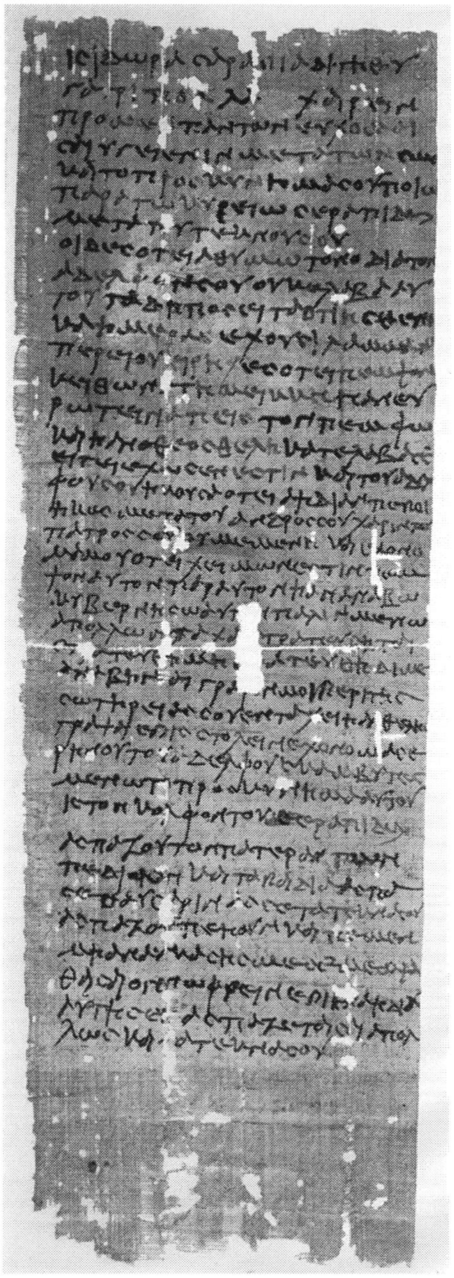

FIGURE 7.7 P.Mich. VIII 514 (III AD)
© UNIVERSITY OF MICHIGAN PAPYRUS
COLLECTION (P.MICH.INV. 5805)

exuberant style.[120] The difference is primarily noticeable at the macro-level: margins are smaller, with a narrow upper and left margin (0.86 and 0.68 cm respectively), but a more spacious lower margin (5.98 cm). Typographically speaking, this document has a two-line initial lay-out part

---

117   ἐρρῶσθαι is not at the beginning of a line, but the closing greeting is right aligned.

118   Bagnall and Cribiore 2006, 294.

119   Bagnall and Cribiore 2006, 269.

120   As Bagnall and Cribiore (2006, 269) note, there is some variation in the handwriting, which becomes smaller, faster, and more bent to the right towards the end of the letter. The document also contains a number of corrections.

that is modestly set apart from the main section, mainly because of the vertical blank space (*vacat*) before χαίρειν. The text does not have a formal closing, but the scribe has made an effort to visually set apart the relatively long salutations (ll. 31–38) from the main part of the text, through the introduction of a line space between lines 30 and 31.

The same sort of sensitivity to framing can be seen in the opening section of the text: the scribe has separated the health wish and *proskynêma* formula from the rest of the text by not filling out the last line of the opening section (l. 7). The scribe has filled out all the other lines of the text, either by writing until the edge of the document or through the use of line fillers, especially with letters such as *alpha* and *upsilon*. Compared to our previous sample document, the scribe of P.Mich. VIII 514 is much less hesitant to split words, with eleven word splits in thirty-eight lines. The most noticeable word split in this regard can be found in the prescript, where the kinship term θυ|γατρὶ is split over two lines (ll. 1–2), thus making the initial lay-out part visually less attractive.

Linguistically speaking, there is some attention to macro-level framing, with an elaborate opening section, containing both a health wish and a *proskynêma* formula. The closing section is less diverse since it only contains salutations. At the micro-level, the asyndetic connection of sentences is very noticeable: καί is used only once, at the beginning of line 15. Sentences and clauses are often rather short, as can be seen in lines 20 to 26: πέμ|ψον αὐτὸν παρ' αὐτόν· ἠὰν (l. ἐὰν) ἀναβῶ | κυβερνήσω αὐτ[ὸ]ν πάλιν. μένω | Ἀπολλῶν. τάχα στρατεύσηται· | στρατευθῇ μὴ σ[τ]ρατευθῇ δῖ (l. δεῖ) με | ἀναβῆναι. γράψον μοι περὶ τῆς | σωτηρείας (l. σωτηρίας) σου ἐν τάχει "send him to his own place; if I go upcountry I shall manage him again. I am waiting for Apollos. Perhaps he will enlist in the army; whether he enlists or not, I must go upcountry. Write to me soon about your well-being" [trans. Bagnall and Cribiore].[121] The text also contains some subordinate clauses, which are not, however, very diverse: ὅτι is used five times, three times for a complement clause, and two times for a causal clause. Because of the use of recitative ὅτι (ll. 12–13), the text gives an impression of directness, which is reinforced by the direct address of one of the people who are saluted, Onnophris (ll. 35–37). Even though the body of the text contains various thematic elements (a brother who has died, the sending of goods, problems with the husband/ father, another brother who is thinking of enlisting), no effort seems to be made to linguistically structure the text.

Our third sample document, SB VI 9122 (ca. 31–64 CE; Fig. 7.8), is also a family letter, sent by Herennia to her father Pompeius. Visually speaking, this document is perhaps the least attractive of the three discussed here: rather than the typical rectangular shape, it takes a square form, with height and width of almost equal size (14.6 × 15.4 cm). The document has significant margins, especially at the bottom (4.41 cm), where the closing greeting has been written, presumably by Herennia herself. The upper margin is slightly larger than in our previous two sample documents (1.68 cm); the left margin is relatively small (0.89 cm).

Typographically, this document only highlights two, rather than three lay-out parts: the closing greeting is separated from the main part of the text through multiple line spaces. There is a significant gap in the middle of the document, so that it is difficult to ascertain whether attention was paid to framing at the meso-level: this does not seem to have been the case. A lack of attention to typographic framing can also be spotted at the micro-level: no effort has been made to use line fillers or to write until the right edge of the document, resulting in variable line endings. The scribe splits words five times in thirteen lines, with a noticeable non-syllabic word split at lines 6 to 7 (μ-|ή). Initial letters of each new line do not seem to be perfectly vertically aligned, while horizontally, lines waver somewhat.

Linguistically speaking, the macro-level framing is quite elaborate: the opening section contains a greeting, health wish, and salutation, but everything is connected through καί in one long sentence: Ἐρε[ννία] Πομπηίῳ τῷ [. . . . .] [π]λεῖστα χαίριν (l. χαίρειν) καὶ διὰ | παν[τὸς] ὑγενειν (l. ὑγιαίνειν), κα[ὶ τὴν] [μη]τέραν (l. [μη]τέρα) μου ἀσπάζομαι "Herennia to Pompeius … very many greetings and all good wishes for his health, and I salute my mother." The closing section consists of salutations, a farewell greeting, and a date. Similar to our first document, P.Mich. III 221, sentences mainly consist of short commands that are connected asyndetically or through καί. The body of the letter does start with two instances of δέ (l. 3: ἐρωτ[ῶ] δὲ …; l. 4: πληρόθητι (l. πληρώθητι) δέ): the first could perhaps be taken to signal the start of the body, but it is not clear why δέ should be used in the second sentence, and not for any of the other commands in the body.[122] Lack of attention to thematic structure can also be seen in the closing section (ll. 11–14), where the salutations are suddenly interrupted by the phrase μὴ ἡμῶν ἐπιλάθηστε (l. ἐπιλάθησθε) (l. 12),

---

121   Particularly noticeable is the phrase στρατευθῇ μὴ σ[τ]ρατευθῇ (l. 24), where asyndeton is employed for a disjunctive semantic relation ("whether … or …").

122   Perhaps the scribe was not able to maintain the use of δέ while writing down Herennia's words?

FIGURE 7.8 SB VI 9122 (ca. 31–64 AD)
© UNIVERSITY OF OSLO PAPYRUS COLLECTION (P. 1444)

"do not forget us," presumably referring to the set of commands/requests made in the letter body.

Obviously, no definitive conclusions can be drawn about framing and dictation on the basis of three sample documents. The discussion above did bring a number of elements to light, however, that may be elaborated, confirmed, or refuted by follow-up research. Typographically speaking, writers pay most attention to framing at the macro-level, adopting significant margins and structuring the text in two or three lay-out parts. When it comes to the micro- and meso-levels, our sample documents gave a less homogeneous picture: writers pay most attention to the micro-level, especially the end of the line; explicit attention was paid to the meso-level in only one document.

Linguistically, there is least divergence from typography when it comes to macro-level framing: all three sample documents have elaborate openings and closings; arguably, these would have been easiest for the scribe to interfere with.[123] A noticeable lack of attention to linguistic framing can be found at the micro-level, however, with lots of short clauses and sentences that are asyndetically connected. At the meso-level, the thematic structure of the documents that we have discussed is not clearly signaled: it is often chaotic and rather unclear.

---

123 Compare Halla-aho 2018, 235: "the opening salutations are those parts in a letter that most easily could reflect the practices of the scribe instead of those of the author."

4   Discourse Planning as a Communicative Strategy

As mentioned in Section 1, the main reason why Bagnall and Cribiore pay such attention to the linguistic and typographical characteristics of women's letters is that there is not much contextual information available. By paying attention to these features, they hope to learn more about the *conditions* behind the textualization of women's letters. That is, they hope to ascertain the degree to which women participated in the writing event, by either not participating in the writing event (giving a scribe directions), directly participating (writing the letters themselves), or indirectly participating (dictating to a scribe).

These different types of involvement have in turn been connected to degrees of literacy,[124] which ranged from completely illiterate over "slow writers" to literate. Although opportunities for Greek women to obtain an education began to expand in the fourth century and in the Hellenistic period,[125] in general it has been assumed that women were less literate than men,[126] and that therefore "the level of female literacy in Graeco-Roman Egypt was negligible."[127] Factors that would have determined whether a girl was educated include social and economic class, as well as geographical place and historical time.[128] During the Roman period, for example, opportunities for a Greek education were more plentiful in the *metropoleis* than in the villages, and were more available to the elite classes who could afford private tutoring for their children.[129]

While female literacy is of course an important factor to take into account, I would like to suggest that we approach textualization in a less deterministic fashion. If we take the example of a fully literate woman, textualization would have involved a considerable element of choice: she would have to decide whether to write herself or to employ a scribe; in both cases, various degrees of discourse planning would have been possible. In this context, I believe we should pay closer attention to the correlation between textualization (discourse planning) and aspects of social context. Recent papyrological scholarship has drawn attention to the social relevance of communicative features: Jean-Luc Fournet, for example, has argued that "l'analyse matérielle d'un document peut être

porteuse de sens,"[130] not only when it comes to text type, but also with regard to the socio-cultural context of writing and the provenance of the document.[131] It is important to realize, however, that the relevance of such material features (among others) goes beyond modern-day scholarship: since we are dealing with autographs, we must assume that variation in communicative features also carried social meaning in antiquity, and that the original addressee(s), too, would have been able to draw meaning from particular communicative choices. From that point of view, a lesser degree of discourse planning should not necessarily be viewed as a communication failure resulting from an imperfect degree of literacy (a perspective sometimes adopted by modern editors); rather, it may alternatively be viewed as a communicative choice conveying, for example, a heightened sense of involvement.

To conclude this chapter, I want to highlight the social contexts from which particular textualization strategies originated, without attempting an in-depth treatment of the matter. In previous research I have started from very specific social factors, such as social distance, agentive role, or degree of imposition.[132] Here, however, I want to take a wider view and start from the different functions communication may have, and how textualization supports these.

As mentioned in Section 1.2, social semioticians recognize three main functions, "ideational," "textual," and "interpersonal," which they connect with different contextual parameters, called "field" (what the discourse is about), "mode" (the ways in which interactants come into contact), and "tenor" (the interactants and their relationship) respectively.[133] Framing as a system is of course narrowly connected to the textual function (and mode), but this does not exclude correlations with other functions and parameters of context.[134] A similar approach was applied to Middle English letters by Alexander Bergs,[135] who argued that letters can be divided into different socio-pragmatic text types, depending on the degree to which the ideational and interpersonal functions play a role,[136] the linguistic features of which he then goes

---

124   See, e.g., Huebner 2018, 165.
125   See Pomeroy 1981, 310.
126   See, e.g., Sheridan 1998, 189.
127   Sheridan 1998, 191.
128   See Pomeroy 1981, 314.
129   See Rowlandson 1998, 300.

130   Fournet 2007, 353.
131   Compare Bentein 2017 and 2019 from a linguistic point of view.
132   See, e.g., Bentein 2017.
133   For further background, see, e.g., Hasan 1999.
134   Compare Matthiessen 2002 on the relevance of clause complexing at the textual and interpersonal level.
135   Bergs 2004.
136   As Bergs (2004, 210) notes, these different functions rarely occur in an isolated fashion: letters can simultaneously describe an event, express a person's thoughts and feelings, and invoke a reaction in the hearer. Compare Bagnall and Cribiore 2006, 13 on women's letters being perfect examples of what the epistolary

on to investigate.[137] Basing his thinking on the work of Karl Bühler,[138] Bergs refers to the ideational function as "descriptive" (relating states or events in the world), and splits up the interpersonal function into "expressive" (relating the thoughts or feelings of the speaker) and "appellative" (invoking a reaction in the hearer), terminology that I adopt here.

In what follows, I briefly outline the relationship between degrees of discourse planning in the corpus of women's letters and the three functions of communication distinguished by Bergs. In doing so, it is important to keep in mind that 1) multiple social factors will have played a role in determining a textualization strategy, and 2) purely practical factors, such as the availability of a scribe, place of writing, and financial situation, will have played a role, too.[139]

4.1 The Appellative Function

Bergs recognizes the importance of the appellative function in two types of letters, called "orders" and "requests." With these two types, the social relation between the interactants is usually unequal: orders being made by superiors and requests by inferiors. As Bergs notes, people making requests will typically try to avoid language use that may be somehow offensive to the addressee, which contrasts with people giving orders.[140]

The relevance of this principle was recently explored by Clarysse with regard to Greek papyrus letters written by landowners and other types of superiors to their stewards and agents.[141] Clarysse shows that in these letters, few philophronetic formulae and polite phrases are used. Such letters are also attested in our corpus, which contains about ten letters written by women in a superior position. In line with Clarysse's observations, most of these show a moderate degree of discourse planning, especially linguistically speaking: they tend to be limited to a short opening and closing formula, and consist of short commands that are asyndetically connected.[142] Some of these letters pay

more attention to typographic framing, an attempt being made to visually structure the text at the macro-level.[143]

The reverse situation, requests made by inferiors to superiors, is less clearly present in our corpus, the prototypical instantiation of which would be petitions written by women to an official. The requests that are made in our corpus are typically formulated to an equal (family, friend, acquaintance) and involve a relatively low degree of imposition: to buy and send things (e.g., SB VI 9122 [ca. 31–64 CE]), to take care of someone (e.g., P.Col. VIII 215 [100 CE]), to register something (e.g., P.Giss. 97 [II CE]), to come over (e.g., SB XVI 12981 [191–209 CE]), to send money (e.g., SB V 7743 [I–II CE]), and so on. It should therefore come as no surprise that such letters are often rather minimal in terms of discourse planning, with little attention to linguistic and often also typographic framing.

In Bergs's framework, a request "involves asking the person for vital, important things, and a strong dependence on the fulfilment of this request,"[144] so that one could doubt whether the above-mentioned documents should really be classified as requests. Letters in which more vital requests are made can be found in our corpus, too: in P.Oxy. XXXVI 2789 (242–299 CE), for example, Cleopatra asks her father to give 5 *artabas* of barley to a mason because she is being harassed by a *dekaprôtos* (a tax collector) and is about to be thrown in jail; in P.Giss.Apoll. 21 (117 CE), Arsis writes to Apollonios the *strategos* that her son Chaeremon needs a second burial,[145] and that she can turn to nobody except Apollonios; and in SB VI 9271 (I–II CE), Paulina asks her brother Titus to come quickly because she is being mistreated by her husband. The generally much higher degree of linguistic and typographic discourse planning in these documents may be taken to reflect the urgency of the matters at hand, even when requests are made to family members and acquaintances. A good example of this is SB VI 9271: despite the fact that Paulina is writing to her brother and guardian, and that she is using an ostracon to do so, an effort has been made to copy visual framing practices that are typical for papyrus letters.

4.2 The Expressive Function

A second major function of letters is for initiators to express their feelings and thoughts towards the addressee.

---

theorists call "the mixed style" (that is, they do not focus on a single main subject). Good examples from our corpus include, e.g., SB V 7572 (104 CE); P.Giss.Apoll. 21 (117 CE); P.Bour.23 (140–144 CE).

137 For comparable approaches in the field of papyrology, see, e.g., Logozzo 2015; Clarysse 2018.

138 Bühler 1934.

139 Cf. Halla-aho 2018, 230.

140 Bergs 2004, 212.

141 Clarysse 2018.

142 See, e.g., P.Bad. II 35 (87 CE); SB VI 9610 (II CE); P.Oxy. LVI 3855 (280–281 CE).

143 See, e.g., P.Mil.Vogl. II 76 (ca. 138–147 CE); P.Sel.Warga. 12 (II CE); P.Oxy. VI 932 (175–199 CE). Contrast, however, P.Bad. II 35 (87 CE).

144 Bergs 2004, 215.

145 δευτέρα ταφή is interpreted by Michael Kortus (1999, 201) as "second mummy-wrapping," which could be connected to Arsis' request in the second part of the letter to buy linen.

Such letters are different from orders and requests in the sense that they are usually written between equals, and that maximal and minimal discourse planning need not indicate degree of respect towards the addressee. On the contrary, studies by Wallace Chafe and Deborah Tannen[146] have drawn attention to the close relationship that exists between oral strategies in language and the degree of involvement between the initiator and the addressee, The descriptive a factor that is also taken into account by Cribiore with regard to women's letters when she notes that "sometimes ... the sender cared to have a more active part in writing the epistle and dictated the whole body of the letter word for word."[147] Similarly, Halla-aho has suggested that female authors may have preferred to write without the help of a scribe when they wanted to convey personal information or private emotions.[148]

Arguably the most evident case of letters with an expressive function in our corpus are so-called philophronetic letters, the main function of which is to maintain contact between the initiator and the addressee. As a result, a real letter body is often lacking, with such letters mainly consisting of formulaic phrases.[149] A good example is P.Oxy. IX 1217 (III CE), a letter from Eudaemonis to Ptolemaeus, which, apart from an opening and closing greeting (with salutation), consists of a single sentence at lines 3 to 7, καὶ νῦν διὰ τούτων μου τῶν γραμμάτων | γράφω σοι, πρῶτον μὲν ἀσπαζομένη σ[ε], | ἔπιτα (l. ἔπειτα) εὐχομένη παρὰ πᾶσι θεοῖς ὑγιαίνον[τά] | σε καὶ εὖ διάγοντα ἀπολαβεῖν μετὰ | τῶν ἡμῶν πάντων, "I am again writing you this my letter, first sending you salutations, and second praying to all the gods that you may receive them in health and prosperity along with all our friends" [trans. Hunt]. Because of their brevity, such letters are not always easy to characterize in terms of maximal or minimal discourse planning, especially linguistically speaking. Typographically, they are often well presented.[150]

Letters often combine multiple communicative functions,[151] with our corpus containing various documents, for example, which are philophronetic in nature, but in which the initiator also makes a small request related to the maintenance of contact. For example, this might be to

write back (e.g., P.Giss.Apoll. 10 [113–120 CE]), to remain in a certain place (e.g., PSI IX 1042 [III CE]), to send information (e.g., SB XVIII 13591 [III CE]), or to stay out of danger (e.g., P.Giss. Apoll. 10 [ca. 113–120 CE]). Such letters, too, are often well framed, both from a linguistic and typographic point of view.

Our corpus also contains quite a few documents where the body contains more substantial requests or descriptions, but where the expressive function still plays an important part because of the initiator's request[152] to greet a broad range of people.[153] Interestingly, such letters very often display minimal discourse planning, especially linguistically but sometimes also typographically.[154] This could, perhaps, be connected to the role of the descriptive function (see further below).

An alternative approach would be to look at participant structure: Arthur Verhoogt has drawn attention to letter writing practices in modern-day Mali,[155] noting that there it is not a solidary activity, and that apart from the initiator and addressee, several people are involved, most evidently a scribe, but also family members engaging in conversation with the initiator during the letter writing, or directly addressing the scribe. Similarly, when the letter is read to the addressee, other people are present. Verhoogt argues that the large number of salutations in women's letters suggests a similar context of writing, with other people saluting the addressee, and the initiator saluting other people in the addressee's circle. While Verhoogt's argument does not exclude the possibility of other contexts of writing,[156] it helps to explain the lack of discourse planning in some of the letters in our corpus, both from the perspective of writing (dictation, use of a scribe) and of reading (reading out loud to a group of people, no need for elaborate visual frames).

More genuine/private emotions are also expressed in women's letters. For example, women send their thanks

---

146   See, e.g., Chafe 1982; Chafe and Tannen 1987.

147   Cribiore 2002, 150.

148   Halla-aho 2018, 230.

149   Bagnall and Cribiore (2006, 389–94) discuss philophronetic letters under the heading "epistolary types: just greetings and good wishes."

150   See, e.g., P.Giss.Apoll. 15 (113–120 CE); P.Oxy. IX 1217 (III CE). For philophronetic letters with less discourse planning, see, e.g., O.Did. 386 (120–125 CE); P.Oxy. XIV 1761 (175–299 CE).

151   See n. 136 above.

152   Other people may also offer greetings to the addressee, although Arthur Verhoogt (2009) argues that this is less often the case in women's letters than in men's.

153   Most often, this is done at the end of the letter, but there are also letters which begin with the greetings (see, e.g., PSI XIV 1420, ll. 4–6 [III CE]). People are mostly greeted individually, but sometimes also more generally: see, e.g., SB VI 9026, ll. 15–16 (II CE); P.Mich. III 221, ll. 18–20 (297 CE). On greetings, see further Nachtergaele 2015, 63–120.

154   For similar examples, see P.Col. VIII 215 (ca. 100 CE); O.Did. 386 (120–125 CE); BGU II 601 (II CE); BGU III 827 (II–III CE); SB V 8027 (II–III CE); P.Mich. VIII 514 (III CE).

155   Verhoogt 2009.

156   Verhoogt (2009) notes that in autograph letters, too, one sometimes finds greetings by other people, and interprets this as writing not only being an oral activity, but also a social activity, with other people present while one person wrote their own letter.

(e.g., P.Oxy. VI 963 [II–III CE]); urge secrecy (e.g., SB VI 9610 [II CE]); blame people (e.g., P.Giss.Apoll. 19 [113–120 CE]; P.Brem. 64 [113–120 CE]); express their worries and concerns (e.g., P.Giss.Apoll. 8 [115 CE]), as well as their disagreement (e.g., P.Bad. II 35 [87 CE]; Chr.Wilck. 483 [275–299 CE]); express desire and longing for someone (e.g., P.Giss.Apoll. 13 [113–120 CE]); and defend themselves against other people (e.g., SB III 6264 [II CE]). Textualization strategies in these letters vary: for example, there are two letters of condolence in our corpus, BGU III 801 (II CE) and P.Oxy. I 115 (II CE). The second of these engages much more with discourse planning, which corresponds to a different social relationship between the interactants: in BGU III 801 Tasoucharion writes to her brother, while in P.Oxy. I 115 Eirene addresses acquaintances. While it is difficult to make any generalizations, it would seem that especially letters conveying negative emotions (blaming, disagreeing, urging, worrying) invest less in textualization: in such cases, a lesser degree of discourse planning may help to convey the negative message. A striking example is PSI III 177 (II–III CE), a letter in which Isidora urges her husband Hermias to come home because she fears that their son, who hasn't been eating for six days, is dying. Isidora underlines the urgency of the matter by threatening to commit suicide if their son dies in Hermias's absence. The lack of discourse planning, too, may be taken to convey the general sense of urgency.

4.3 The Descriptive Function

To conclude this short discussion, it is worth observing that many of the letters in our corpus also have a descriptive function; that is, they describe facts or states of affairs. Bergs refers to letters with this function as "reports,"[157] and considers them "neutral" compared to other text types such as requests, orders, and phatic letters. Indeed, one could consider the descriptive function different in nature from the appellative and expressive functions: whereas the former is ideational, the latter two are both interpersonal. Given the "neutrality" of the descriptive function, there does not seem to be an inherent need for maximal discourse planning. Letters reporting on business matters, for example, often show little discourse planning. In fact, Bagnall and Cribiore refer to letters with a moderate attention to discourse planning as "business prose,"[158] sometimes also describing writers' linguistic and handwriting skills as "businesslike."[159]

The descriptive function is not limited to business letters, however: it can also be found in letters that report on personal matters. For example, we have letters reporting on a safe arrival (e.g., BGU VII 1680 [III CE]), on the arrival of a corpse (e.g., Chr.Wilck. 499 [II CE]), on problems in the household (e.g., P.Mich. VIII 514 [III CE]; SB XVI 12326 [ca. 297 CE]), on a brother being away (Pap.Choix. 13 [127 CE]), on moving to a new house (e.g., PSI IX 1080 [III CE]), on clothing that is being sent (e.g., P.Oxy. XIV 1679 [III CE]), on problems encountered with sending items (e.g., P.Hamb. II 192 [III CE]), and on health and illness (e.g., P.Brem.64 [113–120 CE]). Contrary to what we see in business contexts, such letters do not always adopt minimal discourse planning. PSI IX 1080, for example, a letter from Diogenis to Alexandros about Diogenis' moving into a new house, has been mentioned on several occasions in this chapter for the great deal of attention paid to both typographic and linguistic framing.

Maximal discourse planning is employed in particular in letters that make longer reports about (important) events that have happened, typically in the legal sphere. In such documents, maximal discourse planning may have been adopted in order to guarantee maximal comprehensibility, or to reflect the importance of the topic. Letters of this type are not very frequent in our corpus:[160] examples include P.Oxy. XLIII 3094 (217–218 CE), with 39 lines, outlining legal proceedings involving three successive prefects; P.Oxy. LXXV 5062 (III CE), with 38 lines, concerning problems with a debtor called Cephalon; and P.Mert. II 83 (175–199 CE), with 25 lines, where the initiator is being summoned because of an attack that she would have made.[161]

It is worth making a comparison with two other documents reporting on legal matters: P.Gen. II 1 74 (139–145 CE), with 26 lines, part of the dossier concerning the trial of Drusilla, and P.Mich. VIII 473 (100–125 CE), with 32 lines, a letter from Tabetheus about her son being guilty of murder. These two letters are also well planned typographically, but much less so linguistically, with sentences often connected through καί or asyndetically, speech represented directly, and a chaotic thematic structure. Both letters were written by a single person to a family member: they give the impression that the expressive function had a more important role to play, especially P.Mich. VIII 473.

---

157 Bergs 2004, 214.
158 See, e.g., Bagnall and Cribiore 2006, 350, 401.
159 See, e.g., Bagnall and Cribiore 2006, 386, 399.

160 Bagnall and Cribiore 2006, 305–23 has a separate section on letters concerning legal matters.
161 A much shorter document involving legal matters is P.Ryl. II 232 (II CE).

Conclusion

In this chapter, I have proposed a novel approach towards the analysis of women's letters: drawing on insights from social semiotics and multimodality, I have suggested that the notion of "framing" is central towards our understanding of communication practices in antiquity, in particular how everyday documents took shape (their "textualization"). I have argued for a complex understanding of the notion, making a division between linguistic and typographic framing, and relating framing features to three different levels. Analyzing framing practices in our corpus, I have proposed that letters can be placed on a continuum ranging from maximal discourse planning (with full attention to how information is framed) to minimal discourse planning (with little to no attention to how information is framed). While many of the letters in our corpus seem to be oriented towards one of these poles, others are more heterogeneous.

Paying attention to notions such as framing, discourse planning, and textualization naturally leads one to consider not only the *who* and *how* of letter writing, but also the *why*; that is, why did an initiator opt for a particular type of discourse planning? Whereas previous scholarship has mainly focused on the connection between textualization and literacy, I have attempted to place textualization in its wider social context by exploring its relationship to three main communicative functions (appellative, expressive, descriptive). In this way, we can reinterpret different types of textualization as (potentially) communicative strategies, rather than seeing them as the direct result of (a lack of) education.

Employing a modern conceptual framework for communication practices in antiquity not only helps to clarify questions concerning textualization, it also systematizes them: previous scholarship did not have a conceptual apparatus to directly compare the linguistic and typographic appearance of letters, beyond commenting on the quality of execution. Evidently, this does not mean that the topic has been exhaustively treated: for example, it would be interesting to expand the notion of framing to lower levels, viewing lexical items or letter clusters as lower-level linguistic and typographic framing features; to compare standards of letter writing and their relationship to framing across different time periods; to further analyze the relationship between textualization and social context, by more explicitly comparing letters sent by or addressed to one and the same person; or to further our understanding of gender divisions in Egypt by comparing contemporaneous letters written by both women and men.

More generally, what was presented and discussed in this chapter is also relevant for our understanding of textuality in antiquity. Specifically, it offers a challenge to the view, expressed by Ken Morrison, that one can speak of "text" and written culture only with the introduction of a standardized layout in the fifth century AD; before that period, the notion of "alphabetic writing" would apply.[162] According to Morrison, for the Greeks (and Romans) texts were never more than "a variant of oral utterance ... and oral dictation ... due to the lack of procedures for transforming *writing* into *text*."[163] As I have tried to show in this chapter, textualization, even in documentary sources, was considerably less homogeneous.

Reference List

Arjava, Antti. 1996. *Women and Law in Late Antiquity*. Oxford: Oxford University Press.

Bagnall, Roger S., and Raffaella Cribiore. 2006. *Women's Letters from Ancient Egypt, 300 BC–AD 800*. Ann Arbor: University of Michigan Press.

Bakker, Egbert J. 1993. "Boundaries, Topics, and the Structure of Discourse: An Investigation of the Ancient Greek Particle Dé." *Studies in Language* 17, no. 2: 275–311.

Bednarek, Monika A. 2005. "Frames Revisited—The Coherence-Inducing Function of Frames." *Journal of Pragmatics* 37, no. 5: 685–705.

Bentein, Klaas. 2016. "'Έγραψέ μοι γάρ ... τὰ νῦν οὖν γράφω σοι. Οὖν and γάρ as Inferential and Elaborative Discourse Markers in Greek Papyrus Letters (I–IV AD)." *RBPh* 94, no. 1: 67–104.

Bentein, Klaas. 2017. "Finite vs. Non-Finite Complementation in Post-Classical and Early Byzantine Greek." *Journal of Greek Linguistics* 17, no. 1: 3–36.

Bentein, Klaas. 2019. "Dimensions of Social Meaning in Post-classical Greek." *Journal of Greek Linguistics* 19, no. 2: 119–67.

Bergs, Alexander. 2004. "Letters: A New Approach to Text Typology." *Journal of Historical Pragmatics* 5, no. 2: 207–27.

Bonifazi, Anna, and David F. Elmer. 2012. "Composing Lines, Performing Acts: Clauses, Discourse Acts, and Melodic Units in a South Slavic Epic Song." In *Orality, Literacy and Performance in the Ancient World*, edited by Elizabeth Minchin, 89–109. Leiden: Brill.

Bühler, Karl. 1934. *Sprachtheorie: die Darstellungsfunktion der Sprache*. Jena: Fischer.

Buijs, Michel. 2005. *Clause Combining in Ancient Greek Narrative Discourse*. Leiden: Brill.

---

162   Morrison 1987, focusing on literary texts.
163   Morrison 1987, 244.

Chafe, Wallace L. 1982. "Integration and Involvement in Speaking, Writing and Oral Literature." In *Spoken and Written Language: Exploring Orality and Literacy*, edited by Deborah Tannen, 35–54. Norwood, NJ: Ablex.

Chafe, Wallace L. 1985. "Linguistic Differences Produced by Differences between Speaking and Writing." In *Literacy, Language, and Learning: The Nature and Consequences of Reading and Writing*, edited by David R. Olson, Andrea Hildyard, and Nancy Torrance, 105–23. Cambridge: Cambridge University Press.

Chafe, Wallace, and Deborah Tannen. 1987. "The Relation Between Written and Spoken Language." *Annual Review of Anthropology* 16: 383–407.

Clarysse, Willy. 2018. "Letters from High to Low in the Graeco-Roman Period." In *Scribal Repertoires in Egypt from the New Kingdom to the Early Islamic Period*, edited by Jennifer Cromwell and Eitan Grossman, 240–50. Oxford: Oxford University Press.

Cribiore, Raffaella. 2002. "The Women in the Apollonios Archive and Their Use of Literacy." In *Le Rôle et Le Statut de La Femme En Égypte Hellénistique, Romaine et Byzantine: Actes Du Colloque International, Bruxelles-Leuven, 27–29 Novembre 1997*, edited by Henri Melaerts and Leon Mooren, 149–66. Paris: Peeters.

Evans, Trevor V. 2012. "Linguistic and Stylistic Variation in the Zenon Archive." In *Variation and Change in Greek and Latin*, edited by Martti Leiwo, Hilla Halla-aho, and Marja Vierros, 25–40. Helsinki: Finnish Institute at Athens.

Fournet, Jean-Luc. 1994. "L'influence des usages littéraires sur l'écriture des documents: perspectives." In *Proceedings of the 20th International Congress of Papyrologists*, 418–22. Copenhagen: Museum Tusculanum.

Fournet, Jean-Luc. 2007. " Disposition et réalisation graphique des lettres et des pétitions protobyzantines: pour une paléographie 'signifiante' des papyrus documentaires." In *Proceedings of the 24th International Congress of Papyrology, Helsinki, 1–7 August, 2004*, edited by Jaakko Frösén, Tiina Purola, and Erja Salmenkivi, 353–67. Helsinki: Societas Scientarum Fennica.

Fournet, Jean-Luc. 2009. "Esquisse d'une anatomie de la lettre antique tardive d'après les papyrus." In *Correspondances. Documents pour l'histoire de l'Antiquité tardive. Actes du colloque international, université Charles-de-Gaulle-Lille 3, 20–22 novembre 2003*, edited by Roland Delmaire, Janine Desmulliez, and Pierre-Louis Gatier, 23–66. Lyon: Maison de l'Orient et de la Méditerranée Jean Pouilloux.

Fournet, Jean-Luc. 2012. "Femmes et culture dans l'Égypte byzantine (V^e–VIIe s.)." In *Les réseaux familiaux: Antiquité tardive et Moyen Âge. In memoriam A. Laiou et É. Patlagean*, edited by Béatrice Caseau, 135–45. Paris: ACHCByz.

Fournet, Jean-Luc. 2020. "Les signes diacritiques dans les papyrus documentaires grecs." In *Signes dans les textes. Continuités et ruptures des pratiques scribales en Égypte pharaonique, gréco-romaine et byzantines*, edited by Nathan Carlig, Guillaume Lescuyer, Aurore Motte, and Nathalie Sojic, 145–66. Liège: Presses Universitaires de Liège.

Haines-Eitzen, Kim. 2000. *Guardians of Letters: Literacy, Power, and the Transmitters of Early Christian Literature*. Oxford: Oxford University Press.

Halla-aho, Hilla. 2010. "Linguistic Varieties and Language Level in Latin Non-Literary Letters." In *The Language of the Papyri*, edited by Trevor V. Evans and Dirk D. Obbink, 171–83. Oxford: Oxford University Press.

Halla-aho, Hilla. 2018. "Scribes in Private Letter Writing: Linguistic Perspectives." In *Scribal Repertoires in Egypt from the New Kingdom to the Early Islamic Period*, edited by Jennifer Cromwell and Eitan Grossman, 227–39. Oxford: Oxford University Press.

Hasan, Ruqaiya. 1999. "Speaking with Reference to Context." In *Text and Context in Functional Linguistics: Systemic Perspectives*, edited by Mohsen Ghadessy, 219–328. Amsterdam: Benjamins.

Homann, Margit. 2012. "Eine Randerscheinung Des Papyrusbriefes: Der Versiculus Transversus." *APF* 58, no. 1: 67–80.

Huebner, Sabine R. 2018. "Frauen und Schriftlichkeit im Römischen Ägypten." In *Literacy in Ancient Everyday Life*, edited by Anne Kolb, 163–78. Berlin: De Gruyter.

James, Patrick. 2014. "Papyri, Language Of." In *Encyclopedia of Ancient Greek Language and Linguistics*, edited by Georgios Giannakis, 11–14. Leiden: Brill.

James, Sharon L., and Sheila Dillon. 2012. "Introduction." In *A Companion to Women in the Ancient World*, edited by Sharon L. James and Sheila Dillon, 1–3. Malden, MA: Wiley-Blackwell.

Johnson, William A. 2011. "The Ancient Book." In *The Oxford Handbook of Papyrology*, edited by Roger S. Bagnall, 255–81. Oxford: Oxford University Press.

Koch, Peter, and Wulf Oesterreicher. 2007. "Schriftlichkeit und kommunikative Distanz." *Zeitschrift für Germanistische Linguistik* 35, no. 3: 346–75.

Kortus, Michael. 1999. *Briefe des Apollonius-Archives aus der Sammlung Papyri Gissenses: Edition, bersetzung und Kommentar*. Giessen: Universitätsbibliothek Giessen.

Krause, Jens-Uwe. 1995. *Witwen und Waisen im frühen Christentum*. Stuttgart: Steiner.

Krawiec, Rebecca. 2002. *Shenoute and the Women of the White Monastery: Egyptian Monasticism in Late Antiquity*. New York: Oxford University Press.

Kress, Gunther R. 2000. "Text as the Punctuation of Semiosis: Pulling at Some of the Threads." In *Intertextuality and the Media: From Genre to Everyday Life*, edited by Ulrike

Hanna Meinhof and Jonathan Smith, 132–54. Manchester: Manchester University Press.

Kress, Gunther R. 2004. *Literacy in the New Media Age*. London: Routledge.

Kress, Gunther R. 2010. *Multimodality: A Social Semiotic Approach to Contemporary Communication*. London: Routledge.

Kress, Gunther R., and Theo van Leeuwen. 1996. *Reading Images: The Grammar of Visual Design*. London: Routledge.

Langacker, Ronald W. 2001. "Discourse in Cognitive Grammar." *Cognitive Linguistics* 12, no. 2: 143–88.

Lefkowitz, Mary R., and Maureen B. Fant. (1982) 2016. *Women's Life in Greece and Rome: A Source Book in Translation*. 4th ed. London: Bloomsbury Academic.

Logozzo, Felicia. 2015. "Register Variation and Personal Interaction in the Zenon Archive." *SSL* 53, no. 2: 227–44.

Luiselli, Raffaele. 2008. "Greek Letters on Papyrus: First to Eighth Centuries; A Survey." *Asiatische Studien: Zeitschrift Der Schweizerischen Asiengesellschaft* 62, no. 3: 677–737.

MacLachlan, Gale L., and Ian Reid. 1994. *Framing and Interpretation*. Carlton: Melbourne University Press.

Matthiessen, Christian M. I. M. 2002. "Combining Clauses into Clause Complexes: A Multi-Faceted View." In *Complex Sentences in Grammar and Discourse*, edited by Joan L. Bybee and Michael Noonan, 235–319. Amsterdam: John Benjamins.

McClure, Laura. 2001. "Introduction." In *Making Silence Speak: Women's Voices in Greek Literature and Society*, edited by Laura McClure and André Lardinois, 3–16. Princeton, NJ: Princeton University Press.

Morrison, Ken. 1987. "Stabilizing the Text: The Institutionalization of Knowledge in Historical and Philosophic Forms of Argument." *Canadian Journal of Sociology / Cahiers Canadiens de Sociologie* 12, no. 3: 242–74.

Mugridge, Alan. 2010. "Writing and Writers in Antiquity: Two 'Spectra' in Greek Handwriting." In *Proceedings of the 25th International Congress of Papyrology*, edited by Trajanos Gagos, 273–580. Ann Arbor: University of Michigan Library.

Nachtergaele, Delphine. 2015. "The Formulaic Language of the Greek Private Papyrus Letters." PhD diss., Ghent University.

Nifosi, Ada. 2019. *Becoming a Woman and Mother in Greco-Roman Egypt: Women's Bodies, Society and Domestic Space*. London: Routledge.

Ochs, Elinor. 1979. "Planned and Unplanned Discourse." In *Discourse and Syntax*, edited by Talmy Givon, 51–80. New York: Academic Press.

Oesterreicher, Wulf. 1997. "Types of Orality in Text." In *Written Voices, Spoken Signs*, edited by Egbert J. Bakker and Ahuvia Kahane, 190–214. Cambridge, MA: Harvard University Press.

Pomeroy, Sarah B. 1981. "Women in Roman Egypt: A Preliminary Study Based on Papyri." In *Reflections of Women in Antiquity*, edited by Helene P. Foley, 303–22. London: Routledge.

Pomeroy, Sarah B. 1984. *Women in Hellenistic Egypt: From Alexander to Cleopatra*. New York: Schocken Books.

Porter, Stanley E., and Matthew Brook O'Donnell. 2007. "Conjunctions, Clines and Levels of Discourse." *Filología Neotestamentaria* 20: 3–14.

Ready, Jonathan L. 2019. *Orality, Textuality, and the Homeric Epics: An Interdisciplinary Study of Oral Texts, Dictated Texts, and Wild Texts*. Oxford: Oxford University Press.

Richards, Ernest Randolph. 2004. *Paul and First-Century Letter Writing: Secretaries, Composition, and Collection*. Downers Grove, IL: InterVarsity Press.

Rowlandson, Jane. 1998. *Women and Society in Greek and Roman Egypt: A Sourcebook*. Cambridge: Cambridge University Press.

Royce, Terry D. 2007. "Intersemiotic Complementarity: A Framework for Multimodal Discourse Analysis." In *New Directions in the Analysis of Multimodal Discourse*, edited by Wendy Bowcher and Terry D. Royce, 63–109. Mahwah, NJ: Lawrence Erlbaum Associates.

Salmenkivi, Erja. 2017. "Some Remarks on Literate Women from Roman Egypt." In *Women and Knowledge in Early Christianity*, edited by Ulla Tervahauta, Ivan Miroshnikov, Outi Lehtipuu, and Ismo Dunderberg, 62–72. Leiden: Brill.

Sarri, Antonia. 2018. *Material Aspects of Letter Writing in the Graeco-Roman World 500 BC–AD 300*. Berlin: De Gruyter.

Sheridan, Jennifer A. 1998. "Not at a Loss for Words: The Economic Power of Literate Women in Late Antique Egypt." *Transactions of the American Philological Association* 128: 189–203.

Thibault, Paul J. 2007. "Writing, Graphology, and Visual Semiosis." In *New Directions in the Analysis of Multimodal Discourse*, edited by Terry D. Royce and Wendy Bowcher, 111–46. Mahwah, NJ: Lawrence Erlbaum Associates.

Turner, Eric Gardner. 1987. *Greek Manuscripts of the Ancient World*. 2nd ed. Edited by Peter J. Parsons. London: Institute of Classical Studies.

van Leeuwen, Theo. 2005. *Introducing Social Semiotics*. London: Routledge.

Verhoogt, Arthur. 2009. "Dictating Letters in Greek and Roman Egypt from a Comparative Perspective." https://sites.lsa umich.edu/wp-content/uploads/sites/235/2015/02/dicta ting1.pdf.

Walker, Sue. 2001. *Typography and Language in Everyday Life: Prescriptions and Practices*. Harlow: Longman.

Wilfong, Terry G. 2002. *Women of Jeme: Lives in a Coptic Town in Late Antique Egypt*. Ann Arbor: University of Michigan Press.

Wolf, Werner. 2006. "Introduction: Frames, Framings and Framing Borders in Literature and Other Media." In *Framing Borders in Literature and Other Media*, edited by Werner Wolf and Walter Bernhart, 1–40. Amsterdam: Rodopi.

## CHAPTER 8

Towards a Socio-Semiotic Analysis of Greek Medical Prescriptions on Papyrus

Nicola Reggiani

> Non è la materia che genera il pensiero, è il
> pensiero che genera la materia
> GIORDANO BRUNO

∴

Introduction*

In the general framework of the rising interest in the multimodal communication strategies deployed by Ancient Greek documentary texts, of which the present volume is a perfect representative, it seems worth taking into consideration a comparison with the paratextual devices employed in other categories of papyrological sources, namely paraliterary texts, which usually partake in the very same everyday circulation as the documents themselves.[1] "Paraliterary" defines an uneasy category of texts, mostly pertaining to the genres of technical works, scientific treatises, school handbooks, reference manuals, and the like. The papyri that are commonly labelled as having medical content fall into this paraliterary category and are quite a diverse group, which is particularly suitable to socio-semiotic analysis thanks to their wide circulation among both physicians and laymen, their technical content, their specialized vocabulary, and the paratextual devices employed to convey special meanings.[2]

Among medical papyri from Ptolemaic to Byzantine Egypt, prescriptions constitute a comparatively wide sub-corpus, amounting to ca. 150 items, which is about forty percent of the wider medical papyri group. These items show a variety of textual structures, amongst which we usually distinguish: 1) titles of recipes (likely labels for medicinal containers or shelves), 2) simple lists of ingredients (for pharmaceutical use or commercial inventories), 3) prescriptions or recipes (with more or less detailed directions for the composition and/or use), and 4) *receptaria* (collections of recipes, for the physician's reference).[3] Consequently, as just mentioned, they are of uneasy categorization: sometimes they are considered as proper documentary items, and therefore catalogued in documentary resources such as the *Heidelberger Gesamtverzeichnis* (HGV), while sometimes they are seen as undefined paraliterary texts and thus recorded in literary catalogues such as the *Leuven Database of Ancient Books* (LDAB) or the *Mertens-Pack³* (M-P³).[4] In their borderline nature as quasi-documentary texts, they seem to be among the best *comparanda* for a general discussion about the social semiotics of papyri.

As specialized texts, they employ not only a corpus-specific technical vocabulary, but also a complex set of paratextual (non-textual, non-linguistic) strategies in order to convey their scientific content to a somewhat wide range of different recipients with diverse levels of medical expertise: physicians, pharmacists, and laymen.[5] Their semiotic charge can be described as a graphic and expressive jargon that exhibits a variety of common, well-recognizable, standard schemes.[6] In the following paragraphs, these general schemes will be analyzed first of all with regards to graphical and layout markers that can be considered indicators of fragmentation (i.e., separators of

---

* This paper falls within the framework of the PRIN 2017 National Project "Greek and Latin Literary Papyri from Graeco-Roman and late antique Fayum (IV BC–VII AD): Texts, Contexts, Readers" (P.I. Lucio Del Corso, University of Cassino), University of Parma Research Unit (coordinator Nicola Reggiani).

1 A recent survey on paratextual strategies in written texts from ancient Egypt is now provided by the collective volume Carlig et al. 2020.

2 For a recent survey of "medical papyrology" and further bibliographical directions on the Greek medical papyri, see Reggiani 2019a. An overall and comprehensive introduction to the topic, with a now unfortunately outdated catalogue of texts, is provided by Andorlini 1993. I use the term "paratext" to broadly refer to any linguistic or para-linguistic sign that is not directly part of the main text but contributes to convey its meaning: layout devices, graphic marks, abbreviations, symbols, annotations, etc.

3 To date, there is no detailed comprehensive discussion of Greek medical prescriptions on papyrus. I refer to Reggiani, forthcoming, where I attempt an overall categorization of Greek medical papyri from the viewpoint of materiality. On single aspects of medical prescriptive papyri see Andorlini 2017, 3–36; 2018b; 2019; Reggiani 2018; 2019c.

4 See Reggiani 2017, 78; Reggiani 2019b, 168–71.

5 On laymen dealing with practical medicine see Reggiani 2022b with earlier bibliography.

6 See Andorlini 2017, 15–36.

single prescriptive textual units): horizontal dividers (*para-graphos*, *diple obelismene*), line displacements (*ekthesis*, *eisthesis*), blank spaces, graphical signs (*koronis*), line fillers, and formulaic expressions. In the second section, I will then consider schemes of more a structural nature, especially the use of three distinct textual phases, each of which feature peculiar characteristics. In the third and final section I will consider a special group of indicators, namely monograms used to convey particular technical meanings.

1 Indicators of Fragmentation

Prescriptions are born as fragments, not only due to their papyrological nature. At their very origins, they belong to oral forms of knowledge transmission. Each prescription is an oral fragment, conveying a specific and unique message in a single unit of text, with its own internal structure, which must be preserved in order to guarantee a correct transmission of its message.[7]

In collections of recipes, each textual unit is kept separated and independent by means of paratextual frames, the most obvious of which is a graphic mark, such as the *paragraphos*, a usually short horizontal interlinear stroke that typically divides text blocks.[8] This is a common feature in documentary as well as literary texts, where it is employed with the very same purpose. The *paragraphos* can occur alone, as in P.Oxy. LXXX 5249 (Oxyrhynchus [III CE]) or P.Ryl. I 29[9] (unknown provenance [III CE], parchment codex), and it is not infrequently lengthened to assume the shape of a longer line, which clearly attests to its fundamental role as a separator. We find such an extended *paragraphos* in SB XXIV 15917 (Ankyron [II CE]), for instance, where the two extant lines start from the middle of the left-hand intercolumnar space and reach the middle of the column width (Fig. 8.1). SB XIV 12175 (unknown provenance [II CE]) seems to show a similar feature, since a long horizontal stroke between the upper break and line 1, though mutilated on both sides, can evoke an extended *paragraphos*.

A somehow more elaborated interlinear divider is the segmented line crossing the whole column width in the much later MPER N.S. XIII 10 (unknown provenance [V CE]) and SB XIV 11964 (unknown provenance [V/VI CE])—the latter being not a proper *receptarium* but a papyrus sheet preserving three recipes in two columns.

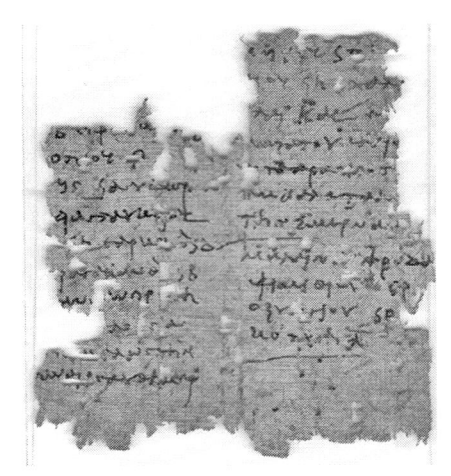

FIGURE 8.1   SB XXIV 15917 (P.Heid. inv. G 845)
PHOTO: ELKE FUCHS.
© INSTITUT FÜR PAPYROLOGIE,
UNIVERSITÄT HEIDELBERG

A similar example can also be seen in the elegant, dotted lines employed in the surviving leaves from two equally late parchment codices, MPER N.S. XIII 8 (unknown provenance [V CE]) and BKT III, 32–33 (unknown provenance [V/VI CE]). Certainly, such graphical variations do attest to the particular care taken in compiling the recipe collections.

More frequently, the *paragraphos* is accompanied by other graphic or layout devices, with the very same function of highlighting the beginning of a new prescriptive unit. An effective layout arrangement is the displacement of the first line of the new text, so that it appears extended with respect to the left-hand margin of the writing column—such an effect is called *ekthesis*. The combination of *paragraphos* + *ekthesis* is very early, since we find it in some of the most ancient *receptaria*. For example, in P.Ryl. III 531 (unknown provenance), which dates back to the third or second century BCE,[10] the *paragraphoi* are systematically enhanced by a considerable extension of the starting line of each prescriptive unit. The very same combination can be found in much later examples, such as P.Paramone 3 (unknown provenance [II CE]), SB XVIII 13310 (= P.Haun. III 47, unknown provenance [II CE]), and P.Oxy. LXXX 5243 (Oxyrhynchus [II/III CE]), which points to a well-established custom. *Ekthesis* of the first line and an extended *paragraphos* are employed in P.Oxy. LXXIV 4977 (Oxyrhynchus [late II–III CE]; discussed further below).

Another way of graphically highlighting the beginning of a new recipe was to enlarge the size of the very first letter of the first line. This is, again, usually in combination

---

7   See Reggiani 2019c.
8   See Barbis Lupi 1994.
9   See Andorlini 2018a, 78–80.

10   See Andorlini 2018a, 65–68.

FIGURE 8.2 P.Yale inv. 1443, fr. 1

IMAGE PROVIDED IN OPEN ACCESS BY THE YALE
PAPYRUS COLLECTION, BEINECKE RARE BOOK &
MANUSCRIPT LIBRARY

with *paragraphoi*. We find this in P.Yale inv. 1443 (= Pap. Congr. XXIV, pp. 427–33, Tebtunis [late I–early II CE]; Fig. 8.2) and P.Oxy. LXXX 5248 (Oxyrhynchus [II/III CE]).

It is not infrequent that only line displacements were used as dividers. P.Harr. I 46 (unknown provenance [I CE]),[11] for example, is a very fragmented piece that nevertheless preserves the turning point from one prescription to another, with the first line of the latter extending considerably to the left, without any other apparent sign—at least from the transcription, since I was not able to check the original or a photograph of it. The same layout can be seen in P.Oxy. LXXIV 4978 (Oxyrhynchus [mid II–mid III CE]) as well. Certainly, it was systematically applied in P.Oxy. LXXX 5247 (Oxyrhynchus [II/III CE]), which preserves the remains of two columns of an originally wider collection of recipes: in what survives of the second column, each prescription begins on a new line, projecting into the left-hand margin by about 1 cm, with the end of the previous line left blank; additionally, it seems that the first letter may be slightly enlarged. The existence of such a scheme in later items, like Pap. Flor. XLIV 3, a fragment from a parchment codex from Antinoupolis dated to the second half of the third century CE, or MPER N.S. XIII 14v (unknown provenance), dating back to the seventh century CE, proves its successful diffusion. In fact, *paragraphoi* and line extensions, either alone or in combination, seem to be the most frequent devices used to separate single items in recipe collections.

In P.Ross.Georg. V 57v (Arsinoites [III CE]) the *ekthesis* of the first line of each new recipe is combined with a blank space (*vacat*) dividing the respective text units. The *vacat* is another method employed in the medical collections: it could be used either alone or in combination with other dividers, though in the few extant examples it is impossible to reconstruct the original layout. Indeed, in P.Oxy. LXXX 5246 (Oxyrhynchus [II/III CE]) and P.Coll. Youtie I 4 (Oxyrhynchus [III CE]), where the prescriptions are clearly separated from each other with blank spaces, the columns' lack of left-hand margin prevents us from ascertaining the possible existence of further indicators.

MPER N.S. XIII 1 (unknown provenance [II/III CE]), where a huge *vacat* is employed certainly without *paragraphos*, is a special case, because it is not part of a large collection, but is a single sheet containing just two versions of the same recipe; nevertheless, the use of blank space to divide the text blocks is meaningful and noteworthy. In P.Oxy. IV 661v (Oxyrhynchus [II–early III CE]) short blanks are used along with *ekthesis* of the first lines. However, I think that this method must not have been widely diffused, because it implied a certain consumption of writing surface and ancient scribes usually tended to economize.

A more practical use of blanks was certainly what can be called the "inline *vacat*," which is a short gap between the end of a text section and the beginning of the next, when both fall onto the very same line. We find clear cases of this in P.Chic. 4v (Karanis [II/III CE]),[12] at line 6, where the end of the previous recipe is further marked by a high dot (*ano stigme*), and most likely at line 13, as well as in SB XVI 13080 (unknown provenance [III CE]) at line 3. In both cases, due to the fragmentary state of the items we are unable to state whether the inline blank was joined to a *paragraphos*, as was the case with BKT III, 30–31 (unknown provenance [II CE]), where a short interlinear stroke is added between the line where the separating *vacat* occurs and the line following. A very special instance is P.Ant. III 135 (Antinoupolis), a fragment of a seventh-century papyrus codex, where the turning point between two prescriptions, on the same line, is graphically stressed with a double dot (*dikolon*) and a *paragraphos*, which can therefore be defined as "inline" as well.

Most of the abovementioned devices can be diffusely found in documentary papyri with the same purpose, as are the peculiar diagonal strokes or slashes systematically used on the left in PSI Congr.XXI 3 (Tebtunis [I BCE])[13] to mark the first line of each new recipe (Fig. 8.3). This is

11   See Andorlini 2017, 69–71.

12   Andorlini 2018a, 76–78.
13   Andorlini 2018a, 11–24.

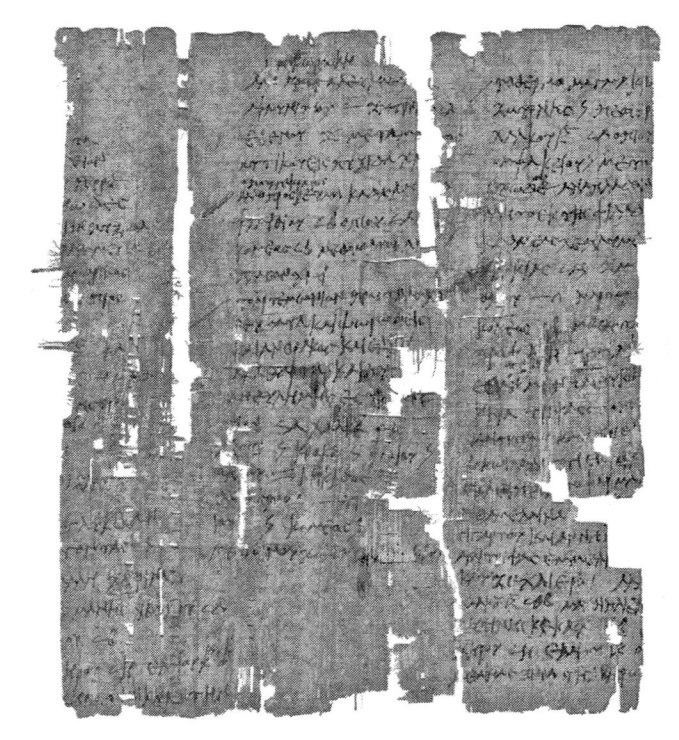

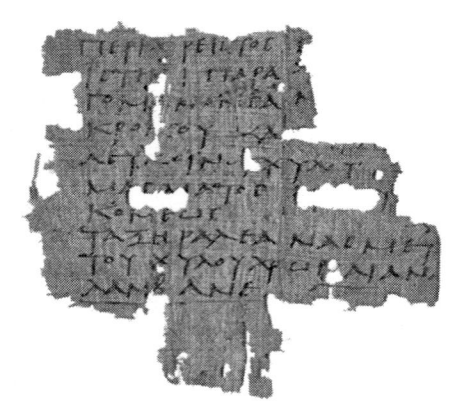

FIGURE 8.4   PSI Congr.XX 5 (PSI inv. 964)
PHOTO COURTESY OF THE
ISTITUTO PAPIROLOGICO
"GIROLAMO VITELLI"

FIGURE 8.3   PSI Congr.XXI 3 (PSI inv. 3051v)
COURTESY OF THE ISTITUTO PAPIROLOGICO
"GIROLAMO VITELLI"

quite a common feature of documentary lists (of people, goods, tax payments, etc.) and is frequently interpreted as a checking device, employed to cross an item out after having transcribed it or accounted for it in a further report. The cited *receptarium*, instead, proves that slashes could be used also as plain ticks aimed at signaling the individual textual items of a group.

Sometimes, more "literary" indicators were used. The *paragraphos*—which, at any rate, is employed in literary papyri as well—is thus replaced by the so-called "forked" *paragraphos* or *diple obelismene*, a horizontal stroke with two divergent tails at the left-hand end (>—).[14] The extant examples of which I am aware deploy irregularly shaped *diplai obelismenai*. The most accurate samples, PSI Congr.XX 5 (unknown provenance [III CE]);[15] Fig. 8.4) and SB XXVIII 17140[16] (Lykopolis [V CE]), exhibit prolonged lines that cross the writing column through almost its entire length. This is also the case with GMP I 13 (Arsinoites [III CE]), though here the sign is traced twice in a very hesitant and rough way, obtaining the effect of two crudely wavy lines.[17] In MPER N.S. XIII 4 (= SB XVI

13002, unknown provenance [III CE]), two interlinear diagonal strokes on the left-hand side look like a hasty attempt to draw the angular tails of a *diple obelismene*, which comes together with an oversized initial letter (see above) and a displacement in *eisthesis* of the title (see below) of the next recipe. All such instances appear in informal texts, copied in irregular handwriting and likely belonging to single sheets with multiple recipes rather than to longer rolls: this suggests that the *diple obelismene*, though of literary flavor, was not used for a literary reason, but was perhaps just a reminiscence of the literary acquaintance of the copyists, or of the very books from which they extracted the prescriptions.

Even more literary in flavor, the *koronis* makes various appearances in the extant medical prescriptive corpus. It is a graphic sign, which initially reproduced a bird before developing into more stylized shapes, and was frequently used in literary papyri to indicate the end of a significant section of text, or a relevant turning point.[18] Its first medical appearance is in SB VIII 9860 (Arsinoites), which is one of the earliest collections of recipes on papyrus, dating to the second century BCE on palaeographical grounds.[19] This is a peculiar item, having being copied by several people from different sources: the extant last six columns of the original roll show three different hands and a variety of language styles and page layouts, which attests to the diversity of the source material. The prescriptions are separated from each other mostly by means of *paragraphoi* and centered titles (see below), but in three cases the beginning of a new text block is further stressed by graphic signs traced on the left of the first line—two

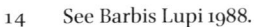

14   See Barbis Lupi 1988.
15   See Andorlini 2018a, 7–10; 2018b, 119.
16   Fournet 1994, 2004, 185–87.
17   Online photo at <https://berlpap.smb.museum/00994>.

18   See Stephen 1959.
19   See Andorlini 2018a, 63–65 (whose reconstruction of the extant portion of the original roll I follow hereafter).

X-shaped marks and a more elaborated doodle, a proper *koronis*, which was probably copied as such from the original source and which is clearly ligatured to an interlinear *paragraphos*.

A second example of *koronis* can be found in GMP I 10 (= P.Rein. I 16 + BKT III pp. 33–34, unknown provenance),[20] another Ptolemaic papyrus, dating back to the late second century BCE. The context is very fragmentary—only the very beginnings of the lines of the incomplete second column of fragment A survive—but the coarsely-written *koronis*, added in the intercolumnar space between lines 3 and 4, next to an interlinear *paragraphos*, must indicate the starting point of a new section of the receptarium. The sign, though affected by a hole and by the generally badly preserved papyrus surface, looks well-traced and can be identified as the "body" of the bird-like shape, with the "crest" on top and schematic "legs" below. Some other marginal traces, below the *koronis*, are of more difficult exegesis.

A third *koronis* appears in P.Köln. XI 437 (unknown provenance; Fig. 8.5), which, although not as early as the previous two papyri, dates between the end of the Ptolemaic age and the beginning of the Roman era (second half I BCE). In this case the sign is traced very well, and the original bird-like shape is easily recognizable in the body, made up of two circles with dots—the "eye" and the "wing"—inside, the upper crescent representing the "crest," and a lower open triangle representing the "legs." It looks appropriate for the general literary flavor of the copy, which is certainly of personal, yet careful production. It occurs at a key turning point of the collection, the transition from the section devoted to emollient plasters (μαλ]άγματα, l. 4, ending at l. 20) to the one concerning liquid painkillers (l. 21, ἄκοπα cυνχρίc[ματα, *l.* cυγχρ-). The new chapter is further highlighted by means of a short interlinear *paragraphos* and a slight indentation (*eisthesis*) of the starting line.

Another element almost certainly derived from literary models is the enlarged and wavy *xi* traced in BKT IX 76 (= SB XX 14501, Hermopolis [VI CE]) at line 9, which appears to be very much similar to the quickest *koronides* to be found in some literary instances. This papyrus—written in an elegant and regular upright hand—does in fact systematically employ long *paragraphoi* and enlarged initials to articulate the prescriptions, but the large curly *xi* is evidently traced with a certain reminiscence of more elaborated graphical signs (Fig. 8.6).

While all of the preceding instances pertain to texts with a literary flavor and aspect, though certainly not

FIGURE 8.5 P.Köln. XI 437, ll. 19–24 (P.Köln inv. 2331)
PHOTO COURTESY OF THE KÖLNER PAPYRUSSAMMLUNG

FIGURE 8.6 BKT IX 76 = SB XX 14501 (P.Berol. inv. G 21173)
© STAATLICHE MUSEEN ZU BERLIN, ÄGYPTISCHES MUSEUM UND PAPYRUSSAMMLUNG

20 Andorlini 2018a, 25–32.

destined for libraries, another case belongs to the very personal production and use of collections of recipes. Specifically, P.Mich. XVII 758 (unknown provenance), the famous so-called "Michigan Medical Codex," is a fourth-century papyrus codex of small format, of which thirteen leaves (amounting to twenty-six pages) survive and in which numerous recipes are collected, seemingly according to the type of medication (pills and lozenges, then wet and dry plasters, at least in the extant pieces). The prescriptions, which find parallels in the known medical literature, typically start with an indented heading (see below), announcing the type of remedy, and are separated from each other with often irregular *paragraphoi* and small blank spaces. The original text, copied at once by a scribe, was subsequently enhanced by the owner of the "book," who corrected a few of the original errors of copying and—more strikingly—added into the ample bottom margins some twenty additional recipes on related topics, doubling the number of recipes in the preserved sections, certainly drawing from his own personal notes or from other pharmacological compilations.

Because empty space was limited, the second hand emphasized the separation between recipes through irregular lines, waves, angular strokes, and marginal markers, among which we find abbreviations (see below) and both wavy and cross-like symbols that might be compared to *koronides*. In folio E recto, for example, a horizontal stroke with an S-shaped tail appended below resembles the last closing mark of PSI 718 (see below) as much as the *koronis* of SB 9860—it is indeed a typical rendering, described by some scholars as a "forked *paragraphos* with a sinuous stroke," which appears in literary papyri through to medieval manuscripts (Fig. 8.7).[21] Although this rendering is frequently considered a late evolution of the simple *paragraphos* or of the *diple obelismene*, I think it more

appropriate to interpret it as a derivation of the fusion between *paragraphos* and *koronis*, as already attested in the Ptolemaic papyri (e.g., SB 9860, in our limited case study). In the same page of the Michigan codex, just next to this *koronis*, another mark, which can be described as a horizontal stroke with a curved leftward tail, is certainly a simpler duplication of the very same sign. Marginal cross-like symbols, as surviving in folios K recto and M recto, can be interpreted as other graphical variants of *koronides*. The purpose of both sign types is clearly to mark the passage between different prescriptions.

With only the peculiar exception of the "inline *vacat*" described above, the prescriptions are usually arranged so that each new text unit begins on a new line, beneath the line in which the previous recipe ends. This circumstance is somehow taken for granted, but nonetheless not obvious, because even line breaks belong to a paratextual strategy that uses the paging layout to articulate the text blocks to preserve their essential unity. From this viewpoint, even in the textual architectures where no further signs are used, the transition between two different recipes is clearly apparent, especially when the last line of the preceding text is short, leaving a considerable final blank, which can be theoretically considered as a sort of *vacat*. In this case, what was stressed of the text unit was rather its end than its beginning.

Sometimes, this essential turning point in recipe collections could be further marked by "line fillers"; that is, graphical signs filling those unwritten spaces that were left at the end of each recipe due to a line break.[22] Generally speaking, line fillers are a common writing strategy in both documentary and literary papyri, where their main and sole function is to maintain the right-hand vertical alignment of the column in the case of shorter lines. Their purpose is thus exclusively what might be called aesthetic,

FIGURE 8.7   P.Mich. XVII 753, Er (P.Mich. inv. 21); at left, the original transcription of the page,
                  and at right, particular *koronis*-signs
                  PHOTO PROVIDED IN OPEN ACCESS BY THE UNIVERSITY OF MICHIGAN
                  LIBRARY

---

21   See, ultimately, Albrecht and Matera 2017.

22   See Barbis Lupi 1992; Di Matteo 2007 (with a particular focus on the Herculaneum papyri).

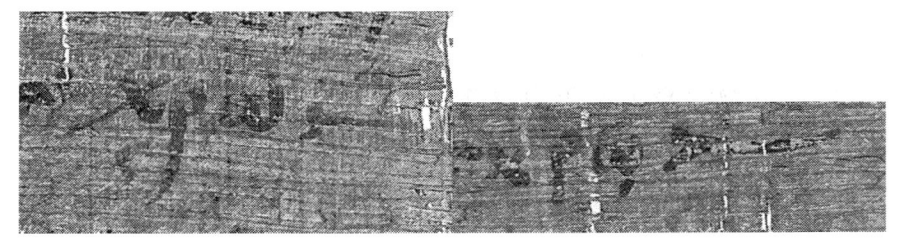

FIGURE 8.8   P.Mich. XVII 753 (P.Mich. inv. 21), with Cr, 6 at left and Dr, 9 at right
PHOTO PROVIDED IN OPEN ACCESS BY THE UNIVERSITY OF MICHIGAN
LIBRARY

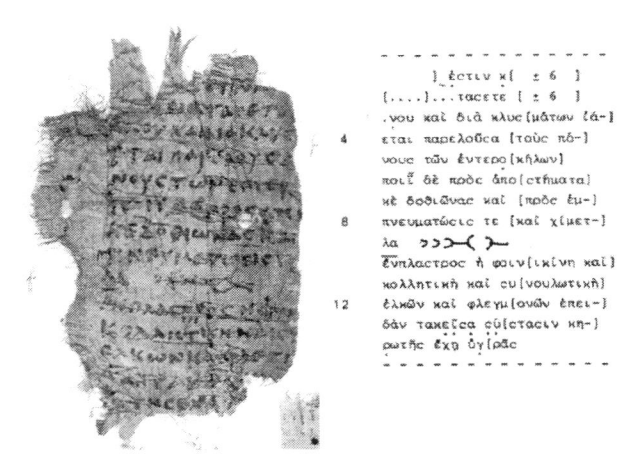

FIGURE 8.9   P.Mich. XVII 753, Fr (P.Mich. inv. 21)
PHOTO PROVIDED IN OPEN ACCESS BY THE
UNIVERSITY OF MICHIGAN LIBRARY

which contrasts with the medical collections, where they were used with the primary aim of visually marking the end of a recipe as an alternative to the simple final *vacat*. In the extant papyri we find few examples of this. As one example, in P.Aberd. 10 (Soknopaiou Nesos [II CE])—the new edition of which by Isabella Andorlini allowed for the reconstruction of a small *ekthesis* of the first line of each recipe[23]—we notice a remarkable extension of the middle stroke of *epsilon* in the word μίσγε (l. 8), at the end of the second prescription surviving on the papyrus scrap.[24]

In other examples, in both SB 12175, line 6, and PSI Congr.xx 5, line 10 (Fig. 8.4), the filling stroke acquires the more elaborated shape of a *diple obelismene*. This feature is repeatedly employed in the abovementioned Michigan Medical Codex as well (folio C recto, l. 6; D recto, l. 9; Fig. 8.8), where it even comes to assume the more complicated aspect of a double specular forked *paragraphos* preceded by three more "forks" (folio F recto, l. 9; Fig. 8.9). Since the scope of the codex is not literary at all, being a practical manual for a physician's individual everyday use,

we might argue that the graphical apparatus was partially inherited and imitated from the original sources—indeed, one cannot fail to notice that the more elaborated signs (the "tailed" *koronides*, the wavy *paragraphoi*, the closing *diplai obelismenai*) belong to the original copying of the texts, while the simpler ones (the cross-shaped *koronides*, the monograms that I will discuss below) belong to the personal additions.

Even more elaborated is the layout of PSI VI 718 (= SB XXVI 16458, Oxyrhynchus [IV/V CE]), a parchment page from a small medical notebook, which combines marginal *paragraphoi* to divide the recipes from each other with closing marks, which deserve deeper attention (Fig. 8.10).[25] The first line of the leaflet is the last line of a prescription certainly started on a preceding page (note that the number on the top of the page, ζ = "7," implies that six leaves, now lost, came before). The last word, λάβε, exhibits an extension of the middle stroke of *epsilon* which resembles—in a shorter fashion—the case of P.Aberd. 10. After this extension, a small S-shaped sign is traced, followed by another angular sign, partially lost in the right-hand break, which corresponds more or less to the left-hand margin of the writing column. A new recipe then begins, on a new line, after a marginal *paragraphos*. The very same sequence of S-shaped sign and angular sign occur at the end of line 4, which is the last line of the second recipe preserved on this page. In this case, the pair of signs is followed by a horizontal stroke up to the right-hand break, and the next recipe starts on the following line, after a marginal *paragraphos*. This third recipe ends at line 11, and again we find a similar sequence of S-shaped sign and angular sign—the latter, here, looks more like a *koronis*, a short horizontal with a curled tail. Unlike the previous cases, the following recipe does not start on a new line, but on the very same line 11, after the closing signs; then it continues along line 12, ending on the next page 8, which did not survive. A *paragraphos*

---

23   Andorlini 2018a, 68–74.
24   It is not possible to detect the same feature at the end of the other extant recipes (ll. 4 and 16).

25   See Andorlini 2018b, 120–22.

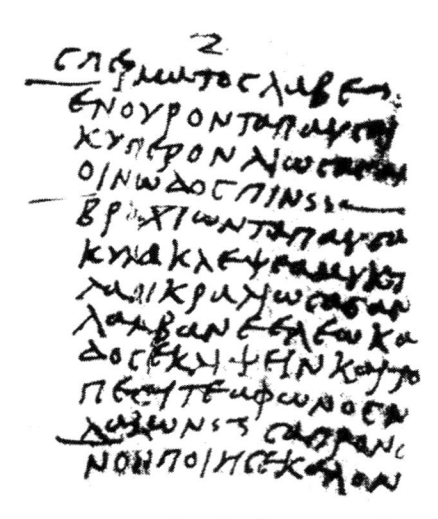

FIGURE 8.10   Drawing from PSI VI 718 =
              SB XXVI 16458 (BML inv.
              13925)

cuts the interlinear space between lines 11 and 12, as in the cases of "inline *vacat*" described above.

A completely different case of line fillers is represented by P.Köln. X 410 (unknown provenance [IV CE]). In this example, filling strokes appear in at least three instances after the columned ingredients. This papyrus is a very fragmentary scrap, so we cannot be certain of what was going on there: we can just follow the editor, Giuseppina Azzarello, in supposing that in this case the signs acted as proper fillers of the blank spaces between the ingredient names and the corresponding quantities.[26]

At times, we also find formulaic expressions that are used as linguistic markers of the specificity of each prescription. Such phrases go beyond their intrinsic linguistic meaning and become readily recognizable semiotic markers, working as semantic components. The most frequent are the terms πρός and ἄλλο. The former, with the meaning of "for" in the sense of "against," typically introduced the therapeutic scope of the medicament; the latter, meaning literally "another one," was frequently repeated at the beginning of each new recipe of the same type or function as the preceding one. Sometimes they were spelled out and regularly inserted in the normal syntax of the text; sometimes they were isolated or abbreviated to further stress their mainly graphic-semiotic role. Among the earliest medical collections, P.Ryl. 531 shows, for example,

both words integrated in the semantic context. πρὸς τοὺς ἀπὸ τῶν ὑστέρων πνιγμούς "against the suffocations from the uterus" (col. ii, l. 3) is the title of a new gynaecological recipe, starting as usual in *ekthesis* after a *paragraphos* (see above); except for a small, almost unnoticeable inline *vacat* separating the whole title from the rest of the prescription (see below), there is no hint that the heading πρός was given a particular stress. Four lines below, ἄλλο ἐὰν μετὰ τοῦ πνίγεσθαι καὶ βήςςῃ, "another one if (she) also coughs beside suffocating" (col. ii, l. 7), again in *ekthesis* after a *paragraphos*, behaves accordingly as the current title of a new remedy of a similar nature.[27]

Nevertheless, the other early Ptolemaic *receptarium*, SB VIII 9860, already gives ἄλλο a special treatment, by isolating and centering it at the beginning of a new prescription (col. iv, l. 18). The variety of sources of this papyrus, as already observed above, are evident also in the fact that elsewhere (col. iii, l. 17) ἄλλο shows no special layout, and the prescription is marked by a *paragraphos* and a marginal cross (see above). The irregular trend of considering ἄλλο as an isolated heading, detached from the syntactic context of the recipe, is apparent from P.Oxy. LII 3654v + II 234v (Oxyrhynchus [II CE]), a composite medical roll combining a catechistic manual with a collection of recipes.[28] In the prescriptive part of this anthology (P.Oxy. II 234), which was very likely taken from the *Euporista* written by Herophilean physician Apollonius Mus, active in Alexandria towards the end of the first century BC, the only readable column (ii) preserves ten remedies for earache, grouped by typology. The different groups are marked by titles in *eisthesis* (ll. 36–37 and 23–24, see below); within each group, the prescriptions are separated from each other by *paragraphoi*, but there is

---

26 The editor proposes the alternative option that the strokes could have been intended to highlight when a quantity was not specified, drawing attention to the fact the amount was not listed by the copyist for several possible reasons. This alternative explanation is more difficult to accept, because if the copyist had wanted to exclude some ingredients from a list or a formulation, I think he would simply have not transcribed them at all.

27 It has been ascertained that P.Ryl. 531 re-elaborates therapeutic material from Hippocrates' gynaecological treatises, namely *Women's Diseases*: see, ultimately, Roselli 2019, 83–85. Both of the mentioned prescriptions (col. ii, ll. 3–6 and 7–10) partially parallel *Mul. Aff.* II 200, and it is interesting to compare their introductory sentences with their Hippocratic counterparts, which run, respectively, as follows: ὅταν πνίγηται ὑπὸ ὑςτερέων "when (she) suffocates from the uterus" and ὅταν δὲ πνίγωςι καὶ ὁμοῦ βήςςῃ "when (she) suffocates and concurrently coughs." It is clear that the catalogue structure of Hippocrates' clinical records, articulated in the formulaic repetition of the adverb ὅταν followed by the direct description of the case in a third-person singular that points to the actual patient, was replaced by a more "impersonal" prescriptive structure based on the verbal markers πρός + abstract mention of the disease and ἄλλο + conditional clause specifying a particular typology of disease. This would become the most common way of articulating prescriptions in the medical papyri and literature from the Ptolemaic age onwards.

28 Andorlini 2017, 240–51.

also an in-text division system, which can be regarded as an enhanced version of the inline *vacat* described above. Since generally there is no line break between the recipes, each of them, except the very first of each group, is introduced by a formulaic ἄλλο isolated between blank spaces: if ἄλλο falls at the line beginning, it has one *vacat* after; if it falls at the line end, it has one *vacat* before; if it falls in the middle of the line, it has two *vacats*, before and after. A horizontal dash is sometimes added at the end of the shorter lines: they are unfortunately omitted in the editorial transcription, and a photo of the papyrus is not available online, but it seems that they can be safely considered as closing marks rather than line fillers.

A comparable instance can be found in the previously mentioned GMP I 10 (at fr. B, col. i, l. 14), where an ἄλλο is preceded by a long blank, though it is uncertain if another blank follows. ἄλλο certainly appears isolated by *vacat* also in its two only occurrences in the third column of P.Oxy. VIII 1088 (see below), at lines 5 and 9, where it shows up at the line beginnings because here the recipes regularly start on new lines. Quite interestingly, these are the only two points of the papyrus that lack a separating *paragraphos*, as if it were considered too strong to function as a divider for formulations of similar type. The best example of this formulaic ἄλλο is perhaps P.Oxy. LXXIV 4975 (Oxyrhynchus [II CE]). Here, the recipes are systematically divided by *paragraphoi* and highlighted by *ekthesis* of the first line, sometimes further stressed by *eisthesis* of the following line (ll. 9 and 14); where ἄλλο occurs (ll. 1 and 17), it is not only isolated by *vacat*, but also rendered in an abbreviated form (α with λ on its top) that underlines its semiotic power even more.

In these last two papyri from Oxyrhynchus—P.Oxy. VIII 1088 and LXXIV 4975—phrases with πρός also appear, but they are not given any special graphical relevance, as they are in several other recipe collections. On some occasions, instead, such a typical introductory preposition is represented through a particular monogram, made up of π and ρ intertwined (℟). This is by no means a specific feature of medical writing, as we find it in many documentary papyri as well (this is the case with ἄλλο, too), but, since this kind of formulation is very peculiar for medical prescriptions, and since it usually appears at the very beginning of the recipes (see below), we might ask whether this monogram was actually used as a symbolic identifier of the starting point of a new recipe. Indeed, in some cases we find it at the very beginning of a prescription, as in PSI X 1180 (see above), *passim* (some instances in the face of other instances of πρός spelled out); P.Oxy. LXXX 5247 (at col. ii, l. 12); and P.Tebt.Tait 43 (at l. 12; Tebtunis [late I–early II CE])—although the two latter papyri are small

fragments, so we cannot say if the feature was regular throughout.

MPER N.S. XIII 9 (unknown provenance [V CE]) and 16 (unknown provenance [VII CE]) are two peculiar cases because they are not proper recipes but medicinal labels; that is, tiny papyrus scraps used to tag medical substances or containers stored in a pharmacy, shop, or private holding. In both cases, the label indicates the purpose of the tagged remedy, and πρός is rendered as a monogram. In P.Oxy. II 234, line 37, the monogram ℟ does appear in the title of a section of the *receptarium* but not at the very beginning, though always referring to the medical purpose (κλυσμοὶ ὠτὸς | [πρ(ὸς)] πόνους "ear washes against pains")—at any rate, the abbreviation is here a tentative supplement.[29] In P.Oxy. LXXIV 4977, line 9, the monogram ℟ does not appear in a heading position, but is used within a sentence that points to the therapeutic scope of the prescription: ποιεῖ δὲ πρ(ὸς) διαθέσεις "use indeed against chronic conditions" (Fig. 8.18); the same happens in P.Oxy. LXXX 5250 (Oxyrhynchus [III CE]),[30] seemingly a single recipe, in which ℟ is employed twice to indicate two different possible usages of the described remedy (see below). In short, there is no hint of a systematic use of the monogram ℟ in medical prescriptions, nor is it exclusive to medical writing; yet, when used, it certainly acted as an effective indicator of a particularly relevant point of the text.

2 Structural Indicators

Every proper prescription typically followed a standard textual architecture, with three distinct phases that facilitated its understanding and use. These phases included, 1) a header, usually containing the title or name of the remedy (προγραφή) and/or its therapeutic indication (ἐπαγγελία); 2) the pharmacological composition (σύνθεσις

---

29   *vac.* κλυσμοὶ ὠτὸς | [πρὸς] πόνους *ed.pr.* (ll. 36–37). The improvement *vac.* κλυσμοὶ ὠτὸς | *vac.* [πρ(ὸς)] πόνους has been proposed by Isabella Andorlini via Papyrological Navigator (<http://papyri.info/dclp/59150>) by analogy with lines 23–24, where a similar two-line heading occurs and the *eisthesis* is applied to both lines; that is, *vac.* ἔνθετα εἰς τ[ὸ] | *vac.* οὓς πρὸς πόνους. The argument is that if we expect an indention at line 37 as well, then the word πρός must be abbreviated, otherwise it would not fit the space. On the other hand, the fact that at line 24 πρός is spelled out leads us to the opposite conclusion: that at line 37 we must supply the whole word and therefore admit the line was not indented. Both options do not agree entirely with what occurs at lines 23–24, so that strict analogy cannot be invoked in either case, and both solutions are equally possible.

30   Andorlini 2018a, 7–10.

or cυμμετρία); and 3) practical instructions for preparation and administration (cκευαcία), which will be discussed in Section 3. Each section commonly shows a particular layout, and although this is not a strict rule, it is not uncommon to find different structural schemes (or even a lack of structural schemes). By considering each of these phases in further detail below, I will show that in those instances where the prescriptions are structured, we can apprehend that there is a certain purpose charging the text's graphical disposition with paratextual meanings.

The highlighting strategies of the first phase, the heading block, almost always overlap with the indicators of fragmentation discussed above, due to the self-evident fact that new recipes start from their title. Sometimes, however, it is clear from the layout that a special stress was given to the title as a separate block, especially when it introduced entire homogeneous sections of pharmacological collections. In P.Oxy. II 234, for example, there is a neat distinction between the single recipes, isolated with the sequences of *vacat* and ἄλλο as described above, and the section titles, indented in *eisthesis*.[31] It is my impression that the two different layout strategies, namely *ekthesis* and *eisthesis*, could be used for two different purposes: the former to mark the starting point of a new prescription, and the latter to highlight the title, mainly of a new section or typological group of remedies.[32]

Another outstanding example is provided by P.Berl. Möller 13 (Hermopolis [III/IV CE]; Fig. 8.11), which preserves one column and a small portion of a second column of a collection of recipes from Heras of Cappadocia, which have been proven to be independent from Galen's excerpts from the same author.[33] At the top of the first extant column (numbered ια "11" in the upper margin), there is a two-line heading in *eisthesis*, πρὸc τὸ μὴ ἀπορρεῖν τὰc ἐν τῇ κε|φαλῇ τρίχαc, "to prevent hair loss on the head," which is clearly the therapeutic destination (προγραφή) of the following prescription, which does not provide the synopsis of the ingredients but moves directly to the cκευαcία, the practical instructions. This text block is followed by a huge unwritten space, which has been convincingly explained as free room left by the copyist for possible future additions of recipes of the same typology as the first; indeed, we can distinguish scanty traces of a *paragraphos* beneath the text block. The general structure of a typical column in this recipe collection is easily learnable from the second column, though mostly mutilated. Its text

FIGURE 8.11   P.Berl.Möller 13 (P.Berol. inv. 11317) © STAATLICHE MUSEEN ZU BERLIN, ÄGYPTISCHES MUSEUM UND PAPYRUSSAMMLUNG

starts at the same level as the first line of the prescription body in the previous column (l. 3), and it is easily arguable that the space on the top must have accommodated an indented heading like the one on the left, now completely lost in the right-hand lacuna. Then five recipes and the first line of a sixth follow, with *paragraphoi* dividing each from the others. Most of these recipes have been identified as belonging to the same typology against headache, so that we may conclude that the indented titles were intended to group analogous prescriptions in a systematic work (in progress) proceeding very likely *a capite ad calcem*; that is, from the head downwards.

The second phase, the pharmacological composition, was usually structured as a columned list of ingredients, with indication of the respective quantity isolated to the right, with the purpose—again—to highlight the relevant information about the makeup of the medicament. Once more I need to stress that this was not a rule; rather, we can in fact pinpoint two different main trends in structuring

---

31   See Lundon 2004.

32   On the use of *ekthesis* and *eisthesis* in the literary papyrus rolls see Savignago 2008.

33   See Marganne 1980; Corazza 2016; Reggiani 2019c, 180–82.

the ingredients of a typical cύνθεcιc section. The first is a columned scheme, while the second is a continuous list, with the substances and their quantities following one another on uninterrupted rows. Both layouts had advantages: the former was clearer as to legibility and usability, while the latter was economical and compact with regards to the exploitation of the writing surface. Not by chance, I think, the former was the preferential format of all the single recipes, those issued or annotated individually, outside the larger collections, from the earliest examples (GMP II 11 = P.Eleph.Wagner 4, Elephantine [late III BCE]) to the latest (SB XIV 12142 = P.Coll.Youtie II 87r, unknown provenance [VI CE]), with very few exceptions.[34]

I believe that an overall consideration of the layout features of the extant *receptaria* could lead to a general categorization between "practical pharmacological manuals," compiled from and for physicians' everyday use, and "systematic pharmacological treatises," with a somehow more "literary" flavor. Rather than listing a catalogue of both, which would be quite a tedious task for the scope of this contribution and which will be gladly reserved for a more comprehensive analysis of the topic, I would like to focus my attention here on two outstanding items, the mixed structures of which allow us to guess their multiple compilation from a variety of different sources—single recipes, personal notes, pharmacological treatises—according to what we already know about the circulation of medical writings in the Hellenistic and Roman world.

The first item, P.Oxy. VIII 1088 (Oxyrhynchus) preserves three columns of a first-century collection of prescriptions copied by an individual in a very personal and cursive handwriting on the verso of a Homeric commentary.[35] In the sixteen recipes surviving in the extant portion of text, a uniform compositional principle is barely perceivable, since the remedies seem to be listed first by bodily part (the skin in col. i, the nose in col. ii), then by medicinal typology (potions in col. iii). This lack of homogeneity is also reflected in the structure of the text. The first two recipes of the first column are arranged on three progressively indented levels: 1) the heading, including the name of the remedy and its therapeutic aim (ll. 1–3 and 8–9); 2) the ingredients, on continuous rows (ll. 4–6 and 10–12); and 3) the final excipient, water, almost centered on the column, with the function of closing (ll. 7 and 13; Fig. 8.12). The third recipe is structured similarly, though on just two

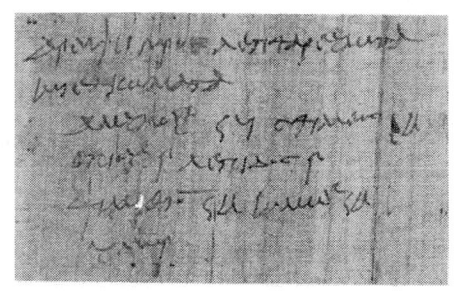

levels: the main body (ll. 14–17) and the final ingredient, considerably indented (l. 18). Then a completely different layout begins: in the prescriptions transcribed from the end of the first to the beginning of the third column, lines are longer and equally aligned, with *paragraphoi* of medium length used only as dividers. The rest of the third column seems to adopt yet another strategy, with the first line of each new recipe extended in *ekthesis*. The second and the third formulations (ll. 52–55 and 56–62) are just variants of the first πότημα πρὸc ἡπ[α]τικ[ο]ύc, a "potion against liver diseases" (ll. 48–51), and—as already noted above—this may explain why they are identified just by *ekthesis* of the first line, without *paragraphoi*. Then a *paragraphos* does separate this first group from a couple of other potions, a πότημα ὑδρωπικῶν, "potion for dropsicals" (ll. 63–65), and a ὑπνωτικὸν πότημα, "sleep-inducing potion" (ll. 66–67), which are characterized by *ekthesis* of the first lines as well. Finally, another *paragraphos* introduces the last two lines, which come back to the "normally-aligned" layout. As John Lundon already correctly saw, such variations, accompanied by small differences in the handwriting and in the abbreviating systems, are not to be blamed on the copyist's whims, but rather ascribed to a compiling process that tends to reproduce the original features of the source material utilized.[36]

The very same situation emerges from the second item, PSI X 1180 (= SB XXVIII 17134), one of the second-century medical papyri pertaining to the priestly library of the temple of the crocodile god Soknebtunis at Tebtunis. Written in a technical, informal, irregular handwriting on the recto of a virgin roll, the text presents an inhomogeneous structure comparable with P.Oxy. VIII 1088. In the sections preserved in large fragment A (Fig. 8.13) and in most of the smaller fragments lettered C to Q, the prescriptions are systematically divided with *paragraphoi* and line extensions with enlarged initial letters; if a recipe ends towards the line end, then the next one starts on the

---

34   Some of these exceptions can be explained by the special context of the transcription: for example, P.Cair.Masp. 67141 (see below), quickly annotated in the free space of an accounting register.

35   See Lundon 2004.

36   Lundon 2004, 121.

following line in *ekthesis*, but if it ends sufficiently before
the line end, then the next recipe starts on the same line,
after a double slanting stroke, with the line below in *ekthesis* anyway. The ingredients are transcribed in the "continuous list" model described above. In a particular section
(col. iv of fr. A) the prescriptions are further marked by
marginal checking strokes as in the abovementioned
case of PSI Congr.XXI 3. In fragment B, instead, though
maintaining the main structure of the *receptarium*, with
paragraphoi, extended lines, and enlarged initials, each
recipe begins after a line break, and the ingredients are
columned (Fig. 8.14). In this case too, Isabella Andorlini,
who re-edited the papyrus with unpublished additions,
correctly stated that such diversity points to the copying
of different source models, juxtaposed with each other
without a personal re-elaboration by the assembler.[37]

Finally, an uncommon characteristic is also worth
mentioning and is certainly featured in writings of a more
literary flavor. Specifically, we can identify the use of diacritical signs to keep the ingredients separated in "continuous lists." For instance, there are double dots (*dikola*) in
BKT III pp. 32–33 (a fragment from a parchment codex,
unknown provenance) and BKT IX 176 (papyrus sheet,

Hermopolis), both dated to the fifth or sixth century CE.
There is also a high dot (*ano stigme*) in P.Oxy. II 234.

---

37   Andorlini 2004, 87–88.

3 Special Indicators

Finally, there are other special indicators that stand as further semiotic indications of the technical message conveyed by prescriptions, including formulaic phrases, meaningful abbreviations, and symbols. We have already encountered the first of these, formulaic phrases, in the cases of ἄλλο and πρός analyzed above. The second, meaningful abbreviations, can be found in ingredients' names or units of measure, which can be abbreviated or not. However, because measures follow the common symbols and abbreviations well-established in the documentary papyri, they do not raise any special interest here.[38] This also applies to most of the abbreviations used for the ingredients, which are very often of the same typologies used in the documents.

It is therefore the third indicator that I would like to discuss here, specifically focusing on a few peculiar monograms, which, owing to their very nature as quasi-symbolic forms can reflect some sort of technical abstraction. A ζ and a ρ overlapped (ℨ) appear in SB XXVIII 17140, l. 25, to indicate ζμύρνη "myrrh." This was a very common ingredient in several recipes,[39] but we do not find the monogram until Byzantine times: in earlier texts the word is spelled out (even in the variant form cμύρνη), or occasionally abbreviated to ζμυρ (in both the previously discussed PSI Congr.XXI 3, ii, 15 and SB XIV 11964, *passim*, where other ingredients are also abbreviated in a similar fashion [Fig. 8.3]) or ζμ (PSI X 1180, fr. A, iv, 16). In another Byzantine recipe, personally transcribed by Dioscorus of Aphroditopolis, a papyrologically famous sixth-century man of letter, in an accounting codex (P.Cair.Masp. II 67141, folio 2r, ll. 20–29), there is a formulation about headache, where ζμύρνη is rendered with a different monogram ζμ. The technical use of the monogram ℨ is certainly late and limited: I could find parallels only in the magical formulations of PGM II 8 (col. iii, ll. 57 and 70; Thebes [IV/V CE]), where myrrh is prescribed as an ingredient to produce an effective ink, which makes me think that it was utilized in certain sapiential environments. On the other hand, the custom of abbreviating words in monograms with ρ cutting through another character is well-attested in all contexts: we have already seen the medical occurrences of ᵽ which was used also in documents as well as in magical papyri, and we will see soon below the case of ☧/ᵽ.

Yet another famous monogram is ⱷ, used to abbreviate ὥρα ("hour") and derivatives in documents as much as in the astrological horoscopes. In other words, although abbreviations and symbols are a common feature of technical writing, fulfilling the need for a recognizable set of semiotic strategies that allowed for the communication of specialized content rapidly, directly, immediately, and safely, I would not stress the medical relevance of ℨ too much. The same can be said, for instance, of the monogram Cℷ for (λίθος) cχιcτός "talc" in P.Oxy. VIII 1088 (col. i, l. 5) and PSI X 1180, A (col. iii, l. 39). The ingredient is widespread in medical recipes, but everywhere else it is spelled out; moreover, the same monogram is largely used in the documents to express common words like χ⟨ε⟩ιρόγραφον and χ⟨ε⟩ιριcτής, for instance.

A much more frequent sign is the *chi-rho* ☧ monogram, which is universally known for other reasons that fall outside our current scope. In medical writings, it points to the imperative idiom χρῶ "use" (from χράομαι) which drives the user's attention to the prescriptive section (cκευαcία), where instructions for the composition and the administration of the medicament are given according to a standard scheme. What is striking about ☧, unlike the monograms just mentioned, is that it soon overcame its simple role of abbreviation and developed into an a-syntactic symbol, involved in a more general semiotic process of abstraction of the linguistic structure of the textual signs.

In the earliest medical papyri, χρῶ appears as one of the recurring verbal forms that indicated the practical phases of production of the medicaments: in SB VIII 9860, for example, it occurs most frequently alone, at the end of the series of instructions, to indicate that the compound was ready to use, and sometimes with some extra direction, like χρῶ ἐν ὕδατι (col. ii, l. 9, "use in water") and χρῶ {πρὸς τὰ} πρὸc | τὰ ῥεύματα | καὶ τὰς περιωδυνί|ας καὶ φλεγμονάς (col. v, ll. 8–11, "use against discharges and excessive pains and inflammations"). Not dissimilar is the situation in PSI Congr.XXI 3, where χρῶι is used—in the graphical variant with ι adscript—either alone as an ending point of the prescription or with details such as μετὰ μέ[λι]τος | Ἀττικοῦ εἰς πυξίδα χρ[ῶι] (col. ii, ll. 3–4, "use with Attic honey in a box"), μεθ' ὕτα[τος] | χρῶι (col. iii, ll. 10–11, "use with water," with phonetic exchange δ → τ; Fig. 8.3). Other examples can be found in later texts, like PSI Congr.XX 5, at lines 8–10, with μετ[ὰ] | τοῦ χυλοῦ χρῶ καὶ ἀνα|λάμβανε, "use and take with the juice" (Fig. 8.4), or also in the Michigan Medical Codex discussed above. This is basically the situation we usually find in later papyri and in the medical literature too.

---

38   That said, it is worth mentioning those few texts where units of measure and quantities are spelled out instead of indicated with symbols and alphabetical characters. These respond to the specific need for clarity and exactness in reporting the pharmacological instructions; see Reggiani 2022a.

39   See Andorlini 2017, 37–40.

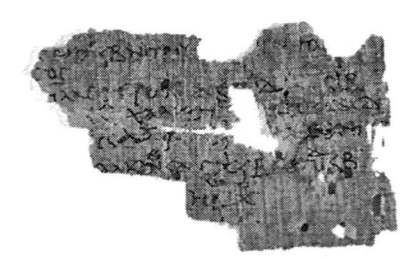

FIGURE 8.15   PSI X 1180 = SB XXVIII, fr. G
(BML inv. 19968; Florence,
Biblioteca Medicea
Laurenziana, Ms. PSI 1180)
BY PERMISSION OF THE
MIC. ANY FURTHER
REPRODUCTION IS
FORBIDDEN BY ANY
MEANS

At a certain point, this recurring term started being irregularly rendered with the monogram ⳨, which itself can be found in documentary and literary papyri for very common words.[40] Just like the full word, we find ⳨ both within sentences and alone. We can see the former in P.Oxy. LXXX 5250, at line 6, χρ(ῶ) δὲ καὶ πρ(ὸς) γαγγραίν[ας "use also against gangrenes," PSI X 1180, fr. A, at line 7, τρίψας μετ' ὄξους καὶ χρ(ῶ) "grind with vinegar and use" (Fig. 8.13), and possibly also in SB XIV 12175, at line 6, where χρ(ῶ) concludes a fragmentary prescription before a closing *diple obelismene*. An example of the latter case can be found in PSI X 1180, fr. G, at line 8, where ⳨ is placed at the conclusion of a recipe, isolated from the preceding instructions at the end of the last line through a small *vacat* (Fig. 8.15); possibly also in the same papyrus, fr. A, at

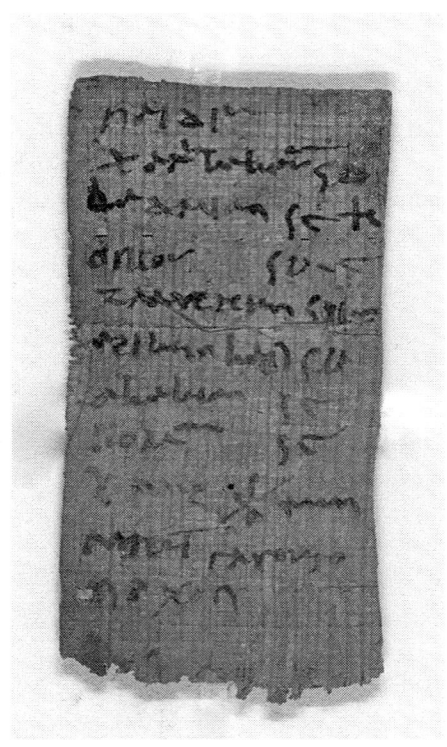

FIGURE 8.16   P.Princ. III 155v (P.Princ. inv.
AM 11224 B)
PHOTO PROVIDED IN OPEN
ACCESS BY THE PRINCETON
UNIVERSITY LIBRARY'S
PAPYRI COLLECTIONS

line 4, where ⳨ follows the last instruction λε⟨ι⟩ο[τριβήσας] "triturate" without any syntactic junction, just before the closing double slash (see above; Fig. 8.13).

It is probably thanks to the symbolic power of the monogram that the medical ⳨ very often loses its syntactic ties with the prescriptive context and becomes a semiotic indicator of the end of the recipe.[41] This is proved by the development of the formulaic phrase ὕδωρ χρῶ, "use with water," where the term for "water" is used in an idiomatic,

---

40   For example: χρυσίον (P.Cair.Zen. I 59021, 6, letter from Philadelphia [258 BCE]); παραχρῆμα (BGU X 1968, 11, contract from Thebes [184 BCE]); and μελίχρως, "honey-coloured" in personal identikits (P.Tebt. III.1 817, 33 and 35, loan contract from Tebtunis [182 BCE]; P.Tebt. III.2 972, 7, 8, 12, register of contract abstracts from Tebtunis [last quarter II BCE]); χρόνος-related terms (SPP XXII 11, 5, receipt from Philadelphia [133 CE]; BKT IV pp. 6–47, 12, 15, 56, philosophical treatise from Hermopolis [II/III CE]). Other monogrammatic abbreviations for the same sequence of characters did exist. For example, χρ(όνος), rendered with a χ bearing a small circle attached to its top right-hand stroke in P.Oxy. I 45, 20 (Oxyrhynchus [95 CE]), which is certainly an evolution of a model of abbreviation where ρ was ligatured to the top right-hand stroke of χ; χρ(ηματισμοῦ?) in SPP XXII 44, 4 (Arsinoites [124 CE]); and χρ(ημάτων) in P.Oxy. XLIV 3193, 13 (Oxyrhynchus [ca. 309 CE]). In later times, probably due to the spread of *chi-rho* as a Christian symbol, the abbreviations almost always come to display the two characters χρ not overlapped and with ρ's leg crossed by a diagonal stroke. Medical papyri are a remarkable exception to this otherwise seemingly general trend.

41   That medical writers entrusted ⳨ with a specific value is perhaps shown by the use of a different monogram, the staurogram ⳨, to render χρ(ήσιμον) or χρ(ηστόν) "most useful," a typical individual annotation of positive experience marginally added by practicing physicians to the relevant prescriptions in their handbooks. We find it in P.Oxy. VIII 1088, on the left of the last recipe of the third column, and in P.Mich. 768, folios H recto and M recto, on the left of two of the recipes added by the owner of the codex. To my knowledge, this form is limited to medical writings, as the overwhelming usage of staurogram in the documents points to the Christian symbolism. Among the documentary papyri, only BGU XIV 2441 (a land register from late Ptolemaic Herakleopolites; col. iii, l. 50), seems to abbreviate χρ(ησίμου) to indicate a portion of productive land, but so far I have not had the occasion to check which abbreviation is used.

FIGURE 8.17   GMP II 5 = P. Tebt. II 273v
COURTESY OF THE CENTER FOR THE TEBTUNIS
PAPYRI, UNIVERSITY OF CALIFORNIA, BERKELEY

FIGURE 8.18   P.Oxy. LXXIV 4977
COURTESY OF THE EGYPT EXPLORATION SOCIETY
AND THE UNIVERSITY OF OXFORD IMAGING
PAPYRI PROJECT

non-inflected nominative form, instead of the more correct forms ἐν ὕδατι or μεθ' ὕδατος (see above). Let us take into consideration, for example P.Princ. III 155v (unknown provenance [II/III CE]; Fig. 8.16).[42] The structure of this single recipe, cursively written on the back of a papyrus sheet used for another single prescription (see below), is clear: the title παιδικ(όν) "paediatric" (i.e., eye-salve), is isolated on the first line; then ingredients and quantities follow, conveniently columned on seven rows; finally, the last three lines (ll. 9–11) host the instructions ὕδωρ χρ(ῷ) ἕως γένητ(αι) γλυοῦ (= γλοιοῦ) τὸ πάχος, "use with water until it becomes of the consistency of machine-oil." The fact that the word ὕδωρ is aligned with the preceding substances helps explain, visually, the history of this formulaic syntagm: ὕδωρ was originally the last item in the list of ingredients, followed by the instruction χρῷ; subsequently, the two terms merged together in an almost independent block, acquiring a semiotic relevance of their own.

The process was certainly neither regular nor linear, but we can easily glimpse its results scattered here and there among the extant medical prescriptive papyri. For instance, in a first example, GMP II 5 (= P.Tebt. II 273, Tebtunis [II/III CE]), υδρωρχρωι is written as a compact set at the end of each recipe, slightly indented and almost centered underneath the columned list of ingredients [Fig. 8.17]. In a second case, P.Oxy. LXXIV 4977, at lines 1 to 2, at the end of the first recipe of the extant fragment, κόμ⟨μ⟩εως (δραχμή) α̅ (ingredient item = "gum: drachm 1") is followed, on the same line, after a one-character blank, by ὕδωρ (last ingredient item = "water," with a noticeable

dieresis on the first letter) χρ(ῶ) | μεθ' ὕδατος (= "use with water," as usual). μεθ' ὕδατος is sensibly indented and somehow squeezed under "ὕδωρ �" at the right-hand margin, as if it were added at a later stage (not much later, however, since the long *paragraphos*, which divides this recipe from the following one, deviates to accommodate this final insertion; see Fig. 8.18). My impression is that the writer no longer understood the literal meaning of ὕδωρ— which is, indeed, written with a peculiar ⳁ monogram instead of its last two letters—ὕδⳁ—and felt impelled to add "with water" as a further specification.

In a third example, PSI X 1180, at the end of the columned recipes (see above), υδ✷, with ὕδωρ is rendered through a remarkable abbreviation (υ with δ above) so that the formula seems to completely lose its linguistic significance (Fig. 8.14). Finally, in a fourth type, seen in P.Oxy. VIII 1088, at the end of the first two recipes (see above; Fig. 8.12), and SB XXVIII 17140, at the end of the second recipe, we can see that as a peculiar by-product of the described process, ὕδωρ alone, though theoretically belonging to the list of ingredients, is actually written further indented, almost in the center of the column, as if it were a sign marking the end of the prescription.

The semioticizing (so to say) power of ✷ was not limited to "water," however. As noticed above, the final excipient used to mix the prescribed ingredients could also be some other substance, like vinegar or wine. The latter seems in fact to have undergone an abstraction process similar to

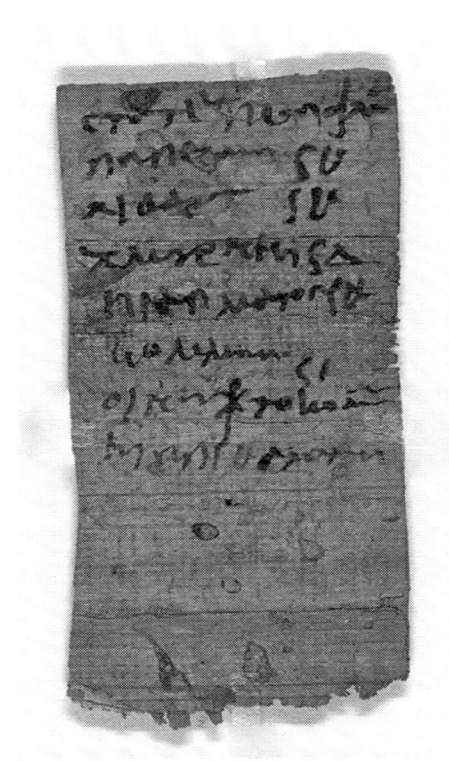

FIGURE 8.19   P.Princ. III 155r = SB XIV 12086
(P.Princ. inv. AM 11224 B)
PICTURE PROVIDED IN OPEN
ACCESS BY PRINCETON
UNIVERSITY LIBRARY'S
PAPYRI COLLECTIONS

Conclusions

Generally speaking, abbreviations are used to mark common or technical terms with the purpose of simplifying and speeding up the writing process and the understanding of the content; in the case of technical terms, we can assume that they were better understood by specialists rather than by laymen.[44] The question is, does this depend on random usage or rather on deliberate choices by the writer? The topic is of primary importance for the socio-semiotic study of textual strategies and leads to interesting further research questions about the relationship between the degree of "symbolification" of the text and its reception. Should we assume that the more a text is charged with semantic signs, the more specialized are its users? Everybody can understand that horizontal lines frame different sections of a text, and that columns point to lists of substances with their quantities, but how many people could understand that ☧ means "use," especially from the fourth century onwards, when the same monogram spread all over the Empire as a Christian flag, or that ⚯ means "myrrh"? To what extent was this part of general knowledge or a specialized doctrine?

The issue of the semiotic power of graphical language has been addressed by W. John Tait in a groundbreaking article, in which he contended that Demotic script could be partially understood by non-scribes, thanks to the presence of readily recognizable standard signs that could guide the reader to comprehend the general sense of the text.[45] His conclusions can be easily exported to any text provided with well-recognizable paralinguistic or non-linguistic features, which become semiotic elements that speak to the reader. I do not think that for the moment we have enough quantitative data to answer these questions with a satisfying degree of certainty, but the issues are striking as regards the socio-semiotic approach to ancient texts and certainly deserve to be exported to documentary texts, for which we certainly do have much more information.[46] A proper way of encoding such features digitally would also be of great help to perform automatic

"water," as we find regular closing phrases like με]τ' οἴνου χρῶι, as found in GMP II 5 in column ii, line 13, "use with wine," which is much less indented than the υδωρχρωι described above, but is nevertheless, noteworthily, in *eisthesis*—flanked by a suspended μετ' οἴνου Χ{ε}ίου ⟦.⟧ ἢ Λεςβίου ("with Chian or Lesbian wine"). In other instances, such as PSI Congr.XXI 3 (col. ii, l. 19), it ends a recipe (Fig. 8.3), while in the most interesting case, P.Princ. III 155r (= SB XIV 12086),[43] the instructing section (the recipe is structured just as the one on the verso described above) begins with οἴνου ☧ (Fig. 8.19). The meaning is clearly "use with wine," but the substance name is given in a senseless plain genitive due to syntactic attraction by the preceding ingredients, listed in the genitive as usual.

---

43   See Andorlini 2019, 6–12.

44   In general, on abbreviations in the literary papyri, see McNamee 1981 and 1985. Abbreviations in the documentary papyri have not been investigated systematically, but see Blanchard 1974 for an introductory essay with analysis of several relevant cases and Gonis 2011 for a survey on this matter.

45   Tait 2001.

46   I have already applied the same methodology to the analysis of the paratextual system of the medical catechisms (manuals

analyses of the material at our disposal. The current general database *Papyri.info*, which has very recently incorporated the *Digital Corpus of Literary Papyri* (DCLP),[47] does not currently allow for encoding in this way (columnation or abbreviation types, for example, cannot be marked up[48]), but I believe that projects like EVWRIT have the potential to generate advanced semantic annotation layers that can very much improve our digital texts and help us to answer deeper questions about our written past.

Reference List[49]

Albrecht, Friedrich, and Margherita Matera. 2017. "Testimonianze di παράγραφοι 'a coda ondulata' in alcuni manoscritti greci e copti." *Νέα Ῥώμη* 14: 5–35.

Andorlini, Isabella. 1993. "L'apporto dei papiri alla conoscenza della scienza medica antica." In *Aufstieg und Niedergang der Römischen Welt*, II 37.1, edited by Wolfgang Haase, 458–562. Berlin: De Gruyter.

Andorlini, Isabella. 2004. "Un ricettario da Tebtynis: parti inedite di PSI 1180." In *Testi medici su papiro. Atti del Seminario di studio (Firenze, 3–4 giugno 2002)*, edited by Isabella Andorlini, 81–118. Florence: Istituto papirologico "Girolamo Vitelli."

Andorlini, Isabella. 2017. *πολλὰ ἰατρῶν ἐςτι ςυγγράμματα, I. Scritti sui papiri e la medicina antica*, edited by Nicola Reggiani. Florence: Le Monnier.

Andorlini, Isabella. 2018a. *πολλὰ ἰατρῶν ἐςτι ςυγγράμματα, II. Edizioni di papiri medici greci*, edited by Nicola Reggiani. Florence: Le Monnier.

Andorlini, Isabella. 2018b. "Tipologia testuale e linguaggio tecnico nelle ricette su papiri: tre casi di ricette conservate dai Papiri della Società Italiana." In *Parlare la medicina: tra lingue e culture, nello spazio e nel tempo*, edited by Nicola Reggiani, 113–27. Florence: Le Monnier.

Andorlini, Isabella. 2019. "From Prescription to Practice: The Evidence of Two Medical Papyri from Roman Egypt." In *Greek Medical Papyri: Text—Context—Hypertext*, edited by Nicola Reggiani, 3–17. Berlin: De Gruyter.

Ast, Rodney, and Holger Essler. 2019. "*Anagnosis*, Herculaneum, and the *Digital Corpus of Literary Papyri*." In *Digital Papyrology II: Case Studies on the Digital Edition of Ancient Greek Papyri*, edited by Nicola Reggiani, 63–74. Berlin: De Gruyter.

Barbis Lupi, Roberta. 1988. "La diplè obelismene: precisazioni terminologiche e formali." In *Proceedings of the XVIII International Congress of Papyrology (Athens, 25–31 May 1986)*, edited by Basil G. Mandilaras, 473–76. Athens: University of Athens.

Barbis Lupi, Roberta. 1992. "Uso e forma dei segni di riempimento nei papiri letterari greci." In *Proceedings of the XIXth International Congress of Papyrology (Cairo 1989)*, edited by A. H. S. El-Mosallamy, 503–10. Cairo: Center for Papyrological Studies.

Barbis Lupi, Roberta. 1994. "La *paragraphos*: analisi di un segno di lettura." In *Proceedings of the 20th International Congress of Papyrologists (Copenhagen, 23–29 August 1992)*, edited by Adam Bülow-Jacobsen, 414–17. Copenhagen: Museum Tusculanum Press.

Blanchard, Alain. 1974. *Sigles et abréviations dans les papyrus documentaires grecs. Recherches de paléographie*. London: Institute of Classical Studies.

Carlig, Nathan, Guillaume Lescuyer, Aurore Motte, and Nathalie Sojic, eds. 2020. *Signes dans les textes II*. Liège: Presses Universitaires de Liège.

Corazza, Francesca. 2016. "New Recipes by Heras in P.Berol. Möller 13." *ZPE* 198: 39–48.

Di Matteo, Tiziana. 2007. "Segni di riempimento nei papiri ercolanesi." In *Proceedings of the 24th International Congress of Papyrology (Helsinki, 1–7 August 2004)*, edited by Jaakko Frösén, Tiina Purola, and Erja Salmenkivi, I, 259–65. Helsinki: Societas Scientiarum Fennica.

Fournet, Jean-Luc. 1994. "Un papyrus médical byzantin de l'Académie des Inscriptions et Belles-Lettres." *Travaux et Mémoires* 12: 309–24.

Fournet, Jean-Luc. 2004. "La bibliothèque d'un médecin ou d'un apothicaire de Lycopolis?" In *Testi medici su papiro. Atti del Seminario di studio (Firenze, 3–4 giugno 2002)*, edited by Isabella Andorlini, 175–97. Florence: Istituto Papirologico "G. Vitelli."

Gonis, Nikolaos. 2011. "Abbreviations and Symbols." In *The Oxford Handbook of Papyrology*, edited by Roger S. Bagnall, 170–78. Oxford: Oxford University Press.

Lundon, John. 2004. "POxy VIII 1088: problemi e proposte." In *Testi medici su papiro. Atti del Seminario di studio (Firenze, 3–4*

---

structured in questions and answers) on papyrus, which utilize the same strategies (*paragraphoi, diplai obelismenai, eisthesis, exthesis, vacat*, punctuation, diacritics, etc.) for the same purpose (to highlight a special structure of the text): see Reggiani 2020. The paratextual system of the medical doxographical treatise known as the *Anonymus Londinensis* (P.Lond.Lit. 165) has been investigated by Ricciardetto 2016 and 2019.

47 See Reggiani 2017, 250–54, 2019b, 330–34; Ast and Essler 2018.

48 A partial exception is represented by some special symbols like ☧ or ⳨, which do possess their own special encoding in both the TEI/EpiDoc XML and Leiden+ markup languages used by *Papyri.info* (see Reggiani 2019b, 17–20). However, the editorial practice is extremely inconsistent: many of these monograms are resolved as plain χρ( ) abbreviations instead of being encoded with their specific glyphs, and even when they are, there is a painful confusion between *chi-rho* and staurogram; for example, while querying the database for this research, I discovered two staurograms encoded as ☧ (BGU II 668, l. 6; SB XII 11230, *passim*).

49 Papyri are cited with the standard abbreviations listed in the *Checklist of Editions* at http://papyri.info/docs/checklist.

giugno 2002), edited by Isabella Andorlini, 119–30. Florence: Istituto Papirologico "G. Vitelli."

Marganne, Marie-Hélène. 1980. "Une étape dans la transmission d'une prescription médicale : P. Berol. Möller 13." In *Miscellanea Papyrologica*, edited by Rosario Pintaudi, 179–83. Florence: Gonnelli.

McNamee, Kathleen. 1981. *Abbreviations in the Greek Literary Papyri and Ostraca*. Ann Arbor, MI: American Society of Papyrologists.

McNamee, Kathleen. 1985. "Abbreviations in Greek Literary Papyri and Ostraca: Supplement, with List of Ghost Abbreviations." *BASP* 22: 205–25.

Reggiani, Nicola. 2017. *Digital Papyrology I: Methods, Tools and Trends*. Berlin: De Gruyter.

Reggiani, Nicola. 2018. "Prescrizioni mediche e supporti materiali nell'Antichità." In *Parlare la medicina: tra lingue e culture, nello spazio e nel tempo*, edited by Nicola Reggiani, 128–44. Florence: Le Monnier.

Reggiani, Nicola. 2019a. "Isabella Andorlini e la Papirologia medica." In *Papiri, medicina antica e cultura materiale. Contributi in ricordo di Isabella Andorlini*, edited by Nicola Reggiani and Alessia Bovo, 53–62. Parma: Athenaeum Edizioni Universitarie.

Reggiani, Nicola. 2019b. *La papirologia digitale. Prospettiva storico-critica e sviluppi metodologici*. Parma: Athenaeum Edizioni Universitarie.

Reggiani, Nicola. 2019c. "Transmission of Recipes and Receptaria in Greek Medical Writings on Papyrus: Between Ancient Text Production and Modern Digital Representation." In *On the Track of the Books: Scribes, Libraries and Textual Transmission*, edited by Roberta Berardi, Nicoletta Bruno, and Luisa Fizzarotti, 167–88. Berlin: De Gruyter.

Reggiani, Nicola. 2020. "Digitizing Medical Papyri in Question-and-Answer Format." In *"Where Does It Hurt?" Ancient Medicine in Questions and Answers*, edited by Michiel Meeusen and Erika Gielen, 181–212. Leiden: Brill.

Reggiani, Nicola. 2022a. "Exactitude in Ancient Pharmacological Theory and Practice: Cases from the Greek Medical Papyri." In *The Limits of Exactitude*, edited by Nicoletta Bruno, Giulia Dovico, Olivia Montepaone, and Marco Pelucchi, in press. Berlin: De Gruyter.

Reggiani, Nicola. 2022b. "Medical Literary and Documentary Culture in Graeco-Roman Fayum." In *Scientific Traditions in the Ancient Mediterranean and Near East. Joint Proceedings of the 1st and 2nd Scientific Papyri from Ancient Egypt (SPAE) International Conferences (Copenhagen, May 31, 2018, and New York, Sept. 19–20, 2019)*, edited by Amber Jacob and Sofie Schiødt, in press. New York: ISAW.

Reggiani, Nicola. Forthcoming. *The Working Process and Writing Practice of Ancient Doctors: The Material Testimony of the Greek Papyri*. Leiden: Brill.

Ricciardetto, Antonio. 2016. "Spazio scritto e spazio non scritto nelle dossografie mediche su papiro." In *Spazio scritto e spazio non scritto nel libro papiraceo. Esperienze a confronto*, edited by Natascia Pellé, 183–224. Lecce: Pensa Multimedia.

Ricciardetto, Antonio. 2019. "Comparaison entre le système d'abréviation de l'Anonyme de Londres et ceux de la Constitution d'Athènes et des autres textes littéraires du Brit. Libr. inv. 131." In *Proceedings of the 28th Congress of Papyrology (Barcelona, 1–6 August 2016)*, edited by Alberto Nodar and Sofia Torallas Tovar, 405–16. Barcelona: Publicacions de l'Abadia de Montserrat.

Roselli, Amneris. 2019. "Un corpo che prende forma (*addendum*): papiri ippocratici e dintorni." In *Greek Medical Papyri: Text—Context—Hypertext*, edited by Nicola Reggiani, 75–88. Berlin: De Gruyter.

Savignago, Lorenza. 2008. *Eisthesis. Il sistema dei margini nei papiri dei poeti tragici*. Alessandria: Edizioni dell'Orso.

Stephen, Gertrude M. 1959. "The Coronis." *Scriptorium* 13: 3–14.

Tait, W. John. 2001. "Exuberance and Accessibility: Notes on Written Demotic and the Egyptian Scribal Tradition." In *Essays and Texts in Honor of J. David Thomas*, edited by Traianos Gagos and Roger S. Bagnall, 31–39. New Haven, CT: American Society of Papyrologists.

CHAPTER 9

Imagining Faith: Images, Scripts, and Texts of Early Christian Inscriptions from the Roman Near East

James Wolfe

Introduction

In 1862, Melchior de Vogüé discovered what was to become a rather famous Syriac inscription (AAES IV 8) on the lintel of a baptistery in Dēḥes, a small town located between Antioch, the capital of the Roman province of *Syria Prima*, and Qinnašrīn. As Enno Littmann explained, at first de Vogüé thought that it was an Armenian inscription.[1] In 1879, however, Eduard Sachau correctly recognized that it was written in Syriac, but that the letters were rotated ninety degrees and read left-to-right, similar to the famous trilingual inscription from Zebed which Sachau himself had discovered. Littmann published the inscription from Dēḥes in 1904 in the fourth part of the publications of Princeton's archaeological expedition to Syria from 1899 to 1900 and dated it ca. 500 CE.[2]

Along with an image of the cast of the inscription, Littmann included a transliteration, translation, and extensive commentary. I follow his reconstruction of the text:

ܗܕܐ ܒܝܬ ܡܥܡܘܕܝܬܐ ܕܐܠܗܐ (ܚ)ܝܐ ܘܩܕܝܫܐ
ܕܩܝܡ ܠܡܪܢܝܫܘܥܡܫܝܚܐ ܘܟܠܗ ܥܕܬܗ
ܨܠܘ ܥܠ ܝܘܚܢܢ ܐܪܕܝܟܠܐ

This is the baptistry of God, living and holy, who raised Our Lord Jesus Christ and his entire church.
Pray for Yuḥanon the architect.[3]

I agree with Littmann's suggestion that this inscription contains two distinct parts. The first, which runs the entire horizontal length of the lintel, contains the description of the building on which it was found and a short phrase recalling scripture.[4] The second, which continues vertically on the vertical stone that made up the right doorjamb, invites the viewer to pray for the architect, presumably of the baptistry, whose name was Yuḥanon. Not only are these two texts set apart physically, with each text occupying a different stone, they are also distinguishable by their script. The horizontal text is written with large finely sculpted separated characters that were rotated ninety degrees in order to be read left-to-right, while the vertical text is written in a cursive script. Following visual cues, then, the viewer of this lintel would encounter two distinct texts that convey distinct messages: one descriptive and the other prescriptive.

Although unusual for the Syriac language, there are several Syriac inscriptions from the late Roman period that have separated letter forms read from left-to-right.[5] Another inscription from Kalb-Lauzeh (AAES IV 1) is also written with separated letters and read from left-to-right. Littmann supposed a date of ca. 550 CE for this inscription because of the similarities in the letter forms with the one from Dēḥes.[6] Unfortunately, the fragment of white marble on which the inscription is found was no longer *in situ* but was being used as spolia in a modern wall (see Fig. 9.1).

AAES IV 1

+ܣܓܘܕܐ ܕ (ܐ)ܒܐ ܘܕܒܪ(ܐ)
ܘܕܪܘܚܐ ܕ(ܩ)ܕܫ(ܐ ܝܘ)ܚܢܢ
ܒܪ ܙܟܪܘܢ

The worshipper of the Father and the Son
and the Holy Spirit: Yuḥanon
son of Zakrōn.[7]

Sadly, due to the quality of the image, it is nearly impossible to make out the inscription; however, the photograph does reveal that the space in which the letters were carved was set apart from the rest of the stone by a rectangular

1 Littmann 1904, 23. For the purposes of this chapter, I will provide a standard bibliographical reference when citing the remarks of the publisher or editor of a volume, while all references to the inscriptions themselves will follow the numbering in the published edition. Littmann 1904 = AAES IV; Prentice 1908 = AAES III; Prentice 1914a = PPUAES III B.5; Prentice 1922 = PPUAES III B.6.
2 Littmann 1904, 27.
3 AAES IV 8.
4 Littmann supposes Rom 6.3ff, 8.11; Cor 15.22ff. See AAES IV 26–27.
5 See Littmann 1904 *passim* for a discussion.
6 Littmann 1904, 23ff.
7 AAES IV 1.

 | DOI:10.1163/9789004526525_011

FIGURE 9.1   AAES IV 1 (Kalb-Lauzeh, white marble stone)

box, whose relief borders distinguished the space for the text from the rest of the stone. The text of the inscription begins with a small cross to the left of the first letter, sem-kat̲ (∞), hardly visible in the squeeze in the upper left-hand corner.[8] Because of the quality of the stone and the letter forms, Littmann supposed that the stone must have originally been part of the large church at Kalb Lauzeh, especially given it is rare to find white marble as a building material in northern Syria from the late Roman period.[9]

If it is true that this stone and its accompanying inscription were part of the large church at Kalb-Lauzeh, it must have contributed to the monumentalism of that church and how individuals interacted with and experienced the church visually. Furthermore, it seems as though these two inscriptions from Kalb-Lauzeh and Dēḥes may have been engaging with the visual typologies of monumental epigraphy in late Roman Syria through their use of materials, scripts, and other non-linguistic markers to help guide the viewer's reading of the text itself. More specifically, it is possible that by using separated Syriac letters that were read from left-to-right the stonecutters were mimicking monumental inscriptions in Greek.

When de Vogüé discovered AAES IV 8, it was the only known Syriac inscription from Dēḥes: all others that had been found were in Greek.[10] As a result, de Vogüé hypothesized that it was created by an individual who chose the Syriac script for the sole purpose of broadcasting

miaphysitism.[11] Although possible, considering that the non-Chalcedonian Syriac Orthodox Church was not established as an independent church with its own hierarchy until the 540s, it would be surprising if not chronologically impossible for an individual in the first decades of the sixth century to use the Syriac script as a symbol of miaphysitism.[12] The early miaphysite movement that eventually did result in the formation of a separate Syriac Orthodox Church was bilingual in the early sixth century, with several of its leading members, such as Severus of Antioch, writing exclusively in Greek. Therefore, it is unlikely that the use of the Syriac language or its script was singularly sufficient to signal belonging to a supralocal miaphysite community, especially in the first decade of the sixth century.

That is not to say, however, that whoever created this inscription could not have chosen the Syriac script for confessional reasons. If the inscription from Dēḥes does date to ca. 500 CE, it would place its creation in the reign of Anastasius, who was not only tolerant of but even supportive of the miaphysites. As John Watt contends, the development of the miaphysite church under Anastasius "gave impetus for the employment of Syriac as a literary language in competition with Greek" and that it was this period "in which Syriac prose literature appeared on the scene as a vital player in the intellectual life of the Roman empire."[13] It is tempting to suppose, then, that a similar motivation may have contributed to the choice to use the Syriac script in an inscription like the one from Dēḥes; however, it raises the question of whether or not the Syriac script was used by miaphysites to broadcast their identity in the early sixth century? Was the Syriac script alone sufficient to do so at this time?

I will return to these questions about the Syriac script and miaphysite identity again below. As noted above, however, more recent scholarship has shown that the Syriac language was not a marker of the miaphysite church in Syria and the Near East until the Islamic period.[14] Miaphysite identity, therefore, was not tied to a specific language or script in the late Roman or early Byzantine periods, and so I doubt that de Vogüé and Littmann would argue now that the use of the Syriac script in inscriptions

---

8   For the squeeze, see Littmann 1904, 9.
9   AAES IV 11.
10   Littmann 1904, 23. As Littmann notes, however, the Princeton archaeological expedition from 1899 to 1900 had discovered several other Syriac inscriptions in Dēḥes and the surrounding area. More on this below (Littmann 1904, 26).

11   Littmann 1904, 26ff.
12   According to Littmann 1904, 26, de Vogüé erroneously suggested that the monophysite (miaphysite) church in Syria had already fully separated itself from the orthodox church by the year 500 CE. This is certainly not the case, as scholarship has demonstrated numerous times since. See ter Haar Romeny et al. 2009 for the fullest discussion on this topic.
13   Watt 2006, 276.
14   ter Haar Romeny et al. 2009.

from late Roman Syria was a definitive marker of miaphysite identity. Nevertheless, Littmann, who noted that the Princeton archaeological expeditions had found several additional Syriac inscriptions in Dēḥes that were unknown to de Vogüé, ultimately agreed with de Vogüé that AAES IV 8 was the work of a miaphysite.[15] Moreover, Littmann assumed that the church at Kalb Lauzeh must have housed a miaphysite congregation because of the Syriac inscription on white marble he found as part of the Princeton expedition (AAES IV 1), even though this inscription was no longer *in situ*.[16]

I believe that neither is necessarily true. If not to broadcast miaphysite identity, though, why did the individuals responsible for these two inscriptions (AAES IV 1 & 8) choose to use the Syriac script? Why did they manipulate the Syriac script so that it could be read from left-to-right? Instead of assuming that the Syriac language or script was necessarily a marker of confessional identity, this chapter investigates how we should understand the choice of script and how scripts could function as a visual form of communication that conveyed meaning independent of lexical information.

To answer these questions, in this chapter I will examine a selection of Greek, Syriac, and multilingual inscriptions from late Roman Syria in order to identify the possible communicative goals motivating the choice of script and the use of scripts and letters as images, not simply as texts. I contend that the Greek and Syriac scripts in inscriptions from late Roman Syria could function as communicative images that supplemented the lexical information supplied by the text of the inscription by engaging in and reaffirming generic, institutional, and societal expectations for inscriptions in public spaces. As a result, Greek, Syriac, and multilingual inscriptions deployed their scripts as discursive texts and images. Moreover, for some inscriptions, it was the script and other visual markers that conveyed the primary message, not the text *qua* language.

First, I examine Syriac inscriptions and bilingual inscriptions (Greek and Syriac) that replicate visual typologies of Greek epigraphy from Roman Syria, including funerary, commemorative, and monumental inscriptions like the ones from Dēḥes and Kalb-Lauzeh discussed above. Second, I analyze Greek inscriptions that include the acrostics XMΓ and IXΘΥΣ as well as other Christian symbols, many of which cite the liturgy of the miaphysite church. A subset of these are *tituli picti* that appear on late Roman amphora produced and shipped from (greater) Syria. I argue that the choice of script and its use in

inscriptions from Roman Syria was itself a discursive act that could express personal identity and adherence to a set of values that, in turn, signaled belonging in certain communities. The expectations of multilingual communities in Roman Syria contributed to the development of a particular epigraphic habit that was realized in inscriptions that deployed both the Greek and Syriac script.

1 Visual Typologies and Scripts of Belonging

Before turning to inscriptions from late Roman Syria, I want to begin with a contemporary example that illustrates how scripts can be used independent of language to broadcast identity and belonging in a community. The phrase μολὼν λαβέ, which is loosely translated "come and take [them]," was, according to Plutarch, what Leonidas said in response to Xerxes' request that the Spartans turn over their weapons to the Persians at the battle of Thermopylae in 480 BCE.[17] Today, far-right conservatives, white nationalists, and defenders of the right to bear arms in the United States have adopted μολὼν λαβέ as a motto of resistance against big government and those whom they fear will take away their guns. This motto can be found on flags, bumper stickers, patches, and t-shirts, all of which are for sale online.

FIGURE 9.2   Bumper sticker (*c.*2019)

In an example on a bumper sticker (see Fig. 9.2), the English translation of μολὼν λαβέ, "come and take them," is written in Greek letters that approximate the Latin script.[18] The resulting text *qua* language is, of course, completely illegible. Visually, however, the resulting text *qua* image is legible. Through both the image of the Spartan helmet at the center and the hybrid script that surrounds it, the decal effectively invokes the Spartans' resistance against the Persians. Moreover, because the English text written in Greek letters is easily discernible even for English-speakers with no knowledge of the Greek alphabet, the phrase μολὼν λαβέ becomes both authentically American and authentically Spartan at the same time, allowing English-speakers to feel empowered to appropriate symbols of Greek resistance. I believe that this decal and other images that redeploy Spartan imagery and the Greek alphabet broadcast belonging within a specific community. In this case, one that is defined by holding values of white nationalism, right-wing conservatism, and pro-gun politics in the United States.

According to de Vogüé and Littmann, the Syriac script in the inscription from Dēḥes was functioning in the same way as this modern decal: the mere use of the Syriac letters was enough for them to conclude that it was created by a member of the miaphysite church, despite there being no further evidence that the individual or community that lay behind the creation of the inscription adhered to a different confessional community than their contemporaries who created the Greek inscriptions in Dēḥes. As I stated above, it has been demonstrated that Syriac was not singularly sufficient to signal miaphysitism in Roman Syria in the early sixth century, nor was Greek singularly sufficient to signal Chalcedonian orthodoxy. In this section, I want to examine how inscriptions, like the one from Dēḥes, used the Syriac script and other non-lexical items to replicate not only the visual typologies of monumental inscriptions found in contemporary Greek inscriptions in the region, but also the experience of viewing, reading, and aurally consuming Greek inscriptions. I agree, then, that the Syriac script could be used to signal belonging in a community, but that it was not exclusively used to broadcast miaphysitism.

The interplay between Greek and Syriac in the late Roman Near East, and especially in Syria and Mesopotamia, has interested scholars recently.[19] Moreover, the script of Syriac inscriptions has garnered significant attention in scholarship, with all major publications on this topic discussing the script at length.[20] As Han Drijvers and John Healey explain, early Syriac epigraphy is distinguished from the epigraphy of other Middle Aramaic dialects only through the use of inscriptional Estrangela.[21] The Estrangela script was the predominant script of the Syriac manuscript tradition in the late Roman period and the only Syriac book hand until the development of the Serṭo script in the sixth century, which was eventually adopted by the Syriac Orthodox Church. Inscriptional Estrangela was also used for Christian Palestinian Aramaic inscriptions, which are, for that reason, typically included in the published *corpora* of Syriac epigraphy.[22]

Although there are several known Syriac inscriptions with separated letters read from left-to-right, the inscription from Dēḥes is one of the earliest. Therefore, it appears to be a relatively late development in the Syriac epigraphic habit, perhaps beginning only in the sixth century. A well-known Syriac manuscript housed in the British Library (Add 14558), and dated to 557 CE, preserves a lesser-known colophon that includes what appears to be the name of the scribe in Greek letters and then again in Syriac letters, separated, rotated ninety degrees, and read left-to-right.[23] Writing with separated letters from left-to-right, then, was not exclusive to inscriptional Estrangela.

Why stonecutters and the individual whose name appears in the colophon of Add 14558 adopted this technique for writing the Estrangela script from left-to-right is difficult to say. The experience of reading inscriptions like the ones from Dēḥes and Kalb Lauzeh would have been very different from the experience of reading not only Syriac manuscripts, but also most other Syriac inscriptions

---

18   "Car Sticker Vinyl 10*10CM Molon Labe Spartan Helmet Fuel Tank Cover Decals Creative Fashion 3D Stickers On Car Styling Creative." https://www.aliexpress.com/item/32904632814.html, accessed on 27.08.19.

19   Andrade 2014 provides a nice survey and detailed bibliography. Other major works are Brock 1994, Bagnall 2011, Chatonnet and

       Desreumaux 2011, Butts 2013, and Fournet 2020, just to name a few. For the history of the Syriac language and its place in the evolution of Aramaic, see Butts 2013; Gzella 2015, 2021.

20   See Littmann 1904, 1914. For Syriac epigraphy in general, Lidzbarski 1898 is still invaluable, along with Hogg 1901; Cook 1904; Naveh 1982. More recently, Millar 1995; Drijvers and Healey 1999; Trombley 2001a, 2001b; Butts 2013; Healey 2009. There is no standard or exhaustive repository of Syriac inscriptions, which remains a *desideratum*. The best resource is either Healey 2009 or "A Comprehensive Bibliography on Syriac Christianity" curated by The Center for the Study of Christianity at The Hebrew University of Jerusalem as an online webpage; see http://www.csc.org.il/db/browse.aspx?db=sb&sL=E&sK=epigraphics&sT=keywords.

21   Brock 1978, which unfortunately is now outdated.

22   In fact, AAES IV 8 shares many grammatical and orthographic features with Christian Palestinian Aramaic (CPA); see Taylor 2002, 312ff.

23   Reproduced by Land 1862, plate VII. This manuscript is included in Hatch 1946, plate 24.

and graffiti. Not all Syriac inscriptions were read from right-to-left, however, as many of the known Syriac inscriptions from late Roman Syria are written vertically, just like Yuḥanon's salutation in the inscription from Dēḥes. Many of these, though, are single vertical lines of text, and so it is impossible to make conclusions about their horizontal directionality. Perhaps the stonecutters responsible for AAES IV 1 and 8 attempted to mimic the directionality of Greek inscriptions on lintels that similarly encouraged the reader to move left-to-right across the stone before proceeding to move vertically down. Examples of these are found throughout the region, including those from Bābiskā and Zebed (see below).[24]

Littmann suggested that the choice to use separated letters instead of a cursive script in Syriac inscriptions may have been in imitation of Greek epigraphy.[25] Rather than simply mimicking the letter forms of monumental Greek epigraphy, however, I suggest that Syriac inscriptions written with separated letters demonstrate an awareness that cursive scripts were not commonly used for monumental inscriptions in Greek (or Latin). If true, these inscriptions would provide evidence, then, of Syriac stonecutters engaging with the generic expectations and visual typologies of monumental epigraphy in late Roman Syria regardless of language or script. This type of evidence, I argue, is also found in a set of inscriptions from the town of Mektebeh. Most inscriptions in Mektebeh, whether Greek or Syriac, have been found on pieces of black basalt with the text carved in relief. Whereas there are no known Syriac inscriptions in relief elsewhere, in Mektebeh Syriac inscriptions are exclusively in relief.[26]

If we consider a specific example, a Syriac inscription on a lintel made out of basalt contains the phrase "He who dwells in the secret place of the Most High" carved in relief (see Fig. 9.3).[27] From the scan of the cast, one can easily see that the letters are not only carved in relief but are separated. Because of the size of the piece of black basalt and quality of the inscription, it was likely a lintel of a church. The vertical lines of the Syriac text are read from left-to-right. Using a different technique than the stonecutter from Dēḥes, possibly one that was characteristic of local stonecutting practice in Mektebeh, the stonecutter of this inscription encouraged the reader's gaze to move from left-to-right over the stone while still employing separated letters. At the same time as the stonecutter was engaging directly with their local audience through the visual

FIGURE 9.3 AAES IV 19 (Mektebeh [VI CE], black basalt). Scan of cast

typologies of inscriptions at Mektebeh, the lexical information conveyed by the text of the inscription demonstrates an engagement in supra-local Christian discourses through the citation of scripture.

For all three of these inscriptions, then, it is the script as an image that communicates adherence to a local community by demonstrating an awareness of the visual typologies of monumental epigraphy. The manipulation of the directionality of a script, letter forms, and carving techniques together produce a viewing experience that approximated the viewing of Greek monumental epigraphy in their community. The visual semiotics of the scripts functioned independently of the lexical information they conveyed.

This is most apparent in a pair of inscriptions from Bābiskā, also published by Littmann.[28] On side-by-side panels of a two-story stoa in the center of the town, two Syriac inscriptions were carved using, once again, separated letters that are read vertically from left-to-right.[29] The panels of the parapet made up one side of a large quadrangle in Bābiskā and faced inwards into what was probably one of the town's *fora*.[30]

As can be seen from the photograph of AAES IV 15, the square panel carries a square frame, inside of which is a raised dovetail plate (the same goes for AAES IV 14). The dovetail plate on the left contains a cross in the left dovetail, while the one on the right (see Fig. 9.4) contains another cross in the right dovetail. The Syriac inscriptions are carved in between the two crosses, beginning at the top right of the left dovetail plate, and ending in the lower right of the square frame having overflowed the spaces created by the dovetail plates.

The inscriptions record that the stoa was built in the year 596 according to the era of Antioch (547 CE) by Yuḥannā son of Zakkay. A group of "brothers" (ܐܚܐ) named Sargon, Theodore, and Bakkhos had previously purchased the garden. Both inscriptions are in the voice of Yuḥannā, as evidenced by the mention of "my days"

24   For Bābiskā, see AAES III 71; for Zebed, see AAES IV 23 and 24.
25   Littmann 1904 *passim*.
26   Littmann 1904, 6.
27   AAES IV 19.

28   AAES IV 14–15.
29   Littmann (1904, 33) suggests that these inscriptions were imitating Greek lettering found on monumental inscriptions.
30   See Lavan 2006.

FIGURE 9.4 AAES IV 15 (Bābisḳā [547 CE])

FIGURE 9.5 AAES III 154 (378 CE). Ḥāss

(ܒܝܘܡܝ) in AAES IV 14, and by the use of the personal pronoun "I" (ܐܢܐ) and the first-person singular form "I built" (ܒܢܝܬ) in AAES IV 15.

AAES IV 14	AAES IV 15
+ܐܠܗܐ	ܒܝܘܡܝ
ܒ[ܪܟ] ܐܢܬ [ܠ]ܢ	ܐܚܐ
ܐܣܛܘܐ	ܣܪܓܘܢ
ܗܕܐ ܒܢܝܬ	ܘܬܐܕܘܪܐ
ܚܡܫܡܐܐ	ܘܒܟܘܣ
ܘܬܫܥܝܢ	ܙܒܢܘ
ܘܫܬ	ܓܢ̈ܐ
ܒܫܢܬܐ	+ܐܢܐ
ܕܐܢܛܝܘܟܝܐ	ܐܚܐ
	ܝܚܢܐ
	ܒܪ ܙܟܝ
	ܒܢܝܬ
	ܘܫܡܠܝܬ

AAES IV 14: God, bless us! This stoa was built in the year five hundred and ninety-six according to the era of Antioch.

AAES IV 15: In my days, the brothers Sargon and Theodore and Bakkhos bought the gardens. + I, brother Yuḥannā son of Zakkay built and finished it.

Although I think that it is reasonable to divide these examples into two separate inscriptions, I do not believe Littmann divides them at the right spot. In his publication of the inscriptions, Littmann divided the texts according to the panel upon which the text was inscribed. Instead, I suggest that the inscriptions should be considered either a single text in two parts or two separate texts with the first ending after the word "gardens" (ܓܢ̈ܐ) and the second beginning with the pronoun "I." This reading of the text would follow the guidance given by two small crosses which were placed at semantically significant points: one at the beginning of the inscription in the top right corner of the left dovetail (as noted in my transliteration), and one between the word "gardens" and the pronoun "I". Read this way, these inscriptions would convey two discrete, interrelated messages to the viewer, which I believe was the intention of the stonecutter.

It is no longer a problem, then, that the letters of the inscription overflow the dovetail plates, because they were not used to denote two separate inscriptions. Nor was it an error on the part of the stonecutter to have the text overflow the dovetail plates, but rather a visual reference to a common feature of Greek inscriptions on dovetail plates from late Roman Syria. For example, above the entrance to a rock-cut tomb in Ḥāss, a large dovetail plate in relief contains incised Greek letters (see Fig. 9.5). The inscription, which describes the construction of the tomb at the direction of Agrippa and Domna, is dated to 378 CE and begins in the top left corner of the dovetail plate. The text concludes, having overflowed the plate, in the bottom right.

> Ἔτους θπχ, Ἀρτεμισίου ε̄, ἐπὶ σπουδῆς Ἀγρίππα τοῦ Μαρίνου καὶ Δόμνα τῆς Σέγνα, γυνεκὸς αὐτοῦ, ἐτελιώθη.
>
> In the year 689, the 5th of Artemisios, at the order of Agrippa son of Marinos and Domna the daughter of Segna, his wife, this tomb was completed.[31]

Thanks to the clarity of the photograph, we can see that the façade of the rock-cut tomb is raw in most places except for the dovetail plate and the archway that frames

31 AAES III 154.

the entrance to the tomb. It appears as though the dovetail plate would have provided the stonecutter of the inscription with a prepared, smooth surface, more conducive for the cutting of Greek letters, while the rest of the rock-cut surface would not have been so. Although most of the text fits on the dovetail plate, at least part of the last line spills out.[32]

Of course, it would have been highly unlikely that the stonecutter of the Syriac inscriptions from Bābiskā saw this exact inscription from Ḥāss; however, both inscriptions from Bābiskā and this inscription from Ḥāss demonstrate the willingness of a stonecutter to ignore physical demarcations for the sake of the clarity and consistency of the script. Moreover, the viewer of either the two Syriac inscriptions or the Greek inscription would begin in the upper left-hand corner of the dovetail plate and move from top left to bottom right, while being encouraged to move their gaze freely over the borders of the dovetail plate. In fact, for all of the Syriac inscriptions I have discussed in this section, the manipulation of the script by the stonecutters produced a text that would have been read with the same directionality as a Greek inscription.

As a result, these Syriac inscriptions do more than mimic Greek letter forms. By manipulating the Syriac script into one that has separated letter forms turned ninety degrees and read left-to-right, the stonecutters responsible for these Syriac inscriptions were able to reproduce the directionality of Greek (and Latin) inscriptions.[33] In other words, not only do they imitate the Greek script, they also create a viewing experience that approximates viewing and reading Greek inscriptions. In doing so, inscriptions like the ones from Bābiskā communicate their monumentality in several registers simultaneously: first, they approximate the visual typologies of contemporary Greek (and Latin) monumental inscriptions found in Roman Syria; second, they convey individual identity and adherence to their local civic and supra-local Christian communities through lexical information; third, they curate a viewing experience with which their audiences

would be familiar. The viewer would be able to follow visual markers, proceeding left-to-right as though reading a Greek inscription. Even if the viewer was unable to read Greek, the stonecutters responsible for these Syriac inscriptions were careful to approximate the experience of reading Greek inscriptions for a hypothetical non-Greek-speaking audience.

2 Symbols of Church and Meaning

As we have seen above, the scripts of Syriac inscriptions could function as communicative images that conveyed information independent of the text *qua* language and shaped the experience of their audiences through visual cues. In this way, they appear to function much like Greek inscriptions from late Roman Syria. Whether or not Syriac stonecutters were directly imitating specific inscriptions is beside the point, although there is evidence that this may have been going on at the local level.

For example, in the city of Brād, located northwest of Aleppo, a two-story house in ruin contains a doorframe with an inscription on the lintel (Fig. 9.6). The inscription, which is dated to 256 in the era of Antioch (207–208 CE), contains numerous place names, including two Aramaic

FIGURE 9.6 PPUAES III B.6 1175 (Brād [207–208 CE]), lintel with solar imagery)

32 There does appear to be some weathering of the rock, however, and so it is impossible to say exactly where the bottom of the dovetail plate was. Nevertheless, because the last two lines of the text follow the curve of the arch, it seems likely that the text has overflowed what was the lower boundary of the plate, since the rest of the text is adjusted to the boundary of the dovetail plate. Moreover, if we attempt to reconstruct the lower boundary by drawing an imaginary line parallel to the upper, which starts in the bottom left corner of the dovetail plate (which is barely visible in the image) and extends to what would have been the bottom right corner, we see that at least part of the last line of the text would overflow this lower boundary.

33 Littmann 1904, 7.

names transliterated into Greek: Καπερ Ναβου and Ρεζιθα. Many of the names of the individuals in the inscription are certainly Roman, while others are possibly Greek. One, Zebinos, appears to be Semitic.

> Ἀγαθῇ Τύχῃ. Οὐρβικός,
> Ἀνδρόνικος καὶ Μάρκος, οἱ Λογγίνου
> υἱοί, σὺν τέκνοις, ἔκτισαν ἔτους ϛνϛ΄.
> Ἀντώνιος καὶ Σώπατρος, ἀδελφοί, ἔ-
> κτεισαν, οἰκοῦντες ἐν Κάπερ Νάβου, καὶ Κάσ-
> σανδρος ἀπὸ Ῥεζιθα, καὶ Ζεβινος ἀπὸ Καπρο ...
> Μνησθῇ Σώπατρος, ὁ ἐπαξάμενος τὸν λίθον.

To Good Fortune. Ourbikos, Andronikos, and Markos, the sons of Longinos, with their children built this in the year 256. Antonios and Sopatros, brothers, built this, being residents of Kaper Nabou, and Kassandros from Rezitha and Zebinos from Kapro ... May Sopatros be remembered, who installed this stone.[34]

Once again, I suggest that this text should be read in two discrete parts. At the beginning of the first part of the text, there is a small circle with rays extending outwards, perhaps representing the sun. Following this symbol, the text begins with a dedication to Good Fortune (Ἀγαθῇ Τύχῃ), followed by a list of three brothers, who are identified as the sons of Longinos. The text explains that these three brothers constructed the building that once housed this large lintel. Finally, the date is given using Greek letters. This first part of the text inhabits the entirety of the two raised panels below the capstone.

The beginning of the second part of the text is marked by the same sun symbol. This second part of the inscription explains that another set of two brothers who were residents of Kaper Nabo, Antonius and Sopatros, along with Kassandros and Zebinos, were responsible for building some other part of the structure (unnamed). The final line of the inscription is a prayer, like the one found on the lintel from Dēhes, that compels the viewer to remember Sopatros, who was responsible for placing the stone on which the inscription was carved. In this inscription, therefore, we see a much earlier use of a religious symbol as a marker to divide discrete parts of a text than the example from the stoa in Bābiskā. Nevertheless, the symbols function in the same way, effectively guiding the viewers' reading of the text.

Because of temporal and geographic distance between this inscription and the two Syriac inscriptions from Bābiskā, it is hard to imagine that this inscription in particular was the model for the stonecutter who used crosses instead of suns to demarcate discrete parts of the text of their Syriac inscription. Another inscription from Brād, however, appears to be in direct conversation with this Greek inscription from the third century. On a lintel of a large gateway to a courtyard in the center of the ancient city, a Greek inscription dated to 491 CE begins with the same dedicatory phrase: Ἀγαθῇ Τύχῃ.[35]

> + Ἀγαθῇ Τύχῃ. Ἀργύριος Πελαγιοῦ ἔκτισεν ἐκ θαιμελίων ἐν μη(νὶ) Ὑπερβερετέου, χρόνιος ἰνδ. ιε΄, τοῦ μφ΄ ἔτους, διὰ Κοσμᾶ, τεχνίτου.

> + To Good Fortune. Argyrios son of Pelagios built this from its foundations in the month of Hyperbereteos during the 15th indiction of the year 540, through the work of Kosmas the architect.

Unlike the inscription dated to 206 to 207 CE, this inscription is inscribed on a dovetail plate in relief. In the dovetails there are two ornamental disks, while the text begins with a cross rather than a symbol of the sun. The use of the cross suggests that the individual named in the inscription, Argyrios son of Pelagios, was a Christian. Only a single cross marks the beginning of the text which runs, therefore, as a continuous text both grammatically and visually.

The use of the cross in Christian epigraphy, of course, had numerous uses beyond being an indicator of semantic breaks and could convey a range of meanings. In the following inscriptions from late Roman Syria, the image of the cross must have been used to broadcast adherence to a supra-local Christian community and the belief in the tenets of that community. Another inscription from Brād, found on a lintel of a doorway near the north church, begins with the image of the cross before the text of the inscription.[36]

> + Τοῦτο ν[ικᾷ].

> + This conquers.

This short phrase recalls Constantine's vision in which he was shown the image of the cross, while explaining the purpose behinds its inclusion in front of the text of the

---

34   PPUAES III B.6 1175.

35   PPUAES III B.6 1176.
36   PPUAES III B.6 1181.

inscription.[37] It is this here image of the cross that conquers, the text seems to be saying.

Several inscriptions from the region similarly instrumentalize the image of the cross while echoing the legend surrounding Constantine's vision. At Il-Barah, an inscription produced by a *comes* named Priskos contains three crosses.[38] The text of the inscription is not only circumscribed by two crosses, but divided in the middle by a cross, where there is again a semantic break.

A cross marks the beginning of a small graffito found on a wall in Midjleyya as well; however, since the Greek verb "conquer!" (νίκαε) is written in retrograde (from right-to-left), the cross falls on the right side of the text.[39] There are examples of Greek inscriptions written retrograde (from right-to-left), but most are from the archaic period.[40] Therefore, scholars have supposed that this inscription from Midjleyya was imitating the practice of writing Syriac (and other Semitic languages) from right-to-left in the region. Not only is the text of the inscription clearly written from right-to-left, but the fact that the cross falls on the right of the text, in my opinion, also confirms that the individual responsible for the graffito intended the viewer to move their gaze from right-to-left and signaled this fact to the viewer by placing the image of the cross at the beginning of the text.

Thanks to a set of inscriptions found in a rock-hewn tomb in Shnan, we know that individuals in late Roman Syria considered the cross to be a "sign."[41] This is no surprise and goes without saying. Nevertheless, I suggest that it is important to emphasize that these crosses were not simply religious imagery, but also functioned as visual cues for the viewer that helped guide the reading of the text of a given inscription and provided hints as to how to understand the text of the inscription semantically. In addition, it is clear from other inscriptions in the region that acronyms could function just like the cross—that is, as signs—even though they are inherently textual insofar as they convey lexical information by default.

Another inscription from the same tomb in Shnan includes numerous acronyms that appear to communicate both linguistic and numeric information.[42] Because of the location of this inscription, we can conclude with confidence that AAES III 254 (V–VI CE) is funerary in character, which may explain the esoteric nature of some

of the more enigmatic choices on the part of the stonecutter. Unfortunately, no image exists of this lengthy inscription, but we are still able to deduce the ways in which the numerous acronyms in the inscription communicated lexical and non-lexical information.[43] The text again begins with an image of the cross, while each line concludes with the acronym ΒΥΜΓ, except for the seventh (this concludes with ΒΜΓ). Prentice noticed that this acronym has the same numerical value (2,443) as the refrain "ΙΗΣΟΥΣ Ο ΧΡΕΙΣΤΟΣ" ("Jesus the Anointed One," or literally "Jesus the Christ," since ΧΡΕΙΣΤΟΣ is technically meaningless).[44] The numerical equivalence of the acronym and the invocation of Christ is made possible only because of the choice to spell ΧΡΙΣΤΟΣ as ΧΡΕΙΣΤΟΣ.[45]

Furthermore, as Prentice notes, the acronym ΒΥΜΓ may communicate linguistic information as well as numeric information. There are many examples of Greek inscriptions from the region that include the acronym ΧΜΓ, on which there has been significant previous scholarship.[46] Although there is no consensus as to the meaning of this acronym, it was certainly a common characteristic of Christian epigraphy in late Roman Syria.[47] Suggestions for the meaning of the acronym ΧΜΓ are many, but scholars mostly agree that "Christ born of Mary" is likely the meaning for some of its uses. Therefore, Prentice suggested a possible reading of the acronym in the inscription from Shnan—Β(οήθι), Υ(ἰος) Μ(ονο)γ(ενής) "Help, only-begotten Son"—but this is only conjectural.[48]

Regardless, I contend that acronyms in Greek inscriptions from late Roman Syria functioned as both images and textual abbreviations that could communicate multiple discrete messages simultaneously. Much like the acronym ΒΥΜΓ that concludes each line in the inscription from Shnan, the acronym ΧΜΓ is found at the beginning of several inscriptions from the region.[49] One inscription on the lintel of a house from Midjleyya contains a large cross in a circle at the center of a raised plate, surrounded on either side by an ornamental disk. At the left is the acronym ΧΜΓ, which constitutes the only textual element of

---

37   According to Eusebius *Vita Constantinii* 1.28.

38   AAES III 203: + Μεγάλη ἡ δύναμις τῆς ἁγίας Τριάδος. + Ὁ κόμης Πρίσκος ἐν τούτο νικᾷ. +.

39   AAES III 210.

40   See Bourogiannis 2000.

41   AAES III 255: Τὸ σημῖων τοῦτο νικᾷ.

42   For more on Shnan, see Greisheimer 1999.

43   Prentice includes a detailed transliteration and reproduction of the inscription in his publication; see AAES III 254.

44   See also Prentice 1906.

45   This seems to have been somewhat common in early Christian circles. For more on the various spellings of Christ in late antiquity, see Edwards 1991; Caulley 2011.

46   See Prentice 1908; 1914b, 169ff (at p. 172 Prentice provides a short list of inscriptions that include the acronym ΧΜΓ); 1914b; Robinson 1986; Derda 1992b.

47   Prentice 1914b.

48   Prentice 1908, 11–12.

49   Some include AAES III 212, 219; PPUAES III B.6 1154, 1156.

the inscription.[50] If we take this acronym to function primarily as an image, however, rather than a series of three letters representing a textual phrase, the entire inscription can be read as a series of symbols.

Nevertheless, it is perhaps more productive to think of acronyms like χмг as functioning at the lexical and symbolic level simultaneously. For example, on the arch of a house in Serdjillā, a dipinto in red paint includes a circumscribed *chi-rho* symbol at the top. On either side of the bottom of the rho are the Greek letters A and Ω. The text of the inscription is as follows:

Ἐμμ]ανουήλ, χмг. Χριστός νικᾷ.

Emmanuel, χмг. Christ conquers.[51]

Semantically, several of the possible reconstructions of the acronym would fit the rest of the inscription and would even provide what would amount to a Christian exegesis of the meaning of the name Ἐμμανουήλ in Hebrew, עִמָּנוּאֵל ("God with Us"). That is to say, Christ is Emmanuel because he was born of Mary. At the same time, however, the acronym may also have marked a semantic break between the invocation of Christ and the affirmation "Christ conquers."[52]

The acronym χмг also appears frequently on late Roman amphorae. As Tomasz Derda notes, all but two of the sixteen inscriptions found on amphorae that contain the formula θεοῦ χάρις κέρδος begin first with the acronym χмг.[53] Two amphorae that were likely produced in Syria in the sixth century CE begin with the acronym χмг, before continuing with the formula θεοῦ χάρις κέρδος and a description of their contents.[54] This acronym, therefore, would have been recognizable throughout the Mediterranean in the sixth century. It is likely that the acronym functioned as a sort of apotropaic image that protected the contents of the amphora; Prentice has suggested that this was one of the uses of the acronym and may explain its frequent appearance on lintels in late Roman Syria.[55]

Similarly, the non-lexical semiotics of χмг are also manifest in inscriptions containing the acronym ιχθυς, which stands for Ἰησοῦς Χριστός Θεοῦ Υἱός Σωτήρ (Jesus Christ Son of God, Savior) but is also the Greek word for "fish." The use of the fish as an image of Christian identity

was widespread throughout the Christian world at a very early date.[56] In an inscription on a rock-cut tomb in Refadeh, the acronym ιχθυς is followed by the phrase Ἰησοῦς Χριστός Θεοῦ Υἱός Σωτήρ completely spelled-out.[57] I suggest that this inscription clearly demonstrates that the acronym had evolved into an image that had become effectively independent from the lexical information it represented. In this inscription, the acronym functions as a visual symbol of the Christianity that the individual responsible for the inscription chose to broadcast, while the following text explicates the theological implications of that individual's Christianity. The text is not, therefore, redundant or repetitive, but complementary to the visual semiotics of the acronym.

Prentice noticed that many Greek inscriptions from Syria cited the liturgy, and many also made references to scripture and popular forms of the doxology. In an article published in 1902, Prentice noted several examples of such inscriptions and demonstrated that phrases from the liturgies of the eastern Christian churches, including miaphysite liturgies, frequently appeared in Greek inscriptions from the region around Antioch. Not only were excerpts from the Liturgy of St. Mark, the Liturgy of St. James, and extant Syriac liturgies all found by Prentice in Greek and Syriac inscriptions, but Peter the Fuller's addition to the Trisagion, "who was crucified for us" (ὁ σταυρωθεὶς δι᾽ ἡμᾶς), can be found in several Greek inscriptions.[58]

Perhaps the most thoroughly examined liturgical phrase found in Greek inscriptions from Roman Syria, however, is the so-called "One-God" formula. Scholars have long argued that these "One-God" inscriptions were markers of recently Christianized communities in which individuals were broadcasting their new belief in one god as opposed to a multitude of gods.[59] That this liturgical phrase was adopted by many early Christian communities in late Roman Syria is immediately clear from the epigraphic record; however, because the phrase frequently contains spelling variations, it is also likely that it was learned orally, possibly through repetition in the liturgy. Moreover, virtually all of the spelling variations can be explained by the reflexes of itacism: the collapsing of several vowels and diphthongs in post-classical Greek to [i].[60] As a result, in contrast to the semiotics of scripts and images I have examined so far, the spelling variations

50   AAES III 212.
51   AAES III 219.
52   See above.
53   Derda 1992a, 135–36.
54   II.1 and II.6 according to Derda's (1992a) numbering.
55   Prentice 1908, 1914b.

56   There is so much secondary literature on the image of the fish in Christianity that it would be superfluous and futile for me to choose only a few to cite here.
57   PPUAES III B.5 1150.
58   Prentice 1902.
59   Prentice 1908, 18ff; Trombley 2001b, 313ff.
60   For example, PPUAES III B.6 1169: ΙΣ ΘΕΟΣ.

in the "One God" formula found in inscriptions remind us that many individuals were only familiar with the liturgy aurally and thus would have interacted with inscriptions aurally as well as visually.

The use of scripts, acronyms, and short phrases to broadcast adherence to confessional communities and to communicate meaning separate from the language they represent visually, therefore, is well attested in Greek and Syriac inscriptions from late Roman Syria. I began this chapter, however, by briefly problematizing Littmann's and de Vogüé's assumptions that the use of the Syriac script in an inscription from Deḥes was sufficient evidence to conclude that the individual responsible for the inscription was a miaphysite. As I argued above, although the Syriac script was a tool that stonecutters could use to signal belonging, it was not done to signal belonging within miaphysite communities exclusively. By replicating the directionality of the process of reading and viewing Greek inscriptions, the Syriac script of many inscriptions engaged with the reader's expectations when viewing and reading Greek (and possibly Latin) inscriptions from Roman Syria.

I also alluded earlier to the fact that the miaphysite movement in the early sixth century was bilingual, with many leaders of the miaphysite church writing exclusively in Greek. Inscriptions from late Roman Syria, and especially from the region around Antioch, confirm this. A Greek inscription from Bshindelinteh, found *in situ* in the wall of what appears to have been a small church, contains the Trisagion with the phrase "who was crucified for us."[61] As a result, Prentice, who published the inscription, suggested that the church in Bshindelinteh served a "Jacobite" (miaphysite) community.[62] He supposed, therefore, that the inscription, which is undated, probably dates to the reign of Justinian, during which time the miaphysite church developed its own hierarchy separate from the Constantinopolitan church. He also supposed that it could date to the patriarchate of Severus of Antioch, one of the most important leaders of the miaphysite movement who wrote exclusively in Greek, in the first two decades of the sixth century.[63]

In this inscription from Bshindelinteh, a large cross in the center divides the Greek text inscribed on either side of the lintel. Before the first word of the inscription, ἅγιος "holy," there is a small cross. The only indication that this inscription was most likely the work of a member of a miaphysite community is the inclusion of Peter the Fuller's

addition to the Trisagion. The non-lexical markers, such as the large cross at the center and the smaller cross that commences the inscription, are, as we have seen, typical for inscriptions from Roman Syria regardless of language or confession.

Peter the Fuller's miaphysite addition to the Trisagion at one point did become, as Prentice notes, a sort of "war-cry" for the miaphysite church.[64] Although Prentice later supposed that the inscription from Bshindelinteh should be dated to the reign of Justinian, he hypothesized that the stonecutter responsible for the inscription must have included the miaphysite addition either to appease Severus of Antioch or to proudly broadcast miaphysitism in order to gain favor with Severus.[65] Either way, I agree that it is probable that the church at Bshindelinteh served a miaphysite congregation, and that the inscription on its lintel was purposefully broadcasting adherence to a supra-local community through the inclusion of the miaphysite formula in Greek.

The same, therefore, could be said of several other inscriptions, all of which are in Greek, that also contain the miaphysite addition from late Roman Syria.[66] In fact, there are no known Syriac inscriptions that contain the miaphysite addition to the Trisagion dated to the sixth century, when the controversy about Peter the Fuller's addition was at its height. Moreover, as Prentice notes, there is little evidence that Peter the Fuller's addition was widely used in Syriac-speaking communities at this time. The Syriac liturgies do not contain the miaphysite addition, while the Armenian liturgy is the only non-Greek liturgy in which there is evidence that the miaphysite addition took hold.[67]

Of course, the miaphysite church that grew into the Syriac Orthodox Church eventually found a footing in Syriac-speaking communities in the course of the sixth century. The Syriac inscriptions I have examined in this chapter, however, do not display the same miaphysite features that their contemporary Greek counterparts do. That does not necessarily mean that any one of them was not produced by a member of a miaphysite community, but that the individuals responsible for their creation chose not to include these conspicuous markers of miaphysitism. Instead, they produced Syriac inscriptions that

61   AAES III 6.

62   Prentice 1908, 34.

63   Prentice 1908, 34.

64   Prentice 1902, 82ff. The much-later *Chronicle*, attributed to Theophanes the Confessor, records many of the controversies and instances of violence that arose from the miaphysite implications of Peter the Fuller's addition to the Trisagion. See Theophanes *Chronographia* Am5956.

65   Prentice 1902, 85.

66   AAES III 205, 295; PPUAES III B.5 1103.

67   Prentice 1902, 85–86.

engaged in the typologies of monumental Greek epigraphy from late Roman Syria, including the directionality of the script and the use of non-lexical symbols to aid the viewer in reading the text. On the other hand, only Greek inscriptions have provided us with firm evidence for miaphysite communities and their expression in the local epigraphic habit in late Roman Syria.

Conclusions

By arguing that Syriac inscriptions demonstrate adherence to both local and supra-local communities through an engagement with the visual typologies of Greek monumental epigraphy and that Greek inscriptions broadcast adherence and belonging to the miaphysite church through the use of liturgical phrases, in this chapter I have problematized the assumption that the Syriac language and the Syriac script itself were used on their own to broadcast adherence to the miaphysite church in the multilingual environment we find in late Roman Syria.[68] The evidence I have examined from Syriac and Greek inscriptions indicates that individuals were able to deploy scripts as images that, independent of language, demonstrate an awareness of the visual typologies of those communities' particular epigraphic habits. Moreover, Syriac inscriptions were not necessarily exclusively produced in miaphysite communities, nor was the use of the Syriac script an expression of a Syrian proto-national movement.

In some Syriac inscriptions, the visual typologies of Greek funerary inscriptions were adopted for dedicatory inscriptions on civic structures, such as the two-story portico from Bābiskā. The use of possibly religious symbols to indicate semantic breaks in two inscriptions from Brād suggest that stonecutters could manage how individuals interacted with the text of an inscription through non-lexical cues. In other words, the reading of the inscriptions was a discursive process between the stonecutter, the inscription as image, and its audience. Similarly, inscriptions that contain images of the cross frequently explicate belief in the symbolic power of the cross in the text of the inscription at the same time as they use the image of the cross to guide the viewers' experience in reading the text.

For example, many inscriptions that contain an image of the cross place it at important syntactic points in the text, marking whether it should be read from right-to-left or left-to-right (regardless of script or language) and where it could be broken down into smaller phrases. Often, where there is a semiotic break in the text, we also find a cross. Acronyms, such as XMΓ and ΙΧΘΥΣ, appear to have been used by stonecutters as visual aids for the reader of the inscription, just like the crosses and other symbols I examined above, especially when the expansion of the acronym would not fit the grammar of the rest of the inscription.

Finally, I suggest that we should abandon any readings of Syriac inscriptions that assume that the use of the Syriac script was only able to broadcast adherence to specific confessional communities. Instead, it is clear that stonecutters and Syriac-speaking individuals responsible for Syriac inscriptions were able to manipulate the Syriac script in order to have effective goal-oriented communication. Moreover, Greek inscriptions, not Syriac inscriptions, that contain quotations from the miaphysite liturgy provide more secure evidence for the existence of miaphysite communities. As a result, it is necessary to examine each inscription and its choice of script as a communicative act in order to understand how the individual responsible for the inscription intended the audience to interact with it. I agree, therefore, with M. C. A. Macdonald, who argued that it is dangerous to assume scripts and the languages they represent were reflections of identity a priori.[69] Scripts and languages were tools that could be appropriated and adapted by individuals regardless of their identity, ethnicity, or the communities in which they lived.

For example, on a set of three panels that once made up a monumental parapet of a church in Zebed there are three Syriac inscriptions written in the Greek and Syriac scripts.[70] Although written in multiple scripts, the inscriptions are all in the Syriac language. As can be seen in Figure 9.7, the panels are quite large and are decorated with intricate designs in the center. The text of each inscription is carved in the margin above the center design. From the north end of the parapet (on the far-right of the image) to the left, the inscriptions fall in this order: AAES IV 24-22-23. I will discuss these briefly in this order.

AAES IV 24
Ζαωρθα σαμασθα

Za'ortha the deaconess.

---

68   I choose to describe late Roman Syria as a multilingual environment because of the presence of Greek, Latin, Syriac, Christian Palestinian Aramaic, and other languages in the region. Whether or not individual multilingualism was prevalent at this time is another issue. For the challenges of distinguishing between individual and societal bi- or multilingualism, see in general Cooley 2012, esp. 304, n. 643. For the case of Syria, see Taylor 2002 and Butts 2013.

69   Macdonald 1998.
70   AAES IV 22–24 = IGLS II 313, 314, 312 (respectively).

FIGURE 9.7 AAES IV 22–24 (Zebed [IV CE, undated], parapet)

AAES IV 22

‏ܪܒܘܠܐ ܐܢܐ+ ܥܒܕ ܬܚܬ ܬܪܘܢܘܣܐ 1
‏ܕܘܟܪܢܗ ܢܗܘܐ ܡܢ ܠܥܠܡܝܬܐ 2

                                       Μωρανας   3

1   + I Rabula made the throne.
2   May his memory be blessed forever!
3   Moranas (name)

AAES IV 23

1   Ραβουλα Βασσονι(ς). Σεργις
2   Βερε(χ) δουχραναν

1   Rabula the son of Basso. Sergius
2   bless our memory!

For obvious reasons, these inscriptions have garnered much scholarly attention. Littmann's detailed discussion is extremely informative, especially for issues of dialect and orthography.[71] By now, we should be familiar with the appearance of the cross at the beginning of the text in the Syriac script in AAES IV 22 (which I have included in my transliteration). It falls in the upper right-hand corner of the panel because, as I have argued, it was being used to indicate the starting point for the viewer. On the other hand, the cross that is found at the beginning of the text of AAES IV 23 (which is visible in the image above) falls in the upper left-hand corner of this panel in order to mark the starting point for the viewer, who should proceed left-to-right.

Three persons are named in these inscriptions. The Syriac inscriptions written in the Syriac script (AAES

IV 22) and in the Greek script (AAES IV 23) appear to be in the voice of the same Rabula, son of Basso. The name Moranas, in Greek letters, is likely the name of the stone-cutter, and is possibly a corrupted form or variation of the more popular name Maronas.[72] Finally, the name of the deaconess Za'ortha is found in AAES IV 24.

Although we can make guesses as to why Moranas, if he indeed was the stonecutter, chose to use multiple scripts to write the Syriac language, these three inscriptions remain puzzling. Why use multiple scripts when one was sufficient? Theoretically, an individual would have had to have been fluent in Syriac and competent in both the Syriac and Greek scripts to successfully read these inscriptions. We know of many individuals who were;[73] however, were these inscriptions only intended for such individuals? How were other individuals supposed to interact with these three inscriptions visually?

Even though Moranas was apparently proficient in the Greek and Syriac scripts, he did not choose to imitate the directionality of the Greek inscriptions in his inscription in the Syriac script. Instead, he curated an experience for the viewer that played with the directionality of the two scripts, resulting in the viewer's gaze moving horizontally towards the pillar that stood in between AAES IV 22 and AAES IV 23 two separate times, before their gaze would move vertically down the left and right margin. This would, in theory, focalize the viewer's gaze on whatever was below this central pillar (which can be seen at the far left of the image). I contend, then, that whatever was there below this pillar was significant and, at least according to Moranas, deserved attention. The two inscriptions on the panels on either side of the pillar, then, were guiding the viewer's experience in the church as a whole, not just the experience of reading or viewing the inscriptions themselves.

I believe that these three inscriptions combined with the others examined in this chapter underline the necessity for a renewed interest in Syriac epigraphy. The study of Syriac epigraphy in the late Roman Near East has lapsed in recent years for several reasons, one of which is that we lack a central repository of Syriac inscriptions. Although the publications of Syriac inscriptions from the beginning of the twentieth century are good, many republished the same inscriptions and were either unaware of this fact or made no reference to other publications. As a result, it is difficult to see the forest through the trees and to situate Syriac epigraphy in its local and supra-local discursive contexts. In this chapter, I have attempted to demonstrate

71   Littmann 1904, 46ff.

72   AAES IV, 23. Littmann 1904, 47ff.
73   See Butts 2013.

that, in order to arrive at a fuller picture of how Greek and Syriac inscriptions were viewed and read by a late antique audience from late Roman Syria, we require new perspectives that take into consideration the semiotics of their scripts both as images and as texts. Read in this way, we can better understand how viewers interacted with inscriptions in their communities in the late antique Near East and situated themselves in their supra-local communities in the late Roman empire.

Reference List

Andrade, Nathanael. 2014. "Assyrians, Syrians and the Greek Language in the Late Hellenistic and Roman Imperial Periods." *JNES* 73, no. 2: 299–317.

Bagnall, Roger S. 2011. *Everyday Writing in the Graeco-Roman East*. Sather Classical Lectures 69. Berkeley: University of California Press.

Bourogiannis, Giorgos. 2000. "Between Scripts and Languages: Inscribed Intricacies from Geometric and Archaic Greek Contexts." In *Understanding Relations Between Scripts II: Early Alphabets*, edited by Philip J. Boyes and Philippa M. Steele, 151–80. Philadelphia: Oxbow Books.

Brock, Sebastian. 1978. "Syriac Inscriptions: A Preliminary Checklist of European Publications." *Annali dell'Instituto Orientale di Napoli* 38: 255–71.

Brock, Sebastian. 1994. "Greek and Syriac in Late Antique Syria." In *Literacy and Power in the Ancient World*, edited by Alan K. Bowman and Greg Woolf, 149–60. Cambridge: Cambridge University Press.

Butts, Aaron Michael. 2013. *Language Change in the Wake of Empire: Syriac in its Greco-Roman Context*. PhD. diss., University of Chicago.

Caulley, Thomas Scott. 2011. "The 'Chrestos/Christos' Pun (1 Pet 2:3) in 𝔓72 and 𝔓1251." *NT* 53: 376–87.

Chatonnet, Françoise Briquel, and Alain Desreumaux. 2011. "Syriac Inscriptions in Syria." *Hugoye: Journal of Syriac Studies* 14, no. 1: 27–44.

Cook, Stanley A. 1904. "North-Semitic Epigraphy." *The Jewish Quarterly Review* 16, no. 2: 258–89.

Cooley, Alison E. 2012. *The Cambridge Manual of Latin Epigraphy*. Cambridge: Cambridge University Press.

Derda, Tomasz. 1992a. "Inscriptions with the Formula θεοῦ χάρις κέρδος on Late Roman Amphorae." *ZPE* 94: 135–52.

Derda, Tomasz. 1992b. "Some Remarks on the Christian Symbol ΧΜΓ." *JJP* 22: 21–27.

Drijvers, Han J. W., and John F. Healey. 1999. *The Old Syriac Inscriptions of Edessa and Osrhoene: Texts, Translations, and Commentary*. Handbook of Oriental Studies 42. Leiden: Brill.

Edwards, M. J. 1991. "Χρηστός in a Magical Papyrus." *ZPE* 85: 232–36.

Fournet, Jean-Luc. 2020. *The Rise of Coptic: Egyptian versus Greek in Late Antiquity*. The Rostovtzeff Lectures. Princeton: Princeton University Press.

Griesheimer, Marc. 1999. "Le sanctuaire de Schnaan (Gebel Zawiye, Syrie du Nord)." *Topoi* 9, no. 2: 689–717.

Gzella, Holger. 2015. *A Cultural History of Aramaic: From the Beginnings to the Advent of Islam*. Handbook of Oriental Studies 111. Leiden: Brill.

Gzella, Holger. 2021. *Aramaic: A History of the First World Language*. Grand Rapids, MI: Eerdmans.

Hatch, William Henry Paine. 1946. *An Album of Dated Syriac Manuscripts*. Boston: The American Academy of Arts and Sciences.

Healey, John F. 2009. *Aramaic Inscriptions and Documents of the Roman Period*. Textbook of Syrian Semitic Inscriptions 4. Oxford: Oxford University Press.

Hogg, Hope W. 1901. "North-Semitic Epigraphy." *The American Journal of Semitic Languages and Literatures* 18, no. 1: 1–8.

Land, J. P. N. 1862. *Anecdota Syriaca. Tomus Primus*. Lugdunum Batavorum: Brill.

Lavan, Luke. 2006. "Fora and Agorai in Mediterranean Cities During the 4th and 5th C. A.D." *Late Antique Archaeology* 3, no. 1: 193–249.

Lidzbarski, Mark. 1898. *Handbuch der nordsemitischen Epigraphik nebst ausgewählten Inschriften*. Vol. 1. Weimar: Verlag von Emil Felber.

Littmann, Enno. 1904. *Semitic Inscriptions*. Part IV of the Publications of an American Archaeological Expedition to Syria in 1899–1900. New York: The Century Co.

Littmann, Enno. 1914. *Semitic Inscriptions: Publications of the Princeton University Archaeological Expeditions to Syria in 1904, 1905 and 1909. Division IV; Section B*. Leiden: Brill.

Macdonald, M. C. A. 1998. "Some Reflections on Epigraphy and Ethnicity in the Roman Near East." *JMA* 11: 177–90.

Millar, Fergus. 1995. *The Roman Near East 31 BC–AD 337*. Cambridge, MA: Harvard University Press.

Naveh, Joseph. 1982. *Early History of the Alphabet: An Introduction to West Semitic Epigraphy and Paleography*. Leiden: The Magnes Press, Brill.

Prentice, William Kelly. 1902. "Fragments of an Early Christian Liturgy in Syrian Inscriptions." *TAPA* 33: 81–100.

Prentice, William Kelly. 1906. "Magical Formulae on Lintels of the Christian Period in Syria." *AJA* 10, no. 2: 137–50.

Prentice, William Kelly. 1908. *Greek and Latin Inscriptions*. Part III of the Publications of an American Archaeological Expedition to Syria in 1899–1900. New York: The Century Co.

Prentice, William Kelly. 1914a. *Division III: Greek and Latin Inscriptions in Syria. Section B (Northern Syria) Part 5 (The*

Djebel Halakah). Publications of the Princeton University Archaeological Expeditions to Syria in 1904–1905 and 1909. Leiden: Brill.

Prentice, William Kelly. 1914b. "ΧΜΓ, a Symbol of Christ." *CPh* 9, no. 4: 410–16.

Prentice, William Kelly. 1922. *Division III: Greek and Latin Inscriptions in Syria. Section B (Northern Syria) Part 6 (Djebel Sim'an)*. Publications of the Princeton University Archaeological Expeditions to Syria in 1904–1905 and 1909. Leiden: Brill.

Robinson, Georgina. 1986. "ΚΜΓ and ΘΜΓ for ΧΜΓ." In *Tyche: Beiträge zur Alten Geschichte Papyrologie und Epigraphik. Band 1*, edited by Gerhard Dobesch, Hermann Harrauer, Peter Siewert, and Ekkehard Weber, 175–77. Vienna: Verlag Adolf Holzhausens.

Taylor, David G. K. 2002. "Bilingualism and Diglossia in Late Antique Syria and Mesopotamia." In *Bilingualism in Ancient Society: Language Contact and the Written Word*, edited by James Noel Adams, Mark Janse, and Simon Swain, 298–331. Oxford: Oxford University Press.

ter Haar Romeny, Bas, Naures Atto, Jan J. van Ginkel, Mat Immerzeel, and Bas Snelders. 2009. "The Formation of a Communal Identity among West Syrian Christians: Results and Conclusions of the Leiden Project." *Church History and Religious Culture* 89, nos. 1/3: 1–52.

Trombley, Frank R. 2001a. *Hellenic Religion and Christianization c. 370–529*. Vol. 1. Leiden: Brill.

Trombley, Frank R. 2001b. *Hellenic Religion and Christianization c. 370–529*. Vol. 2. Leiden: Brill.

Watt, John W. 2006. "Two Syriac Writers from the Reign of Anastasios: Philoxenus of Mabbug and Joshua the Stylite." *Harp* 20: 275–93.

## CHAPTER 10

The "Exposed Writings": Semiotic Contributions to the Analysis of Linguistic Variability in Archaic Greek Inscriptions

Sarah Béthume

Introduction

In a letter of August 2, 1981, addressed to Lilian Hamilton Jeffery, the specialist in Greek epichoric alphabets, Charalambos B. Kritzas wondered about "the curious aspiration" or "not expected aspiration" in an Argive inscription.[1] He asked, "how could we explain this phenomenon? Was that a guide for the correct pronunciation?" These comments illustrate the kinds of issues arising for epigraphists, linguists, and dialectologists when confronted with the multitude of (ortho)graphic variants in archaic and classical Greek inscriptions, where it is an extremely puzzling task to determine their nature and, in particular, whether they have a phonetic-phonological reality in the spoken language.[2] This also perhaps explains why the interpretations that are given often reflect a conception of linguistic variability that does not adequately account for the epigraphic data, especially for the archaic and epichoric documents. Indeed, they reveal an insufficiency of sensitivity to the particular nature of the source material available for the study of the Ancient Greek dialects. Yet, the constant (ortho)graphic variability needs to be reconsidered, and this can be done fruitfully with different tools from both sociolinguistics and (socio)-semiotics.

In this chapter, I address this problem in reference to inscriptions from the corpus of the Western Argolid. The first step will be to investigate two terms and their compounds, forming a "case file" that could be named "the 'hypercorrect' aspiration," where I compare the occurrences of these variants and the explanations given for them. This case exemplifies the weaknesses of the common explanations, which are studied in the second section. In the third and final section, I consider the whole communication situation of the "epigraphic message" in which the problematic sign ⊟ appears: sender(s), receiver(s), context of enunciation, and issues of reception. I emphasize the characteristics of the visual channel through which the message is conveyed and the different layers of meaning embedded in it. I ground this approach to the epigraphic documents on theoretical considerations, both pragmatic and semiotic, and in particular on the 2018 epistemological essay by Jean-Marie Klinkenberg and Stéphane Polis, "On Scripturology."[3]

1 The "Hypercorrect" Aspiration: Analysis of the Evidence, *Status Questionis*, and Evaluation of the Interpretations

In archaic inscriptions from Western Argolid, at the beginning of certain words, a graphic sign (the closed *heta*: ⊟) occurs sporadically and is associated with the sound of the aspirate /h/. The disparity of the data in Argolid itself and the exceptional character of this spelling, compared to other Greek regions, has led researchers to an interpretation of an "hypercorrect aspiration." I will first examine the evidence.

1.1 (*h*)αϝεθλο-:

The word (h)αϝέθλον is contained in six inscriptions engraved on a set of inscribed bronze Argive prizes: four bronze *hydriai* with a feminine *protome*, including the one preserved in the Metropolitan Museum of Art (Fig. 10.1), a *lebes*, and a tripod.[4] All were produced between the end of

---

1 LSAG[2] 1990, 444–445E = SEG XLI 284. The text has been presented at three lectures: 1) at the 8th International Congress of Epigraphy (Athens, 1982); 2) at the ENS in Paris, in March 1982, see Ruzé and Van Effenterre 1994, 273; and 3) in Oxford, on March 11, 1983, see Jeffery's notes on the *Poinikastas* website: http://poinikastas.csad.ox.ac.uk/. It has not yet been published in its entirety. For the convenience of the reader, the bibliographical references of the various editions and commentaries are included at the end of the chapter.

2 See Donati 2015, 2 on the Latin epigraphy.

3 They state that the word "scripturology" refers to the study of writing "perceived in its generality, as the semiotic apparatus articulating language facts and spatial facts" (9/57). Other inspiring theoretical perspectives anchored on semiotic and pragmatic principles are found, e.g., in Detienne 1988a; Svenbro 1988; Susini 1989; Fraenkel 1994; Alfieri Tonini 2007; Luraghi 2010; Klock-Fontanille 2014; Klinkenberg 1996, 2018b. Recent reviews of the literature on the specificities of writing can be found in Klock-Fontanille 2014 and Klinkenberg 2018b. My title "exposed writings" is taken from those of Susini 1989 and Fraenkel 1994.

4 This collection of documents has been described in detail by Pierre Amandry (1980 and 2002). Hereafter, the *hydriai* are named after their place of discovery or, when this is unknown, after their place of

---

FIGURE 10.1   The *hydria* of the Metropolitan Museum of Art
METROPOLITAN MUSEUM, NEW YORK:
PUBLIC DOMAIN

FIGURE 10.2   The mouth of the Met *hydria* with the prize
inscription. From G.M.A. Richter 1928, 189, fig. 8

the Persian Wars and the end of the Peloponnesian War.[5] These six prizes present an almost identical formula, although in some cases the text has been partially obliterated by corrosion: Πὰρ Ηέρας (:) Ἀργείας (:) (ἐμὶ) (:) (τὸν) (h)αϝέθλον.[6] The well-preserved but shorter inscription on the mouth of the Met *hydria* is shown in Figure 10.2.

The following syntactic variations can be regarded as minor: 1) the presence vs. absence of the verb ⟨EMI⟩ in the

first person singular (p. sg.);[7] 2) the presence vs. absence of the article in the neuter genitive plural (gen. nt. pl.);[8] and 3) the presence vs. absence of "punctuating" signs.[9] However, the word (h)αϝέθλον raises two further (ortho)-graphical and/or phonetic-phonological issues: 4) the presence of the intervocalic *digamma*, which is consistent in all the documents, and 5) the presence vs. absence of the sign ⊟, denoting an initial aspirated consonant /h/. This letter is only documented on the *hydriai*, where it can be read on two of them and has been restored with certainty on the other two.[10] By contrast, the initial

conservation: the *hydria* of the Metropolitan Museum of Art in New York = the Met *hydria*; the *hydria* of the Ny Carlsberg Glyptothek in Copenhagen = the Copenhagen *hydria*; the Pompeii *hydria* and the Sinope *hydria*. It is noteworthy that the archaeological contexts do not allow the dating for any of these documents because 1) either the vases come from the antiques market (Copenhagen, Met), 2) the excavations were executed in an unscrupulous manner (*lebes*, Sinope), or 3) these objects were found in much later tombs, which reflects other uses fulfilled in the meantime (*lebes*, tripod, Sinope, Pompeii). See, for the tripod, Andronikos 1979, 1984; for the *lebes*, Smith 1926 and Williams 2014; for the Pompeii *hydria*, Lazzarini and Zevi 1988–89, 1992, Pappalardo 2016, and Varone 2016; for the Sinope *hydria*, Akurgal and Budde 1956.

5   Amandry 1980, 216.

6   The restoration of the *lacunae* in the text is nevertheless guaranteed by 1) the space available on the support, 2) the stylistic—and dating—criteria of the support, and 3) the form of the lettering (Lazzarini *apud* Lazzarini and Zevi 1988–89).

7   This is the so-called type of "oggetti parlanti" (Burzachechi 1962 and Amandry 1971, 619, n. 78). Jesper Svenbro (1988, 476) prefers to speak of "égocentriques" supports or monuments.

8   The text of the *hydria* from the Met contains neither the verb ⟨EMI⟩ nor the article ⟨TON⟩, whilst the other texts bear at least traces of these two elements of the formula. For the more concise variant, the editors have suggested interpreting the term ⟨haϝεθλον⟩ as a nomin. sg. (Lazzarini *apud* Lazzarini and Zevi 1992, 42) or a gen. pl. partitive (Amandry 1971, 619, n. 79). Besides the gen. pl., the analysis of Jeanne and Louis Robert (1981, 40) of ⟨haϝεθλον⟩ as an acc. sg. is not justified because 1) it would involve an implied transitive verb that is not found in any other document and 2) in so doing, it ignores the parallel with the other Greek prize formulas, as listed by Amandry (1971, 615–618; completed in 1980, 211, n. 4).

9   The "punctuating" signs, either in the shape of three vertical dots ⠇ or of three vertical dashes ☰, occur respectively on the *hydria* from Pompeii and on the *hydria* of the Met. These signs are usually called "interpunction" but, as they perform a variety of functions, the term "punctuation" or "punctuating signs" will be preferred in reference to their primary nature as small, prick-like marks on the object-support (στιγμή in Greek, *punctum* in Latin).

10   It is preserved on the *hydriai* of the Met and from Sinope. On the other hand, the space for this sign and for the *digamma* is visible on the Copenhagen *hydria*: Πὰρ [Η]έρας Ἀ[ργείας ἐ]μι τὸν

aspiration is omitted in the formula on the *lebes* from Athens and on the tripod from Vergina.

Moreover, it is worth mentioning two other occurrences of the initial aspiration: these are two derivatives, hαϝεθλοθέται and hαϝέθλιμον (ἀργύρον).[11] These terms have been cut on bronze plaques discovered by Kritzas in 2000/2001, during rescue excavations near the north-eastern area of the Argive agora.[12] According to Kritzas, this batch of about 134 plaques, dating from the end of the fifth to the beginning of the fourth century BCE, are the financial archives of the sanctuary of Athena Polias, which may have acted as a "central bank" of Argos.[13] The temple also kept in its treasury the goods of Hera, supplying the religious, administrative, and military needs of the city.[14] Interestingly, the four semi-annual hαϝεθλοθέται probably played a role in the production of the Hera competition prizes. Kritzas reports that, assisted by two secretaries, these officials were in charge of the organization of the competitions in honor of the goddess (Ηεκατόνβουα). For this task, they received payments of 10,000 *drachmai* and managed the money described as "hαϝέθλιμον," which may have been intended for the purchase of animals or food for public celebrations.[15] Or, more significantly, this money, earned through selling the skins of the sacrificed animals, possibly served to produce competition prizes.[16]

Although this fact has not attracted the attention of specialists, the presence of the *digamma* is noteworthy when compared to the other occurrences of the term or of its root in the archaic inscriptions from the Argolid. The oldest known occurrence is a metric epitaph of Hyssematas, a man fallen in battle. The Doric capital on which it has been cut was unearthed in the south-west of the Heraion, perhaps near the hippodrome. Jeffery gave an approximate date of 525 to 500 BCE,[17] based on the design of the Doric capital and on the lettering (in particular, the *san* M is still used for the sibilant /s/ before the introduction of the *sigma* Σ). In the Homeric compound ἀε⟨θ⟩λοφόρον, the notation of the intervocalic *digamma* is omitted. Moreover, despite the *scriptio plena*, the two vowels have a monosyllabic scansion, which could suggest that the hiatus was maintained only artificially (graphically).[18]

A second occurrence is a hexametric dedication presumably to the (W)anakoi (i.e., the Dioscuri) by Aischyllos to celebrate his victories in games. The *stele* was found reused in the church of Haghios Georgios in Argos. The inscription is dated by Jeffery to between 500 and 480 BCE on the basis of the lettering and especially because of the replacement of the *san* by the *sigma*.[19] In the expression ἐν ἀέθλοις, the scansion of the vowels in hiatus is dissyllabic.

A third occurrence, found in the inscription of the second line on the *hydria* of Sinope, where the word appears once again as ἄεθλα, is also noteworthy. Nevertheless, the line constitutes a second inscription, as inferred by the difference in the alphabets, in the small letter size, and in the space between the letters. This inscription, although difficult to read, can now be restored with confidence thanks to the parallel offered by a *kalpis* with a Siren ornament, preserved in the Michael C. Carlos Museum of Atlanta: Ἐκ Φ[οκέ]ον ἄεθλα π[αρ] Δ[ι]ο[σ]κόροιν.[20] This variant of

---

[h]α[ϝέ]θλον (edition of Amandry 1980, after cleaning). The restoration of the text of the *hydria* from Pompeii, whose final part is severely corroded (Πὰρ Ηέρας ː Ἀργείας [ː ἐ]μ[ὶ ː τὸν ː hαϝέθλον], from Lazzarini *apud* Zevi and Lazzarini 1992), is largely ensured thanks to the formal resemblance of the *hydria*, and in particular, of the *protome* of its handle, with the other three *hydriai*, and therefore, because of their relative contemporaneity (Lazzarini *apud* Lazzarini and Zevi 1988–89; 1992; Amandry 2002).

11 Kritzas 2006, 413–14; 2007, 150–151. Only the second term is discussed by Nieto Izquierdo (2008, 257) and cited by Alain Blanc (2008, 404).

12 The texts of these plaques have not yet been published, but their financial and administrative content has been presented in several papers by Kritzas (e.g., 2006, 2007, and 2013).

13 Kritzas 2007, 136. The palaeography suggests a date in the late fifth century BCE, but the content of some texts includes references to the Corinthian War (394–386 BCE) and to internal disorder in Argos, which led to Σκυταλισμό (370 BCE). Hence, the documents are probably later. Despite their storage in different deposits, Kritzas assumes that all these plates must be relatively contemporary.

14 Kritzas 2007, 136.

15 Kritzas 2006, 414, n. 50.

16 Kritzas 2007, 150. However, when comparing the chronology of the documents studied (the bronze prizes, all limited to the fifth century BCE, and the plates), these sums of money could not have contributed precisely to the elaboration of the prizes.

17 Jeffery 1990 (LSAG²), 168, no. 15. Lloyd Daly (1939, 169) states that Hyssematas fell at the battle of Sepeia. This attack from Sparta is not precisely dated: traditionally, in 494 BCE, but other scholars date it back to 520 BCE.

18 Nieto Izquierdo 2008, 151, n. 94. The scansion could also be due to the gaucherie of the metric and syntactic composition of the text (Friedländer and Hoffleit 1948), combined with the clumsy execution of the engraving: the *ductus*, the shape of the letters, and the mistaken substitution of Φ instead of Θ in ΑΕΦΛΟΦΟΡΟΝ (on which see below).

19 Jeffery 1990 (LSAG²), 169, no. 17.

20 The *kalpis* with the Siren ornament bears the inventory number 2004.25.1. Its inscription is legible, with more recent letters incised from punched dots (with *omega* instead of *omicron*; and with the unapocopated preposition): Ἐκ Φωκέων ἄεθλα παρὰ Διοσκόροιν. The ethnic designation Φωκέων seems to be best interpreted as referring to the inhabitants of the region of Phokis in central Greece (Φωκεύς, plural Φωκεῖς, genitive Φωκέων) and not of the city of Phokaia in Asia Minor (Φωκαιεύς, gen. pl. Φωκαιέων or Φωκαέων). This latter hypothesis has been proposed by Jasper Gaunt (2005, 16), while the former is formulated by Amy Sowder Koch (2015, 17, n. 27, 28) and Athanasios

the term was thus erroneously integrated by Enrique Nieto Izquierdo into his analysis of the dialects of Argolid.[21] The inscription was most probably engraved on the *hydria* after having been given to a winner of the Argive Hera's games. Consequently, it is important to consider that the variants ͱαϝέθλον and ἄεθλα do not coexist within the same inscription, but in two inscriptions produced in different places, by two craftsmen, at different moments in the life of their common object-support.

The *digamma* is remarkably preserved in the studied documents (prizes and bronze plaques), even though they are several decades later than the two inscriptions mentioned above, in which the letter is missing. According to Sophie Minon, the late retention of *digamma* in the alphabet is characteristic of Argos and Laconia.[22] The letter disappeared in the official inscriptions of the Argive Plain from the middle of the fourth century BCE and even from ca. 400 in private epigraphy.[23] Before this period, it was maintained in all positions except after a sonorant, and, with a few exceptions, in intervocalic position and in longer words.[24] The adoption of the "reformed" Attic alphabet in the region may have hastened the disappearance of the phoneme: the graphic sign has become confined to certain lexical categories.[25] Concerning the terms derived from the lemma ἆθλον, in the post-classical inscriptions of Argolid, the contraction of the vowels is systematic and the notation ⟨ΑΘΛΟ-⟩ is generalized.[26] It reflects either a late contraction (after the adoption of the ionized Attic alphabet), with [ae] > [aː], or a borrowing from the *koine*.[27]

If we compare the Argive corpus with the inscriptions from the rest of the Greek linguistic domain, we find only three other occurrences of the same root containing an intervocalic *digamma*: 1) [ἄ]ϝεθλα in an Arcadian dedication by an athlete to Athena Halea, from ca. 525 to 500 BCE;[28] 2) ἀϝέθλον in a sinistroverse dedication to Athena by the Olympionic Kleom(b)rotos, on a bronze plaque found in Sybaris, dating from the seventh to the sixth century BCE;[29] and 3) πενταϝέθλεον on a fragment of a stone *halter* from Isthmia, probably also an agonistic dedication, and from the first half of the sixth century BCE.[30] In addition, in the Homeric language, the fall of the /w/ intervocalic is recent.[31] Yet, in the forms deriving from this stem, the vowels in hiatus contract only exceptionally: the monosyllabic scansion betrays the recentness of the passage.[32]

As can be seen, the Argive *corpus* witnesses a remarkable frequency of the variant with intervocalic ⟨ϝ⟩, compared to the other regions of the Greek world. Furthermore, the chronology of the Argive documents reveals that it is attested later. But let us now consider the second aspect of the problem posed by ͱαϝεθλο-.

As already observed, the "unexpected" notation of an initial aspiration regularly generates embarrassment for both editors and for commentators, whether linguists or epigraphists.[33] Jeffery interpreted the aspiration in the word Ͱέρας as having possibly "encouraged" the initial aspiration in the term ͱαϝέθλον. She suggested that Kritzas examine all the Argive facts to determine whether an aspirate in a preceding word could cause "the irrational use of h in a following word." I reproduce here the text of the draft of her correspondence with Kritzas, with the corrections, additions, and diacritical marks in Jeffery's hand, as

---

Sideris (2019, 138, n. 29–30). This new reading of the Sinope *hydria* invalidates the previous itinerary through the city of Pheneos in Arcadia, suggested by Kritzas and taken up in Dubois 1990, 516, no. 424; Amandry 2002, 31; Cogan 2011, 137.

21   Nieto Izquierdo 2008, 151.

22   Minon 2014, 47.

23   Minon 2014, 41. The letter has never been documented in Eastern Argolid (Epidauros), probably because of the later epigraphic data (not earlier than ca. 500 BCE), see Minon 2014, 47.

24   Nieto Izquierdo 2008, 233.

25   Nieto Izquierdo 2008, 236.

26   Epidaurian documents: a) a law dating from ca. 220 to 216 BCE (IG IV² 1 44), l. 2, ἀθλήμασιν; b) a decree of the second century BCE (IG IV² 1, 99 II), ll. 15–16, τῶν ἀθλη|τᾶν and l. 19, πένταθλος. Documents from the Argive Plain: c) an inscribed *patera* foot discovered in Candia (near Argos), from the second century BCE (SEG XI 373), l. 1, ἄθλου.

27   Nieto Izquierdo 2008, 152. The outcome of this recent contraction differs significantly from that of older contractions where [ae] > [εː]: e.g., the verb NIKE = νίϙε (with E noting [εː]) in the dedication by Aischyllos.

28   IG V, 2, 75; Rhomaios 1912, 353, fig. 1; Dubois 1986, 12–13; Jeffery 1990 (LSAG²), 215, no. 5, pl. 40. The debate about the initial /h/ of Athena's epiclesis (correct for Nieto Izquierdo 2008, 261–62 vs. hypercorrect for Dubois 1986) echoes the problems discussed here.

29   Sybaris-Thourioi, Francavilla Marittima, Arena 2002 (IGASMG IV), 2; Guarducci EG I 1967, 110–11, no. 3, fig. 14; Hansen 1983 (CEG I), no. 394; Jeffery 1990 (LSAG²), 456 1a; Dubois 2002, IGDGG II 5; see SEG XXVII 702; XXIX 1014; XXXV 1053; LVII 971 for complete references.

30   Broneer 1959, 322, no. 1, fig. 4 and pl. 73a; Hansen 1983 (CEG I), no. 355. See SEG XVIII 140; XXII 207; XXVI 407 for the bibliography. In Lazzarini's transcription (1976, no. 829), the word is a participle or a noun in the genitive plural. The editor (Broneer 1959, 322) reports Jameson's reading πενταϝεθλεον{ν}ίϰα as a noun. Oscar Broneer himself favors a variant of the term πεντάθλίον (Pind., *Isth*. I, 26), that could be evidence of the introduction of the pentathlon in the Isthmian Games.

31   Chantraine 1942, 28.

32   Chantraine 1942, 32, §15.

33   In Kritzas's words.

they are visible (and readable) in the photograph on the Poinikastas website:

> the preceding h̲ε̲ρ̲α̲ς̲ [...] might possibly have caused/influenced this second use of heta [...] I have no good answer to these "intrusive" (?) aspirate [...]. I note that in 2 of the inscriptions which you cite there is a preceding aspirate (h̲ερας, and h̲ιερόν). Might this, perhaps, cause the irrational use of h in a following word? (As for the other example // ϝʰεδιεστάς, C. D. Buck, Gr. Dialect, p. 283), [ed.] the preceding ϝ would (?) have similarly ~~influenced~~ encouraged the following h̲? [...]. Perhaps, it would be worthwhile to check them and see in how many cases there was in Argos some sort of aspirate letter preceding the "intuitive" use of ⊟ in all these attested abnormalities (ϝh̲εδιεστάς, παρh̲οδελονόμον, etc.).

Puzzled by this aspirate, some researchers have qualified it as "pleonastic," "anomalous," "hypercorrect," or "ultracorrect," without further explaining the exact meaning they give to those epithets.[34] All accept the explanation of an influence of the name of ⟨⊟EPA⟩ (thereby reaffirming Jeffery's idea) and refute any etymological reconstruction for the aspirate.[35] But their wording does not always clarify whether they are describing a graphic or a phonetic fact.[36] Maria Pilar Fernández Álvarez is an exception: she supports an etymological aspiration maintained in our Argive documents without the dissimilation of the aspirates (in reference to Grassmann's law).[37] However, her reasoning for doing so is contradictory: "haϝεθλον [...], sin disimilación, parece a primera vista irregular, pero, como

indicamos, con frecuencia en las inscripciones se usa sin motivo el espíritu áspero."[38]

As pointed out by Georges-Jean Pinault, the etymology of ἀεθλο- is controversial.[39] Notwithstanding, on account of a semantic problem but not of a formal obstacle, he discards the reconstruction that would have allowed us to consider the initial aspirate as etymological: $*(h)a\text{-}weth^lo\text{-} < *sm\text{-}wedh^h\text{-}lo\text{-}$, in the sense of "hitting together" or "place where adversaries hit each other" composed of the "copulative prefix $*sm\text{-}$ 'together.'"[40] His assumption does not validate the initial aspiration: he proposed the root $*h_2ewh_1\text{-}$ "to favor, to mark a preference for, to help," which has counterparts in the Latin auidus, auēo, -ēre "to desire ardently" and in Sanskrit $av^{i\text{-}}$ "to be favorable," nt. avana- "favor, protection."[41] Through these parallels, Pinault tries to reconstruct a common conception of the "Indo-European populations":[42] ἄ(ϝ)εθλον $< *h_2\acute{e}wh_1\text{-}d^hlo\text{-}$ in the meaning of "'ce par quoi se réalise la faveur'; dans le cadre d'un concours, il s'agit de l'aide, de l'encouragement accordé aux concurrents [...] celui qui gagne est considéré comme 'favorisé' par la chance, par sa valeur personnelle, ou par les dieux, ou par tout cela ensemble."[43]

In light of the recent discovery of the bronze plaques in the archives of Athena's Treasury, in which are attested the signs of the initial aspirate and the intervocalic digamma in the root, the hypothesis of a contamination from the theonym bears limited relevance. Although the phonetic context was not specified by Kritzas, such an analogy, sporadic and exceptional, should not have been exerted in these presumably different contexts.

---

34 *Pleonastic*: Lazzarini apud Lazzarini and Zevi 1988–89, 43. "Pleonastico" should probably be understood in the etymological sense of "repeated, overabundant." Lazzarini connects this fact to the "uso incoerente dello spirito aspro nelle iscrizioni argive arcaiche." *Anomalous*: Nieto Izquierdo 2008, 257 and 259: in opposition to the forms labeled as "correctas" or "con la aspiración notada correctamente." *Hypercorrect*: Pinault 2006, 394; Nieto Izquierdo 2008, 234 and 261, where these forms are also classified among the "contaminaciones analógicas." *Ultracorrect*: Nieto Izquierdo 2008, 21 and 256, n. 249.

35 Pinault 2006, 394; Nieto Izquierdo 2008, 261, n. 266.

36 In a rather opaque formulation by Nieto Izquierdo (2008, 261), the aspiration of Ἥρα would have "contaminated" "los juegos en honor de esta diosa." In her quoted letter, Jeffery used interchangeably both the sign ⊟ and the notation "h," which seems to denote a phonetic fact. On the other hand, Pinault (2006, 394) clearly speaks of "graphie hypercorrecte," while Lazzarini describes the (graphic) sign as "pleonastico" and not the (phonetic) aspirate.

37 E.g., Lejeune 1987, 56–58, §45. The dissimilation is rejected in Pinault 2006, 394 and Nieto Izquierdo 2008, 261, n. 266.

38 Fernández Álvarez 1981, 144 (my emphasis).

39 Pinault 2006, 393 f. His status questionis should be consulted. He stresses the uncertainty of the general works. Indeed, Hjalmar Frisk (GEW: 22) and Pierre Chantraine (DELG: 21) consider that all the reconstructed protoforms are unsatisfying. Robert Beekes (EDG: 23) tentatively reinstates the root $*h_2uedh\text{-}$ "contest" but he relies on an Indo-European origin ("the word looks Indo-European").

40 Pinault 2006, 394–96. This root implies a notion of violence that he judges inadequate in contrast to what he traces as the primary meaning of the term. The hypothesis is not new, and has recently been endorsed by Kölligan (in an unpublished comment); also Pinault 2006, 395, n. 73.

41 Pinault 2006, 397.

42 Pinault concludes, "En définitive, le sens profond de gr. ἄ(ϝ)εθλον [...] témoigne, par la conservation de la même racine dans le même contexte, de l'antiquité indo-européenne de la conception du "concours" ritualisé" (2006, 407, my emphasis).

43 Pinault 2006, 398.

1.2 hοδελο-

Another root has led to the same type of interpretations. Ηοδελο- is present in an inscription written on a bronze plaque, found about two hundred meters from the sanctuary of Apollo Deiradiôtes, in the vicinity of Argos, and dating according to Alan Johnston from ca. 460 to 450 BCE.[44] This is the very word that led Kritzas to solicit Jeffery concerning "the curious aspiration of the ὀδελόνομοι": ΠΑRΒΟΔΕΙΟΝΟΜΟΙΣ ("παρ᾽ hοδελονόμοις" "in the presence of *hodelonomoi*,"[45] ll. 15, 17) and ΒΟΔΕΙΟΝΟΜΟΝ (gen. pl., partitive, complement of the verb ἀϝρέτευε, l. 19).

Jeffery's advice to examine whether this "abnormal aspiration" could have been conditioned by the prior presence of an Β is, for this text, questionable. First, the three instances of the term suggest that it cannot be a mere incidental misspelling but rather that the engraver really meant to inscribe it. Second, the possible distance for the effects of the "contextual contamination" is not specified. In the present text, for the first occurrence of ΠΑRΒΟΔΕΙΟΝΟΜΟΙΣ, one can first find the letter in the previous line (i.e., in another sentence) six times, and then again in the following line, also six times. In this context, Β notes the abbreviation of the numeral 100 ("hεκατόν"), according to the acrophonic principle, and its signifier corresponds to the multiple of the Argive *drachma*.[46] If this reasoning is followed, one should also take into account the aspirate in the sequence of abbreviations denoting the numeral 1000 X ("χίλια," with the aspirated stop [kʰ]). Concerning the second occurrence of the term (l. 17), the same numeral Β is repeated five times in the previous line (i.e., the previous sentence) and eight times in the same line/phrase. In order to explain the last example (l. 19), one can resort to the adjective Β[ΕRΑ.]ΕΥΣ in the preceding line and clause; this adjective is then repeated in the same line and clause ("hεραιεύς" means "Heraiaeus, belonging to the Heraiees").[47]

In addition, the word ΒΟΔΕΙΟΣ is preserved in a fragmentary boustrophedon inscription on rough grey poros, from Mycenae, incorporated in a Hellenistic wall. Dating the inscription back to ca. 550 to 525 BCE, its editor, Georgios Mylônas, erroneously transcribed the form as ϝοβελός (with an initial *digamma* and a *beta* instead of *delta*).[48] After him, all scholars have reproduced the *editio princeps*, except Ronald S. Stroud, who rightly corrected the form on the basis of a squeeze.[49] Then, the recommendable reading is hοδελός, as confirmed by a careful observation of the photographs.[50] Françoise Ruzé and Henri Van Effenterre correctly identify the sign Β (noting "hοβελος"), but they explain it as the numeral, while ignoring the parallel with the compound hοδελόνομοι.[51]

The "very strange" occurrence of the initial aspirate is again characterized by Nieto Izquierdo as "hypercorrect," subject to "contamination."[52] He attempts to explain it without conviction by an analogy with other terms containing an aspiration and belonging to the same lexical field: χαλκός (a monetary unit equivalent to 1/8 of an *obolos* or, here, hοδελός) and possibly δραχμά (att. δραχμή).[53] In Nieto Izquierdo's opinion, frequent enumeration of these three terms in decreasing order in the financial accounts may have resulted in the aspirated pronunciation of the word initial, which would have been secondarily extended to the compounds. This explanation confirms that, according to him, in this case, the aspiration was

---

44 LSAG² 1990, 444–45E. In her drafts, Jeffery noted that the lettering was contemporary with the bronze *hydria* from the Met, and earlier than the stele of the Argives fallen at Tanagra (see below).

45 The text—unpublished—is available in Jeffery's archives on *Poinikastas* website. According to the etymology, these officials could be "those who regulate the official weights or the coinage." Ruzé and Van Effenterre (1994, 272) merely indicate "magistrats financiers [...] connus à Trézène à la fin du IIIᵉᵐᵉ siècle" (with reference to IG IV 757 where the initial aspiration is omitted).

46 Kritzas 2009, 2013, 281.

47 This corresponds to a subdivision of the Argive population, probably a *phatria* (or *phratria*): Kritzas 1992; Piérart 1997; *contra* Charneux 1984, 207–27.

48 Mylônas 1964, 71, pl. 72γ. Though his drawing clearly displays Β as the first letter and D in third position, his transcription is discordant in its use of an unconventional sign: [. In his next article, Mylônas (1965, 161) transcribed ϝοβέλος (= ϜΟΒΕΛΟΣ). This reading was then replicated in Robert and Robert 1968, 464, no. 258.

49 The correct reading is found in SEG LVI 419 (suggested by Stroud) and followed by Nieto Izquierdo (2008, 258 and 261). The erroneous reading is found in the following editions: Orlandos 1964, 69–70 and 72, fig. 82; Robert and Robert 1968, 464, no. 258; Ruzé and Van Effenterre 1995, 227, no. 62 (with an imprecise drawing). Fernández Álvarez 1981 does not report the word.

50 The high-quality photograph given in Orlandos 1964, 72, fig. 82 allows us to identify the third letter as a *delta*, since there is a curve to the right of the vertical stroke. Although the light on the stone might suggest that a short oblique stroke rose from the vertical one, the shape does not correspond to the *beta* used in Argos and Mycenae, whose upper stroke slopes down or remains straight (Jeffery 1990 [LSAG²], 151: Ϸ). This apparently oblique line can be attributed to the irregularity of the grain of the stone or to a sharp mark cut during its reuse. This problem underlines the crucial importance of a thorough examination of the epigraphic documents, even in linguistic descriptions.

51 Ruzé and Van Effenterre 1995, 227. Yet, in their 1994 edition of the previous inscription (at 272–74, no. 65), they retained the initial aspiration.

52 Nieto Izquierdo 2008, 261.

53 Nieto Izquierdo 2008, 261. His lack of conviction is palpable from his wording: "de manera *totalmente tentativa* y a falta de otra explicación *más verosímil*" (my emphasis).

orally sounded and that the "contamination" is not only a graphic phenomenon.

Yet, a consensus has not yet been achieved on the etymology of the term. The labial consonant of ὀβελός (Ionian, Attic ὀβολός, Thessalian ὀβελλός, Homer) alternates with a dental ὀδελός (Doric and Boeotian dialects, Arcadian). This alternation is commonly explained as a different result of an Indo-European labiovelar *gʷ.[54] Nevertheless, Beekes considers the word "clearly Pre-Greek" in light of the multiple difficulties of reconstructing a "pre-form":[55] he regards the resorting to the "analogy-explanation" for the dialectal extension (outside Aeolic) of the labial as unsatisfactory, and believes that the Thessalian geminate remains unexplained, as does the initial ὀ-.[56] Moreover, in the enumeration of the dialectal forms, no lexicographer quotes the Argive variant with the initial aspirate that appears in our texts.

In summary, these accounts for haϝέθλον and hοδελός mainly rely on the notions of hyper-/ultra-correction (Pinault, Nieto Izquierdo), abnormality (Jeffery, Nieto Izquierdo), or irregularity (Pinault).[57] They are chiefly grounded on the etymology, despite its uncertainty. The authors pay little attention to the exact nature of the phenomenon, whether it is a graphical one (an (ortho)-graphical or engraving error) or whether it impacts on phonetics. Lastly, they fail to circumscribe the conditions for the occurrence of these variants by studying the characteristics of the documents themselves. Let us now examine these assertions with reference to the definition of hypercorrection and by decomposing the theoretical assumptions underlying the concept. Thence, the pitfalls of this method will be highlighted.

2   The Veil of the Standard: Back to the Notion of Hypercorrection

According to the sociolinguistic literature, hypercorrection consists of the reconstruction by a speaker of a form or a syntactic structure through the erroneous application of a rule or a model, by analogy with other cases where the rule is opportunely applied.[58] This phenomenon is possible owing to the coexistence of several variants within a community, but also within the competence of the individual speakers, who are thus "polylectal." First, it may represent an attempt to compensate for the evolution of the language by restoring an obsolescent form that is considered more correct (i.e., hyperarchaisms, due to the coexistence of diachronic variants).[59] Second, it happens in situations of "linguistic insecurity" (in particular in a formal style) which lead the speaker to pay strong attention to their speech in such a way as to exaggerate sociolinguistic traits or markers (variable features) that are deemed to belong to the prestige or standard variety to be imitated (reflecting the coexistence of diastratic varieties).[60] Third, hypercorrection may cause the formation of hybrids derived from several dialectal varieties in diglossic or bilingual communities (i.e., from the coexistence of diatopic varieties).[61]

Despite the technicality of its definition, some commentators of our inscriptions use the specialized term "hypercorrection" as an interchangeable synonym for "irregularity" and "abnormality"—in other words "incorrectness" or "misspelling"—without clarifying whether it has a phonetic correspondent. This is shown by the adjectives qualifying the aspirate: "irrational use," "without motive," "inconsistent," "abusive," "intrusive."[62] However, I would argue that there are several obstacles to the widespread use of this notion, some of which are intrinsically dependent on the specificity of the epigraphic corpus. Beginning with the issue of an engraving mistake, I will then consider that of spelling errors, before returning to the question of the "unexpected" 𐌇 and whether it can in fact be considered a hypercorrection.

---

54   For Bailly (1950, 1349), the etymology is controversial. Frisk (*GEW*, 344–45) elaborates an explanation for each dialectal variant: a) the Attic vocalism /o/—ὀβολός—is due to assimilation; b) the Thessalian gemination ὀβελλός is secondary; c) the labial outside the "Aeolic" (i.e., in Ionian and Attic) must be analogical; d) the initial /o/ remains unexplained (although a connection with βέλος is mentioned). Chantraine (*DELG*, 772) reiterates Frisk's comments but states that the initial /o/ "ne peut être qu'une prothèse."

55   Beekes *EDG*, 1042–43.

56   See also what he says about this initial (*EDG*, 1041, s.v. ὀ 2).

57   Elsewhere, they use epithets that insist on the lack of reason for this sign: "incoerente" (Lazzarini), "irrational" and "intrusive" (Jeffery), "sin motivo" (Fernández Álvarez), "abusive" (Pinault). I will return to this point below.

58   Chambers and Trudgill 1998, 42, 82; Dubois 2002, 235; Schilling-Estes 2004, 379–82; Brixhe 2010, 231, 240; Holmes 2013, 255–56; Bubeník 2018, 162.

59   Dubois 2002, 235; Schilling-Estes 2004, 380; Brixhe 2010, 240.

60   E.g., Labov 1972, cited by Chambers and Trudgill 1998, 82–83; Schilling-Estes 2004, 380; Holmes 2013, 255–56. This is often the case for "(lower) middle-class" speakers, or for some authors, of semi-literate speakers, with an imperfect command of the standard (Brixhe 2010, 231, 240, 242).

61   Bubeník 2018, 162; Minon 2009, 2013.

62   See n. 58.

2.1   *Engraving Mistake?*

If one interprets this terminology as referring to a simple engraving fault made by a slightly educated, inattentive craftsman who neglected the transcription of the commissioned text, it is necessary to explain the recurrence of this sign of aspiration in different sets of inscriptions produced by different hands (the bronze plaques and the prize vessels). Even in the case of the *hydriai*, it is very improbable they were inscribed by the same hand.[63] A careful comparison of their lettering, in relation to the shape of their female *protome*, leads to the conclusion that there are chronological discrepancies between them, so that we may assume that, although they were produced for different games, they were certainly manufactured by the same local bronze workshop.[64]

The Sinope *hydria* is the oldest in terms of both the inscription and the stylistic characteristics of the *protome*:[65] it can be dated between 470 and 458/457 BCE.[66] Conversely, the Copenhagen *hydria* is the most recent: ca. 450 to 440 BCE.[67] Thus, the Met and the Pompeii *hydriai* must be placed between these two other prizes but they exhibit some relevant differences (the form of the punctuation sign and of the *pi*, shorter vs. longer formula). The *lebes* and the tripod, whose inscriptions lack the sign ⊟, can be dated to 430 to 420 BCE, because their letters have a curved *ductus* and are later epichoric allographs (the *gamma* Λ, the dotted *theta* ⊙, the *nu* Ͷ). Lastly, the bronze plaques from the Treasure of Athena are significantly later according to Kritzas' dating to the late fifth century BCE to the first half of the fourth century BCE.[68]

Further doubts arise concerning the hypothesis of an engraving error if we examine the care taken in the drawing of the letters on every Argive prize, and especially on the *lebes* and the tripod where they are engraved with punched dots, probably by the same hand, with an undeniable aesthetic aspect.[69] This precision corresponds to the delicate plastic execution of the supports (*hydriai*, *lebes*, tripod), unanimously praised by their editors. These elements of execution, together with the prestige of these trophies, would suggest that a banal engraving mistake can be excluded.[70]

What is more, the frequent corrections that one may observe in archaic epigraphic documents reveal a fair degree of literacy among the craftsmen, who not only copied the text (which they could have done without understanding what they were copying) but were also fairly capable of proofreading it and identifying their mistakes.[71] For example, the tripod from Vergina features an *omikron* that has obviously been added between the *lambda* and the *nu*, after the process of engraving the letters by punched dots. Louis Robert stresses the infrequency of *lapsus calami* even in geographically isolated areas.[72] Finally, the use of punctuation signs on the *hydriai* of the Met and from Pompeii is indicative of a certain metalinguistic reflection on the part of the scribes and engravers, because the subdivision of the utterance by means of this sign presupposes its analysis in accented units, a notion which prefigures that of the word.[73]

Graphic variants—albeit isolated—are often treated inconsistently by specialists. Some benefit from this, since they are not dismissed as hypercorrect or incorrect, but are erected as standard or even as an original form, almost as a protoform. In the Argive inscriptions already

---

63   *Contra* Amandry 1980, 213. The influence of a single model is accepted in Lazzarini *apud* Lazzarini and Zevi 1988–89, 43.

64   Diehl 1964, 24; Zevi *apud* Lazzarini and Zevi 1988–89, 37; Amandry 2002, 30; Sowder Koch 2009, 159. It is worth noting that, in the general opinion, the prize vases were made for the occasion of the games and not reused vases: their style is therefore consistent with the time of their inscription: see Amandry 1971, 608, n. 60; *contra* Zevi *apud* Lazzarini and Zevi 1988–89, 37.

65   Von Bothmer 1974, 16; Sowder Koch 2009, 144.

66   The benchmark for the Argive documents of this period is given thanks to the absolute date of the *stele* listing the Argives fallen in the battle of Tanagra and erected in the Kerameikos in Athens (in 458/457 BCE); see Jeffery 1990 (LSAG²), 162–64, 169, no. 30. The letters of the Sinope *hydria* are somewhat earlier, based on the form of the *gamma* and of the *lambda*), but the historical context prevents us from dating it back earlier than 470 BCE.

67   Amandry 2002, 30.

68   We do not have precise information concerning the palaeography of the bronze plaques on which the studied terms were written.

69   Amandry 1980, 251; Lazzarini *apud* Lazzarini and Zevi 1988–89, 43.

70   E.g., for the quality of the *lebes* see Smith 1926, 256; of the *hydriai* see Zevi *apud* Lazzarini and Zevi 1988–89, 33–37; and of the tripod see Andronikos 1984, 165.

71   Jacquemin 1999 lists numerous corrections in Delphi. See also Robert (1955, 212), who warns that "un mauvais travail pouvait être refusé, rejeté et recommencé." Nevertheless, the disqualification of the stonecutters is a most common explanation of epigraphic difficulties. On the contrary, Rudolf Wachter (1992) has emphasized the interest of the linguistic study of the errors and corrections in epigraphic documents.

72   Robert 1955, 218, n. 3.

73   Morpurgo Davies 1987, 271, 275. The Argive plain differs from most Greek regions (with the exception of Attica) in its frequent use of punctuating signs (Jeffery LSAG² 1990, 153; Morpurgo Davies 1987, 270–71). It must be pointed out that the two areas of the Argolid (Western and Eastern) used different alphabetic systems. In the Argive plain, in the Western Argolid, various cities shared the same alphabet: especially Mycenae, Tiryns, the Heraion, and Argos. These centers remained independent until Argos took control of the plain in about 470 to 460 BCE.

mentioned as parallels, it is sufficient to compare the status given to two forms which pose similar problems: the form ΑΕΦΛΟΦΟΡΟΝ has been unanimously corrected to ἀε⟨θ⟩λόφορον. This emendation is quite plausible because of the resemblance of the shape of Φ and Θ (both are rounded letters) and because of the Φ correctly written in the second term of the compound: this is clearly a case of "graphic contamination" and therefore of misspelling.[74] On the other hand, although it constitutes an isolated variant both in the Argive field and in Greek texts in general, [Σ]-ΠΑΔΙΟΝ (: σπάδιον) has been promoted as the Argive and even original form.[75] No one has noticed that the shape of ⟨Π⟩ was relatively close to that of ⟨Τ⟩ and could have entailed a purely graphic error.

Finally, this attack against the engraver's skill ignores the diversity of the protagonists involved in the elaboration of the message delivered by the inscriptions. Louis Robert traces the complex production process, which may vary if the inscription is commissioned by an official entity or by a private individual.[76] Does the variant record the idiolect of the craftsperson who delivers the finished product (engraver, painter, bronzeworker) or of a secretary, who (at least for official inscriptions) provides them with a copy of the text to be displayed, or is it the variant of the commissioner who dictates the text to them? In any case, it is not so easy to incriminate the engraver.

2.2 *Spelling Error?* Ortho*graph, Norm(s), and Standard(s)*

The concept of "hypercorrection" and even the less precise notions of "irregularity" and "abnormality" involve the ideas of "rule," "norm," a search for "correction," and excessive attempts to reach a "linguistic standard."[77] However, in view of the omnipresent variability in the archaic Greek inscriptions of any region, one may wonder whether epichoric dialects have ever been subjected

to standardization, codification, institutionalization, and elaboration, even at a very local level. The supposed standard is rather an evanescent *phantasma.*[78] It is sufficient to observe the variability of the spelling within the same inscription, for the same word, which reveals a great deal of "orthographic" freedom: this is the case of the reduplication of the signs for certain consonants, and of *iota* in intervocalic or postconsonantal position.[79]

If there is any convention, it should have been a tacit one. At the very least, it can be identified with the local graphic convention by which letters were associated with sounds/phonemes.[80] This convention was probably learnt by the engravers and other literate people, and was constantly actualized through the production of each inscription and text; for example, in workshops. The developments of the letter shapes show how much this supposed "custom" is exposed to constant re-elaboration and to extremely localized fashions.

A plurality of norms, not formulated in grammars, or rather of trends, had a centripetal influence on the written utterances, if we consider that the highest possible degree of formalism manifests itself in writing.[81] This is especially so since the "exposed writings," namely the epigraphic documents, are likely to constitute a climax, given that

---

74   For Nieto Izquierdo (2008, 284), this is not a phonetic development whereby "/tʰ/ > /θ/, /pʰ/ > /f/ con posterior neutralización de /f/ y /θ/ en /f/."

75   Its retention is based on the testimony of the glosses and the *Etymologicum Magnum*: so, Buck (1968, §88) and Nieto Izquierdo (2008, 377–78) have categorized στάδιον as secondary in connection with the adjective στάδιος. Bechtel's phonetic explanation (II, 1923, 473, §32.2) involving consonant dissimilation into adjacent syllables is rejected by Nieto Izquierdo (2008, 378). Today, the *stele* is too damaged precisely at this section of the line, so that the particular spelling has unfortunately disappeared: it now rests on an old drawing by Fränkel for the IG IV (1902), based on an unpublished squeeze by Le Bas (see Fränkel 1902, IG IV 561).

76   Robert 1955.

77   Consani 2004, 203.

78   As James Clackson has shown in his presentation at the *EVWRIT* colloquium, "Standard Languages, Language Standards and Language Norms in the Greco-Roman World," this concept remains tenacious among modern authors. He defined the explicit formulation and codification of the standard(s) as decisive criteria for its/their emergence.

79   For the consonants /m/ (before /n/) or /s/ (in anteconsonantic context and even in external *sandhi*), see, e.g., IG IV² 1, 40 and 41 (from Epidauros): with reduplication: no. 40, ll. 7–8, μέδιμμνον; 8–9, ἡμίδιμμνον; 12, τοὶ ἰαρομμνάμονες; 10, τὸ σσκέλος; no. 41, l. 1, τôι Ἀσσκλαπιôι; *versus* without reduplication: no. 40, ll. 11–12, 15–16, τὸ δ' ἄτερον σκέλος; 15 τὸ σκέλος; no. 41, l. 5, τοῦ Ἀσκλαπιοῦ; 7, τôι Ἀσκλαπιôι; 12–13, τοὶ ἰ[αρο]μνάμονες. For the double *iota*, see, e.g., Jeffery (LSAG² 1990, 168, no. 8; 444) = SEG XI 314; SEG LXV 210 (from the Larisa, the acropolis of Argos), l. 2, Ἀθαναίιας; 4, τᾶι Πολιιάδι; 5–6, χρεστερίιοισι; 6, Ἐράτυιιος, τᾶς θιιô *versus* l. 4, τᾶι Ἀθαναίαι; 6, τᾶς Πολιάδος. Both these graphic phenomena are also remarkably attested in the *Schlangenschrift* inscriptions from Tiryns, see Verdelis, Jameson, and Papachristodoulos 1975, 189.

80   This is an irresistible conclusion if we consider the major differences from one epichoric alphabet to another; see Jeffery's and Guarducci's comprehensive studies, and also Luraghi (2010, 84–86), who focus on the north-eastern Peloponnesian graphic systems.

81   Brixhe 1997, 398; Chambers and Trudgill 1998, 48, 59–61, 70–72; Consani 2004, 202. These "norms" can thus have been spontaneously constituted by the hierarchization of linguistic variants in society according to the "jeu des variables produites par les détenteurs du pouvoir effectif ou symbolique" (Brixhe 1997, 394).

their public, often monumental character, was intended to last.[82] Moreover, the recurrence of the formulae denotes a uniformity, an acculturation shared throughout the Greek world (for many formulae, inspired by literary authors such as Homer): they constitute "epigraphic genres."[83] According to Monique Bile, Claude Brixhe, and René Hodot, writing delivers a metalanguage,[84] and it must be understood that it "constitue toujours un acte formel, où l'individu engage toute sa compétence ; si humble soit-il, le message écrit a toujours comme modèle implicite la langue dominante."[85]

Among experts, the mention of a "correct use" is based either on 1) the majority of the forms attested in either the same region and, therefore, supposedly in a local dialect, or, in all Greek inscriptions. Alternatively, it is based on 2) the etymology as reconstructed by intradialectal, interdialectal, or interlinguistic comparison.[86] Occasionally, it is also based on 3) the variants used in official epigraphy.[87] The first two criteria deserve to be questioned for two reasons.

The first reason is that the value of the most-attested variant, reified as a "standard," must be minimized by virtue of the chronological and geographical "discontinuity" of epigraphic data, both within and between regions.[88] Indeed, the Greek dialects are classified by Emmanuel Dupraz and Wojciech Sowa as "langues d'attestations fragmentaires."[89] This discontinuity is reinforced by the random preservation and finding of the texts, as well as by their fragmented condition (sometimes, with the impossibility of any restoration).[90] If one assumes this criterion (as well as the third), then the forms haϝεθλο- and hοδελο- should be included in the Argive standard and considered as correct.

Second, the criterion of the etymology conditioning either the inclusion of a variant into the "grammar of the dialect" or its eviction is also debatable for multiple reasons: a) Researchers do not always reach a consensus on the etymology at the morphological or semantic level; b) The proto-Greek or proto-Indo-European root is often based on the frequency of attestations of a form, which is redundant to the first criterion; and c) the etymology is influenced by theoretical biases, such as the genetic kinship of Greek dialects and of the Indo-European languages.[91] This theory assumes the idea of a primordial linguistic unity, followed by a diversification due to migrations and to subsequent encounters with substrate and adstrate languages.[92] The influence of the substrate on Greek dialects varies significantly from one linguist to another. Beekes' etymological dictionary, for example, shows the predominance of the substrate explanation (especially as an expedient in the case of consonantal or vocalic variability from one dialect to another). On the contrary, Frisk and Chantraine are more optimistic about the possibility of an Indo-European reconstruction. Finally, we also have d), whereby the description and the very name attributed to certain phenomena reveal a preconception based on an original form, expected for etymological reasons and therefore considered to be correct: this is the case with *psilosis*, whose meaning presupposes a loss from an original state (and not, which would have been more neutral, an absence).[93] However, some authors use this notion even in cases where the etymology is uncertain; for example, for ἱαρός and ἵππος, and their compounds.[94]

In synthesis, the first two criteria seem to be based on corresponding preconceptions: on the one hand, that of the synchronic unit of the local standard; on the other hand, that of the prehistoric diachronic unit, namely the reconstructed root. Both these descriptions of epigraphic data only flatten the variability which was still widespread in the archaic inscriptions.

2.3 Hyper-*Correction*

Ultimately, the graphic or linguistic facts studied here do not involve hypercorrection as two defining features of the phenomenon are not met: 1) the agency of the lower

---

82 Bubeník 1989, 40; Minon 2015, 276, and 280: publication and display are key features for any inscription, even from private individuals.

83 The idea of "acculturazione epigrafica" is developed by Giancarlo Susini (1984 and 1989, 296): his comments on the Roman world are largely transposable to the Hellenic context. In his contributions, the concept is related to the phenomenon of colonization: I take the responsibility for transposing it to the Greek *poleis* and their populations. The formula "genre épigraphique" is used by Dupraz and Sowa 2015.

84 Bile, Brixhe, and Hodot 1984, 161–63, 199; see also Rosén 1984, 226; Brixhe 1991, 314; Klinkenberg and Polis 2018, 30/76; Klinkenberg 2018b, 102–3.

85 Brixhe 1997, 398.

86 E.g., for Buck (1968, 55) "unetymological" is contrary to "regular."

87 Minon 2015, 280.

88 García Rámon 2018, 32, 54, 60.

89 Dupraz and Sowa 2015.

90 Brixhe 2006b, 42; García Rámon 2018, 54.

91 Some critiques of this theory are formulated by Bile, Brixhe, and Hodot 1984; Brixhe 2006a, 2006b; in Jonathan Hall's account of the history of Greek dialectology (1997, 153–81); *contra* García Rámon 2006, 2018.

92 Such as the famous Dorian Invasions. This explanation is grounded on an equation, language = population, see Hall 1997, 22, 32, 143–81.

93 Buck 1968, 53, and Lejeune 1987, 281, § 321.

94 Nieto Izquierdo 2008, 260f.

middle-class speakers (due to linguistic insecurity in a formal register, and to their striving to reach a higher social status) and 2) the implication of forms or phonemes/sounds that are undergoing change, leading to an arbitrary reintroduction, in order to adhere to a supposedly original form.[95] On the one hand, the inscriptions containing the so-called "hypercorrect" variants all belong to official epigraphy: the Argive bronze prizes were commissioned by the authorities of the city-state, organizing the competition in honor of Hera.[96] The bronze plaques, in which are contained the compounds of haϝεθλο- and hοδελο-, are administrative and financial documents, recording transactions: some of them may have been publicly exposed on the walls of temples or other official buildings.[97] Despite its very fragmentary character, the boustrophedon inscription on stone from Mycenae was certainly made by the local authority.[98] The speaker is therefore unlikely to be a middle-class person, but these variants belong rather to an official usage, which could nearly be regarded as a norm.

On the other hand, the phoneme /h/ was not obsolete in Argolid when these inscriptions were produced.[99] According to Nieto Izquierdo, the sound was still lively in view of the small number of forms featuring an unexpected aspiration or, on the contrary, the absence of aspiration.[100] In contrast to the general opinion, the sound [h] is not limited to the initial position before a vowel, or after the voiceless stop (/pʰ/, /kʰ/, /tʰ/), but the sign can also note an intervocalic aspirate resulting from the release of a secondary sibilant /s/.[101] It is also found, following the

sonorants (/m/, /n/, /l/, /r/, /w/), at the beginning of words or in intermediate position.[102] Minon reports that in the region surrounding Argos the "closed *heta*" disappeared from the official inscriptions only shortly before 350 BCE, to be replaced by the open sign H, that transcribes the long open vowel /ɛː/ in the Ionic alphabet.[103] At that moment, the aspiration was no longer written down, regardless of its origin. Nevertheless, despite the disappearance of the letter due to the spread of the "new" common alphabet, the sound was preserved over a long time, at least in Attica and in the *koine*, as shown by the loanwords in Latin and the Semitic languages.[104] In Argolid, the persistence of the hiatus following the late loss of the intervocalic sibilant /s/ encourages to conclude that the sound persists quite late.[105] In short, the conditions are therefore not fulfilled to qualify the "unexpected" 目 as hypercorrect.

3 The Contribution of Socio-Semiotics through the Three Signifiers of Written Utterances: Grapheme, Grammeme, and Scripteme

The entire data set presented here is exemplary of the difficulty in apprehending the relationship between the written and the spoken language. To reach this goal, it seems fundamental to include the specificities of the epigraphic corpus and of the written medium by referring to the semiotic theory of writing; namely, the "scripturology" proposed by Klinkenberg and Polis.[106] Instead of postulating, as did Margherita Guarducci and Vít Bubeník, a pure transparency of the alphabetical system and "the isomorphism between language spoken and language written," we can consider that epigraphic documents and their texts are not mere *trans*criptions of oral utterances, but written utterances that are *in*scribed with their own

---

95   Schilling-Estes 2004, 380.

96   Amandry 1980, 251.

97   As indicated by holes on some bronze plates, see Kritzas 1992, 235 for the plate with the term hοδελόνομοι. Bronze plaques were frequently nailed on to hard supports (*stelai*, building walls, or statue bases) and the cities displayed their official texts on the walls of the main temples probably by this means (Detienne 1988c, 42). According to Jacques Des Courtils (1981, 609–610), in the city of Argos, it was on the walls of the temple of Lycian Apollo that the official bronze plaques were nailed.

98   It is not clear whether it is a law (Johnston 1990 [LSAG²], 445A) or a financial document (Ruzé and Van Effenterre 1995, 226–27, no. 62). The latter hypothesis derives from the recognition of 目 as the numeral.

99   Brixhe (1991, 318) has doubts about its quality as a phoneme in Greek dialects; *contra* Bubeník 1983, 77; Probert 2010, 90; Alonso Déniz 2013.

100 Nieto Izquierdo 2008, 259. *Contra* Buck (1968, 54) and Lejeune (1987, § 320–21), for whom the graphic fluctuations reflect its "débilité" in most of the Greek domain, including in non psilotic dialects (such as Argive).

101 In most of the dialects, there is contextual restrictions of the phoneme, see Lejeune 1987, § 320; Probert 2010, 90; Alonso Déniz 2013. The intervocalic /h/ substituting for a sibilant /s/ is

characteristic of the Western Argolid, Laconia, Elis, and Cyprus (Lejeune 1987, § 88, 319; Alonso Déniz 2007, 183–268; 2009; 2013). This development occurs in the Argive plain between the first quarter of the fifth century and the first century BCE.

102 The spellings M目, N目, Λ目, P目, F目, from Indo-European **sm, *sn, *sl, *sr, *sw*, denote only the voiceless feature of the preceding sonorant, and not an aspiration (Bubeník 1983, 80; Lejeune 1987, 280, § 319). This is explained by the fact that the aspirate delays the vibration of the vocal cords during the articulation (Probert 2010, 91, 94).

103 Minon 2014, 41.

104 Lejeune 1987, 321; Alonso Déniz 2013.

105 These vowels in hiatus do not contract, even when they are identical.

106 Klinkenberg and Polis 2018.

communicative aims.[107] Their enunciation and the communicative situation in which they are inserted are quite particular.

Klinkenberg and Polis stress that writing, like language, constitutes a semiotic system in its own right, conforming to its own rules, and endowed with its own characteristics. Admittedly, it has an important linguistic component, which is predominantly accounted for by linguists and dialectologists, but writing involves more than just "transcoding" the language into the visual channel:[108] it is not a mere "sémie substitutive."[109] Thanks to its spatial and material component (which mainly attracts the attention of epigraphists), writing acquires properties that affect the syntagmatic organization of its units and enable it to transcend the temporal and spatial limits of oral utterance. Indeed, through the visual channel, allowing a "tabular exploration" of at least two dimensions simultaneously, the receiver-reader can process seven times more information than through the auditive channel (i.e., 10^7 bits/second).[110] The "topo-syntax" of written utterance induces an indexical relationship of "synousia" with the "object-support" and the "scriptural field" that is isolated on the support by the utterance itself.[111] Owing to this relationship by which it is semanticized and given a distinct cultural status, the object becomes the support for the utterance and the scriptural field is segregated from the rest of the "perceptual field."[112] Consequently, any graphic stimulus is endowed with three signifiers: grapheme, grammeme, and scripteme. These are associated with three functions (~ signifieds) which operate *simultaneously*, so that writing is a "pluricode."[113]

Klinkenberg's remark that "les aspects matériels de la communication font de plein droit partie du travail de la signification" works particularly well for the study of epigraphic sources.[114] That is, the analysis of the texts must be carried out by a keen examination of the support whose materiality is constantly manifested.[115] The awareness of the double significant dimension of writing (linguistic and spatial—i.e., iconic and plastic) tends to reconcile the two traditionally divorced disciplines, dialectology and epigraphy.[116]

Linguists chiefly focus on the first type of graphic signifier, the grapheme. The minimal units of the world's writing systems refer on the "content plane" to linguistic units of first and second articulation, and this, in varying degrees.[117] Yet this first level of meaning immediately involves difficulties when dealing with the reconstruction of a language system from the past, such as the Ancient Greek dialects. Apart from the autonomous functions, the graphemes also perform "heteronomous" functions, which are always associated with other adjacent units, in an indexical relationship, insofar as they alter their function.[118] We are far from the ideal of grapheme-phoneme biunivocity claimed for the Greek alphabet.[119]

This description also has the advantage of incorporating graphic signs that are little considered and nonetheless omnipresent in Argive inscriptions: punctuation signs. In accordance with Klinkenberg's classification, such signs are polyvalent:[120] they fulfil morphosyntactic, intonative, and demarcative functions, for their presence indicates the boundaries (= demarcative) of the accent units (= intonative), which constitute functional syntactic groups (particularly in Greek: proclitic or enclitic + noun). Other signs do not fit well with the traditional model of a transparent alphabet, such as the numeral signs, whose system relies on an acrophonic principle. Although they have an autonomous logographic value[121]—for example, the sign ⊟ means "100 *drachmai*"—the same sign usually

---

107 The dichotomy is stated by Svenbro (1988, 461), and the autonomy of the written word is proclaimed by Detienne (1988b, 10; 1988c, 56). On the contrary, the "isomorphism" between spoken and written language is stated by Bubeník 1989, 25. Such idealistic considerations are widely shared: e.g., by Guarducci (1967, 60–61), Powell (1991), and other contributors to the book *Phoinikeia grammata*. This presumption leads researchers to use alphabetic symbols and phonological notations interchangeably, as did Ruijgh 2007.

108 Klinkenberg 2018a, 112.

109 Klinkenberg (2018a, 104) cites the expression to E. Buyssens (1943, 49).

110 The Groupe μ 1992, cited by Klinkenberg 2018a, 113; 2018c, 39. In contrast, the "exploration" of oral utterances is "linear" (i.e., the units are processed successively and not simultaneously), due to their organization following a "chrono-syntax."

111 Klinkenberg and Polis 2018, 17–18/65–66.

112 Klinkenberg and Polis 2018, 20/68.

113 Klinkenberg 1996, 236; 2018c, 75–76.

114 Klinkenberg 2018a, 113. According to Klinkenberg and Polis 2018, 21/69, all the constituent elements of the graphic stimulus are semiotized: these are 1) the substrate—i.e., the object-support with its scriptural field; 2) the material form of the script, such as paint, engraving groove, etc.; 3) the instrument of its production (or of its reception), such as a pen, brush, chisel; and 4) the mode of inscription (subtraction for engraving, addition for painting).

115 Indeed, "the object-support and the scriptural field [...] are phenomenologically primary, both in production [...] and in reception" (Klinkenberg and Polis 2018, 20/67–68).

116 I retain here only the categories applicable to Greek epigraphy and refer to Klinkenberg and Polis 2018 for an exhaustive overview of the classification.

117 Klinkenberg and Polis 2018, 22–23/69–70.

118 Klinkenberg and Polis 2018, 32/78–79; Klinkenberg 2018b, 90–92.

119 See above and Klinkenberg and Polis 2018, 22/69–70.

120 Klinkenberg 2018b, 93–101.

121 Klinkenberg and Polis 2018, 25/72.

has a phonetic-phonological value of the aspirate consonant /h/.

However, if we turn to the second and third signifiers of the same graphic stimuli in inscriptions, it is clear that, in contrast to the grapheme, they are rarely *systematically* analyzed in order to extract a precise meaning from them. They are, in Klinkenberg's words, "en rapport avec le processus matériel de l'écriture."[122] To remedy this oversight, I will now consider the grammeme and the scripteme: I will adapt their definition to the epigraphic sources for the purpose of reexamining the grapheme and the linguistic problems that arise from it.

The grammeme, consists of "une 'texture' de l'écrit"; that is, the plastic form of the graphic objects composing the written utterance, and their combinations.[123] Concretely, variations are actualized depending on the diversity of the possible choices of writing types, font, style, palaeography, shape of the characters, color, size, *ductus*, etc. These signifiers can have not only symbolic functions, denoting a geographical, chronological, or sociological meaning (signified), but they may also correspond to indicial functions.

Turning to archaic Greece, on the one hand, geographical meanings are remarkably illustrated by the numerous epichoric alphabets, which indicate the origin of an inscription, both geographically and chronologically, as Jeffery's work has shown. Thus, in the materials discussed, the characteristically Argive shape of *lambda* ⊢ and *gamma* ∧ certainly points to Argos and its vicinity (the Heraion, Mycenae, and Tiryns). From a chronological point of view, the pattern of the lettering and possibly the disappearance of some character (occasionally replaced by others) allows us to date a document within a quarter of a century. In our texts, the presence of *sigma* Σ instead of *san* M for denoting the sibilant gives the *terminus post quem* from the end of the sixth century BCE onwards.[124] The symmetry and squareness of *alpha, epsilon, digamma,* and *mu*, the evolutionary form of *theta* (with a cross ⊕ vs. with a dot ⊙), the appendix to the *rho* (Ɽ not P), and the size of *omikron* (small vs. larger) are evidence to support a fairly close dating of the documents.[125] The direction of writing also falls into this function: sinistroverse, boustrophedon, or dextroverse, which, according

to Jeffery, also depended on the relationship of the written utterance to its support.[126]

Concerning the third symbolic function, at a more sociological level, the consistency of the shape of the characters (especially *alpha* and *nu*), the regularity of the *ductus* and the correction made on the tripod of Vergina demonstrate a high degree of skill and professionalism on the part of the Argive bronzeworker.[127] These latter variables may also correspond, on the other hand, to the second, indicial, functions in that they are "causally motivated by the status or the dispositions of the writers."[128] The distinction between private vs. official epigraphy also relies on these clues.

The third type of signifier, the scripteme, involves conceiving the written utterance as a "basic unit [...] complex and contextualized."[129] The utterance, taken as a whole, performs indexical functions which appear quite decisive for epigraphic documents.[130] This means, on one hand, that the text operates as an "indexer" that refers to its context (e.g., its support), within an "external centrifugal indexicality" (pointing to the context to which it confers a special status). This is clearly the function of dedications, epitaphs, property labels, milestones (*horoi*), and artists' signatures, since they mark the support to which they are affixed and contiguous as "offering, tomb, property, work, etc. of X." The inscriptions engraved in the bronze of the Argive prizes are also a kind of label that performatively guarantees the function and the origin of the object.[131] On the other hand, the laws, decrees, accounts, and so on, engraved on steles or on removable bronze plaques, like those found by Kritzas, and on the *poros* fragment from Mycenae, are "indexed" by their context (namely the building wall where they were displayed or the scriptural field of the *stele* where they were engraved, etc.). In this "external centrifugal indexicality," the context "confers its values on the written utterance" by allowing us (or more generally the addressee) to "make an inferential gamble on the nature of the text it bears."[132]

Epigraphists, archaeologists, and linguists have to deal with this bundle of signifiers—the grapheme, grammeme, scripteme—in order to deduce the full meaning of documents and to reconstruct the enunciation of these utterances. This theory of writing prompts a more exhaustive

122 Klinkenberg 2018b, 105.

123 The expression "texture de l'écrit" and its subsequent explanations are from Klinkenberg and Polis 2018, 36–38/83–85.

124 Jeffery 1990 (LSAG²), 152. This can be applied to all the studied inscriptions except the epitaph of Hyssematas: thus, despite the *boustrophedon*, the *poros* block of Mycenae shows a *sigma* and not a *san*.

125 Lazzarini *apud* Lazzarini and Zevi 1988–89; Amandry 1980, see Jeffery's principles (1990 [LSAG²], 151–53).

126 Jeffery 1990 [LSAG²], 44.

127 For this reason, Amandry (2002) claims that the inscription was made by a craftsman in the service of the city.

128 Klinkenberg and Polis 2018, 37/84.

129 Klinkenberg and Polis 2018, 41/87.

130 Klinkenberg and Polis 2018, 42/88.

131 Lazzarini and Zevi 1988–89, 36, 42.

132 Klinkenberg and Polis 2018, 44/90.

and comprehensive linguistic approach which takes into consideration the graphic utterances and their significant relationship with their support and context (architectural, urbanistic, and, more broadly, socio-cultural). This approach calls for the gathering of all the information relating to the archaeological object and to the historical context of their production and reception. The case of the Argive bronze prizes is particularly exemplary of the interest of this approach. I will conclude this article by applying to it the analysis of the three signifiers and signifieds.

Conclusion: Back to the Data

The Argive bronze prizes constitute an exceptional group, as they are the largest and most richly decorated ensemble of preserved prizes, with the exception of the Panathenaic *amphorai*.[133] They enjoyed remarkable prestige both at the time of their production and in the fate they met after being won, especially with regard to their geographical dispersion throughout the Greek world (Pompeii, Athens, Sinope, at the south of the Pontic Sea, and Vergina in Macedonia). Specialists have insisted on the quality of the decoration of the *hydriai*, either of the feminine *protome*, completely individualized by the details of her face, hair, peplos drapery, and posture, but also of the vase itself with its decorated handles and attachments.[134] These objects do not belong to mass production.[135] The vases, as well as the inscription, were clearly made in the vicinity of Argos, as can be seen both from the iconographic typology and the shape of the letters.[136]

When their archaeological context is known, it can be observed that these objects, after having been awarded as prizes, had considerable prestige. They were frequently dedicated to the deities in the city of the winner as a sign of his piety:[137] this is most probably the case with the Sinope *hydria*, according to Kritzas's hypothesis explaining the incision of the second inscription.[138] Or, most

often, they were kept in the victor's estate, perhaps for several decades or even several generations, before being used later as a cinerary urn or as part of the funerary furniture.[139] Such examples are the *hydria* from Sinope, the bronze *lebes* found in a huge tumulus, the so-called "tomb of Aspasia," near the Piraeus, but also the tripod from Vergina, which was found in Tomb II of the Macedonian royal family, attributed to Philip II.[140] It can be assumed that the *hydria* of Pompeii experienced a similar destiny.[141]

Both these last artifacts share the most memorable story. The tripod from Vergina is said to have been won by an ancestor of Alexander the Great, probably Archelaos, an illegitimate son of Perdiccas, who ascended the throne in 413 BCE. The Macedonian sovereigns sought early on to prove their "Hellenicity" by claiming to be kin to the Temenid dynasty of Argos. As a result, Alexander I obtained permission from the *Hellanodikai* to compete in the Olympic Games ca. 500 BCE.[142] Given the lapse of nearly a century between its production and its burial in the tomb, the tripod was probably displayed in the royal palace, as a "trophée précieux à l'appui de leurs prétentions généalogiques."[143] In the royal tomb, the coexistence of this object with highly valuable items is indicative of its importance for the dynasty.[144]

The Pompeii *hydria* was found, along the Via dell'Abbondanza, in a house (IX, 13, 1–3) belonging to a rich

133 Amandry 1980, 234; Zevi *apud* Lazzarini and Zevi 1988–89, 36; Cogan 2011, 134.

134 Mertens 1985, 5 and no. 23; Zevi *apud* Lazzarini and Zevi 1988–89, 36; Sowder Koch 2009, 138–58.

135 Zevi *apud* Lazzarini and Zevi 1988–89, 36.

136 Mertens 1985, no. 23; Amandry 2002, 30.

137 Amandry 1971, 621; 1980, 217, n. 14; Cogan 2011, 137.

138 According to his hypothesis (quoted in Dubois 1990, 515–16, no. 424; Amandry 2002, 31; Cogan 2011, 137), the winner of the Argive contest would have been an Arcadian who dedicated his trophy to the Dioscuri, in his hometown Pheneos. With the new reading, it is only the origin of the winner that is different: he would have come from Phokis in central Greece. The artifact would then have been taken from the treasure of the Twin Gods

and "réutilisé par les organisateurs du concours comme prix offert [à un] vainqueur [qui aurait été] originaire de Sinope." As is frequently the case with inscriptions on bronze prizes, these give evidence of a local cult and of games that are otherwise unknown.

139 Amandry 1971, 621; 1980, 251; Cogan 2011, 138; Sowder Koch 2015, 27. The reuse of these vessels in a funerary context explains the very good state of preservation of a large number of examples (including those acquired by museums on the black market), see von Bothmer 1974.

140 For the Aspasia's tomb, see Smith 1926, 256; Williams 2014. The *lebes* was contained in a custom-made marble crater. They were surrounded by an alabastron and gold myrtle leaves, proof of the high rank of the deceased (see Zevi *apud* Lazzarini and Zevi 1988–89, 38). Because of the symbolic association of the myrtle wreath with the protection of democracy, Dyfri Williams (2014, 430–31) hypothesizes that the deceased belonged to the family of Konon III. For the Royal Tomb of Vergina, see Amandry 1980, 217, n. 14; Andronikos 1979; 1984, 165f.; Zevi *apud* Lazzarini and Zevi 1988–89, 38. Some authors refute this attribution, see Hall 2002, 155, n. 131. In any case, the description provided by Andronikos of the extreme wealth of the architecture as well as of the furniture demonstrates the royal status of the deceased.

141 Lazzarini and Zevi 1988–89, 39–40; 1992, 94.

142 Lazzarini and Zevi 1988–89, 38; Amandry 2002, 31; Hall 2002, 154–56.

143 Amandry 2002, 31.

144 Andronikos 1984, 166. This is all the more obvious as the intrinsic value of the tripod is quite low compared to the artistic quality and precious metals of the other funeral paraphernalia.

freedman, C. Iulius Polybius.[145] It was likely reused at least twice, as evidenced by the loss of its horizontal handle (common for *hydriai* reused as cinerary urns) and by the hole drilled in the body of the vase, with traces of welding around it (the *hydria* would have been used as a pouring vase). Eventually, the *hydria* probably became part of a collection of antiques, since the disappearance of the spout was anterior to the eruption of Vesuvius.[146] The great chronological hiatus between its production and its last ornamental function can be explained with reference to Strabo (VIII, 6.23) who mentions the depredations in tombs at Corinth by Caesar's settlers. For the rich Pompeian freedman, who had entered politics and carried out important works in his *domus*—combining restoration of Samnite elements with modernization—shortly prior to the eruption, the exhibit in the *triclinium* of such an antique, authenticated by its inscription, acted as a status symbol.[147]

Clearly, the Argive bronze prizes have had a special destiny and served as status symbols for the winners of the Argive competitions, for their descendants, and for whoever holds them. This emerges from their subsequent uses. Additionally, they were produced in a context that is highly relevant to the city of Argos: according to Pierre Amandry, they date from a relatively short period between the end of the Persian Wars and that of the Peloponnesian War. One or two decades after the battle of Sepeia against Sparta and after the servile interregnum (Paus., VIII, 27.1), Argos flourished, extending its influence on the Argive plain.[148] It seized Mycenae (ca. 468–460 BCE), as well as Tiryns, among others, but also the Heraion.[149] In this major sanctuary, perhaps

from the middle of the fifth century BCE onwards, Argos undertook a program of restoration of the temple, with the production of chryselephantine statues of Hera and Hebe.[150] In this historical context, the prizes may document the very creation of the games at the Heraion under the auspices of Argos (Amandry), or at least, their reorganization (Lazzarini and Hall).[151] In any case, the spread of the prizes with the attributive adjective Ἀργείας, qualifying the theonym of the patron goddess of the sanctuary, guaranteed the panhellenic reputation of the newly (re)instituted Heraian Games and that of Argos, as well as the personal glory of the victors and of their mother city.[152] At the same time, in Hall's opinion, the tenth Nemean of Pindar, dating from 464 BCE, could have been commissioned by the Argives in order to glorify the new religious organization at the Heraion.[153]

In this context, the inscriptions on the bronze prizes do play a significant role. On the one hand, the formula "παρ᾽ Ἥρας Ἀργείας" could betray an appropriation of the sanctuary by Argos, for it constitutes a fusion between two standard prize-formulae and, therefore, a kind of innovation:[154] usually, it was composed 1) of the name of the deity or hero celebrated in the games (with or without the prepositions παρά or ἐπί) and/or 2) of the toponym where the games took place (in the genitive, with/without the preposition ἐκ, or followed by the suffix -θεν).[155] Instead, in the Argive formula, the adjective derived from the toponym agrees with the theonym.

On the other hand, the plastic conservatism of the artifact (the *hydriai*) and in particular the severe style of the female *protome*, perhaps intentional, have been emphasized.[156] This concerns the scriptemic signifier,

---

145   See Varone 2016 for a portrait of this *homo nouus* and of his family.

146   Zevi *apud* Lazzarini and Zevi 1988–89, 41. It was found alongside other antique objects, such as a statue of Apollo in the severe style and a crater in relief (Zevi *apud* Lazzarini and Zevi 1988–89, 33, 41; Pappalardo 2016, 329).

147   Zevi (*apud* Lazzarini and Zevi 1988–89) view it as a mixture of traditionalism and local particularism, on the one hand, and of the manifestation of comfort and luxury (consistent with the fashion of the *Vrbs*), on the other. This search is explained by a claim to legitimacy from a *homo nouus*.

148   Amandry 1980, 234; their dating is doubtful.

149   On the history of this sanctuary, see Billot 1997, especially 39, 53, n. 403; on the domination of the Argive plain by Argos, see Moggi, 1974. The sanctuary is frequently referred to in the literature as the "Heraion of Argos" (Argive Heraion), but Hall (1995) has demonstrated that for much of the archaic period it was merely a common sanctuary for the cities of the Argive plain, including Argos (see also Amandry 1980, 235; Lazzarini *apud* Lazzarini and Zevi 1988–89, 44; Zevi and Lazzarini 1992, 39).

150   The moment of the beginning of the works is problematic (Amandry 1980, 235, 240; Hall 1997; Kritzas 2006). These works continued until the fourth century BCE.

151   Amandry 1980, 241; Lazzarini *apud* Lazzarini and Zevi 1988–89; Hall 1995.

152   Amandry 1980, 241; Zevi *apud* Lazzarini and Zevi 1988–89, 36; Cogan 2011, 134, 138.

153   Hall 1997, 612.

154   Although the adjective Ἀργεῖος can also refer to the Argive plain.

155   Amandry 1971, 619; 1980, 217; Lazzarini *apud* Lazzarini and Zevi 1988–89, 42.

156   Zevi *apud* Lazzarini and Zevi 1988–89, 36–37. Lazzarini (*apud* Zevi 1988–89, 43) assumes that the form of the letters is "archaizing." Actually, it is rather "archaic" and epichoric, as in other contemporary Argive documents until the end of the fifth century BCE (see Jeffery 1990, 150 f.; Minon 2014). Indeed, on the *hydriai*, some letter shapes are advanced (*alpha, epsilon, digamma, mu, pi*), while others remain conservative (the so-called "closed *heta*" Ⱶ), as in the Argive plain until the last quarter of the fifth century BCE. The statement of conservatism could possibly be applied

in view of the relationship of indexicality established between the graphic utterance and its object-support: the status of the latter, as one of the prizes awarded to the winner of the games for Hera, is defined by the inscription. Moreover, at the level of the grammemic signifier, the strong local characterization of the letter shapes constituting the prize inscription is significant, especially as the prizes were intended to spread throughout the Greek world.[157]

Finally, regarding the graphemic signifier, the conservatism of the iconic support, combined with the local identity conveyed by the letters of the inscription, could echo the conservative connotation derived from the preservation of the intervocalic *digamma*. As shown by the relative chronology of the Argive and other Greek variants, this phonetic variant is clearly a sort of fossil, especially in the fifth century BCE. Is it therefore exaggerated to consider that the initial sign **B** in the same term could have constituted a kind of hyperarchaism or hyperdialecticism? This phenomenon seems typical of the official language of Argos, for the other older inscriptions from private individuals do not show any examples of it. This sound (or grapheme?) would thus have been (re)introduced in this local variety forming some kind of standard, at least a graphic one,[158] especially since the preservation of *digamma* and of the "closed *heta*" is indeed described as characteristic of Argos, and since the Greeks were eager to express their local political identity through writing.[159] In these circumstances, the famous "h hypercorrect" would have been constitutive of the official local variety, given its recurrence in the prizes but also in the bronze plaque texts and in the Mycenian law.

Nevertheless, it does not meet the technical definition of hypercorrection. Nor does it seem to be an irrational use, a mere misspelling. The contribution of semiotics and its tools allows us to link, more systematically and more confidently, the information relating to the support (scripteme) and the material form (grammeme) of the written utterance with the signifying dimension contained in the graphemic signifier, at the purely linguistic level. Taking into account all these intermingled signifiers for the same graphic utterance, I can conclude by suggesting the following interpretative hypothesis: in view of the weakness of the articulation of the initial aspirate (a mere breath), the sign of the aspirated **B** could have been introduced through a phonetic phenomenon of reinforcement (by introducing a breath where there was none). Indeed, this phenomenon is characteristic of the upper social classes, affecting phonetically strong positions in the words (in this case the beginning of words), in highly formal situations and emphatic and careful registers (as are official inscriptions, intended for exposure and durability).[160] This would constitute an exemplary case where sociolinguistics meets sociosemiotics.

References and Transcribed Text of the Studied Inscriptions (as Encountered Above)

1. *Hydria* in the Metropolitan Museum of Art (New York, inv. 26.50, gallery 156), ca. 460–450 BCE; archaeological context unknown. *Editio princeps*: Richter 1928, 182–91, fig. 1/8, pl. 13. *Further editions and commentaries*: SEG XI 355; XXX 366; Diehl 1964, 23–25, cat. B 78; Jeffery 1990 (LSAG²), 169, no. 26, pl. 29; Amandry 1971, 615, no. 3B; 1980, 212–17, fig. 1; Mertens 1985, 5–6, fig. and no. 23; Amandry 2002; Sowder Koch 2015, 13, 16, 26, 29, figs. 1–2, cat. 1.4.
   Text: Παρ Ηέρας ≡ Ἀργείας ≡ haϜέθλον.

2. *Hydria* from Sinope, in the Museum of Anatolian Civilization of Ankara (inv. 11047), ca. 470–460 BCE; found in a tomb. *Editio princeps*: Akurgal and Budde 1956, 12–15, pl. 5, fig. a–b. *Further editions and commentaries*: SEG XXX 1456; XXXIX 394; XXXIX 1365; LVI 2046; Diehl 1964, 23–25, pl. 5, figs. 1–3, cat. B 77; Amandry 1971, 615, no. 3A; 1980, 212–17, fig. 2; Dubois 1990, 515–16, no. 424; Amandry 2002; Sowder Koch 2015, 16–18, 29, cat. 1.5; Sideris 2019, 138.

---

to the form of the letters of the tripod and of the *lebes*, which is fairly consistent with that of the *hydriai*. Furthermore, it must be stressed that, in addition to their archaeological context dating a century later, the *lebes* and the tripod are considered difficult to date on the basis of their formal characteristics. It is primarily the inscription that enables the dating.

157   For modern researchers, it is this very characterization that allows us to deduce the origin of prizes, independently of the linguistic signified of the utterance.

158   According to Minon (2014, 32, 48, 52), the authorities initiated a reflection on the current graphic system and ensured its modernization from the second half of the fifth to the first half of the fourth century BCE (contemporaneous with the inscriptions studied). Nino Luraghi (2010, 88) speaks of scribes appointed by the city to control its written expression.

159   Both signs are still largely preserved in the plaques of Athena's Treasure (Kritzas 2006, 2007). For the expression of political identity through the use of the local alphabets, see, e.g., Piérart 1991 and Luraghi 2010.

---

160   This phenomenon of phonetic reinforcement is described by Julián Méndez Dosuna (2004, 173).

Text: first line/inscription: Πὰρ Ηέρας Ἀργείας ἐμὶ τὸν haϝέθλον; second line/inscription: Ἐκ Φ[οκέ]ον ἄεθλα π[αρ] Δ[ι]ο[σ]κόροιν.[161]

3. *Hydria* from Pompeii, preserved in the Archaeological Museum of Naples (inv. Pompeii 21803), ca. 460–450 BCE; found in a Pompeian *domus* of C. Iulius Polybius (IX 13, 1–3). *Editio princeps*: Zevi and Lazzarini 1988–89, figs. 1–10, 12–15; 1992. *Further editions and commentaries*: SEG XXXIX 1061; 42.921; Amandry 2002; Sowder Koch 2015, 15–16, cat. 1.6; Pappalardo 2016, 330–33, fig. 2.

    Text: Πὰρ Ηέρας ⫶ Ἀργείας [⫶ ἐ]μ[ὶ ⫶ τὸν ⫶ haϝέθλον].

4. *Hydria* in the National Museum of Copenhagen (previously in the Ny Carlsberg Glyptothek, inv. I.N. 3293, Br. 36), ca. 450–430 BCE; archaeological context unknown. *Editio princeps*: Diehl 1964, 23–24, cat. B 82; Johansen 1969, 54–65; figs. 1, 3, ph. *Further editions and commentaries*: SEG XXX 367; Amandry 1971, 615, no. 4; von Bothmer 1974, 16; Amandry 1980, 212–17, fig. 3; 2002; Sowder Koch 2015, 16, cat. 1.7.

    Text (Amandry 1980, after cleaning): Πὰρ [Η]έρας Ἀ[ργείας ἐ]μι τὸν [h]α[ϝέ]θλον.

5. *Lebes* in the British Museum (inv. 1816,0610.115),[162] ca. 430–420 BCE; found in Aspasia's tomb. *Editio princeps*: Smith 1926, 253–57, D, fig. 3, pl. XIV. *Further editions and commentaries*: SEG XI 330; 30.52; Amandry 1971, 615, no. 3C; 1980, 213, 216, fig. 4; Jeffery 1990 (LSAG²) 170, no. 43; Amandry 2002; Williams 2014.

    Text (Amandry 1980, after cleaning): [Πὰρ] hέ[ρα]ς Ἀ[ρ]γε[ί]ας ἐμὶ τὸν ἀϝέθλον.

6. Tripod from the Royal Tomb of Vergina, preserved in the Thessaloniki Museum, ca. 430–420 BCE. *Editio princeps*: Andronikos 1979 and 1984, 165–66, figs. 133–34; *Further editions and commentaries*: SEG XXIX 652; 30.648; 39.1365; Johnston 1990 (LSAG²), 444 H.

    Text: Πὰρ Ηέρας Ἀργείας ἐμὶ τὸν ἀϝέθλον.

7. Metric epitaph of Hyssematas, commissioned by Qossina, ca. 525–500 BCE; found in the vicinity of the Heraion. *Editio princeps*: Daly 1939, 165 s., figs. 1–4, ph., squeeze. *Further editions and commentaries*: SEG XI 305; XXII 262; XXXIII 294; XLV 2250; Friedländer and Hoffleit 1948, no. 136; Hansen 1983 (CEG I), no. 136; Moretti 1983, 44–41, no. 1; Jeffery 1990

(LSAG²), 168, no. 15; McGowan 1995, 615–632, fig. 11; Guijarro Ruano 2015, 121–124.

Text: Ϙόσινα hυσεμάταν θάψα [π]-|έλας hιποδρόμοιο, ἄνδρα ἀ-|[γα]θ[ό]ν, πόλοις μνᾶμα καὶ | [ἐσ]ομένοις | ἐν πολέμοι [φθ]ίμενον, νε-|αρὰν hέβαν ὀλέσαντα, σό-|φρονα, ἀε⟨θ⟩λοφόρον, καὶ σ-|οφὸν hαλικίαι.

8. Metric dedication of Aischyllos, son of Thiops, commemorating his multiple victories, reused in a wall of the Haghios Georgios church, now in the Museum of Argos (inv. E 272), ca. 500–475 BCE. *Editio princeps*: IG IV 561. *Further editions and commentaries*: SEG XI 328; 14.317; Vollgraff 1930, 30–33, no. 5; Friedländer and Hoffleit 1948, no. 51; Hansen 1983 (CEG I), no. 364; Jeffery 1990 (LSAG²), 169, no. 17, pl. 27; Guijarro Ruano 2015, 132–33; Nieto Izquierdo 2019, 66–69, ARG. 12.

    Text: [– ⏑⏑ – ⏑⏑ ϝαν]-|άρον ἀνέθεκε [..]-| [.]ν τε ⫶ Αἴσχυλλο[ς] | Θίοπος· τοῖς δαμ-|οσίοις ἐν ἀέθλο-|ις ⫶ τετράκι τε σ-|πάδιον νίκε κα[ὶ] | τρὶς τὸν ὁπλίτα[ν].[163]

9. Bronze prize *kalpis* with a Siren ornament, given at the games for the Dioscuri, from the Phokians, now preserved in the Michael C. Carlos Museum of Atlanta (inv. 2004.025.001), not earlier than the end of the fifth century BCE; no information about the archaeological context.[164] Not yet published. *Commentaries*: SEG LXV 2046; Gaunt 2005, 16; Sowder Koch 2015, 18, 35, n. 29; Sideris 2019, 138, n. 29–30.

    Text: Ἐκ Φωκέων ἄεθλα παρὰ Διοσκόροιν.

10. Fragment of a rough grey *poros* block, presumably containing a prescriptive text, late sixth century BCE. *Editio princeps*: Orlandos 1964, 69–72, ph.; Mylônas 1964, 71, ph./dr.; 1965, 161. *Further editions and commentaries*: SEG LVI 419; Robert and Robert 1968, no. 258; Johnston 1990 (LSAG²), 445, no. 1a; Ruzé and Van Effenterre 1995, no. 62 (inaccurate drawing).

    Text: [---τ]οχου χρ[---] | [----]ευσι χρος[----] | [-----] hοδελός [----].[165]

161 This is the most recent restoration based on the discovery of a bronze *kalpis* (now in the Michael C. Carlos Museum of Atlanta) with an almost identical inscription, see Gaunt 2005, 16; Sowder Koch 2015, 17; and Sideris 2019, 138.

162 Good quality photographs of the vase itself and of the inscription on its mouth are available on the British Museum's website: https://www.britishmuseum.org/collection/object/G _1816-0610-115.

163 The underlined letters are no longer legible due to the subsequent deterioration of the *stele*.

164 Good quality photographs of the vase itself and of the inscription on its mouth are available on the Michael C. Carlos Museum's website: https://collections.carlos.emory.edu/objects/11584 /kalpis-inscribed-as-a-prize-awarded-at-games-sacred-to -the?ctx=4228397c3254a8a02dc354936fb3d771e027c1a9&idx=11. For linguistic reasons (ethnic), I favor the location of the games in Phokis (central Greece) instead of that suggested on the website, Phokaia (in Turkey). The dating mentioned here depends on the shape of the letters and especially on the *omega*.

165 I produce an edition adapted to my reading of the document on photographs. This reading of the last word is confirmed by Stroud (*apud* SEG LVI 419).

11. Bronze plaque found near the sanctuary of Apollo Deiradiôtes, in the vicinity of Argos, with the accounts of the fourth Argive tribe, the Hyrnathioi, ca. 460–450 BCE. Not yet published. *Commentaries:* SEG XLI 284; XLVIII 403, 407; L 346; Johnston 1990 (LSAG²), 444–45 E; Kritzas 1992, 235 f.; Ruzé and Van Effenterre 1994, 272–74, no. 65; Piérart 1997, 332–33.[166]

Reference List

Supplementum epigraphicum graecum: SEG XI 330, 355; XXIX 652; XXX 648, 366–67, 1453, 1456; XXXIX 394, 1061, 1365; XLII 921; LX 624; LXI 1587; LXV 2046, 2129.

Akurgal, Ekrem, and Ludwig Budde. 1956. *Vorläufiger bericht über die ausgrabungen in Sinope.* Türk tarih kurumu yayinlarindan. V. Seri no. 14. Ankara: Türk tarih kurumu basimevi.

Alfieri Tonini, Teresa. "Iscrizioni esposte ed iscrizioni nascoste nel mondo Greco." *ACME. Annali della Facoltà di Lettere e Filosofia dell'Università degli Studi di Milano* 60, no. 3: 22–35.

Alonso Déniz, Alcorac. 2007. *Estudios sobre la aspiración de /s/ en los dialectos griegos.* PhD diss., Complutense University of Madrid. Published online: https://eprints.ucm.es/7894/1/T30236.pdf.

Alonso Déniz, Alcorac. 2009. "Difusión de la aspiración de la /s/ intervocálica en el Peloponeso en el I milenio a. C." *CFC(G)* 19: 9–27.

Alonso Déniz, Alcorac. 2013. "Aspiration." In *Encyclopedia of Ancient Greek Language and Linguistics.* Leiden: Brill, http://dx.doi.org/10.1163/2214-448X_eagll_SIM_00000419.

Amandry, Pierre. 1971. "Collection Paul Canellopoulos, I: Armes et lébès de bronze." *BCH* 95, no. 2: 585–626.

Amandry, Pierre. 1980. "Sur les concours argiens." *BCH,* Supplément 6, Études argiennes: 211–53.

Amandry, Pierre. 2002. "Hydries argiennes." In *Essays in Honor of Dietrich von Bothmer,* edited by Andrew J. Clark and Jasper Gaunt, 29–32. Amsterdam: Allard Pierson Series.

Andronikos, Manolis. 1979. "The Finds from the Royal Tombs at Vergina." *PBA* 65: 355–67.

Andronikos, Manolis. 1984. *Vergina: The Royal Tombs and the Ancient City.* Athens: Ekdotikè Athènôn.

Bailly = Bailly, Anatole. 1950. *Dictionnaire grec – français.* Revised edition by Louis Séchan and P. Chantraine. Paris: Librairie Hachette.

Bakker, Egbert J., ed. 2010. *A Companion to the Ancient Greek Language.* Malden: Wiley-Blackwell.

Baurain, Claude, Corinne Bonnet, and Véronique Krings, eds. 1991. *Phoinikeia Grammata. Lire et écrire en Méditerranée, Actes du colloque de Liège, 15–18 novembre 1989.* Collection d'études classiques, 6. Travaux du groupe interuniversitaire d'études phéniciennes et puniques, Studia Phoenicia, 13. Namur: Société des Etudes classiques.

Bechtel, Friedrich. 1921–24. *Die griechischen Dialekte.* 3 volumes. Berlin: Weidmann.

Beekes, EDG = Beekes, Robert. 2010. *Etymological Dictionary of Greek. Volumes I–II.* Leiden Indo-European Etymological Dictionary Series, 10/1–2. Leiden: Brill.

Bile, Monique, Claude Brixhe, and René Hodot. 1984. "Les dialectes grecs, ces inconnus." *BSL* 79, no. 1: 155–203.

Billot, Marie-Françoise. 1997. "Recherches archéologiques récentes à l'Héraion d'Argos." In *Héra. Images, espaces, cultes. Actes du colloque international du Centre de Recherches Archéologiques de l'Université de Lille III et de l'Association P.R.A.C. Lille, 29–30 novembre 1993,* edited by Jacqueline La Genière, 11–56. Naples: Publications du Centre Jean Bérard.

Blanc, Alain. 2008. "Compte rendu de 6. ΦΩΝΗΣ ΧΑΡΑΚΤΗΡ ΕΘΝΙΚΟΣ. Actes du Ve congrès international de dialectologie grecque (Athènes 28–30 septembre 2006), sous la direction de M. B. Hatzopoulos, avec la collaboration de Vassiliki Psilakakou." *Revue des Études Grecques* 121, no. 1: 403–5.

Bothmer, Dietrich von. 1974. "Two Bronze Hydriae in Malibu." *The J. Paul Getty Museum Journal* 1: 15–22.

Brixhe, Claude. 1991. "De la phonologie à l'écriture : quelques aspects de l'adaptation de l'alphabet cananéen au grec." In Baurain, Bonnet, and Krings, 1991, 313–56.

Brixhe, Claude. 1997. "Langues et sociétés antiques." *Comptes rendus des séances de l'Académie des Inscriptions et des Belles-Lettres* 141, no. 2: 391–414.

Brixhe, Claude. 2006a. "De la filiation à l'héritage. Réflexion sur l'origine des langues et des dialectes." In *Peuplements et genèses dialectales dans la Grèce antique,* edited by Claude Brixhe and Guy Vottéro, 7–37. Coll. Etudes anciennes, 31. Nancy: A.D.R.A.

Brixhe, Claude. 2006b. "Situation, spécificités et contraintes de la dialectologie grecque. À propos de quelques questions soulevées par la Grèce centrale." In *Peuplements et genèses dialectales dans la Grèce antique,* edited by Claude Brixhe and Guy Vottéro, 39–69.

Brixhe, Claude. 2010. "Linguistic Diversity in Asia Minor during the Empire: Koine and Non-Greek Languages." In Bakker, 2010, 228–52.

Broneer, Oscar. 1959. "Excavations at Isthmia: Fourth Campaign, 1957–1958." *Hesperia* 28, no. 4: 298–343.

Bubeník, Vít. 1983. *The Phonological Interpretation of Ancient Greek: A Pandialectal Analysis.* Phoenix, Supplementary Volume XIX. Toronto: University of Toronto Press.

Bubeník, Vít. 1989. *Hellenistic and Roman Greece as a Sociolinguistic Area.* Amsterdam Studies in the Theory and History

---

166 The re-transcription of the text of the bronze plaque was available on *Poinikastas.* Unfortunately, the images are no longer available on this website.

of Linguistic Science, Series IV; Current Issues in Linguistic Theory, 57. Amsterdam: John Benjamins.

Bubeník, Vít. 2018. "North–West Doric Koina and the Issue of 'Koineization': Sociolinguistic Concerns." In Giannakis, Crespo, and Filos, 2018, 149–66.

Buck, Carl Darling. 1968. *The Greek Dialects: Grammar, Selected Inscriptions, Glossary.* Chicago: University of Chicago Press.

Burzachechi, Mario. 1962. "Oggetti parlanti nelle epigrafi greche." *Epigraphica* 24: 3–54.

Chantraine, Pierre. 1942. *Grammaire homérique, volume I. Phonétique et morphologie.* Paris: Klincksieck.

Chantraine, *DELG* = Chantraine, Pierre, e. a. 1968–80. *Dictionnaire étymologique de la langue grecque. Histoire des mots. Tome I–IV-2.* Paris: Klincksieck.

Chambers, Jack K., and Peter Trudgill. 1998. *Dialectology.* 2nd edition. Cambridge: Cambridge University Press.

Charneux, Pierre. 1984. "Phratries et Kômai d'Argos." *Bulletin de correspondance hellénique* 108, no. 1: 207–27.

Cogan, Gwenola. 2011. "Les concours des cités à l'époque de Pindare: panhelléniques et *chrêmatites?*" *Mètis* 9: 125–48.

Consani, Carlo. 2004. "Per una visione variazionistica del greco antico." In *Zhì. Scritti in onore di Emanuele Banfi in occasione del suo 60° compleanno,* edited by Nicolà Grandi and Gabriele Iannaccaro, 201–13. Rome: Caissa.

Daly, Lloyd W. 1939. "An Inscribed Doric Capital from the Argive Heraion." *Hesperia,* no. 2: 165–69.

Des Courtils, Jacques. 1981. "Note de topographie argienne." *Bulletin de correspondance hellénique* 105, no. 2: 607–10.

Detienne, Marcel, ed. 1988a. *Les savoirs de l'écriture en Grèce ancienne.* Cahiers de philologie, Volume 14, Série apparat critique. Lille: Presses universitaires de Lille.

Detienne, Marcel. 1988b. "L'écriture et ses nouveaux objets intellectuels en Grèce." In Detienne, *Les savoirs de l'écriture,* 7–26.

Detienne, Marcel. 1988c. "L'espace de la publicité : ses opérateurs intellectuels dans la cité." In Detienne, *Les savoirs de l'écriture,* 29–81.

Diehl, Erika. 1964. *Die Hydria. Formgeschichte und Verwendung im Kult des Altertums.* Mayence: Verlag Philipp von Zabern.

Donati, Margherita. 2015. "Variazione e tipologia testuale nel corpus epigrafico *CLaSSES I.*" In *Ancient Languages between Variation and Norm,* edited by Giovanna Marotta and Francesco Rovai, 21–38. Special issue of *Studi e saggi linguistici* 53, no. 2.

Dubois, Jean, e. a. 2002. *Larousse. Grand dictionnaire. Linguistique et sciences du langage.* Paris: Larousse.

Dubois, Laurent. 1986. *Recherches sur le dialecte arcadien.* 3 vols. Bibliothèque des cahiers de l'institut de linguistique de Louvain, 33, 34 and 35. Louvain-la-Neuve: Cabay and Publications linguistiques de Louvain.

Dubois, Laurent, e. a. 1990. "Bulletin épigraphique." *REG* 103, no. 492–94: 435–616.

Dupraz, Emmanuel, and Wojciech Sowa, eds. 2015. *Genres épigraphiques et langues d'attestation fragmentaire dans l'espace méditerranéen.* Cahiers de l'ERIAC, no. 9, Fonctionnements linguistiques. Mont-Saint-Aignan: Presses universitaires de Rouen et du Havre.

Fernández Álvarez, Maria Pilar. 1981. *El Argólico occidental y oriental en las inscripciones de los siglos VII, VI y V a.C.* Theses et Studia Philologica Salmanticensia, 19. Salamanca: University of Salamanca.

Fraenkel, Béatrice. 1994. "Les écritures exposées." In *Écritures,* edited by Jacques Anis, 99–110. Special issue of *Linx* 31.

IG IV = Fraenkel, Maximilianus. 1902. *Inscriptiones Graecae. IV. Inscriptiones Graecae Aeginae Pityonesi Cecryphaliae Argolidis.* Berlin: Georg Reimer.

Friedländer, Paul, and Herbert B. Hoffleit. 1948. *Epigrammata: Greek Inscriptions in Verse from the Beginnings to the Persian Wars.* Berkeley: University of California Press.

Frisk, *GEW* = Frisk, Hjalmar. 1960–72. *Griechisches etymologisches Wörterbuch.* 3 vols. Heidelberg: Winter.

García Ramón, José Luis. 2006. "La fragmentación dialectal griega: limitaciones, posibilidades y falsos problemas." *Incontri linguistici* 29: 61–81.

García Ramón, José Luis. 2018. "Ancient Greek Dialectology: Old and New Questions, Recent Developments." In Giannakis, Crespo, and Filos, 2018, 29–106.

Gaunt, Jasper. 2005. "New Galleries of Greek & Roman Art at Emory University: The Michael C. Carlos Museum." *Minerva* 16: 13–17.

Giannakis, Georgios K., Emilio Crespo, and Panagiotis Filos, eds. 2018. *Studies in Ancient Greek Dialects: From Central Greece to the Black Sea.* Berlin: De Gruyter.

Guarducci *EG I* = Guarducci, Margherita. 1967. *Epigrafia Greca. Volume I. Caratteri e storia della disciplina. La scrittura greca dalle origini all'età imperial.* Rome: Istituto poligrafico dello stato.

Guijarro Ruano, Paloma. 2015. *La lengua de las inscripciones métricas del Peloponeso (siglos VII–IV a.C.),* PhD diss., Complutense University of Madrid. Published online: https://eprints.ucm.es/id/eprint/39779/1/T37902.pdf.

Hall, Jonathan Mark. 1995. "How Argive was the 'Argive' Heraion? The Political and Cultic Geography of the Argive Plain, 900–400 B.C." *AJA* 99, no. 4: 577–613.

Hall, Jonathan Mark. 1997. *Ethnic Identity in Greek Antiquity.* Cambridge: Cambridge University Press.

Hall, Jonathan Mark. 2002. *Hellenicity: Between Ethnicity and Culture.* Chicago: University of Chicago Press.

Hansen, Peter Allan. 1983. *Carmina epigraphica graeca saeculorum VIII–V a. Chr. N.* Texte und Kommentare, 12. Berlin: Walter de Gruyter.

Holmes, Janet. 2013. *An Introduction to Sociolinguistics,* 4th edition. London: Routledge.

Jacquemin, Anne. 1999. "Le rédacteur et le lapicide: 'barbouillage dialectal' et repentir dans les inscriptions de Delphes." In *Urkunden und Urkundenformulare im Klassischen Altertum und in den orientalischen Kulturen, Symposium Heidelberg, 3–5 novembre 1994*, edited by Raif Georges Khoury, 71–81. Heidelberg: Universitätsverlag C. Winter.

Jeffery or Johnston,[167] LSAG² = Jeffery, Lilian Hamilton. 1990. *The Local Scripts of Archaic Greece: A Study of the Origin of the Greek Alphabet and its Developments from the Eight to the Fifth century B.C.*, revised edition with a supplement by Alan Johnston. Oxford: Clarendon Press.

Johansen, Flemming. 1969. "En klassisk græsk Bronzehank." *Meddelelser fra Ny Carlsberg Glyptotek* 26: 54–65.

Klinkenberg, Jean-Marie. 1996. *Précis de sémiotique générale.* Points Essais, Sciences humaines. s.l.: De Boeck Université.

Klinkenberg, Jean-Marie. 2018a. "Entre dépendance et autonomie. Pour une définition de l'écriture dans les sciences du langage et du sens." In *Signatures. (Essais en) Sémiotique de l'écriture*, edited by Jean-Marie Klinkenberg and Stéphane Polis, 103–129. Special issue of *Signata* 9.

Klinkenberg, Jean-Marie. 2018b. *Entre langue et espace. Qu'est-ce que l'écriture.* Brussels: Académie royale de Belgique (L'Académie en poche, 111).

Klinkenberg, Jean-Marie, and Stéphane Polis. 2018. "De la scripturologie." In Klinkenberg and Polis, *Signatures*, 9–56. Special issue of *Signata* 9. English version of the text "On Scripturology," 57–102. N B: For the convenience of the reader, both versions are quoted with /.

Klock-Fontanille, Isabelle. 2014. "Penser l'écriture: corps, supports et pratiques." *Communication & Langages* 182: 29–43.

Kritzas, Charalambos B. 1992. "Aspects de la vie politique et économique d'Argos au Vᵉ siècle avant J.-C." In *Polydipsion Argos. Argos de la fin des palais mycéniens à la constitution de l'État classique. Bulletin de correspondance hellénique. Supplément XXII*, edited by Marcel Piérart, 231–40. Paris: Diffusion de Boccard.

Kritzas, Charalambos B. 2006. "Nouvelles inscriptions d'Argos: les archives des comptes du trésor sacré (ivᵉ s. av. J.-C.)." *CRAI* 150, no. 1: 397–434.

Kritzas, Charalambos B. 2007. "Ετυμολογικές παρατηρήσεις σε νέα επιγραφικά κείμενα του Άργους." In *ΦΩΝΗΣ ΧΑΡΑΚΤΗΡ ΕΘΝΙΚΟΣ. Actes du Vᵉ congrès international de dialectologie grecque (Athènes, 28–30 septembre 2006)*, edited by M. B. Hatzopoulos, with the collaboration of Vassiliki Psilakakou, 135–60. Special issue of *Μελετήματα* 52. Paris: Diffusion de Broccard.

Kritzas, Charalambos B. 2009. "Οβολοί αργολικοί." In *KEPMATIA ΦΙΛΙΑΣ τιμητικός τόμος για τον Ιωάννη Τουράτσογλου*, edited by Stella Drougou, 9–23. Athens: Hellenic Ministry of Culture and Numismatic Museum.

Kritzas, Charalambos B. 2013. "Οι νέοι χαλκοί ενεπίγραφοι πίνακες από το Άργος. II. Πρόδρομη ανακοινώση." In *Στα βήματα του Wilhelm Vollgraff. Εκατό χρόνια αρχαιολογικής δραστηριότητας στο Άργος / Sur les pas de Wilhelm Vollgraff. Cent ans d'activités archéologiques à Argos. Actes du colloque international organisé par la IVᵉ EPKA et l'école française d'Athènes, 25–28 septembre 2003*, edited by Dominique Mulliez and Anna Banaka-Dimaki, 275–301. Recherches franco-helléniques IV. Athens: École française d'Athènes.

Lazzarini, Maria Letizia. 1976. "Le formule delle dediche votive nella Grecia arcaica." *Atti della Accademia nazionale dei Lincei*, year CCCLXXIII, serie VIII, vol. XIX, fascicule 2 (Memorie. Classe di scienze morali, storiche e filologiche): 47–354.

Lazzarini, Maria Letizia, and Fausto Zevi. 1988–89. "Necrocorinthia a Pompei: una idria bronzea per le gare di Argo." *Prospettiva* 53–56: 33–48.

Lejeune, Michel. 1987. *Phonétique historique du mycénien et du grec ancien.* Tradition de l'humanisme IX. Paris: Klincksieck.

LSJ = Liddell, Henry George, and Scott Robert. 1968. *A Greek-English Lexicon*, revised and augmented throughout by Sir Henry Stuart Jones, with the assistance of Roderick McKenzie. Oxford: The Clarendon Press.

Luraghi, Nino. 2010. "The Local Scripts from Nature to Culture." *ClAnt* 29. 1: 68–91.

McGowan, Elizabeth P. 1995. "Tomb Marker and Turning Post: Funerary Columns in the Archaic Period." *AJA* 99, no. 4: 615–32.

Mertens, Joan R. 1985. "Greek Bronzes in the Metropolitan Museum of Art." *The Metropolitan Museum of Art Bulletin* 43, no. 2: 1, 5–64.

Méndez Dosuna, Julián. 2004. "¿Sociofonología y sociomorfología en griego antiguo?" In *Registros lingüísticos en las lenguas clásicas*, edited by Antonio López Eire and Agustín Ramos Guerreira, 173–191. Classica Salmanticensia III. Salamanca: Ediciones de la Universidad de Salamanca.

Minon, Sophie. 2009. "La communication interdialectale au milieu du Vᵉ siècle a. C. Argien et crétois dans les deux règlements argiens des relations entre Cnossos et Tylissos." In *ΦΩΝΗΣ ΧΑΡΑΚΤΗΡ ΕΘΝΙΚΟΣ. Actes du Vᵉ congrès international de dialectologie grecque (Athènes, 28–30 septembre 2006)*, edited by M. B. Hatzopoulos, with the collaboration of Vassiliki Psilakakou, 169–210. Special issue of *Μελετήματα* 52. Paris: Diffusion de Broccard.

Minon, Sophie. 2013. "Dialectal Convergence." In *Encyclopedia of Ancient Greek Language and Linguistics*, Leiden: Brill. http://dx.doi.org/10.1163/2214-448X_eagll_COM_00000096.

Minon, Sophie. 2014. "Les mutations des alphabets péloponnésiens au contact de l'alphabet attique ionisé (ca 450–350

---

167 I distinguish when the information is provided by Lilian Hamilton Jeffery or by Alan Johnston.

av. J.-C.).” In *Diffusion de l'attique et expansion des* koinai *dans le Péloponnèse et en Grèce centrale. Actes de la journée internationale de dialectologie grecque du 18 mars 2011, université Paris-Ouest Nanterre*, edited by Sophie Minon, 29–55. Hautes études du monde gréco-romain 50. Geneva: Librairie Droz S.A.

Minon, Sophie. 2015. “Variationnisme et épigraphie grecque antique.” In Dupraz and Sowa, *Genres épigraphiques*, 275–304.

Moggi, Mauro. 1974. “I sinecismi e le annessioni territoriali di Argo nel V secolo A.C.” *Annali della Scuola Normale Superiore di Pisa*, Classe di Lettere e Filosofia 4, no. 4: 1249–63.

Morpurgo Davies, Anna. 1987. “Folk-Linguistics and the Greek Word.” In *Festschrift for Henry Hoenigswald: On the Occasion of his Seventieth Birthday*, edited by George Cardona and Norman H. Zide, 263–80. *Ars Linguistica* 15. Tuebingen: Gunter Narr Verlag.

Mylônas, Georgios E. (1964) 1966. “9. Ἀνασκαφὴ Μυκηνῶν.” *Πρακτικὰ τῆς ἐν Ἀθήναις ἀρχαιολογικῆς ἑταιρειας*: 68–77.

Mylônas, Georgios E. 1965. “Ἀνασκαφαὶ Μυκηνῶν.” *Ἀρχαιολογικὸν Δελτίον 20. Μέρος Β΄ι—Χρονικά*: 160–163.

Nieto Izquierdo, Enrique. 2008. *Gramática de las inscripciones de la Argólide*. PhD diss., Complutense University of Madrid. Published online: https://eprints.ucm.es/8475/1/T30692.pdf.

Nieto Izquierdo, Enrique. 2019. *L'Argolide*. Coll. Paradeigmata : recueil d'inscriptions grecques dialectales, vol. 4. Nancy and Paris: Association pour la diffusion de la recherche sur l'Antiquité and éditions de Boccard.

Orlandos, Anastasios K. 1964. “Κεφάλαιον Α΄· Ἀνασκαφαί. 9, Μυκῆναι.” *Τὸ Ἔργον* 11: 68–77.

Pappalardo, Umberto. 2016. “I bronzi.” In *Caio Giulio Polibio. Storie di un cittadino pompeiano*, edited by Vincenzina Castiglione Morelli, Ernesto De Carolis, and Claudio Rodolfo Salerno, 329–58. Rome: Istituto per la Diffusione delle Scienze Naturali.

Piérart, Marcel. 1991. “Écriture et identité culturelle. Les cités du Péloponnèse nord-oriental.” In Baurain, Bonnet, and Krings, 1991, 565–76.

Piérart, Marcel. 1997. “L'attitude d'Argos à l'égard des autres cités d'Argolide.” In *The Polis as an Urban Centre and as a Political Community: Symposium August 29–31, 1996; Acts of the Copenhagen Polis Centre* 4, edited by Mogens Herman Hansen, 321–51. Copenhagen: Munksgaard.

Pinault, Georges-Jean. 2006. “Compétition poétique et poétique de la compétition.” In *La langue poétique indo-européenne. Actes du colloque de travail de la Société des Etudes Indo-européennes. Paris, 22–24 octobre 2003*, edited by Georges-Jean Pinault and Daniel Petit, 367–411. Collection linguistique XCI. Leuven and Paris: Peeters.

Powell, Barry B. 1991. “The Origins of Alphabetic Literacy among the Greeks.” In Baurain, Bonnet, and Krings, 1991, 357–370.

Probert, Philomen. 2010. “Phonology.” In Baker, 2010, 85–103.

Rhomaios, Konstantinos. 1912. “ΤΕΓΕΑΤΙΚΑΙ ΕΠΙΓΡΑΦΑΙ.” *BCH* 36: 353–86.

Richter, Gisela M. A. 1928. *Antike Plastik Walther Amelung zum sechzigsten Geburtstag*. Berlin: Walter de Gruyter.

Robert, Louis. 1955. “Épigraphie et paléographie.” *CRAI*, no. 2: 195–222.

Robert, Jeanne, and Louis Robert. 1968 “Bulletin épigraphique.” *REG* 81, nos. 386–88: 420–529.

Robert, Jeanne, and Louis Robert. 1981. “Bulletin épigraphique.” *REG* 94, nos. 447–49: 362–485.

Rosén, Haiim B. 1984. “Le transfert des valeurs des caractères alphabétiques et l'explication de quelques habitudes orthographiques grecques archaïques.” In *Aux origines de l'hellénisme. La Crète et la Grèce. Hommage à Henri van Effenterre*, 225–36. Publications de la Sorbonne. Histoire ancienne et médiévale, no. 15. Paris: Centre G. Glotz.

Ruzé, Françoise, and Henri Van Effenterre. 1994. *Nomima. Recueil d'inscriptions politiques et juridiques de l'archaïsme grec. I. Cités et institutions*. Publications de l'École française de Rome, 188/1. Rome: École française de Rome.

Ruzé, Françoise, and Henri Van Effenterre. 1995. *Nomima. Recueil d'inscriptions politiques et juridiques de l'archaïsme grec. II. Droit et société*. Publications de l'École française de Rome, 188/2. Rome: École française de Rome.

Schilling-Estes, Natalie. 2004. “Investigating Stylistic Variation.” In *The Handbook of Language Variation and Change*, edited by J. K. Chambers, Peter Trudgill, and Natalie Schilling-Estes, 375–401. Oxford: Blackwell.

Sideris, Athanasios. 2019. “An Archaic Hydria in Sinope.” In *International Symposium on Sinope and Black Sea Archaeology: “Ancient Sinope and the Black Sea,” 13–15 october 2017*, edited by Hazar Kaba, 133–49. Sinope: Sinope University.

Smith, A. H. 1926. “The Tomb of Aspasia [Plate XIV].” *JHS* 46: 253–57.

Sowder Koch, Amy. 2009. *Greek Bronze Hydriai*. PhD diss., Emory University. Published online: https://etd.library.emory.edu/downloads/cr56n162q?locale=es.

Sowder Koch, Amy. 2015. “Far from the Fountain: Inscriptions on Bronze Hydriai and the Uses of Water Jars in Ancient Greece.” *BABESCH* 90: 13–42.

Susini, Giancarlo C. 1984. “L'analisi dei primi processi di acculturazione epigrafica.” In *Épigraphie hispanique: problèmes de méthode et d'édition*. Paris: de Boccard.

Susini, Giancarlo C. 1989. “Le scritture esposte.” In *Lo spazio letterario di Roma antica. II. La circolazione del testo*, edited by Guglielmo Cavallo, Paolo Fedeli, and Andrea Giardina, 271–305. Rome: Salerno editore.

Svenbro, Jesper. 1988. “J'écris, donc je m'efface. L'énonciation dans les premières inscriptions grecques.” In Detienne, 1988a, 459–79.

Varone, Antonio. 2016. "Indagine su un cittadino al di sopra di ogni sospetto: Giulio Polibio." In *Caio Giulio Polibio. Storie di un cittadino pompeiano*, edited by Vincenzina Castiglione Morelli, Ernesto De Carolis, and Claudio Rodolfo Salerno, 95–116. Rome: Istituto per la Diffusione delle Scienze Naturali.

Verdelis, Nikolaos, Michael H. Jameson, and Ioannis Papachristodoulos. 1975. "Ἀρχαικαὶ ἐπιγραφαὶ ἐκ Τίρυνθος (Πίνακες 46–51)." Ἀρχαιολογικὴ ἐφημερίς: 150–205.

Vollgraff, Wilhelm. 1930. "Ad titulos Argivos." *Mnemosyne* 58, nos. 1/2: 20–40.

Wachter, Rudolf. 1992. "Der Informationsgehalt von Schreibfehlern in griechischen und lateinischen Inschriften." *Sonderdruck aus würzburger Jahrbücher für die Altertumswissenschaft*, Neue Folge 18: 17–31.

Williams, Dyfri. 2014. "Πρός μυρρίνην: Reconstructing a Fourth-Century Tumulus near the Piraeus." In Ἔγραφσεν καὶ ἐποίησεν: *Essays on Greek Pottery and Iconography*, edited by Panos Valavanis and Eleni Manakidou, 419–39. Thessaloniki: University Studio Press.

Zevi, Fausto, and Maria Letizia Lazzarini. 1992. "Hydria bronzea da Pompei (tavv. IX–XI)." *Atti e memorie della Società Magna Grecia*, 3rd series, 1: 91–97, pl. IX–XI.

PART 3

A Quantitative Approach to Linguistic Variation in Papyri

∵

Ὀκτώ or ὀκτώι: Reconsidering Orthographic Hypercorrection in Antiquity

Geert De Mol

Introduction*

Documentary papyri offer a rich source for the study of spelling variation because they are autographs from antiquity. Although Greek spelling was more or less standardized in the fifth century BCE, papyri present many spellings that reflect drastic changes on the phonological level (among other levels) in later periods. These phonological changes have already been studied extensively, mainly on the basis of these spelling variations,[1] but a systematic study of the social meaning of spelling variation in Greek has yet to be carried out.[2]

Furthermore, little systematic work has been undertaken on hypercorrection in ancient texts, mainly because scholars of modern sociolinguistics have for the greater part concentrated on spoken language in modern languages, which allows for experimentation with native speakers. For Latin antiquity, literature on hypercorrection mainly encompasses remarks in more general works,[3] with studies on hypercorrection specifically remaining scarce.[4] For Greek, there is even less to be found. Therefore, one aim of this paper is to apply the theoretical basis of modern-language approaches and use them to our advantage for Greek papyri. For this purpose, a corpus-based approach will be used, with special attention to the Abinnaeus and the Heroninos archives.

In this case study, I will focus on the variation in expressing the numeral "8" in papyri. Three main possible spellings present themselves: the correct—at least according to the classical norm—⟨οκτω⟩; the hypercorrect spelling ⟨οκτωι⟩, which was influenced by the loss of a phonological difference between ⟨ω⟩ and ⟨ωι⟩; and the use of the number η´, equivalent to our number "8." Papyri offer abundant material for the study of this phenomenon because documentary papyri in particular frequently deal with objects or people to be counted or to be accounted for (e.g., in accounts, contracts, and lists of various kinds). In what follows, I will mainly focus on the full-word forms of the number "8," although the mere fact that the full-word form of the numeral is chosen over the shorter numerical form is in itself already a meaningful choice.

As another motivation for this case study, the orthographic hypercorrection ⟨οκτωι⟩ for the correct ⟨οκτω⟩ is remarkable because it never offers a correct form for the indeclinable ὀκτώ, in contrast to the dative cases of a number of nominal declensions, where ⟨ωι⟩ is a perfectly legitimate case ending. This makes ⟨οκτωι⟩ a rather unique case of hypercorrect iota adscript.[5] However, this spelling is never found in a position where it can be interpreted as a dative case, which excludes the possibility of carry-over effects from this source, at least from a morphological point of view.

Beyond the variation between ⟨οκτω⟩ and ⟨οκτωι⟩, deviation from the norm (commonly seen as a mistake and hence labelled "unlicensed variation" by Mark Sebba[6]) and standardized variant spellings (so-called "licensed variation," which is not seen as a spelling mistake) do offer an orthographic choice in a number of other cases.[7] Carry-over to the spelling of ὀκτώ might be explained this way. Specifically, writers may have been so used to writing iota adscript after a final *omega* that they employed it everywhere, whether this was morphologically licensed or not.

I will analyze here the possible difference in (social) meaning between these alternative spellings. Possible factors influencing spelling choice include, first, the relation between the sender (or, in a more general sense, including

* The research for this chapter was conducted within the ERC Starting Grant project EVWRIT ('Everyday writing in Graeco-Roman and Late Antique Egypt. A socio-semiotic study of communicative variation', PI Klaas Bentein), a project which has received funding from the European Research Council under the Horizon 2020 research and innovation programme (Grant Agreement No. 756487).

1 See, for example, Teodorsson 1977.

2 This is one of the aims of the EVWRIT project at Ghent University (https://www.evwrit.ugent.be/). In what follows, I will use data from the project's database, which is being set up as a tool for the socio-semiotic study of ancient documentary texts. I would like to thank Klaas Bentein, PI of the EVWRIT project, for his extensive feedback on earlier versions of this chapter, as well as Giovanbattista Galdi, Joanne Stolk, Yasmine Amory, and Filip De Decker for their feedback and suggestions. Unless otherwise specified, translations are my own.

3 Such as Adams 2013, 73–80.

4 Such as Quirck 2017 on hypercorrection in the Appendix Probi.

5 Although, for the spelling ⟨ηι⟩, the indeclinable Egyptian month name Μεσορή, sometimes spelled ⟨Μεσορήι⟩ in papyri, does offer a parallel.

6 See Sebba 2007.

7 The examples *par excellence* are once again the nominal dative case endings.

genres other than letters, the "initiator") and the addressee (or, for genres other than letters, the "receiver") and their respective social positions. The relation between sender and addressee can be called their "relative social position" and can be known even if their exact social status or "absolute social position" is unknown. A second factor is the genre of the text in question, while a third is idiolect (i.e., the dialect of an individual) and personal preferences.[8] I have chosen these contextual, social factors rather than purely linguistic ones because hypercorrection is essentially a phenomenon caused by the social implications of a linguistic variable, rather than by its linguistic properties themselves.[9] Otherwise, there would be no motivation for certain language users to speak or write "properly," which is exactly the attitude that causes hypercorrection.

Guided by a corpus-wide view of recorded uses, I intend to investigate the influence of these contextual factors on the variation between and distribution of ⟨οκτω⟩, ⟨οκτωι⟩, and ⟨η⟩. For this purpose, I will draw on the EVWRIT database, which contains documentary papyri from Egypt dating from the third century BCE up to the eighth century AD. I will also draw on the Trismegistos database, including offering a more focused look at the Abinnaeus and the Heroninos archives.[10]

In investigating this influence, I will first provide some background on the notion of "hypercorrection" (§ 1), before sketching the general condition of the orthography of iota adscript in the papyri (§ 2). Zooming in on the spelling of ὀκτώ, I will then investigate the influence of absolute and relative social positions (§ 3), and the genre of the text in question (§ 4). In more general terms for iota adscript, I will also investigate to what degree idiolect and/or personal preferences had an influence on spelling (§ 5). I conclude that the hypercorrect form occurs more in more formal genres, as can be expected, but it is, surprisingly, more often used by superordinates while addressing subordinates, instead of the other way around. However, the overrepresentation of tax receipts in the corpus mandates caution for this conclusion.

1 Hypercorrection

As mentioned above, here I intend to apply the theoretical basis of modern-language approaches to understand hypercorrection within my papyrological corpus. For this reason, it is useful to first consider our terms and clarify

how this field specifically applies to papyri. Drawing on these terms, I will then set out the possible hypotheses guiding this case study.

First, William Labov, the founding father of sociolinguistics as a discipline, defined hypercorrection in two different ways. Both definitions are still in use today:

> *Definition 1*: "To describe this phenomenon, the term *hypercorrection* will be used, since the lower-middle-class speakers go beyond the highest-status group in their tendency to use the forms considered correct and appropriate for formal styles."[11]
> *Definition 2*: "This is of course an extension of the usual use of the term to indicate an irregular misapplication of an imperfectly learned rule, as in the hypercorrect case marking of *whom did you say is calling?*"[12]

The first definition clearly has a more sociolinguistic flavor to it. In what follows, I will use this first definition, because in the papyrological material, explicit information on social status, however scarce, is more available than explicit information on a person's level of education. Hence, it is more often possible to assess if a certain status group has more of a tendency to use certain features than it is to assess if this is due to a gap in a person's knowledge.

The social background of the scribe of a papyrus cannot be retrieved for all papyri, nor systematically for all papyri with the same degree of certainty, but there are still a lot of cases where we can make a basic distinction in relative terms. For instance, if the initiator of a letter addresses someone as δέσποτα, we can generally assume that the addressee has a higher status than the initiator, regardless of the specific nature of their relationship.[13] Although this kind of information has been used in papyrological studies already, it has not been widely utilized for the sociolinguistic study of the language and more specifically the spelling of the papyri.

It is also worth noting that in our case, the scribe was sometimes only the person holding the pen and not the person taking the initiative to write. Hence, scribe and initiator were not always or not even usually the same person. The influence of the people delegating the writing to a scribe on the spelling varies and is uncertain. Sociolinguistic work on modern languages operates under

---

8 As mentioned in Sebba 2007.
9 See Labov 1972 and 1990.
10 Accessible via http://www.trismegistos.org/.

11 Labov 1972, 126; see also Janda and Auger 1992, 199.
12 Labov 1972, 126; see also Janda and Auger 1992, 199; Labov 1990, 246.
13 Dickey 2001 cites a few exceptions to this rule and mentions that it was also used within family circles, but overall, it seems to have been more deferential than κύριε in Imperial times.

the assumption that higher class equals higher literacy; however, the higher classes of antiquity did not (necessarily) write more, since this could be performed by other people, who might have a higher or at least equal degree of literacy, but lower social status, while the fact that the higher classes delegated writing might indicate a lack of time, rather than a lack of writing skills.[14]

Returning to Labov's second definition of hypercorrection, the designation "irregular misapplication" implies that it is statistically a marginal phenomenon when compared to the total amount of linguistic data.[15] The percentages of texts with correct and/or hypercorrect iota adscript are indeed very low (on average 0.715 % for ⟨ωι⟩ and 0.378 % for ⟨ηι⟩; I will return to these figures below) but this is not the case for ὀκτώι in relation to the lemma: in the Trismegistos database, there are 2,300 instances of the lemma ὀκτώ, 273 (11.87 %) of which are spelled as ὀκτώι. It is remarkable that more than one tenth of all (fully written) instances of something so trivial and simple as the number eight are spelt in a way that deviates from the common norm.[16]

The field of sociolinguistics also provides a further useful distinction of terms, with Richard Janda and Julie Auger distinguishing between quantitative and qualitative hypercorrection. The first, quantitative hypercorrection, is a phenomenon where members of a less prestigious social group use a prestige variant of a certain feature more often than the highest-prestige group. This occurs only in certain speech styles—mostly formal. In less formal styles, speakers are simply less motivated to make this effort and thus do not do so.[17] One can argue that although a private letter is more informal than a petition to a high magistrate, writing involves by nature a higher degree of formality than speaking, since speaking can be conceived as a less-consciously executed act in some cases, whereas writing is always a conscious act.[18] This might account for the appearance of more formal elements in informal texts. Janda and Auger note that "the proportion of hypercorrection becomes much higher in settings favoring more self-monitoring."[19] The same could be true for written texts in antiquity, although we will have

to make do without explicit information on the writer's attitude.

The second form, qualitative hypercorrection, is defined by Janda and Auger as "primarily momentary but perhaps also longer-term situations where members of a social group which is not most prestigious engage in [...] four-part behavior." The behavior sees those members 1) try to exclude a linguistic feature which they normally use in that environment but feel to be less prestigious; 2) substitute it with a variant that they feel is more prestigious; 3) in so doing, produce an utterance that is not correct to the language users who use it naturally; while 4) this utterance is not correct because the prestige group uses the replaced element in the relevant environment, or even a different third variant.[20]

Janda and Auger thus locate the major difference between the two kinds of hypercorrection in the fact that in

> the qualitative sort, the frequency with which the relevant element is employed in a criterial set of environments is (aside from true speech-errors) zero for native users and non-zero for non-native users. In the quantitative sort, on the other hand, both native and non-native users employ the relevant element with a non-zero frequency in a criterial set of environments.[21]

This means that if the addition of iota adscript is a qualitative hypercorrection, so-called native users of the iota adscript would never use it hypercorrectly, and as a result never write the (always hypercorrect) ⟨οκτωι⟩.

In what follows, I investigate whether the use of ⟨οκτωι⟩ for ⟨οκτω⟩ should be considered as a case of quantitative or qualitative hypercorrection in Janda and Auger's terms. This should be answerable by testing which of the following hypotheses holds true. First, if it is a case of quantitative hypercorrection, ⟨οκτωι⟩ will be more frequent in more formal texts. Second, if it is a case of qualitative hypercorrection, ⟨οκτωι⟩ would not be used by members of the highest-prestige group, although they might (and in practice indeed do) use iota adscript in other words. This might also lead to more lasting changes, because, as Janda and Auger argue, "while qualitative hypercorrection rarely affects all members of a given word-class, it quite often leads to categorical and lasting changes in one or more word-forms belonging to such a class."[22] Third, if it is a

---

14   See Halla-aho 2018, and chapter 7 of this volume.

15   See Janda and Auger 1992, 221.

16   For other lemmas with the same hypercorrection, the average is 4.39 percent.

17   See Janda and Auger 1992, 199–202.

18   See Herman 2000, 8 on Vulgar Latin: "The mere fact of writing necessarily involves the use of certain conventions based on the literary tradition or, at the very least, the standard orthography, even in the case of barely literate writers and whether they are aware of it or not."

19   Janda and Auger 1992, 221.

20   Janda and Auger 1992, 201.

21   Janda and Auger 1992, 212.

22   Janda and Auger 1992, 202.

case of qualitative hypercorrection, there will always also be cases of plain incorrect forms, which prove the linguistic insecurity of the scribe.[23]

To test these possibilities, it will be important to establish whether or not ὀκτώι is used by high-status users, whether or not it is accompanied by other incorrect forms, and whether or not it is more frequent in formal texts. However, this raises another question: how often are high-status users allowed to employ the hypercorrect form before it becomes a normal mistake instead of a hypercorrection, since simply picking one form is not the same as hypercorrection, which implies a conscious choice?[24] This might mean that the use of ὀκτώι for ὀκτώ is not a hypercorrection at all.

According to Janda and Auger, both forms of hypercorrection can co-occur when two conditions are fulfilled. The first is when "the use of a variable's prestige-value in an imitated speech-variety is non-categorical, so that quantitative overshoot by an imitating group is possible";[25] that is, there are other correct variants in the given linguistic environment allowing for quantitative overextension. The second is when one of the possible variants of the feature is a zero-element—that is, a simple non-use—which allows for qualitative overextension in a context normally requiring the zero-variant. For ὀκτώι versus ὀκτώ, this would mean that it is always a qualitative hypercorrection, since ωι is never correct in this form and "quantitative overshoot" is therefore not possible. This would also mean ὀκτώι occurs in texts written by all classes of people. I will cover this in the following section.

2 Iota Adscript

Due to the loss of the second element of the sound cluster /ωι/, the two spellings ⟨ωι⟩ and ⟨ω⟩ become phonological equivalents.[26] This is also the case for other combinations of long vowels with iota in Greek. This leads to the general tendency in the papyri to spell ⟨ω⟩ for both ⟨ωι⟩ and ⟨ω⟩. Modern editions usually correct this to ⟨ῳ⟩ where this is morphologically correct, but iota subscript was not in use in antiquity.

Willy Clarysse sketches the historical situation well, although he does not provide any exact numbers, when he explains that although "the historical orthography (sc. with iota) rapidly disappears" in the second-century papyri, in the third and fourth-century papyri "the use of

the iota is confined to the dative singular in the heading or the address of letters, petitions etc., where it occurs with increasing rarity," while documents from the fifth century onwards "nearly always display the phonetic spelling."[27] Clarysse's summary also holds for the EVWRIT data. Specifically, Table 11.1 displays the number of texts using at least one iota adscript (the percentages of texts using iota adscript as a percentage of the texts from that period in the database are indicated in parentheses).

Looking at the table, it becomes clear that the iota adscript was barely written in Egypt, even from a very early stage. This cannot exclusively be ascribed to the fact that the preserved texts did not provide any occasion to write it in a correct way (such as datives on ⟨ωι⟩ or ⟨ηι⟩), however, as one example of its use can be found in the first line of BGU XVI 2608 (TM 23331). This example is a letter from Herakleides to his brother Athenodoros, found in the Herakleopolites and dated to around the first century BCE, which reads, Ἡρακλείδης Ἀθηνοδώρωι τῶι ἀδελφῶ[ι], "Herakleides to Athenodoros, [his] brother."

The data in Table 11.1 also make it clear that the spelling ⟨οκτωι⟩ occurs most commonly in the first centuries CE in contrast to the development of iota adscript in general. However, although the difference in tendency is remarkable, it might just be a side-effect of the disproportionate number of texts for the first three centuries AD. It was therefore worth checking the possibility that a lack of texts isn't clouding this assessment, and so I compared the numbers of texts with ⟨οκτωι⟩ and ⟨οκτω⟩ to the total number of texts (with percentages in parentheses). Looking at Table 11.2, it seems that in periods in which few texts with the lemma ὀκτώ have survived, both variants occur in similar amounts compared to periods with more texts. In the fourth to sixth centuries CE, however, the hypercorrect spelling almost completely disappears, with only two cases compared to 327 cases of ⟨οκτω⟩. This shows that the development for individual lemmas might be quite different from the development of the spelling of iota adscript in general.

TABLE 11.1 Number of texts using at least one iota adscript

Centuries	⟨ωι⟩	⟨ηι⟩	# texts
V–IV BCE	13 (2.14 %)	6 (0.99 %)	607
III–I BCE	52 (0.67 %)	36 (0.46 %)	7,776
I–III CE	12 (0.04 %)	12 (0.04 %)	28,427
IV–VI CE	1 (0.01 %)	4 (0.02 %)	16,851

---

23 Janda and Auger 1992, 213.
24 Janda and Auger 1992, 205–6.
25 Janda and Auger 1992, 214.
26 See Vierros 2012, 108–9.

27 Clarysse 1976, 151.

TABLE 11.2 Number of texts with ⟨οκτωι⟩ and ⟨οκτω⟩

Centuries	# texts containing ⟨οκτωι⟩	# texts containing ⟨οκτω⟩	# texts
V–IV BCE	0 (0 %)	4 (0.66 %)	607
III–I BCE	9 (0.12 %)	92 (1.18 %)	7,776
I–III CE	184 (0.65 %)	902 (3.17 %)	28,427
IV–VI CE	2 (0.01 %)	327 (1.94 %)	16,851

TABLE 11.3 Relation between writer and addressee for ⟨οκτωι⟩ and ⟨οκτω⟩

Relative social position	⟨οκτωι⟩	⟨οκτω⟩
Bilateral	5	21
Equal (writing to equal)	9	36
Family (writing to family)	6	25
Subordinate (writing to superordinate)	17	165
Superordinate (writing to subordinate)	71	416
Unknown or uncertain	87	663

3 The Relation between Initiator and Receiver and Their Respective Social Positions

The relation between the initiator and receiver is one factor that could have influenced the occurrence of iota adscript. Although the social status of the initiator and receiver cannot always be determined exactly in absolute terms, as noted above, sometimes their relative positions can be determined, especially if an entire archive is preserved. Compared to the level of detail about language users in modern sociolinguistics, however, historical data offer very haphazard information and papyri are no exception to that.

In the EVWRIT project database, there are 195 texts containing one or more instances of ⟨οκτωι⟩ with that exact spelling, including instances where ⟨οκτωι⟩ is part of a composite numeral, such as ὀκτωικαιδεκάτου in P.Fam.Tebt. 15, 2 (TM 10732; Tebtynis [114/115 CE]) or τεσσαράκοντα ὀκτώι in BGU VIII 1753, II, 20 (TM 4835; Hereakleopolites [63 BCE]). The following spelling variants are attested, each with the number of texts in which they occur and with hypercorrect ones with iota adscript marked in italics:

⟨οκτω⟩	1326
⟨οκτωι⟩	*195*
⟨ωκτω⟩	32
⟨ωκτωι⟩	*4*
⟨οκκτω⟩	3
⟨ωκκτω⟩	1
⟨ωκτο⟩	3
⟨οκτο⟩	45
⟨οκκτο⟩	2

It seems that only the two most-common spellings of ὀκτώ that end in ⟨ω⟩ take a hypercorrect iota, because they are the only ones with a frequency that is high enough to show this variation in the corpus. The form *⟨οκτοι⟩, for example, would be possible, since ⟨οκτο⟩ occurs in forty-five texts, but it does not appear. This is logical, because the chance of it appearing is smaller, since it is a variation

of the already less-common variant ⟨οκτο⟩. Another factor might be that the spelling ⟨οι⟩ would point to the pronunciation /i/, which is not the case for ⟨ο⟩, so contrary to the pair ⟨ωι⟩ vs. ⟨ω⟩, a difference in pronunciation might play a role here.

The relation between writer and addressee for the 195 texts with ⟨οκτωι⟩ and the 1326 texts containing the spelling ⟨οκτω⟩ are summarized in Table 11.3. It is clear that ⟨οκτω⟩ is the dominant spelling, although ⟨οκτωι⟩ is relatively common for a hypercorrect form. Texts where the relative social position is marked as "bilateral" are texts where there is only an initiator but no real receiver. This can be the case in contracts where both parties make an agreement on something, using formulas in the first-person plural—such as, ὁμολογοῦμεν "we agree"—or in the third person—such as, ὁμολογεῖ "he/she agrees." More often, however, contracts are drawn up as a letter written from one party to another. Hence, a contract of marriage can be counted as being a case of "family writing to family," while this is in practice not the case. The low percentage of letters in this corpus (80 out of 1,326 containing ⟨οκτω⟩, for example, compared to 334 contracts) is an indication that we must be cautious in interpreting these results.

What seems to be clear, however, is that superordinates tend to use both ⟨οκτωι⟩ and ⟨οκτω⟩ a lot more than just the number η': only 340 out of 4,642 texts (7.32 %) containing η' are sent by a superordinate, as compared to 71 out of 195 (36.41 %). This is also misleading, since these texts containing ⟨οκτωι⟩ are mainly tax receipts, which we know were written by a (superordinate) official to (subordinate) citizens. We can't be sure of this for other receipts or for a lot of other texts, so we cannot exclude the possibility that the incompleteness of our information distorts our image at this point.

For extra information, we can also look at the reverse situation, where subordinates address a superordinate. An excellent example of this is the Abinnaeus archive (TM

Arch ID 1), a substantial portion of which is made up of petitions addressed to Abinnaeus, the *praefectus alae* of a fortress in Dionysias who was also responsible for policing the area in the mid-fourth century CE. This gives us an insight into the kind of problems the civilian population brought to Abinnaeus's attention. In this case, we have to look more broadly than just the spelling of ὀκτώ, but still certain tendencies can be meaningful to our investigation, not least because petitions are a more formal genre as well (a point I will return to below). In light of the definition of hypercorrections established in Section 1, this kind of situation where lower-class people address a superordinate in a formal text would be a typical context where we would expect orthographic and other hypercorrections.

In the Abinnaeus archive, however, there seems to be no apparent relation between spelling and social status: both "higher-ranked" and "lower-ranked" writers use the same irregular spellings. To illustrate this, I cite two documents as examples, one from someone who is ranked higher than Abinnaeus (P.Abinn. 3) and one from someone ranked lower (P.Abinn. 31). P.Abinn. 3 is a threatening letter from Flavius Macarius, written for him by a scribe, with a subscription in his own hand.

(1) Φλ(αούιος) Μακάριος διασημό(τατος) ἐπίτρ(ο-
     πος) δεσποτικ(ῶν) κτήσεων | Φλ(αουίῳ) Ἀμιννέῳ
     πρ(αι)φ(έκτῳ) κάστρων Διονυσιάδος | χαίρειν. ἡ
     ἐξουσία τοῦ κυρίου μου Φλ(αουίου) Φηλικισσίμου
     τοῦ | διασημο(τάτου) κόμιτός τε καὶ δουκὸς προ-
     νοίαν ποι|ουμένη τοῦ δεσποτικοῦ οἴκου προσέ-
     ταξεν | τῇ ἐμῇ ἐπιμελία (l. ἐπιμελείᾳ) βοήθιαν (l.
     βοήθειαν) στρατιωτικὴν ‖μοι‖ | παρασχεθῆναι εἰς
     τὴν ἀπαίτησιν τῶν δεσ|ποτικῶν κανόνων ἐκ τῶν
     ὑπὸ τὴν σὴν φρον|τίδα στρατιωτῶν. σπούδασον
     οὖν κατὰ | τὰ γραφέντα σοι ὑπὸ τοῦ αὐτοῦ κυρίου
     μου | τοῦ διασημο(τάτου) δουκὸς στρατιώτας ἀπο-
     στῖλαι (l. ἀποστεῖλαι) | εἰς τὴν αὐτὴν ἀπαίτησιν
     διὰ τοῦ ἀπο|σταλέντος ὀφ(φικιαλίου) ὑπό τε τοῦ
     αὐτοῦ κυρίου μου | τοῦ διασημο(τάτου) δουκὸς
     οὐ μὴν ἀλλὰ καὶ τοῦ κυρίου | μου τοῦ διασημο(τά-
     του) καθολικοῦ, γειγνώσκων (l. γιγνώσκων) | ὡς
     εἰ μὴ βουληθῆς (l. βουληθείης) τούτους ἀποστῖλαι
     (l. ἀποστεῖλαιε) ἀνε|νεχθήσεται εἰς γνῶσιν τοῦ
     αὐτοῦ κυρίου μου | δουκὸς ὡς σου τὴν ἀπαίτησιν
     τοῦ δεσπο|τικοῦ οἴκου ἐνεδρεύσαντος. (hand 2)
     ἐρρῶσθαί σε, κύριε ἄδελ|φαι (l. ἄδελ|φε), πολλοῖς
     χρόνοις | εὔχομαι.
     Verso
     (Hand 3) Φλ(αούιος) Μακάριος Φλ(αουίῳ)
     Ἀμιννέῳ π(ραι)π(οσίτῳ)

Flavius Macarius the most illustrious Overseer of the Imperial Domains to Flavius Abinnaeus, praefectus of the camp of Dionysias, greeting. His excellency my lord Flavius Felicissimus the most illustrious Count and Duke, making provision for the imperial revenues, has given orders to my heedfulness that a military detachment should be furnished from the troops under your command for the collection of the Imperial taxes. See to it zealously therefore that in accordance with the instructions given to you by my said lord the most Illustrious Duke you send soldiers for the said collection by the official sent by my said lord the most illustrious Duke and also by my lord the most illustrious Catholicus, knowing that if you should refuse to send them it will be brought to the knowledge of my said lord the Duke that you have impeded the collection of the Imperial revenues. I pray for your health, my lord and brother, for many years. (Addressed) Flavius Macarius to Flavius Abinnaeus the praepositus.

trans. BELL et al. 1962

P.Abinn. 31 is a letter of recommendation written and signed by Thareotes, who was, also judging by his handwriting, far from an experienced writer.[28]

(2) τῷ δεσπότῃ μου καὶ πάτρωνι πραιποσίτῳ |
     κάστρων Διονυσιάδος | Θαρεώτης ἐν θ(ε)ῷ χαίρειν.
     | πρῶτον μὲν εὔχομέ (l. εὔχομαί) σοι (l. σε) εὐθυ-
     μοῦντα ἀπολα|βῖν (l. ἀπολα|βεῖν) τὰ παρ' ἐμ[ο]ῦ
     γράμματα· εὔχομε (l. εὔχομαι) γὰρ καὶ παρὰ τῷ
     κ(υρί)ῳ | τὴν ὁλοκληρίαν Κωσταντίου καὶ Δόμνου.
     | παρακαλῶ σε δέ, δέσποτά μου, παρατιθόμενός
     (l. παρατιθέμενός) | σοι τὸν υἱὸν τοῦ ἀδελφοῦ μου
     Συρίωνα. ἠτῖ (l. αἰτεῖ) σε δὲ | καὶ ἀξιοῖ κατηχεύσεν
     (l. κατακούσειν) αὐτῷ ὡς ἐμοί· οὕτως γὰρ ἐγὼ |
     εἶπα ὅτι τινὸς ἐὰν χρίαν (l. χρείαν) ἔχῃς ὁ δεσπότης
     μου | παρέχετέ (l. παρέχεταί) σοι ἐκεῖ. ἀπέστιλά
     (l. ἀπέστειλά) σοι δὲ διὰ Ἀμμωνίο(υ) | σκοιτέως (l.
     l. σκυτέως) χεννιω (l. . χεννίω⟨ν⟩) βίκους β, γάρου
     μαυρα α, | γλυκοιδίων (l. γλυκυδίων) ὀμφακηρὰ
     (l. ὀμφακηράν) α· ἐπιστολὴν δὲ αὐτῷ | οὐκ ἐποίη-
     σα, τοὺς δὲ στρουθοὺς ἀρραβῶνα δέδω|κα. Θάρσι
     (θάρσει) αὐτοὺς ἔνουσιν (l. ἔνεισιν) οἱ στρουθού (l.
     στρουθοί). ἐπιδὴ (l. ἐπειδὴ) οὖν ἔτι | μικκοί εἰσιν
     καὶ λεεικοί (l. λευκοί) λειδω.[. . .]ι ἄφες γένοντα

(l. γένωνται) | μεγά[λα], κἀγώ (l. καὶ ἐγώ) ἔρθω (l. ἔλθω) μετ' ἐσοὶ πρ[ὸ]ς τὸν Φαμενώθ· | ἐν ἐτύμως (l. ἑτοίμῳ) δὲ ἔχε τὰς (l. τὰ) σιππῖα (l. σιππεῖα), φέρω γὰρ τοὺς κοινη|γοὺς (l. κυνη|γοὺς) ἐρχόμενος, ἵνα τὰ λίνα ποιήσομεν (l. ποιήσωμεν). ἀποστέλλω δὲ | πρός σε καὶ τὰ καμήλια τὰ ἀπὸ τῆς μέσης μετὰ γραμμά|των ἀναδιδάσκοντά σοι ἄν τι χρίαν (l. χρείαν) ἔχωσιν οἱ τὰ στρω|τῖα (l. στρου|θεῖα), εἵνα (l. l. ἵνα) αὐτοῖς ἀπογάλης (l. ἀπαγγέλης)· πολλοὶ γὰρ αὐτοῖς κακὸ (l. κακὸ⟨ν⟩) παρέ|χουσιν τὰ δὲ ἀντιλαβὲν (l. ἀντιλαβεῖν) ἀκέραια· κἀγώ (l. καὶ ἐγώ) οὐκ ἀφῶ αὐτοὺς | [- ca.15 -]αρ .[.] . . . .[. . . . .] . . . .[. . . .] . . . ̣ν | λυσομε .[. .] . ἐρρῶσθαί σε εὔ[-χομαι] | τῷ δεσπότῃ μου πραιποσίτῳ Θαρεώτης.

To my master and patron, the praepositus castrorum of Dionysias, Thareotes, greeting in God. First I pray for you that you may receive my letter in good spirits; for I pray also to the Lord for the health of Constantius and Domnus. I beg of you, my master, (on behalf of) Syrion my brother's son whom I present to you. He asks and begs of you that you will show the same attention (?) to him as to me; for this is what I said: "whatever you have need of my master furnishes you with it there." I have sent you by Ammonius the cobbler 2 jars of quails, 1 pot (?) of fish paste, 1 flagon (?) of grape syrup. I did not do a letter for him, but I have given the chickens by way of earnest money. Do not worry about them, the chickens are inside. Now as they are still small and white (?) ... Let them grow big (?), and I will come to visit you in Phamenoth; and keep the hempen cords ready, for I shall bring the huntsmen when I come, so that we may make the nets. I am sending you also the camels from the middle farm (?) with a letter informing you of whatever is needed by the men in charge of (?) the chickens, that you may give them instructions (?), for many people are doing them harm, and help to keep them safe (?). I won't let them go ... I pray for your health ... (Addressed) To my master the praepositus, Thareotes.

trans. BELL et al. 1962

The differences between the ways the senders of these two letters request something are visible not in the spelling, but in the general tone and grammar. Thareotes makes mistakes against the case system, while the scribe in

P.Abinn. 3 makes no such mistakes. Thareotes also makes more mistakes in a text of similar length.

In the Abinnaeus archive, the non-standard spellings occur regardless of genre. All types of variations[29] occur in all genres. One characteristic variation for the Abinnaeus archive is ⟨μ⟩ for ⟨β⟩ in Ἀμινναίῳ, which may be a reaction to the fricative pronunciation /v/ of ⟨β⟩ and foreshadow the Modern Greek spelling ⟨μπ⟩ for the sound /b/.

In summary, we can tentatively conclude that the full-word form of the numeral eight was used more in formal contexts where we are certain that hierarchical relations play a role, such as between subordinates and superordinates rather than between equals or family members. Nevertheless, it cannot be said without any doubt that a certain group of people uses the hypercorrect form with iota adscript more than others. On this basis, we cannot conclusively qualify this hypercorrection as qualitative or quantitative.

4   Genre of the Text

The abovementioned 195 texts with ⟨οκτωι⟩ and the 1,326 texts with ⟨οκτω⟩ in the EVWRIT database containing one or more instances of ὀκτώ can be divided into genre categories, grouped according to their context of use. Specific genres are only given when a significant number of texts of that genre contains an instance.

Looking first at the most commonly occurring genre, of the receipts containing the spelling ⟨οκτω⟩, 389 are tax receipts (i.e., 58.67 % of receipts with ⟨οκτω⟩ and 29.34 % of all texts with ⟨οκτω⟩). For ⟨οκτωι⟩ this is so in sixty-six cases (i.e., 69.47 % of receipts with ⟨οκτωι⟩ and 33.85 % of all texts with ⟨οκτωι⟩); thus, tax receipts are overrepresented for both the correct and hypercorrect spellings, but the hypercorrect spelling occurs more in this genre only because the number is more often written in full in this specific kind of text, not because the hypercorrection occurs proportionately more in them. The reason for this is simple: the tax receipts have a standard formula that can be paraphrased as "[number written in full] + γίνονται + [number]." An example can be found in O.Tebt.Pad. 10 (201/202 CE):

---

29   That is, the following: iotacisms: ⟨ι⟩, ⟨ει⟩, ⟨η⟩, ⟨οι⟩, ⟨υ⟩; ⟨ντ⟩ for ⟨τ⟩; ⟨η⟩ for ⟨αι⟩; ⟨ε⟩ for ⟨αι⟩ and vice versa; ⟨ρ⟩ for ⟨λ⟩; ⟨ο⟩ for ⟨ω⟩ and vice versa; ⟨ξ⟩ for ⟨κσ⟩ or ⟨κς⟩; ⟨ο⟩ for ⟨α⟩; ⟨νγ⟩ for ⟨γγ⟩; ⟨νχ⟩ for ⟨γχ⟩; ⟨ω⟩ for ⟨ου⟩.

(3) (ἔτους) ι ἀριθ(μήσεως) Τῦβι. | διέ(γραψε) Λαυτᾶνις | ὑπὲρ λαγ(ραφίας) τοῦ αὐτοῦ | ἔτους ἄλλας δραχ(μὰς) | ὀκτώ, (γίνονται) (δραχμαὶ) η.

In year ten of the counting, Tubi. Laudanius paid for the poll tax of that same year another eight drachmae, equaling 8 drachmae.

I have not found a similar explanation for the other genres, where the number is either written in full or not, without combining both.

TABLE 11.4   Spelling of ⟨οκτωι⟩ and ⟨οκτω⟩ by genre

Genre	⟨οκτωι⟩	⟨οκτω⟩	% of ⟨οκτωι⟩ compared to ⟨οκτω⟩
Administration[a]	7	128	5.47 %
Business[b]	5	22	22.73 %
Law[c]	77	346	22.25 %
– Contract	74	334	22.16 %
Mixed[d]	0	1	0 %
Private[e]	0	3	0 %
Religion[f]	0	6	0 %
Letter	4	80	5 %
Order[g]	5	61	8.20 %
Receipt[h]	95	663	14.33 %
– Tax receipt	66	389	16.97 %
Uncertain[i]	2	16	12.50 %
Total	195	1326	14.70 %

a   "Administration" encompasses acknowledgements, applications, appointments, bids, certificates, declarations, lists, memoranda, notices, oaths, petitions, registers, and reports.

b   "Business" only contains accounts in this overview. Business letters could also be sorted under this category, but because letters can be of private or administrative nature and the boundaries are often blurry, I choose to treat them separately here.

c   "Law" encompasses agreements, authorizations, contracts, decrees, donations, legal proceedings, ordinances, and registrations.

d   "Mixed" documents and documents of "Uncertain" genre each form separate categories, however few they may be in our case.

e   "Private" here denotes exercises and school texts. Again, part of the letters could be grouped under this heading, but letters are treated separately.

f   "Religion" here only contains mummy labels.

g   "Orders" and "receipts" are treated separately for the same reasons letters are: they can, with good reason, be put into several categories. A receipt for a payment, for example, could be labelled "business," but if it is a tax receipt it would fall into the "administration" category.

h   See previous note.

i   "Mixed" documents and documents of "Uncertain" genre each form separate categories, however few they may be in our case.

TABLE 11.5   Texts with ⟨οκτω⟩ or ⟨οκτωι⟩ as compared to the total number of texts

Genre	⟨οκτωι⟩ (% of genre)	⟨οκτω⟩ (% of genre)	⟨οκτωι⟩ (% of all texts with ⟨οκτωι⟩)	⟨οκτω⟩ (% of all texts with ⟨οκτω⟩)
Contract	18.14 %	81.86 %	37.95 %	25.19 %
Letter	4.76 %	95.24 %	2.05 %	6.03 %
Order	7.58 %	92.42 %	2.56 %	4.60 %
Receipt	12.53 %	87.47 %	48.72 %	50.00 %

The next step is to consider the percentages of texts that have either variant as compared to the total number of texts of that genre containing either ⟨οκτω⟩ or ⟨οκτωι⟩, and the percentages of texts that have either variant compared to all the texts containing only the same variant. I only compared these numbers for contracts, letters, orders, and receipts, because the number of cases for other genres is too low to yield significant results. Looking at the numbers for all texts containing the same variant (see the two last columns of Table 11.5), we see that letters, orders, and receipts are not significantly more likely to have hypercorrect ⟨οκτωι⟩ instead of ⟨οκτω⟩. Contracts, however, are proportionally more likely to have ⟨οκτωι⟩ (37.95 % vs. 25.19 %). Turning to the percentages per genre (see columns two and three), we see that a relatively high percentage of texts has hypercorrect ⟨οκτωι⟩, especially contracts. Overall, this is 11.87 percent for ὀκτώ as a lemma, as previously mentioned. It seems that especially contracts and (tax) receipts are prone to have this hypercorrection.

When we look at these different genres, the preponderance of more formal genres is striking. The hypercorrection is made because writers, probably (though not conclusively) irrespective of social class, have a sense that this form is appropriate in a formal context. This also explains the low numbers of (private) letters in the corpus at hand: adding iota adscript is not felt as necessary in the informal context of private letters, if the need is felt to write it in full at all. This would point to ⟨οκτωι⟩ being a case of quantitative hypercorrection, albeit used by more than one group.

5   Idiolect and Personal Preferences

In order to track the existence of personal preferences and possible ideological factors influencing them, it is necessary to have several texts written by the same (identified) scribe. For this purpose, archives of papyri provide us with identified scribes whose spelling habits we can track. In our case, however, this is a problem, since only 453 of 1,521 texts containing ⟨οκτω⟩ or ⟨οκτωι⟩ are linked to an archive, although this is still a good amount of data. A bigger problem is that these texts are also divided among 148 different archives, and this does not yet guarantee that the texts in the same archive are written by the same scribe(s).

Another problem is that we cannot establish in a systematic way how much room the scribe had to make their own decisions, especially for phenomena that had no real influence on the content of the text, such as spelling. Scott Bucking states that production from memory or by dictation would offer a greater chance of phonologically motivated errors in orthography, whereas copying from a written text would reduce this phenomenon by offering a visual support, especially if the scribe did not read the text in front of them out loud.[30] Hilla Halla-aho, on the other hand, states that scribes did not alter much, based on the observation that letters written by scribes for less-literate people and autographs from less-literate people share many stylistic and grammatical properties.[31] However, spelling was probably the first thing to fall "victim" to scribal alterations, being a more superficial element than word choice or syntax, for example.[32] This means that a scribe would stick to their own spelling habits, regardless of who was dictating and that word choice and syntax came from the initiator, whereas spelling and handwriting came from the scribe.[33]

Given these claims, it is therefore worthwhile to check the texts to see whether the hypercorrect form ⟨οκτωι⟩ occurs on its own or in combination with other cases of iota adscript. This can already be an indication of the scribe's preference in spelling this feature. A simple start is to check consistency in the spelling of ⟨οκτωι⟩. There are 273 occurrences of ⟨οκτωι⟩ in 195 texts, which means that it occurs 1.4 times on average in each text—that is, more than once in many texts.

Only in ten texts, however, are both the correct ⟨οκτω⟩ and hypercorrect ⟨οκτωι⟩ used by the same scribe. Of these, SB X 10270, 41 (TM 16733; Panopolis [III CE]) is a special case, with both forms showing up right next to each other in line 4 for no apparent reason:

(4) Αὐρήλιος Πανίσκος | Πεσόντι ὀρνιθοτρ(όφῳ) | χα(ίρειν). ἔσχον ⟨Τῦβι⟩ θ ᾠὰ | ὀκτὼι ι ὀκτὼ | γ(ίνονται) ᾠὰ δεκαὲξ | (ἔτους) ζ Τῦβι | ια

Aurelius Paniscus to Peson the birdkeeper, greetings. I received on the 9th <of Tubi> eight, on the 10th eight eggs, being sixteen. In the year 7, Tubi 11.

Four other texts, P.Stras. V 408 (Bakchias [II CE]), BGU XV 2531 (Soknopaiou Nesos [end II CE]), O.Wilck. 7 (Dios Polis [II BCE]), and PSI X 1138 (Tebtynis [II CE]), also have both forms of ὀκτώ, but here the difference in form coincides with a change in scribal hand. It is also interesting to note that P.Giss. 94 (TM 11288; Soknopaiou Nesos [67 CE]) switches from ⟨οκτωι⟩ to ⟨ωκτωι⟩ as the hand switches: the main scribe and three other sub-scribes use ⟨οκτωι⟩, whereas a last scribe switches to ⟨ωκτωι⟩. Even here, me might call the use of ⟨οκτωι⟩ over ⟨ωκτωι⟩ relatively consistent. Based on these figures, then, we can conclude that scribes were generally very consistent on their own (with only ten exceptions) and also consistent themselves when more than one scribe was writing (with only four exceptions). This last tendency can be caused by a more experienced scribe influencing the spelling choices of a less literate sub-scribe in some cases.

Furthermore, the hypercorrect form often occurs in combination with at least one more (correct or hypercorrect) iota adscript in the text in words other than ὀκτώ. This is especially so if there are occasions where iota adscript is—according to the scribes' contemporary norms—optional but correct, such as in dative cases in the address.[34] A typical example of this is O.Berenike II 167, dated to the middle of the first century CE:

(5) Σαραπίων Κασίου | Ἀνδουρωι χ(αίρειν)· δι(απόστειλον) Πετεαρποχ(ράτῃ) | Ψενθφοῦτος οἴν(ου) πολ( ) | κεράμια πεντήκοντα|ὀκτώι. Ἐπείφ ια´.

Sarapion son of Cassius to Andurus, greetings. Send fifty-eight jars of wine [...] to Petearpochrates son of Psenthphous. Epeiph 11.

30   Bucking 2007, 238.
31   Halla-aho 2018, 230–32.
32   Thus spelling is not mentioned when Halla-aho (2018, 231) states that "dictated letters and autograph letters by less literate persons share many essential characteristics: the lack of connecting and ordering devices that are normally used in written language (particles and other connectives, hypotactic structures)" and "because the scribe was the person who actually wrote the words down," makes it a "reasonable assumption" that "orthography was always produced by the scribe."
33   See Halla-aho 2018, 232.

34   This last trend is also visible with the use of hypercorrect iota adscript in general: occurrences tend to show up in groups in texts.

However, seventy-two texts are an exception to that rule, although most (70) are too short to give the possibility of using iota adscript in a correct way to begin with, so it is not surprising they do not have another iota adscript. This leaves us with only P.Fam.Tebt. 22 (Tebtynis [122 CE]) and P.Stras. V 404 (Bakchias [126 CE]) as real exceptions. They are the only texts that do not have another iota adscript, despite having the possibility to do so correctly.

The scribal consistency for the use or non-use of iota adscript in general can be exemplified by the Heroninos archive (TM Arch ID 103), which contains texts ranging from 199 to 275 CE and is the largest known papyrus archive from Roman Egypt, consisting of 472 published papyri and some 600 unpublished texts. The core texts of this archive are the 385 papyri containing the business letters and draft accounts of Heroninos, who managed parts of the estates owned by the *eques* Aurelius Appianus in Theadelpheia in Egypt. The other papyri can be divided into five subarchives, which originally did not belong to the Heroninos archive, but were added to it by Heroninos after their respective owners' deaths.

As a manager, Heroninos frequently corresponded with Appianus's representative Alypios, but also with his colleagues Heronas and Eirenaios, who managed other parts of Appianus's possessions. This means that there are examples of both equals writing to equals and subordinates addressing their superordinate, with both appearing in the relatively informal genre of the business letter. Heroninos made drafts of the accounts he had to send to his employer, before sending the actual accounts. As a result, we find the drafts of outgoing accounts in the Heroninos archive, though the submitted versions are now lost. These draft accounts, which were obviously intended for personal use, were written by Heroninos in his cursive hand.

In his treatment of the archive, which has now become the standard text on this topic, Dominic Rathbone cites several elements that can be derived from the context of the archive as a whole and which are helpful for sketching the sociolinguistic context for this study. First, Heroninos and his colleagues were very informal in their letters, addressing each other as *philtatos* ("my dear friend") or *adelphos* ("my brother").[35] This is a typical phenomenon of equals in a close working relationship, both in antiquity and the present day. Second, they also appear to have been free men, and were probably from relatively though not extremely prosperous families.[36] This would explain their education, which they used for their jobs as estate managers rather than for more ambitious endeavors which

were the privilege of higher classes. Third, in terms of absolute social status, Appianus and his employees were of (almost) equal social status, at least in practice, as far as we can tell: the administrators of the Appianus estate were large landowners in their own right, which counters a strict hierarchical relationship.[37] Appianus seems to have treated them as such, with Rathbone observing that "in general the bantering tone of Appianus's letters suggests an owner who knew that he had the professional respect of his managers."[38] All of these elements paint the context of a group of relatively high-status individuals who had been colleagues for many years and who addressed each other accordingly. The same also applies to their superiors: all of the communication seems to have been rather informal.

Having set out the sociolinguistic context, if we then look at the numbers of instances of ⟨ωι⟩ and ⟨ηι⟩ versus ⟨ω⟩ and ⟨η⟩ respectively (see Table 11.6, where the percentages indicate the results in relation to the total number of both pairs of spellings in the archive), we can see almost all of the instances of ⟨ωι⟩ are found in the heading or the address of letters or similar documents.[39] This then confirms the historical claim by Clarysse I noted in Section 2.[40]

Looking in more detail, we can see that most of the time, the iota adscript can be found in the name of the addressee. This can be seen in an example from P.Flor. II 215 (TM 11088; Theadelpheia [253 CE]): Νίννος Ἡρωνίνωι καὶ Π[ο]ντικῷ τοῖς φι(λτάτοις) χαίρειν, "Ninnos to his friends Heroninos and Pontikos, greetings." An exception to this general rule, however, is found in P.Flor. II 229 (TM 31145; Theadelpheia [first half III CE]), although the iota adscript is still to be found in the letter's opening formula: Παλᾶς Ἡρωνείνῳ τῷ φιλτάτωι χαίρειν, "Palas to his friend Heroninos, greetings."

TABLE 11.6   Spellings with iota adscript compared to spellings without iota adscript

⟨ωι⟩	⟨ω⟩	⟨ωι⟩ and ⟨ω⟩	⟨ηι⟩	⟨η⟩	⟨ηι⟩ and ⟨η⟩
73	674	747	5	280	285
9.77 %	90.23 %	100 %	1.75 %	98.25 %	100 %

35   Rathbone 1991, 80.
36   Rathbone 1991, 81.
37   Rathbone 1991, 83.
38   Rathbone 1991, 86–87.
39   The orthographies ⟨ω⟩ and ⟨η⟩ are commonly used in the editions where papyri read ⟨ω⟩ and ⟨η⟩ and classical Greek has ⟨ωι⟩ and ⟨ηι⟩. Where both papyri and classical Greek have ⟨ω⟩ and ⟨η⟩, the editions adopt ⟨ω⟩ and ⟨η⟩.
40   Clarysse 1976, 151.

Another exception is SB XIV 12003 (TM 30106; Theadelpheia [first half III CE]), but this time, the iota is not used in the opening formula or in the address:

(6) Αἴας Λογγίνῳ τῷ υἱῷ | χαίρειν. | ἔγραψά σοι ἄλλοτε περὶ | τῶν ἐριδίων καὶ οὐκ ἔ|πεμψάς μοι αὐτά. δὸς αὐ|τὰ Σαραπάμμωνι \αὐτά/ καὶ | ψωμία καὶ εἰπὲ Εὐτύ|χῃ ὅτι τίς σε ἐσύλησαι | καὶ πέμψον μοι φάσιν. | τοσαυτάκις γὰρ ἔγραψα | περὶ τούτου. ἐρῶισθαι | [σε εὔχομ]αι. Πασα . | [-ca.-?] .σιχλ .

Aias to his son Longinus, greetings. I wrote you earlier about the wool and you didn't send it to me. Give it to Sarapammon and the bread and tell Eutyche that someone has robbed you and send me [her?] answer, because I wrote so many times already about this. I wish you good health. Pasa [...]

The highlighted form ἐρῶισθαι is one of only two hypercorrect uses of iota adscript with ⟨ω⟩ in the Heroninos archive. The other passage, which can be found in P.Laur. III 102v (TM 31520; Theadelpheia [mid-III CE]), once again has the iota used in a personal name in the dative in the greeting formula of a letter: Ὠρίωινι τῶι [ἀδελ]φῷ χαίρειν, "to his brother Horion, greetings."

Turning to the use of ⟨ηι⟩, we only find five instances in the Heroninos archive. Since the instances are not all clearly situated in one category, as was the case with ⟨ωι⟩, I reproduce all five here:

(7) P.Laur. I 8, 5 (TM 28761; Theadelpheia [first half II CE])
[ἀπέχειν ἀπὸ τῆς] φερνῆς ἧς ὀφίλει αὐτῆι ὁ αὐτὸς Πτολ(εμαῖος) κατὰ συνγραφὴν ὁμολ(ογηθεῖσαν) γάμου τετελειωμένην ἐπὶ [-ca.-?]

[receiving from the] dowry that the same Ptolemaios owes here according to the agreed contract of marriage that was struck on [...]

(8) P.Laur. III 106, 5 (TM 41442; Theadelpheia [253 CE])
γράφω σοι ἵν' εἴδῃς καὶ μηκέτι ἀν-| [-ca.-?]

I write to you so you know and nothing [...]

(9) P.Prag. I 67, 1 (TM 30065; Theadelpheia [probably mid-III CE])
δὸς Κασίῳ ὄνον ἕνα. | Μεσορὴι α

Give Cassius one donkey. Mesore 1

(10) SB XXIV 15927, 4 (TM 45371; Theadelpheia [III CE])

κώμηι οἰκί(α) [-ca.-?]

[In the?] village a house [...]

(11) SB XXIV 15927, 13 (TM 45371; Theadelpheia [III CE])

καὶ ἐν τῆι κώ[μηι] [...]

And in the village [...]

In the case of αὐτῆι and τῆι, the iota adscript is used to mark the dative case, while in εἴδῃς it is part of the subjunctive marker. In all three of these cases, the spelling without iota could have been used in a correct way, according to contemporary norms. Κώμηι could also be in this category, but the lack of context leaves the possibility of a hypercorrect nominative form (instead of κώμη) theoretically open in SB XXIV 15927 (not in SB XXIV 15927, after the preposition ἐν). This would however point to a consistency in the scribe's spelling habits.

The Egyptian month name Μεσορήι is a hypercorrect form of Μεσορή. Since no Egyptian month name is inflected in Greek, it cannot be a regular dative case form, although the analogy with the dative case of Greek-inflected nouns ending in ⟨η⟩ is plausible, especially since we are dealing with month names which are by definition often used as a complement of time, a function readily associated with the dative case in Greek. In this specific case, however, it can also be interpreted as Μεσορὴ ια, "Mesore 11," so it is a doubtful case. This would leave us with even fewer cases of iota adscript in the Heroninos archive.

Zooming in on the fifteen texts which were written in Heroninos's own hand, we notice that Heroninos never uses the iota adscript in his draft accounts, although he could have done so correctly in eighty-one instances. The uses which are marked with iota subscript in editions and where he could have used it without going against the norms of his time are once again proper names or designations of persons in the opening formula of letters or in the lists with expenses in the accounts. The following examples, from P.Prag.Varcl. II 2 (TM 14168; Theadelpheia [250 CE]) are illustrative for both categories:

(12) Αὐρηλίῳ Ἀπιανῷ ἐξηγ(ητεύσαντι) βουλ(ευτῇ) τῆς λαμπρο|τάτης πόλεως τῶν Ἀλεξανδρέων καὶ ὡς χρημ(ατίζει) | παρὰ Αὐρηλίου Ἡρωνείνου φροντιστοῦ Θεαδελφ(είας).
ll. 2–4

To Aurelius Appianus, former exegetes and bouleutes of the magnificent city of Alexandria and however he is styled, from Aurelius Heroninos, phrontistes of Theadelpheia.

(13) ἐμοὶ Ἡρωνείνῳ (δραχμαὶ) μ | Πω[λί]ωνι βουκό-
λ(ῳ) (δραχμαὶ) ιζ (ὀβολὸς) | Σιλβανῷ βουκόλ(ῳ) (δραχμαὶ) μη
ll. 31–33

For me, Heroninos, 40 drachmae. For Polion, shepherd 17 drachmae 1 obole. For Silvanus, shepherd 48 drachmae.

In short, we can conclude that Heroninos (and possibly also his colleagues) show a very high degree of consistency in *not* using iota adscript. Personal choice seems to have been an important factor in this.

Finally, evidence for scribal preferences can also be found elsewhere. In a study on the language of bilingual notaries in the Pathyrite area, Marja Vierros states that "the *agoranomoi* in the Pathyrite area show both the maintenance of the historical orthography and confusion between writing the *iota adscriptum* or a plain long vowel. Some individual tendencies and practices can be detected. The context also plays a role."[41] Here one can wonder if by "context," genre and/or social relations are meant. Vierros then goes on to discern three main groups of writers: those who tend to write the iota adscript in the correct places; writers with a "mixed" usage (i.e., writing iota most of the time, occasionally omitting it; mostly not writing iota, except in some words; purely mixed usage without any apparent influences on the choice); and writers who do not write iota at all (Hermias and Ammonios can even be identified in this way).[42]

In conclusion, it is safe to say that personal preferences did play a major role in spelling choices, even more than genre and social relations or background. The same seems to hold true for the spelling of ὀκτώ: hypercorrect forms occur in different genres and are not exclusively made by one specific group of people, although tendencies can be discerned. It is, however, impossible to know if or which ideological factors would be involved. A conservative tendency might be at play, but to be sure about this, other spelling features would need to be considered as well, which is beyond the scope of my current investigation.

Conclusions

In conclusion, we can draw the following sketch concerning the use of ⟨οκτω⟩ and ⟨οκτωι⟩. The full-word form of the number eight is written more in formal contexts where superordinates address subordinates, but taking into account the overrepresentation of tax receipts, it is not entirely clear if superordinates use the hypercorrect form more than others. This does not allow us to qualify this hypercorrection as qualitative or quantitative with certainty.

The hypercorrect form occurs more in more formal genres: contracts, orders, and (tax) receipts. This would make the use of ⟨οκτωι⟩ a case of quantitative hypercorrection. The use of both correct and hypercorrect iota adscript is highly personal: scribes show a high level of consistency in their choice for either ⟨οκτω⟩ or ⟨οκτωι⟩.

Since ⟨ωι⟩ is never correct in this word and the use or non-use of iota is categorical, "quantitative overshoot" is not possible and ⟨οκτωι⟩ should be considered a qualitative hypercorrection according to the definition given by Janda and Auger. However, if we look at the use of iota adscript in general, the use is non-categorical, because the use of iota adscript is correct—though optional—in words other than ὀκτώ. This would point in the direction of a quantitative hypercorrection.

All in all, my preliminary study suggests that the hypercorrect use of ⟨οκτωι⟩ for ⟨οκτω⟩ can be considered a case of quantitative hypercorrection. The case of ὀκτώ defies the classical definition of hypercorrection, however, in that it seems to have been used mainly by superordinates to address subordinates, instead of the other way around, like in petitions from citizens to officials, which would be far more typical environments for hypercorrection. These observations notwithstanding, a broader investigation of the use of iota adscript in general is required (and is underway) to fully ascertain the extent of these claims.

Reference List

Adams, James Noel. 2013. *Social Variation and the Latin Language.* Cambridge: Cambridge University Press.

Bell, Harold Idris, V. Martin, and Eric Gardner Turner. 1962. *The Abinnaeus Archive: Papers of a Roman Officer in the Reign of Constantius II.* Oxford: Clarendon Press.

Bucking, Scott. 2007. "On the Training of Documentary Scribes in Roman, Byzantine, and Early Islamic Egypt: A Contextualized Assessment of the Greek Evidence." *ZPE* 159: 229–47.

---

41   Vierros 2012, 122.
42   Vierros 2012, 122.

Clarysse, Willy. 1976. "Notes on the Use of the Iota Adscript in the Third Century B.C." *CE* 51: 150–66.

Dickey, Eleanor. 2001. "Kyrie, ΔΕΣΠΟΤΑ, Domine: Greek Politeness in the Roman Empire." *JHS* 121: 1–11.

Halla-aho, Hilla. 2018. "Scribes in Private Letter Writing: Linguistic Perspectives." In *Scribal Repertoires in Egypt from the New Kingdom to the Early Islamic Period*, edited by Jennifer Cromwell and Eitan Grossman, 117–239. Oxford Studies in Ancient Documents. Oxford: University Press.

Herman, József. 2000. *Vulgar Latin*. Translated by Roger Wright. University Park: Pennsylvania State University Press.

Janda, Richard D., and Julie Auger. 1992. "Quantitative Evidence, Qualitative Hypercorrection, Sociolinguistic Variables and French Speakers' "eadaches' with English *h/∅*." *Language & Communication* 12: 195–236.

Labov, William. 1972. *Sociolinguistic Patterns*. Philadelphia: University of Pennsylvania Press.

Labov, William. 1990. "The Intersection of Sex and Social Class in the Course of Linguistic Change." *Language Change and Variation* 2: 205–54.

Quirck, Ronald J. 2017. "Hypercorrection in the sillabyfication Probi." *Philologus* 161: 350–53.

Rathbone, Dominic. 1991. *Economic Rationalism and Rural Society in 3rd-Century AD Egypt: The Heroninos Archive and the Appianus Estate*. Cambridge: Cambridge University Press.

Sebba, Mark. 2007. *Spelling and Society: The Culture and Politics of Orthography around the World*. Cambridge: Cambridge University Press.

Teodorsson, Sven-Tage. 1977. *The Phonology of Ptolemaic Koine*. Göteborg: Acta Universitatis Gothoburgensis.

Vierros, Marja. 2012. *Bilingual Notaries in Hellenistic Egypt: A Study of Greek as a Second Language*. Brussels: Royal Flemish Academy of Belgium for Arts and Sciences.

## CHAPTER 12

Word-Split Frequency in Greek Documentary Papyri (with an Appendix on Syllabification)

Mark Depauw

Investigating the frequency of word-splits in papyrological documentation is not the sexiest topic imaginable. Even those interested in the history of the Greek language and its everyday use in Graeco-Roman Egypt may never have wondered how common it is for scribes to split a word over two lines. What, then, is the origin of this weird research focus? Presumably, my Egyptological background is to blame, because in Egyptian, a lexeme is not commonly split over two lines. At least that is my impression, as to my knowledge the frequency of the phenomenon has not been investigated there either.[1]

One possible answer could be that a dearth of splitting words might be related to the quadratic system of writing hieroglyphs and the visual appeal of the script. But imagining a closer connection between *signifiant* and *signifié* is problematic in itself, and, as far as I can tell, splitting is also rare in Demotic, which does not fit signs into a square in the same way as hieroglyphic, and the cursive signs can hardly be called iconic either. Therefore, there seems not to be a ready explanation for the rarity of splitting words over lines, and given the lack of investigation, the phenomenon may even be imaginary. It was, in any case, this idea that Egyptian and Demotic rarely split words over consecutive lines that led me to formulate the research questions I shall attempt to answer here. Specifically, to what extent did Greek scribes avoid splitting words; did they split words in some genres more than in others; and did they split words in some periods more than others?

Beginning this research, I did not know of any secondary literature to answer these questions—neither for Greek nor Egyptian, as mentioned above.[2] When I asked a colleague in the linguistic department whether the practice had been investigated for handwritten texts, he looked into it. After some time, he came back with the answer that he had not found anything, subtly adding that this was unsurprising, as he could not see in which way this could warrant investigation.[3] Unperturbed by adversity, I decided to pursue this quest by myself, with only the sources as my companion.

In the following, I will offer an account of this research quest, beginning with a description of the data set. This is followed by a test case looking at private and official letters, in which I consider the possibility of chronological interference, the length of split words, and possible issues of abbreviation. A short appendix considers issues of syllabification.

1 The Data Set

Although the full text of Greek papyri has been available through papyri.info for a number of years, I had lacked the technical knowledge to extract it from the GitHub page where it was up for grabs. On top of that, it would have been problematic to have more- or less-standardized genre information. In late 2016, however, a window of opportunity to investigate my research questions presented itself. This came through my co-supervision of PhD candidate Alek Keersmaekers, who was starting a corpus-linguistics study of the complementation system in Greek papyri.[4]

This contact gave me access to his XML files, which had been extracted from *papyri.info*, then tokenized, morphologically annotated, and lemmatized by machine learning algorithms. Together, we set up a MySQL database of the roughly 4.5 million words in the Greek papyri, with all the annotated information. I made this available through Trismegistos Words,[5] so that lexical searches would be easier for anyone interested in specific word forms or the chronological distribution of a lexeme.[6] More important in the context of this current chapter, however, it also made it more feasible for me to investigate word-splits.

---

1 Harco Willems referred me to a note by Ursula Verhoeven, who in turn alerted me to Rössler-Köhler 1985, which is a related but inverse phenomenon.

2 Although see the literature on syllabification in Greek mentioned in note 14 of the appendix below.

3 Email November 24, 2016. I should like to thank him for his efforts to find something.

4 Keersmaekers 2020, supervised by Dirk Speelman, Toon Van Hal, and myself.

5 See https://www.trismegistos.org/words.

6 See Keersmaekers and Depauw 2022.

In one field of the MySQL database the hyphens (as well as the other diacritical brackets of the Leiden system) were hard-coded and could be found through a simple query.

Of course, things are rarely as easy as they seem at first sight. Data are unfortunately always dirty for the topic you want to investigate. Several obstacles impeded a simple count of split words in the database. First, some of the other annotations of the XML were also hard-coded in the same way, and contained a hyphen, as with "|parens-punctuation-closing|" for instance. Apart from these tags with pipes, I also excluded the records containing only a hyphen and the ones consisting of digits.[7] After these manipulations, I found 73,550 split words.

To get an idea of the relative frequency, however, the total number of words needed to be calculated. This is not just equal to the 4,294,533 records in the database, since there are also tokens for interpunction. After again excluding tokens with a pipe as well as digits, I found 3,519,290 words. This means that a proportion of 0.0184 or just under 2 percent of all attested words in Greek documentary texts seem to be split.

The total number of words is a rather unsatisfying statistic, however, since only words at the end of a line can be split, making it a good idea to count the number of lines in a text if we want to know the maximum number of possible splits. For this the highest attested line number cannot be used, as some texts are numbered differently, with columns, or separately for the recto and verso. On top of that, split words have the line numbers of the first and last line over which the word is split (e.g., 2–3), making this a text field that cannot easily be converted to only a number.

A further complication is the 1,213 cases where the first number in a line indication of a split word does not equal the second number minus one. A few of these are cases where a single word is split over three lines or more, but most are plain errors, or human-readable abbreviations of the type "27–8." As I thought it would be too time-consuming to clean all of this up, I settled for a solution whereby I counted, for each Trismegistos (TM) text id, the number of different combinations of a text division (e.g., "A" or "Vo" or "col. 1") with line indications, excluding the split-word line indications. On the basis of a table with this number of lines per text, I calculated that the average Greek papyrological documentary text has 15.12 lines. As the median of eight is lower, some very long texts with many lines distort the average—in other words a skewed right distribution. I also calculated the average number of words per text

as 77.27, with a median of 31 (again, because of the long texts).

This means that the average Greek papyrological text has 5.11 words per line (77.27 divided by 15.12), and that the percentage of split words when compared to all last words in a line rises by 5.11 to 0.094 or just under 10 percent.[8] On average, a text contains 1.43 split words.[9] This general figure conceals marked differences per text, however. Of the list of 51,839 texts, no fewer than 31,599 (61 percent) do not split words at all. These texts without splits on average contain 49.23 words and 10.75 lines, but some count several thousands of words (96 texts > 1000 words; up to 34,036 words) and hundreds of lines (223 texts > 100 lines; up to 4.546 lines). It is clear that many of these texts without split words may be lists, a genre which tends to be laid out with a lot of free space.

2 Private and Official Letters as a Test Case

Having tidied the data, I could now seek to answer my research questions with a first test case. Because of the possible variation according to genre, I opted to look at a single type of document: letters. This choice was inspired by the frequency of the genre, but also by the fact that there are different types of letters: private and official. On top of that there was a very practical motivation: while it can very often be difficult to assign a document to a genre, making it time-consuming, I could rely on the work of Joanne Stolk, who went through all Greek documents and assigned them with a genre in the framework of her studies for TM Text Irregularities.[10] Also, in the case of letters, the work is facilitated by the PhD thesis of Delphine Nachtergaele at the University of Ghent, who studied the epistolary formulae in private letters and therefore also implemented a categorization.[11]

---

7 I decided to exclude digits as they are not really words, but in the end the proportion would have remained very similar when including them: 74,069 splits for 4,013,423 tokens or 0.0184.

8 That is, 0.01845532 times 5.11. Or calculated differently: the total number of words divided by the average number of words per line (4,013,423 / 5.11) gives 785,405.68 words that could in theory have been split. This number divided by 73,550 split words results in a percentage of 0.09430668. Unlike above, I have taken the total number of words including digits, as it would be difficult to exclude lines that only consist of digits or other, non-Greek tokens.

9 0.09430668 times 15.12. The number is identical to the division of the number of split words by the number of texts in the corpus: 1.43 (74,069 / 51,839).

10 Building upon the work described in Depauw and Stolk 2015, which resulted in https://www.trismegistos.org/text irregularities.

11 Nachtergaele 2015.

TABLE 12.1   Split words in private and official letters

	Private		Official	
	Average	Median	Average	Median
# lines	15.26	13	18.77	13
# words	62.96	48	89.24	51
	Average		Average	
# words / line	4.13		4.75	
# split words / text	2.84		2.19	
% split last words	18.58 %		11.65 %	

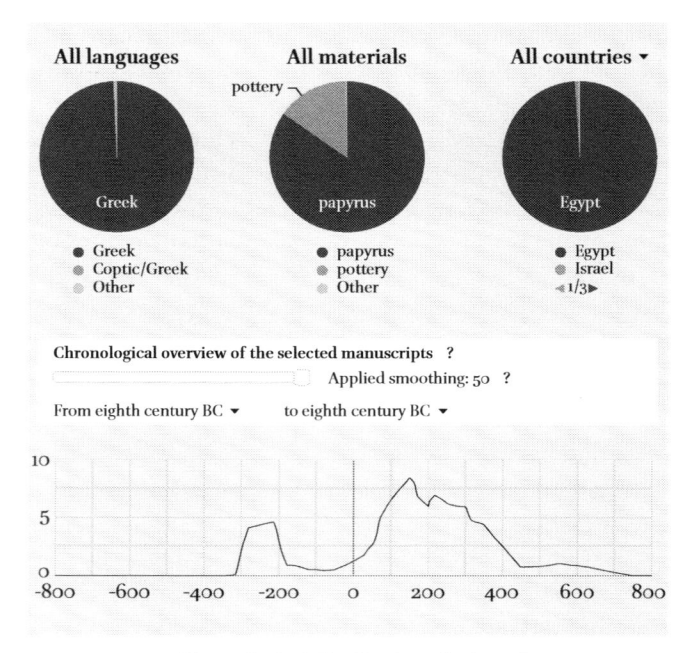

FIGURE 12.1   Chronological distribution of private letters

In TM there are currently 4,199 texts that have been marked as "Letter: private" and 1,863 as "Letter: official." The private letters contain 11,568 split words across a total of 257,152 or 4.5 % (0.045). The official letters contain 4,073 split words across a total of 166,084 or 2.5 % (0.025). The results of repeating the above calculations for the number of lines and words for private and official letters are presented in Table 12.1.

In summary, after this initial count it seems that, at first sight, scribes were less likely to split words in official letters than in private letters. This in turn suggests that splitting words was an undesirable custom. However, I sought to find out whether this is in fact true, or whether something else was at play?

2.1   *Chronological Interference?*

The statistical difference between private and official letters could of course also be explained by a different chronological distribution. If we imagine that avoiding word-splits was a typical early custom that had disappeared over time and that, if the corpus of official letters was on average later in date than the set of private letters, it would look as if the private or official character played a role. In fact, however, only the chronological distribution of the evidence would be to blame.

A look at this distribution of private and official letters (Figs. 12.1–12.2) shows that official letters are about as common in the Ptolemaic as in the Roman period. Roman period private letters, on the other hand, are more frequent than their Ptolemaic counterparts.

It therefore seemed wise to set out the Ptolemaic evidence against the Roman, both for letters in general and for private and official letters separately. If we first look at Ptolemaic versus Roman letters in general, however, in all, the 1,936 Ptolemaic letters count 121,600 words of which 3,587 or 2.9 percent are split, while the 3,490 Roman

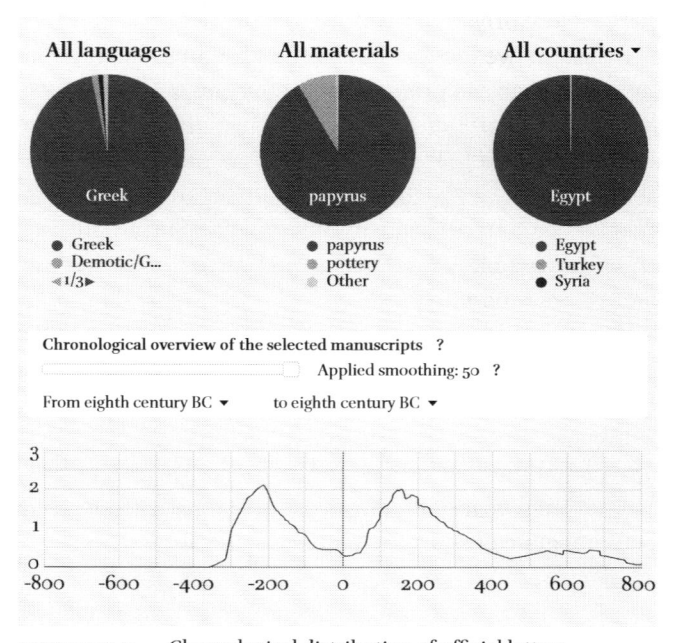

FIGURE 12.2   Chronological distribution of official letters

ones count 264,638 words of which 11,652 or 4.4 percent are split. There is thus a clear chronological difference: Roman period letters tend to contain far more word-splits than the Ptolemaic ones. Table 12.2 summarizes further key points of comparison between the letters.

If we then look at Ptolemaic vs Roman private letters, in all, the 1,179 Ptolemaic private letters count 62,894 words of which 1,952 or 3.1 percent are split, while the

TABLE 12.2 Split words in Ptolemaic versus Roman letters (all types)

	Ptolemaic letters (1,936 total)		Roman letters (3,490 total)	
	Average	Median	Average	Median
# lines	14.62	11	18.06	15
# words	62.81	44	75.83	51
	Average		Average	
# words / line	4.26		3.82	
# split words / text	1.84		3.04	
% split last words	12.57 %		16.82 %	

TABLE 12.3 Split words in Ptolemaic versus Roman private letters

	Ptolemaic private letters		Roman private letters	
	Average	Median	Average	Median
# lines	12.43	10	17.14	15
# words	53.42	40	66.89	51
	Average		Average	
# words / line	4.23		3.69	
# split words / text	1.63		3.40	
% split last words	13.11 %		19.82 %	

TABLE 12.4 Split words in Ptolemaic versus Roman official letters

	Ptolemaic official		Roman official	
	Average	Median	Average	Median
# lines	18.04	14	20.68	14
# words	77.43	49	101.17	52
	Average		Average	
# words / line	4.29		4.17	
# split words / text	2.15		2.23	
% split last words	11.97 %		10.79 %	

TABLE 12.5 Split words in Ptolemaic versus Roman private papyrus letters

	Ptolemaic private papyrus letters		Roman private papyrus	
	Average	Median	Average	Median
# lines	12.47	10	19.10	17
# words	53.74	40	77.68	62
	Average		Average	
# words / line	4.25		3.96	
# split words / text	1.64		3.97	
% split last words	13.17 %		20.78 %	

2,580 Roman ones count 172,570 words of which 9,270 or 5.4 percent are split. There is thus again a clear chronological difference and Roman period private letters tend to contain far more word-splits than the Ptolemaic ones. Table 12.2 summarizes further key points of comparison between the private letters.

Finally, if we look at Ptolemaic vs Roman official letters, in all, the 757 Ptolemaic official letters count 58,616 words of which 1,635 or 2.8 percent are split, while the 910 Roman ones count 92,068 words of which 2,382 or 2.6 percent are split. For official letters, the chronological factor thus seems less important, and the proportion of split words is even higher for the Ptolemaic examples than for their Roman period counterparts. Table 12.4 summarizes further key points of comparison between the official letters.

The picture is thus more complicated than just private against official. Nevertheless, this distinction still seems to be significant, as official letters tend to split less than private ones, regardless of their date. For private letters, chronology seems to play an important role.

One possible explanation might be to assume that a higher proportion of Roman period (and eastern desert) short private letters are on ostraca, thus accounting for this aspect. However, setting out Ptolemaic private letters on papyrus against Roman ones on papyrus still shows the chronological difference. The 1,166 Ptolemaic private letters on papyrus count 62,665 words, of which 1,934 or 3.1 percent are split. The 2,026 Roman ones count 150,383 words, of which 7,890 or 5.25 percent are split. Table 12.5 summarizes further key points of comparison between Ptolemaic and Roman private letters on papyrus.

Based on the initial count offered in section 1, I had noted that scribes were less likely to split words in official letters than in private letters, which suggests that splitting words was an undesirable custom. Asking whether something else was at play, the detailed analysis just offered above suggests that chronology does indeed play a role in the varying frequency of word-splits. Not content that this explains the whole picture, however, I decided to investigate other possible explanations for the difference between private and official letters.

2.2   The Length of (Split) Words

Another way to explain the difference between private and official letters might be a variation in the length of words between the two genres. This is based on the assumption that longer words tend to be split more frequently than shorter ones. At first glance, however, we can see that the average length of words in private letters is 5.33 characters, while in official letters it is 6.19. This means that, if anything, we would expect there to be more split words in official letters. Given these figures, we might ask whether our assumption that longer words tend to be split more is true?

For all papyri, one can calculate the average length of a split word as 8.88, and the average length of a word as 5.98. This does mean that longer words tend to be split more often than shorter ones. Table 12.6 provides a survey of the frequency of splits for words with increasing character lengths.[12] Figure 12.3 presents the data as a bar chart, immediately making it obvious that there is something remarkable about the percentages.

TABLE 12.6   The frequency of split words according to word length

Word length (no. of characters)	# attestations	# split attestations	percentage
2	240,245	178	0.07 %
3	658,088	571	0.09 %
4	311,956	2,345	0.75 %
5	389,333	4,480	1.15 %
6	368,406	6,472	1.76 %
7	439,856	8,645	1.97 %
8	375,567	10,512	2.80 %
9	253,414	11,492	4.53 %
10	189,379	9,973	5.27 %
11	117,254	7,375	6.29 %
12	60,046	4,972	8.28 %
13	25,752	2,766	10.74 %
14	15,897	1,997	12.56 %
15	8,061	1,003	12.44 %
16	3,889	372	9.57 %
17	6,245	186	2.98 %
18	8,58	148	17.25 %
19	182	30	16.48 %
20	90	13	14.44 %
21	21	4	19.05 %
22	17	2	11.76 %
23	69		0.00 %
24	10	1	10.00 %

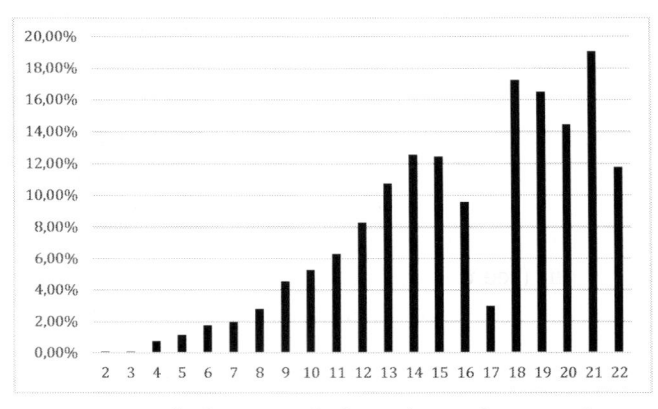

FIGURE 12.3   The frequency of split words according to word length

As I noted above, the assumption is that word-splits become more common as the length of a word increases. After all, it is easier to fit in a shorter word at the end of a line. For words of up to fifteen characters there is indeed a correlation between the number of characters and the frequency of splitting the word over two lines. Yet for words with a character length of sixteen and seventeen there is an unexpected dip in the curve. This mystery is solved by looking at the attestations, but also raises new methodological problems.

As it turns out, of the 3,889 words with sixteen characters, προσδιαγραφόμενα is by far the most common with 999 attestations, and of the 6,245 words with seventeen characters, προσδιαγραφομένων accounts for no fewer than 4,593 cases. As these words are almost always abbreviated to προσδ or even προ, they distort the proportion. Omitting them, the percentages for split words are 12.87 percent for sixteen characters and 11.26 percent for seventeen. No doubt abbreviations of other long words have similar effects on the curve.

2.3   Split or Abbreviate?

This observation raises an interesting methodological problem. In this study I have looked only at the frequency of split words, with the interesting result that word splits seem to be less common in official letters than in private ones. Of course, a word-split can equally be avoided by abbreviating the last word of the line, as is the case for προσδιαγραφόμενα and προσδιαγραφομένων. A thorough study of the phenomenon of splitting would thus also have to look at the frequency of abbreviations of the last

---

12   I have omitted the rows for zero length (41) and also those for single character length. Although zero length is impossible and

a word consisting of a single character cannot be split, there are nonetheless still thirteen cases (out of 283,242 words) where the field contains a hyphen. This illustrates the data are still dirty and need to be cleaned up, which unfortunately was not feasible in the context of this article.

word in a line and quantify how many characters were omitted by means of the abbreviation.

Taking abbreviations into account is only one of the aspects of splitting that warrants further investigation. One could also investigate how many characters are written before the split and how many after. Is there any correlation between syllable structure and the place of the word split (see the Appendix)? Or are characters sometimes crammed in at the end of a line to avoid word splitting? Is there a relation with the evolution of the often very narrow format of the letter or with spelling "mistakes"?

3 Conclusion

My study was just a very preliminary one, yet the quantitative analysis has nevertheless revealed some trends. Specifically, in answer to my research questions, we have seen that Greek scribes did avoid splitting words, that scribes were less likely to split words in official letters than in private letters, and that there is a chronological element to the distribution of word-splitting in Ptolemaic and Roman letters. Finally, the data confirms the assumption that word splitting becomes more frequent in words with more characters, although there are complicating factors at play owing to the use of abbreviations.

The above study could have been improved by a better knowledge of statistics; for example, multivariate regression analysis. I therefore hope someone will pick up the thread where I left it and write a thorough study of word-splits and the layout of text over lines. The material is available through papyri.info or Trismegistos Words, and scholars are increasingly discovering the possibilities of quantitative study building on these materials. The recently developed website Callimachus is a tool which illustrates the possibilities,[13] and no doubt the EVWRIT project will be another landmark in the promising world of digital papyrology.

Appendix: Syllabification

I should have known better than to have assumed that there was no literature on the subject of word-splitting in Ancient Greek (in papyri and elsewhere). Thanks to the peer review, I was alerted to some interesting literature on the subject of syllabification or splitting words by syllables, which has attracted the attention of grammarians since the ancient world and up to this day.

Threatte, along with Mayser and Schmoll, are the standard works for Greek grammar of inscriptions and papyri, and both have sections dealing with the topic.[14] Francis Gignac makes the following observations: there is a universal tendency to end a line with a complete syllable or even word (see the main section of this article); word-splits generally seem to follow the rules as described by the Greek grammarian Herodianus in his work *On Orthography*;[15] seemingly random unsyllabic word-splits are rare, and due to "[s]ubjektive Willkür oder Ungewandtheit der Schreiber, wohl auch aus Rücksicht auf den Raum." The listed examples of these irregularities are partially attributed to these factors: texts are very poorly written; there is insufficient space; ostraca have unusual shapes; or sometimes etymology plays a role. But most papyri follow the rules, meaning that in non-compound words:

1) A vowel between two consonants belongs to the second syllable (and is therefore written on the next line);

2) Geminated consonants are mostly split over two lines;

3) Groups consisting of mute consonants and nasal liquids, as well as κτ, πτ, χθ, φθ, γδ, and μν, are usually combined with the following vowel (and thus written on the next line);

4) Groups of consonants beginning with a nasal liquid are split, and the nasal remains on the first line;

5) Groups of consonants beginning with σ are split, and the σ remains on the first line.

To a large extent, these rules also apply to compound words, often meaning that the etymological origin is not taken into account when splitting. Finally, the rules of syllabification even apply to words that are closely connected to those that follow, such as prepositions or οὐκ.

Lack of time prevents me from going into the various rules for syllabification and the extent to which writers of papyri followed them. But I have looked at the first rule, stipulating that an intervocalic consonant is normally assigned to the line following the split; that is, v-cv rather than vc-v. To eliminate the complications caused by uncertain readings, abbreviations, and signs in lacuna, I have only included split words that contain none of these. I found 23,072 examples of a v-cv split, and only 733 of a vc-v. This means that in no less than 96.92 percent of

---

13 See glg.csic.es/Callimachus/Callimachus_presentation.html.

14 Very elaborate is Threatte 1980, 64–73, which also includes some observations about chronological evolutions. As this article is not about inscriptions, it would lead us too far to compare our evidence with this. I therefore stick to Mayser and Schmoll 1970, 220–24, discussed in what follows. Gignac 1976 seems to remain silent on the subject. For the rules in general, see also Stuart-Jones 1901.

15 TM Author 374 (mid II–III CE): see Lentz 1848, 393ff.

all cases, the rule has been complied with. Moreover, a look at the examples of vc-v shows that many of these are compounds such as ἰσ-αποδῶι, προσ-έχων, or συν-έθεντο,[16] with possible influence of etymological origin. There also seem to be several proper names amongst the exceptions, where similar factors may have played a role; for example, Ψεν-αρψενῆσιν.[17]

To return to the central research question of this article, I investigated the difference between private and official letters. Of the 733 examples that do not follow the rule, 140 or 19.10 percent are private or official letters. This is in line with what could be expected, as the 11,568 split words of private letters and the 4,073 of official letters form 21.27 percent of all split words (see above). Mistakes against the v-cv rule are therefore not more common in letters than in other texts. Although not very marked, there is a difference according to the type of letters: 110 irregular splits of this type are attested in private letters (0.95 percent) versus 30 in official letters (0.73 percent). Although the figures are very low, they point towards a similar conclusion as the main section of this article.

Again, further research is necessary, but the strict compliance with rules as grammarians such as Herodianus have described them is remarkable. It may indeed point to carelessness if no adequate excuse for the irregular split is at hand, and should be considered when the linguistic quality of individual documents is described.[18]

---

16   BGU I 190 (TM 8951 [84–96 CE]), fr. 2, ll. 3–4; BGU I 93 (TM 24885 [II–III CE]), ll. 13–14; BGU I 322 (TM 9054 [216 CE]), ll. 20–21. See also the exceptions to the rule noted in Stuart-Jones 1901, 398 no. 4.

17   BGU II 2023 (TM 9560 [200/201 CE]), ll. 9–10. The village Psenharpsenesis (TM Geo 1955) comes from Egyptian P3-šy-n-Ḥr-p3-šr-n-Ỉs.t or "the lake of Horos the son of Isis." A split after the Greek equivalent of P3-šy-n "the lake of" is more appropriate etymologically.

18   For example, Roger Bagnall and Rafaella Cribiore (2006, 336–37, 346, and 405) state about P. Tebt. 2 413 (TM 28426 [late II CE]) that "spelling and syllabication leave much to be desired," describe the syllabic division of P. Tebt. 2 414 (TM 28427 [II CE]) as "almost nonexistent," point out that the writer of P. Col. 8 212 (TM 17625 [49 CE]) has corrected the end of a line to avoid incorrect syllabic division, and observe trouble with syllabic division at the end of lines in SB 20 14132 (TM 26168 [I CE]).

Reference List

Bagnall, Roger S., and Raffaella Cribiore. 2006. *Women's Letters from Ancient Egypt, 300 BC–AD 800*. Ann Arbor: University of Michigan Press.

Depauw, Mark, and Joanne Stolk. 2015. "Linguistic Variation in Greek Papyri: Towards a New Tool for Quantitative Study." *GRBS* 55: 196–220.

Gignac, Francis Thomas. 1976. *A Grammar of the Greek Papyri of the Roman and Byzantine Periods, Volume I: Phonology*. Milan: Cisalpino-La Goliardica.

Keersmaekers, Alek. 2020. *Variety and Change in the Ancient Greek Papyri: A Corpus-Linguistic Study of the Use of Tense, Aspect and Modality in the Greek Complementation System (3rd century BC–8th century AD)*. PhD diss., KU Leuven.

Keersmaekers, Alek, and Mark Depauw. 2022. "Bringing Together Linguistics and Social History in Automated Text Analysis of Greek Papyri." In *Digital Classics III: Re-Thinking Text Analysis (Classics@)*, edited by Anna Novokhatko. Washington, DC: Center for Hellenic Studies.

Lentz, Augustus. 1848. *Herodiani Technici Reliquae (Grammatici Latini, 3.2.2)*. Leipzig: Teubner.

Mayser, Edwin, and Hans Schmoll. 1970. *Grammatik der Griechischen Papyri aus der Ptolemäerzeit*. Band I.1: Einleitung und Lautlehre. Berlin: De Gruyter.

Nachtergaele, Delphine. 2015. *The Formulaic Language of the Greek Private Papyrus Letters*. PhD diss., University of Ghent. Publication forthcoming in the series Trismegistos Online Publications.

Rössler-Köhler, Ursula. 1985. "Zum Problem der Spatien in altägyptischen Texten: Versuch einer Systematik von Spatientypen." *ASAE* 70: 383–408.

Stuart-Jones, Henry. 1901. "The Division of Syllables in Greek." *CR* 15: 396–401.

Threatte, Leslie. 1980. *The Grammar of Attic Inscriptions, Volume One: Phonology*. Berlin: De Gruyter.

Index of Passages Cited

Literary Texts

Basil of Caesarea
Letter 334 — 57–58

Demetrius
On Style 227.1–3 — 61n53

Gregory of Nazianzus
Letter 51, 4.18–23 — 61n53

Herodianus
On Orthography — 189

John Chrysostom
Letter 68 — 61, 61n59

Julius Victor
Ars Rhetorica (*De Epistolis*) 448.35 — 60, 60n49, 61n60

Libanius
Letter 1123 — 60

Procopius of Gaza
Letter 91 — 22, 22n35

Pseudo-Libanius
Epistolary Styles 2 — 61n53
Epistolary Styles 6 — 61–62n61

Inscriptions

AAES III 6	141n61
AAES III 71	135n24
AAES III 154	136 fig. 154, 136n31
AAES III 203	139n38
AAES III 205	141n66
AAES III 210	139n39
AAES III 212	139n49, 140n50
AAES III 219	139n219, 140n51
AAES III 255	139n41
AAES III 295	141n66
AAES IV 1	131, 131n7, 132n9, 132 fig. 9.1, 133, 135
AAES IV 8	131–133, 131n3, 134n22, 135
AAES IV 14	135–136, 135n28
AAES IV 15	135–136, 135n28, 136 fig. 9.4
AAES IV 19	135n27, 135 fig. 9.3
AAES IV 22 = IGLS II 313	142–143, 142n70, 143 fig. 9.7
AAES IV 23 = IGLS II 314	142–143, 142n70, 143 fig. 9.7
AAES IV 24 = IGLS II 312	135n24, 142–143, 142n70, 143 fig. 9.7
CEG I 355	149n30
IG IV 561	154n75, 162
IG IV 757	151n45
IG IV² 1 40	151n80
IG IV² 1 41	151n80
IG IV² 1 44	149n26
IG IV² 1 99 II	149n26
IG V 2 75	149n28
LSAG² 1990, 162–164, 169, no. 30	153n66
LSAG² 1990, 444–445E = SEG XLI 284	146n1, 163
PPUAES III B.5 1103	141n66
PPUAES III B.5 1150	140n57
PPUAES III B.6 1154	139n49
PPUAES III B.6 1156	139n49
PPUAES III B.6 1169	140n60
PPUAES III B.6 1175	137 fig. 9.6, 138n34
PPUAES III B.6 1176	138n35
PPUAES III B.6 1181	138n36
SEG XI 314 = *LSAG²* 1990, 168, no. 8; 444	154n79
SEG XI 330	162
SEG XI 355	161
SEG XI 373	149n26
SEG XVIII 140	149n30
SEG XXVII 702	149n29
SEG XXIX 652	162
SEG XXX 367	162
SEG XXX 1456	161
SEG XXXIX 1061	162
SEG LVI 419	151n49, 162, 162n165
SEG LXV 2046	161–162

Manuscripts

Patmius 706, fol. 228v — 57n28

Papyri, Ostraca, and Tablets

BGU I 93	190n16
BGU I 190	190n16
BGU I 261	98, 99 fig. 7.14, 100
BGU I 322	190n16
BGU II 380	98n91, 100–101, 101 fig. 7.5
BGU II 385	100
BGU II 602	98, n90, 101
BGU II 610	75
BGU II 668	129n48
BGU III 718	43 fig. 3.1
BGU III 801	100, 109
BGU III 827	98, 98n88, 100, 108n154
BGU IV 1097	100
BGU VII 1544	44n33
BGU VII 1552	44n33
BGU VII 1680	95n63, 96n71 and n74, 97n82, 109
BGU VIII 1753	175
BGU X 1968	126n40
BGU XI 2023	190n17
BGU XIV 2441	126n41
BGU XV 2531	179
BKT III pp. 30–31	115
BKT III pp. 32–33	114, 124
BKT IV pp. 6–47	126n40
BKT VI pp. 55–109	30n6

BKT IX 76 = SB XX 14501	117, 117 fig. 8.6
BKT IX 176	124
ChLA V 284	71n51
ChLA V 285	67, 70–71n51
ChLA XI 472	67, 70
ChLA XVIII 659	79n60
ChLA XXVI 808	79, 79n55
ChLA XLIII 1248	67, 69, 69n35 and n37, 71n57, 75
ChLA XLVII 1404	79n60
ChLA XLVII 1405	79n60
Chr.Wilck. 23 = BGU IV 1035	56, 59
Chr.Wilck. 483	109
Chr.Wilck. 499	97, 109
CPR VII 28	77
CPR IX 68	79n57
CPR XIX 30	58
CPR XXV 11	58n37
CPR XXX 17	58
CPR XXX 20	58
GMP I 10 = P.Rein. I 16 + BKT III pp. 33–34	117, 121
GMP I 13	116
GMP II 5 = P.Tebt. II 273	127, 127 fig. 8.17
GMP II 11 = P.Eleph.Wagner 4	123
Leiden, Rijksmuseum van Oudheden (RMO), inv. no. F 1948/3.5	78 fig. 6.1
MAF inv. 50068	33
MPER N.S. XIII 1	115
MPER N.S. XIII 4 = SB XVI 13002	116
MPER N.S. XIII 8	114
MPER N.S. XIII 9	121
MPER N.S. XIII 10	114
MPER N.S. XIII 14v	115
O.Bankes 14	42
O.Bankes 17	42
O.Bankes 21	42
O.Bawit IFAO 28	48n46
O.Berenike II 167	179
O.BYU Mag. 1–3	51
O.Claud. I 83	44
O.Claud. I 90	44
O.Claud. I 115	44
O.Claud. I 145	47
O.Claud. I 147	47
O.Claud. I 148	47
O.Claud. I 159	47
O.Claud. II 260	41
O.Claud. II 261	41
O.Claud. II 262	41
O.Crum 84	51n52
O.Crum 401	51n52
O.Crum 465	51n52
O.Did. 29	45n38
O.Did. 327	47
O.Did. 328	47, 48 fig. 3.9
O.Did. 339	45, 45 fig. 3.5
O.Did. 343	46 fig. 3.6
O.Did. 360	98, 98n88 and n93, 101
O.Did. 370	47, 48 fig. 3.10
O.Did. 371	47
O.Did. 376	50
O.Did. 386	100n98, 101n105, 108n150 and n154
O.Did. 390	57n20
O.Did. 393	40n17
O.Did. 406	45n41, 47
O.Did. 427	97n86
O.Did. 451	99–101
O.Eleph.DAIK 16	42
O.Eleph.DAIK 32	42–43, 43 fig. 3.3
O.Eleph.DAIK 40	42
O.Eleph.DAIK 42	42
O.Eleph.DAIK 71	42n29
O.Eleph.DAIK 319	48
O.Frange 68	49, 49 fig. 3.14
O.Frange 208	48, 49 fig. 3.11
O.Frange 217	48, 49 fig. 3.12
O.Frange 255	51n52
O.Frange 256	51n52
O.Frange 342	48, 49 fig. 3.13
O.Kellis 145	40
O.Medin.Madi 31	35
O.Mon.Epiph. 380	49, 49n48, 50 fig. 3.16
O.Narm.Dem. III 155–157	50n51
O.Petr.Mus. 4–7	51n56
O.Petr.Mus. 13–16	51n56
O.Sarga 27	40
O.Syene Swiss s/n	44 fig. 3.4
O.Tebt.Pad. 10	177–178
O.Wilck. 7	179
P.Aberd. 10	119
P.Abinn. 1	57n20
P.Abinn. 2	67, 69
P.Abinn. 3	176–177
P.Abinn. 31	176
P.Abinn. 43	57n20
P.Ant. III 135	115
P.Aphrod.Reg.	17n7
P.Babatha 22	19
P.Bad. II 35	98n88 and n89, 100, 107n142 and n143, 109
P.Berl.Möller 13	122, 122 fig. 8.11
P.Berol. inv. 25721	56
P.Bingen 28	30n10
P.Bingen 128	32–33, 32n29
P.Brem. 64	109
P.Brit.Col. inv. 1	34
P.Cair.Masp. I 67002	18, 24, 25 fig. 1.9
P.Cair.Masp. I 67006	25 fig. 1.8
P.Cair.Masp. I 67019 recto	24
P.Cair.Masp. I 67030	26n47
P.Cair.Masp. I 67031	26n47
P.Cair.Masp. I 67064	58n30
P.Cair.Masp. I 67066	59n42
P.Cair.Masp. I 67068	59
P.Cair.Masp. I 67069	56
P.Cair.Masp. I 67092	18
P.Cair.Masp. I 67131	25n46
P.Cair.Masp. II 67138	17n6
P.Cair.Masp. II 67139	17n61
P.Cair.Masp. II 67141	123n34
P.Cair.Masp. II 67242	23
P.Cair.Masp. III 67280	26n47, 27 fig. 1.11

P.Cair.Masp. III 67281	26
P.Cair.Masp. III 67303	24 fig. 1.7
P.Cair.Masp. III 67320 = ChLA XLI 1193	26n47
P.Cair.Masp. III 67321	26n47
P.Cair.Masp. III 67325	18n9 and n10
P.Cair.Masp. III 67341	18n10
P.Cair.Zen. I 59021	126n40
P.Cair.Zen. I 59057	19
P.Chic. 4v	115
P.Col. VIII 212	97, 190
P.Col. VIII 215	98n88, 99, 107, 108n154
P.Col. X 272	18
P.Coll.Youtie I 4	115
P.Coll.Youtie I 30	32
P.Coll.Youtie I 51	34
P.Coll.Youtie I 52	34–35, 90n18
P.Dubl. 32 = SB I 517	18
P.Dura 26	19
P.Dura 56	67, 69
P.Dura 56 B	69n39
P.Dura 56 C	69n39
P.Eleph. 1	19
P.Erl. 55	26n47
P.Euphrates	19
P.Fam.Tebt. 15	175
P.Fam.Tebt. 22	180
P.Fay. 132	34
P.Flor. I 2	31n15
P.Flor. II 215	180
P.Flor. II 229	180
P.Flor. II 259	21n30
P.Flor. III 292	26n47
P.Flor. III 332	93–94, 94n49, 96–97
P.Fouad. I 76	34
P.Fouad. I 88	58n30 and n37
P.Fouad. I 89	58n37, 59n39
P.FuadUniv. 7	34
P.Gen. II 1 74	93–94, 109
P.Giss. 57	58n30, 59
P.Giss. 94	179
P.Giss. 97	98, 107
P.Giss.Apoll. 1	97
P.Giss.Apoll. 5	99
P.Giss.Apoll. 8	94, 108
P.Giss.Apoll. 10	108
P.Giss.Apoll. 13	108
P.Giss.Apoll. 15	97, 108n150
P.Giss.Apoll. 19	109
P.Giss.Apoll. 21	107, 107n136
P.Grenf. II 112	30n6
P.Hamb. I 68	19, 23, 23n37
P.Hamb. II 192	95, 95 fig. 7.2, 97, 109
P.Harr. I 46	115
P.Haun. II 25	59
P.Heid. inv. 1639	34
P.Heid. IV 295	30n6
P.Herm. 17	55
P.Herm. 23	79n57
P.Horak 3	30n6
P.Ital. I 1	81, 81n66
P.Ital. I 2	78n52, 81, 81n66
P.Ital. I 3	81, 81n66
P.Ital. I 8	81
P.Ital. II 31	79n55
P.Ital. II 35	82n72
P.Ital. II 37	82n72
P.Ital. II 47–48	81–82, 82n70
P.Ital. II 50	81
P.Ital. II 53	81, 82n67
P.Köln. I 56	98–99, 101
P.Köln. I 57	34
P.Köln. V 215	30n6
P.Köln. VI 280	34
P.Köln. X 410	120
P.Köln. XI 437	117, 117 fig. 8.5
P.Land.List I–II	18n8
P.Laur. I 8	181
P.Laur. III 102v	181
P.Laur. III 106	181
P.Laur. III 111	26n47
P.Leid.Inst. 42	98n93, 100, 101n103
P.Lips. I 123	74, 82
P.Lips. II 145	32
P.Lond. V 1663	26n47
P.Lond. V 1730	20, 20n24
P.Lond. V 1731	20
P.Lond. V 1736–37	20n23
P.Lond.Lit. 132	29
P.Lond.Lit. 165	129n46
P.Mert. II 63	98, 99 fig. 7.3
P.Mert. II 81	94, 94n53
P.Mert. II 82	94, 94 fig. 7.1, 94n53, 96n78, 97, 100n100
P.Mert. II 83	95–96, 109
P.Messeri 33	36, 36n44, 37 fig. 2.3
P.Messeri 45	25n46
P.Mich. III 202	98, 98n90, 100
P.Mich. III 221	102–104, 102 fig. 7.6, 108n153
P.Mich. VIII 464	100n101
P.Mich. VIII 473	109
P.Mich. VIII 507	96–97
P.Mich. VIII 514	103 fig. 7.7, 104, 108n154, 109
P.Mich. XIII 660 + 661 + SB XVI 12542	25
P.Mich. XVII 753, Cr + Dr	119 fig. 8.8
P.Mich. XVII 753, Er	118 fig. 8.7
P.Mich. XVII 753, Fr	119 fig. 8.9
P.Mich. XVII 758	118
P.Mich. XVIII 768	126n41
P.Mich. XVIII 794	67, 71, 71n56
P.Michael. 46	23n47
P.Michael. 54	23n47
P.Mon.Epiph. 431	49, 50 fig. 3.15
P.Monts.Roca IV 72	42n28
P.Münch. I 2	20n23
P.Narm. 2006 15	50n51
P.Neph. 1	59n41
P.Oslo III 157	34
P.Oxf. 19	98, 100–101, 101n107
P.Oxy. I 34v	31n17
P.Oxy. I 45	126n40
P.Oxy. I 110	34
P.Oxy. I 111	34
P.Oxy. I 114	99
P.Oxy. I 115	97n82, 109

P.Oxy. I 116	93
P.Oxy. I 123	59n42
P.Oxy. II 237	18, 58n37
P.Oxy. III 523	34
P.Oxy. III 524	34
P.Oxy. IV 661v	115
P.Oxy. IV 747	34
P.Oxy. VI 926	34
P.Oxy. VI 927	34
P.Oxy. VI 930	94
P.Oxy. VI 963	109
P.Oxy. VIII 1088	121, 123, 123 fig. 8.12, 125, 126n41, 127
P.Oxy. VIII 1100	32, 32n26 and n27
P.Oxy. IX 1214	35
P.Oxy. IX 1217	93, 95, 97, 97n82, 108, 108n150
P.Oxy. X 1291	95–96
P.Oxy. X 1295	94n50, 97
P.Oxy. XII 1484	34
P.Oxy. XII 1485	34
P.Oxy. XII 1486	35
P.Oxy. XII 1487	34–35
P.Oxy. XII 1579	34
P.Oxy. XII 1580	34
P.Oxy. XII 1581	94n54, 95
P.Oxy. XIV 1679	109
P.Oxy. XIV 1755	34
P.Oxy. XIV 1758	96, 96n69
P.Oxy. XIV 1773	94, 94n49, 96n71
P.Oxy. XVI 1834	59
P.Oxy. XVI 1841	59n43
P.Oxy. XVI 1845	60, 60 fig. 4.3
P.Oxy. XVI 1857	59n40
P.Oxy. XVI 1858	61
P.Oxy. XVI 1859	58, 60–61, 60 fig. 4.4
P.Oxy. XVI 1860	59, 59 fig. 4.2, 61
P.Oxy. XVI 1862	59n43, 60n46
P.Oxy. XVII 2108	30n14
P.Oxy. XVII 2147	34
P.Oxy. XVIII 2182	46 fig. 3.7
P.Oxy. XX 2265	69–70, 71n57
P.Oxy. XXXI 2592	34
P.Oxy. XXXI 2603	61
P.Oxy. XXXIII 2664	31
P.Oxy. XXXIII 2678	34
P.Oxy. XXXIV 2705	32
P.Oxy. XXXIV 2707	32–33
P.Oxy. XXXIV 2717	42n28
P.Oxy. XXXVI 2789	94n52, 96n74, 107
P.Oxy. XXXVI 2791	34
P.Oxy. XXXVI 2792	34–35
P.Oxy. XL 2924	31, 31n21 and n22
P.Oxy. XLI 2950 = ChLA XLVII 1414	31
P.Oxy. XLII 3059	94, 96n69
P.Oxy. XLII 3067	61
P.Oxy. XLIII 3094	109
P.Oxy. XLIII 3129	65n5, 67–68, 67n15 and n16, 68n21, 70n44
P.Oxy. XLIV 3193	126n40
P.Oxy. XLIV 3202	34
P.Oxy. XLVIII 3392	42n28
P.Oxy. XLIX 3501	35
P.Oxy. L 3577	65–68, 65n2,n3,n4 and n5, 66n9 and n12, 68n20 and n21
P.Oxy. L 3579	67–68, 67n19 and n19, 68n21, 70n44
P.Oxy. LI 3616	31, 31n18
P.Oxy. LII 3654v + II 234v	120
P.Oxy. LII 3693	34, 35n37
P.Oxy. LII 3694	35
P.Oxy. LV 3793	67–68, 68n24 and n26–28, 70–71, 70n44
P.Oxy. LV 3794	67–68, 68n25–27, 70n45
P.Oxy. LVI 3866	18
P.Oxy. LIX 4008	58
P.Oxy. LXIII 4369	67, 70, 70n46–48
P.Oxy. LXIII 4394	23–24
P.Oxy. LXVI 4539	34
P.Oxy. LXVI 4540	34
P.Oxy. LXVI 4541	34
P.Oxy. LXVI 4542	34
P.Oxy. LXVI 4543	35
P.Oxy. LXVIII 4670v	31
P.Oxy. LXVIII 4671	31
P.Oxy. LXVIII 4696	71n54
P.Oxy. LXXIV 4975	121
P.Oxy. LXXIV 4977	114, 121, 127, 127 fig. 8.18
P.Oxy. LXXIV 4978	115
P.Oxy. LXXV 5053	43 fig. 3.2
P.Oxy. LXXV 5056	34
P.Oxy. LXXV 5057	33–34
P.Oxy. LXXV 5062	94, 94n54, 97n80, 109
P.Oxy. LXXIX 5215	32–33
P.Oxy. LXXIX 5216	32–33
P.Oxy. LXXIX 5217	32–33
P.Oxy. LXXIX 5218	32–33
P.Oxy. LXXX 5243	114
P.Oxy. LXXX 5246	115
P.Oxy. LXXX 5247	115, 121
P.Oxy. LXXX 5248	115
P.Oxy. LXXX 5249	114
P.Oxy. LXXX 5250	121, 126
P.Oxy.Hels. 45	100
P.Panop. 19	18n9
P.Paramone 3	114
P.Petaus. 29	99
P.Petra I 2	23n40
P.Petra I 39	23n41
P.Petra III 20	20n26
P.Petra IV 41	20n25
P.Petra V 55	20n26
P.Petra V 78	26n47
P.Prag. I 67	181
P.Prag.Varcl. II 2	181
P.Princ. II 67	93, 96
P.Princ. III 155r = SB XIV 12086	128, 128 fig. 8.19
P.Princ. III 155v	126 fig. 8.16, 127
P.Rain.Cent. 125	56, 56 fig. 4.1
P.Rain.Unterricht 77	62
P.Rain.Unterricht 79	62
P.Ross.Georg. V 57v	115
P.Ryl. I 29	114
P.Ryl. II 232	94n50, 109n161
P.Ryl. II 243	93, 94n54, 97

P.Ryl. III 531	114, 120, 120n27
P.Sakaon 1 = P.Strasb. Gr. 1 42	75
P.Sel.Warga. 12	98, 107n143
PSI inv. 4361	34, 35, 35 fig. 2.1, 36 fig. 2.2
PSI III 177	109
PSI III 237	58n37
PSI VI 718 = SB XXVI 16458	118, 119, 120 fig. 8.10
PSI VII 742	59n41
PSI IX 1026	19
PSI IX 1042	94, 96n69, 97, 108
PSI IX 1080	95–96, 96n69, 109
PSI X 1138	179
PSI X 1180 = SB XXVIII 17134	121, 123, 124 fig. 8.13 and 8.14, 125–127, 126 fig. 8.15
PSI XII 1239	18
PSI XIII 1345	58n30
PSI XIV 1406	31n16
PSI XIV 1418	98, 101
PSI XV 1543	35, 35 fig. 2.1
PSI XVI 1576	30, 30n6
PSI Congr.xx 5	116, 116 fig. 8.4, 119, 125
PSI Congr.xxi 3	115, 116 fig. 8.3, 124–125, 128
P.Sijp. 23	67, 69, 69n30
P.Strasb.gr.inv. 1633	18n10
P.Stras. IV 279	58n30
P.Stras. V 404	180
P.Stras. V 408	179
P.Tebt. II 413	98n93, 100, 100n98, 190n18
P.Tebt. II 414	100n96, 190n18
P.Tebt. III.1 817	126n40
P.Tebt. III.2 972	126n40
P.Tebt.Tait. 43	121
P.Vat.Aphrod. 3 B+D	23
P.Yale inv. 1443 = Pap.Congr. XXIV pp. 427–33	115, 155 fig. 8.2
P.Yale I 85	34
Pap.Choix. 13	109
Pap.Flor. XLIV 3	115
PGM II 8	125
SB I 4639 = P.Berol. inv. 11532	30, 65n7
SB III 6264	98, 109
SB IV 7433 = P.Ross.Georg. V 30	57
SB IV 7438	58n30
SB V 7572	98–99, 98n92, 101, 107n136
SB V 7743	107
SB V 7745	33, 35
SB V 8027	100, 100n98, 108n154
SB V 8028 = ChLA X 464	26n47
SB V 8248 = OGIS II 665	32
SB VI 9102	24, 30n7
SB VI 9120	94, 96n71
SB VI 9122	104, 105 fig. 7.8, 107
SB VI 9271	94 fig. 54, 97, 107
SB VI 9610	107n142, 109
SB VIII 9860	116, 118, 120, 125
SB X 10270	179
SB XII 10907	42n30
SB XII 10915	42n30
SB XII 10929	31
SB XII 11230	129n48
SB XIV 11580	100
SB XIV 11585	98n89, 99
SB XIV 11652	34
SB XIV 11882	56
SB XIV 11942	29
SB XIV 11944	34
SB XIV 11964	114, 125
SB XIV 12003	181
SB XIV 12142 = P.Coll.Youtie II 87r	123
SB XIV 12175	114, 119, 126
SB XVI 12326	109
SB XVI 12511	34
SB XVI 12573	59n41
SB XVI 12589	95
SB XVI 12596	34
SB XVI 12745	77
SB XVI 12980	61n57
SB XVI 12981	107
SB XVI 13080	115
SB XVIII 13310 = P.Haun. III 47	114
SB XVIII 13111	59n43
SB XVIII 13266	79n57
SB XVIII 13591	107
SB XVIII 13875	34
SB XX 14132	98, 101n103, 190n18
SB XX 14241	56
SB XX 14503	34
SB XXII 15358 = P.Oxy. I 181 descr.	34
SB XXII 15453	95n79, 100, 100n98
SB XXIV 15917	114, 114 fig. 8.1
SB XXIV 15927	181
SB XXVI 16351	59
SB XXVIII 17140	116, 125, 127
SPP XX 1	18
SPP XX 248	78
SPP XX 259	78
SPP XXII 11	126n40
SPP XXII 44	126n40
T.Alb. 7	82n73

Index of Subjects

Abbreviation   7, 62, 78, 80*n*63, 113*n*2, 118, 121, 125, 126*n*40, 126*n*41, 127–128, 128*n*44, 129*n*48 and *n*49, 139, 151, 184–185, 188–189
Acronym   6, 139–142, 139*n*46
Address   55–56, 58–62, 60*n*45 and *n*47, 71, 94*n*57, 100, 174, 179–181
Addressee   5, 7, 11, 22, 25, 54–62, 57*n*28, 59*n*39, 60*n*45, 61*n*54, 96, 99–101, 106–108, 108*n*152, 158, 172, 175, 180
Amphora   41*n*21, 48, 48*n*45, 133, 140, 159
Ancient medicine   113*n*5
Annotation (in a document)   42, 81*n*66, 113*n*2, 126*n*41
   Digital   4, 10–11, 128, 185
Argive plain   149, 149*n*26, 153*n*73, 160, 160*n*149 and *n*154
Aspiration   6, 146–153, 150*n*36, 151*n*45 and *n*51, 156, 156*n*102
Asyndeton   93, 98, 103–105, 104*n*121, 107, 109
Attic alphabet   149
Authenticity
   of the document   5, 65–66, 69
   position   66–71
Autograph   56, 60–61, 70, 74, 106, 108*n*156, 171, 179, 179*n*32

'Barbarian' document   72
Belonging (script of)   6, 133–137, 141
Bilingual
   Communities   152
   Documents   10*n*69, 50, 133
   Notaries   182
Blank space   5–6, 9, 21, 34, 42, 55, 75, 79, 80, 92–93, 95–97, 95*n*66, 97*n*84, 99, 101–104, 114–115, 118, 120–121, 127. *See also vacat*
Body (of the letter)   22, 45, 47, 55–59, 62, 65, 69–70, 92, 95–96, 96*n*77, 98–101, 103–105, 108
Bronze plates   148, 153*n*68, 156*n*97
Bronze plaque   153, 156, 156*n*97, 158, 161, 163
Bronze prize   146, 148*n*16, 149, 153, 156, 158–160, 159*n*138, 162

Catalogue   72–73, 73*n*8,*n*13*n*16, and *n*17, 76–77, 113, 113*n*2, 120*n*27, 123
Circus programme   32–33
Chancery   5, 30*n*7, 59, 65–71, 68*n*21, 77. *See also style*
Clause combining   92–93, 93*n*47
Codex   7, 17–18, 18*n*10, 57*n*28, 76–78, 81, 114–115, 118–119, 124–125, 126*n*41
Column (of a document)   18–19, 20*n*25 and *n*26, 21, 21*n*32, 23, 25, 27, 30, 33, 34, 43–44, 73–78, 80–81, 81*n*66, 114–123, 126*n*41, 127–128, 185
Concave side   40–41, 40*n*13–16, 46*n*42, 100
Convention   5, 17, 27, 154, 173*n*18
Convex side   40–41, 40*n*13,*n*15–16 and *n*18, 42*n*31, 51
Consular year   65–71, 68*n*26
Contamination   150–152, 154
Coptic   10, 41–42, 42 table 3.1, 50
Copy   19, 20*n*26, 25*n*46, 31, 31*n*19 and *n*25, 69, 75, 81, 81*n*66, 94, 117, 154
Copying (act of)   21*n*26, 45*n*38, 62, 81*n*66, 82, 107, 118–119, 124, 153, 179
Copyist   81*n*66, 116, 120*n*26, 122–123
Cutting (of a document)   17, 40–41, 135
curator   68

data clause   66–71
Deed   18*n*10, 23–24, 25*n*45
Deference   5, 54–56, 58–60, 62
Demotic   7, 50, 128, 184
Diacritical sign   5, 124

Dialect   143, 154–155, 172
   Argive   149, 152, 156*n*100 and *n*101
   Greek   146, 152, 155, 156*n*99, 157
   Middle Aramaic   134
Dictation   9, 89*n*14, 102, 105, 108, 110, 179
Dimension (of ancient artefacts)   5, 29, 31–33, 35–37, 44, 65, 68, 71
diple obelismene   114, 116, 118–119, 126
Diplomatics   21, 27
Direction (of the writing)   6–9, 40–41, 41*n*23, 51, 97*n*82, 135, 137, 141–143, 158
Discourse planning   90, 93–110
   minimal vs. maximal   90
Docket   66, 70, 82
Dorsal note   74, 82, 82*n*72 and *n*73
Dot   117, 147*n*9, 158
   High - (*ano stigme*)   115, 124
   Double - (*dikolon*)   115, 124
   Punched   148*n*20, 153
Double document   19
ductus   5, 66*n*8, 70, 148*n*18, 153, 158

Education   1, 6, 9, 51, 57, 60, 89–90, 106, 172, 180
   Graphic   5, 60–62
   Visual   61
Epichoric alphabet   146, 154*n*80, 158
epistalma   25–26, 25*n*44 and *n*45, 26 fig. 1.10
Epistolography   22, 55, 58, 60*n*52, 61*n*56
Estrangela script   134

Farewell   46*n*43, 47, 93
   Formula   45, 47, 65–69, 71
   Greeting   45, 96, 99–100, 102*n*115, 104. *See also Greetings*
Format (of a document)
   Horizontal   18–20, 24, 35, 41–42, 45, 47, 49, 55
   Square   23, 35, 42, 104
   Standard   17, 68
   Tabular   75, 77, 81
   Vertical   7, 18–20, 22, 35, 45, 47, 49, 55
Formula
   "One-God"   140
      valedicendi   21, 55
Formulaic phrase   92–93, 96, 107–108, 114, 120, 125, 126
Framing
   Macro-level   92–97, 100–104, 107
   Meso-level   92–93, 95–96, 99–100, 103–105
   Micro-level   92–95, 98, 103–105
Function
   Appellative   107, 109–110
   Descriptive   107–110
   Expressive   107–110
   Ideational   3, 91, 106–107, 109
   Interpersonal   3, 91, 106, 106*n*134, 107, 109
   Textual   3, 106, 106*n*134

Genre   5, 7–9, 20–21, 23–25, 23*n*39, 27, 41–42, 42 table 3.1, 44, 51, 54, 96, 113, 155, 155*n*83, 172, 176–178, 178 table 11.4 and 11.5, 180, 182, 184–185, 188
Grammar   3, 10, 76, 76*n*34, 91, 94*n*56, 142, 154–155, 177, 189
Grammeme   156–158, 161

Grapheme   93, 156–158, 161
Greek   2, 5–10, 9*n*64, 23, 29–30, 36, 41–42, 42 table 3.1, 50–51, 56,
     57*n*20, 62, 65–67, 69–71, 73, 75, 76*n*32, 77*n*41 and *n*43, 82, 83*n*75,
     90*n*18, 91–93, 106–107, 110, 113, 113*n*2 and *n*3, 132–144, 135*n*29, 146,
     147*n*8 and *n*9, 149, 152, 153*n*73, 154–155, 155*n*83 and *n*91, 156*n*100,
     157, 159, 161, 171, 174, 177, 180*n*39, 181, 184–185, 184*n*2, 185*n*8, 189,
     190*n*17. *See also under Dialect; Inscriptions; Greek monumental*
     epigraphy
Greek monumental epigraphy   6, 132–135, 135*n*29, 137, 142
Greetings   32, 45–47, 55, 58*n*33, 60, 60*n*47, 65–66, 68–71, 96–97,
     97*n*83, 99–100, 102*n*115, 103*n*117, 108, 108*n*149,*n*152,*n*153 and
     *n*156. *See also farewell greeting*
    Opening   59, 96–97, 100–101, 103–105, 108

Handbook   40*n*12, 60, 113, 126*n*41
Handshift   66*n*8, 67, 69
Handwriting   1, 5, 9, 45, 55–57, 57*n*20, 59, 61–62, 61*n*59, 65–66, 66*n*8,
     68, 77, 91, 93, 103*n*120, 109, 116, 123, 176, 179
Heading (of a document)   25, 36, 65, 118, 120–123, 121*n*29, 174, 178, 180
Height (of the roll)   18, 21, 23, 30
Hera's games   149, 156, 160, 161
Hydria   146–147, 147*n*4, 147–148*n*10, 153, 153*n*70, 159–160, 160–161*n*156
Hyperarchaism   6, 152, 161
Hypercorrection   6–7, 11, 152–155, 161, 171–174, 171*n*4, 173*n*16, 177–178, 182

Identity   5–6, 65, 132–133, 137, 140, 142, 161, 161*n*159
Idiolect   9, 154, 172, 178–182
Ink   3, 33, 40, 65, 69, 125
Inscription
    Aramaic   134
    Argive   146, 149, 150*n*34, 153, 157, 160*n*156
    Greek   6, 133–143, 146–161, 157*n*116
    Latin   76*n*36, 135, 137, 141, 146*n*2
    Syriac   131–135, 132*n*10, 134*n*20, 137–138, 140–142
Inventory (ancient)   40, 43–44, 73*n*17, 76, 79
Involvement   90, 106, 108
Iota adscript   171–182
Irregularity   51, 58, 151*n*50, 152, 154

Koronis   6, 114, 116–119, 118 fig. 8.7

Label   40, 81, 113, 121, 158, 178
Latin   2, 5–6, 10, 20*n*26, 31, 31*n*19, 65–71, 72, 73*n*9 and *n*17, 75–76,
     76*n*33,*n*34 and *n*36, 77*n*41 and *n*43, 78–82, 80*n*64, 134–135, 137,
     141, 142*n*68, 147*n*9, 150, 156, 173*n*18
Latin papyri   76
Layout   1, 3–7, 4*n*38, 9, 17, 17*n*1, 20*n*25, 21, 22 fig. 1.5 and 1.6, 23, 25*n*46,
     26–27, 31–32, 55–56, 75–76, 81, 97, 97*n*79, 111, 113, 113*n*2, 114–116,
     118–120, 122–123, 189
lebes   146, 147*n*4, 148, 153, 153*n*70, 159, 159*n*140, 161*n*156
Legibility   23, 48, 54, 56–57, 76*n*34, 123
Length
    of the document   21
    of the lines   21, 25, 99, 116, 123
    of the text   21, 23–25, 27, 41, 177
    of words   7, 184, 188, 188 table 12.6 and fig. 12.3
Letter
    Cover   74
    Festal   27, 30
    (Graeco-)Roman   55, 60*n*47, 186, 189
    Late Antique   5, 45, 54–62
    Literary   60, 61*n*59

Official   5, 8*n*54, 19–21, 27, 57, 65–66, 69–70, 184–190, 186 fig. 12.2
Philophronetic   108, 108*n*149 and *n*150
Private   21, 54*n*5, 58, 61, 173, 178, 185–187, 186 fig. 12.1, 189–190
Ptolemaic   97, 186
Requesting   61–62*n*61
Women's   1, 6, 9, 89–110, 106–107*n*136, 108*n*152
Letter carrier   59
Lexeme   184
Line ending   78*n*49, 98, 99 fig. 7.3, 104
Line filler   92–94, 94 fig. 7.1, 98, 103–104, 114, 118, 120–121
Linguistic standard   152–155, 152*n*60, 154*n*78
List (ancient)   5, 19*n*14, 36, 36*n*45, 39–40, 43–44, 50*n*52, 72–83, 73*n*17,
     76*n*32 and *n*36, 78*n*49 and *n*50, 79*n*55 and *n*57, 80*n*64, 81*n*66,
     82*n*70, 83*n*75, 113, 116, 120*n*26, 122–124, 127–128, 138, 171, 178, 181
Literacy   8, 45, 90, 106, 110, 153, 173
Liturgical service   30–31, 31*n*15
Liturgy   51, 51*n*53, 133, 140–142
Lycopolis papyri   20

Magical text   8*n*46, 40*n*12, 51, 125
Margin   5, 21, 40, 42, 44–46, 44*n*33, 45*n*38 and *n*41, 46–47*n*43, 48, 60,
     65–71, 65*n*5, 67*n*16, 68*n*26, 69*n*35, 93–94, 97, 97*n*83, 99–105,
     100*n*95, 101*n*105, 114–115, 118–119, 122, 127, 142–143
Materiality   1, 1*n*2, 5, 7–8, 10, 39, 44*n*35, 45, 51, 54*n*4, 113*n*3, 157
Medical papyri   6, 113, 113 n.2 and n.3, 120*n*27, 123, 125, 126*n*40. *See also*
     ancient medicine
Miaphysitism   132–134, 140–142, 141*n*64
Mistake   20*n*24, 81*n*66, 148*n*18, 152–153, 171, 174, 177
Monogram   6, 78, 78*n*48, 114, 119, 121, 125–128, 126*n*40, 129*n*48
Multilingualism   2–3, 9, 133, 142, 142*n*68
Multimodality   3–4, 6–7, 9–10, 54, 92, 102, 110
    multi-modal discourse segmentation   92–93

Notarial office   17, 23
Notary   23–24, 27, 72, 81*n*66, 182. *See also bilingual notaries*
Numeral   74, 80, 82–83, 151, 156*n*98, 157, 171, 175, 177

Orality   90–91
Opistographic document   40
Orthography   6, 93, 102, 102*n*113, 134*n*22, 143, 154–55, 171–172, 173*n*18,
     174, 176, 179, 179*n*32, 180*n*39, 182, 189

Page setup   41–42, 45, 49, 51
Palaeography   66, 76, 76*n*34, 77*n*41, 80, 97*n*79, 116, 148*n*13, 153*n*68, 158
'paléographie signifiante'   4–5, 17, 54
Paragraphos   6, 96–97, 101, 114–123, 127
Paraliterary   2, 6, 113
Paratext/paratextual   6, 8*n*48, 113–114, 113*n*1 and *n*2, 118, 122,
     128–129*n*46
Parchment   70, 76, 77*n*41, 79, 79*n*55 and *n*59, 114–115, 119, 124
Party invitation   5, 33–36, 33*n*36, 90*n*18
Perfibral   7, 18, 18 fig. 1.1, 20–21, 20–21*n*26, 23, 23*n*46, 26–27
Politeness theory   4*n*32, 5, 10, 55, 55*n*6, 62
Postscript/*postscriptum*   42, 45*n*41, 46, 46–47*n*43, 60
Potsherd   2, 5, 7, 39–41, 44–45, 45*n*38, 48, 51, 93
    Concave side of the   40–41, 40*n*13–16, 46*n*42, 100
    Convex side of the   40–41, 40*n*13,*n*15–16 and *n*18, 42*n*31, 51
Pottery   5, 39–40, 41*n*23, 41, 48, 50–51
    Choice of   39–41
    Local   40, 40*n*11 and *n*12
    Imported   40, 40*n*11
    Type of   39, 42, 47

Power (in Roman Egypt)   3, 30, 32, 37
praeses   26*n*47, 27, 65–67, 68*n*21, 69–71, 70*n*48, 71*n*52
Prefect   24, 30–31, 31*n*16,*n*17 and *n*25, 32, 35, 65–71, 68*n*21, 82*n*71, 109
Prescript   21 fig. 1.4, 22, 55–56, 56*n*13, 62, 97, 104
    Hypomnematic   27
Prescription   6, 113–127, 113*n*3, 120*n*27, 126*n*41
Proceedings (legal)   25–26, 25*n*46, 109, 178
Production   1, 7, 27, 40–41, 44*n*33, 47, 125, 148, 154, 157*n*114, 159–160
    of documents   26, 39–41, 40*n*18, 42*n*30, 50–51
    of letters   45
    of lists   44
    of receipts   118
Proof of delivery   74
prostagma   26, 26*n*47
Protocol   81, 81*n*66
protome   146, 148*n*10, 153, 159–160
Public archive   23
Public display   30–31, 155*n*82
"Punctuating" sign   147*n*9

Receipts   5, 7, 18, 18*n*10, 20, 33, 47, 48*n*46, 51, 69, 74–75, 101, 101*n*107, 126*n*40, 175, 177–178
    for beer   33
    Tax   5, 18*n*9, 20–21, 20*n*26, 26*n*48, 39–40, 40*n*12, 41*n*19 and *n*21, 42–43, 42*n*28, 43 fig. 3.1–3.3, 50–51, 77, 172, 175, 177–178, 182
receptarium   114, 116, 117, 120–121, 124
Regularity   40, 40*n*9, 54, 56–57, 158
Request   5, 8, 20–21, 25–26, 25*n*45, 54–55, 54*n*5, 57–58, 58*n*31 and *n*33, 60–62, 61–62*n*61, 95, 96, 98–99, 105, 107–109, 107*n*145, 133, 177
Respect   55–58, 61, 108, 180
Roll   17–19, 21, 23, 25, 27, 29–30, 35, 65, 72, 74–77, 81–82, 81*n*66, 116, 120, 122*n*32, 123
Roman cursive   80
Roman Near East   134, 143

Scribal
    Practice   39, 40*n*18, 43, 45, 46*n*43, 50–51
    Preferences   182
Scribe   2, 5, 9, 20*n*23, 20–21*n*27, 27, 39–41, 40*n*12 and *n*18, 43–45, 44*n*33, 45*n*38, 48, 50–51, 56–57, 59–60, 62, 72, 74–75, 78, 81–83, 81*n*66, 89, 90, 97*n*84, 102–108, 104*n*122, 105*n*123, 115, 118, 134, 153, 161*n*158, 172, 174, 176–177, 179, 179*n*32, 181–182, 184, 186–187, 189
    's posture   40, 44
    Experience of the   41
    professional   57*n*20, 62, 90–91, 102
Scripteme   156–158, 161
Scripturology   6, 146, 146*n*3, 156
Seal   42, 94
Semiosis   89, 92
    Semiotic marker   120
    Semiotic resource   3–5, 7, 9, 29, 37, 54, 89–92, 90*n*24, 101–102
Sender   3, 5, 7, 11, 55–56, 58–62, 59*n*39, 60 fig. 4.3, 65–71, 74, 90*n*18, 108, 146, 171–172, 177
"Series" of ostraca   39, 50–51, 51*n*53
Signature   42, 42*n*29, 158
Shape (of the document)   2, 8, 18, 27, 39–42, 40*n*8,*n*9 and *n*18, 41*n*26, 44–45, 48, 51, 97, 104

Slash (sign)   44, 115–116, 126
Small document   5, 29–30, 33–37, 40*n*9, 41–42, 41*n*21, 101, 118
Social status   65, 156, 172–173, 175–176, 180
Spelling   9, 46*n*43, 139*n*45, 139*n*45, 146, 154, 156*n*102, 171–172, 171*n*5, 174–182, 179*n*32, 190*n*18
    Error   152, 154–156, 171, 189–190
    Habits   179, 181
    Variation   140, 171, 175
Stonecutter   132, 134–139, 141–143, 153*n*71
Style   22, 24, 46*n*43, 56–57, 56*n*16, 59–62, 60*n*45, 65–66, 70*n*47, 71, 103, 106–107*n*136, 158
    Graphic   5, 56, 58
    Chancery   31, 57, 59–60, 65, 67–71, 70*n*44, 102. *See also chancery*
    Epigraphic   31
    Language   116, 152, 172, 173
    Severe   160, 160*n*146
    Writing   17, 57–58, 60, 62, 65
Subscription   23, 30, 31*n*19, 32, 60, 70, 75, 81, 176
Surface (of the document)   21, 33, 34–35 table 2.2, 40–42, 40*n*13 and *n*18, 45–46, 48–49, 48*n*45, 115, 117, 123, 137
Syllabification   7, 94*n*56, 98, 184, 184*n*2, 189–190. *See also word splitting*
Symbol
    chi-rho   78, 78*n*48, 125, 126*n*40, 129*n*48, 140
    chrismon   77
    Christian   5, 77–78, 83, 133, 137–142
    Cross   58–59, 62, 118, 120, 132, 135–136, 138–139, 141–143. *See also Christian symbols*
    Staurogram   62, 77–78, 83, 126*n*41 and *n*48
    Sun   158
Syriac   2, 6, 10, 131–144. *See also inscriptions*
    script   132–134, 141–143

Teacher   62
Textuality   45, 90, 110
Textualization   6, 89–90, 89*n*13, 92, 102, 106–107, 109–110
Titulature   66, 70
Tomb   81, 136, 139–140, 147*n*4, 158–162, 159*n*140
Training   62
Transfibral   5, 18, 19 fig. 1.2, 20
transversa charta   18–21, 22*n*33, 23–25, 27, 29, 30*n*6
Tripod   146, 147*n*4, 148, 153, 153*n*70, 158–159, 159*n*144, 161*n*156, 162
Typology   8, 8*n*55, 42–43, 49, 54, 65, 75–76, 120, 120*n*27, 122, 123, 159

vacat   22, 45–47, 56, 58–59, 58*n*31,*n*32 and *n*33, 80*n*64, 96, 101, 104, 115, 118–122, 126, 129*n*46. *See also blank space*
versiculi transversi   21
Visual aspect   54–57, 57*n*28, 60, 62
Visual communication   3, 6–8, 91, 133
'Visual politeness theory'   5, 55, 62

Women   89, 90*n*18, 106–108, 110
Word splitting   7, 92–94, 94*n*56, 98, 103–104, 184, 186–189. *See also syllabification*
Writing exercise   5, 40*n*12, 57, 61–62, 178